Working-Class War

Working-Class

WAR

American
Combat
Soldiers
and
Vietnam

CHRISTIAN G. APPY

The

University

of North

Carolina

Press

Chapel Hill

& London

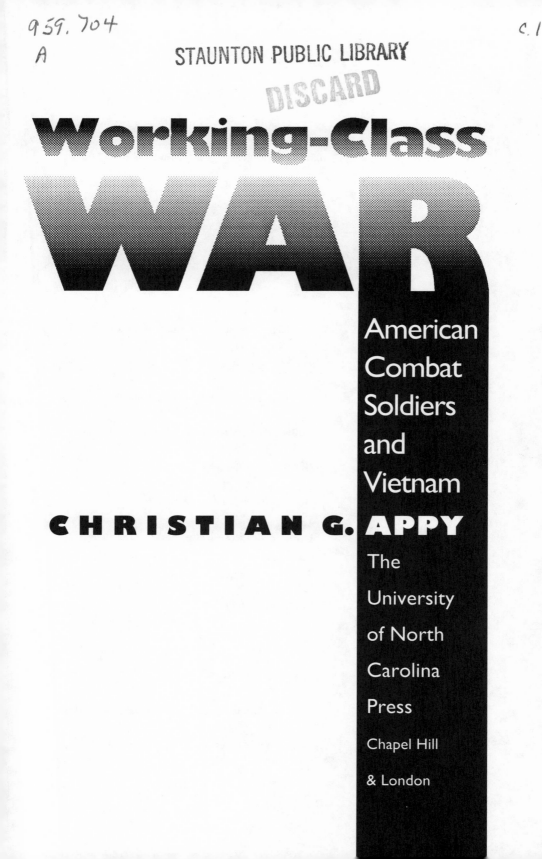

Library of Congress Cataloging-in-Publication Data

Appy, Christian G.

   Working-class war : American combat soldiers and

Vietnam / by Christian G. Appy.

     p. cm.

   Originally presented as the author's thesis (doctoral—

Harvard University).

   Includes bibliographical references and index.

   ISBN 0-8078-2057-1 (cloth : alk. paper). —

ISBN 0-8078-4391-1 (pbk. : alk. paper)

   1. Vietnamese Conflict, 1961–1975—United

States.   2. Soldiers—United States.   I. Title.

DS558.A67   1993

959.704′3373—dc20   92-18318

                                              CIP

97 96 95 94 93 5 4 3 2 1

Lyrics to "Born in the U.S.A." by Bruce Springsteen,

© 1984 Bruce Springsteen, used by permission. ASCAP.

For Meri,

Nathan, and Henry

Contents

Acknowledgments

I began this work as a doctoral dissertation in the History of American Civilization program at Harvard University. Thesis advisers usually discourage their students from choosing subjects as broad as this one. However, my advisers, Stephan Thernstrom and Robert Coles, graciously encouraged me to pursue the topic I found most compelling. I am deeply grateful for their help and generosity.

I am most indebted to the many Vietnam veterans who told me about their lives. The private, in-depth interviews I conducted with approximately 100 veterans are crucial sources for this book. While most of these oral histories were collected from men living in Massachusetts, I also interviewed about two dozen veterans from places as varied as Alabama, Texas, California, Illinois, and Virginia. Almost all were army and marine noncareer enlisted men; they were, that is, the sort of men who comprised the vast majority of American forces in Vietnam. Among that group, I tried to interview people with a wide range of experiences and perspectives—draftees and volunteers, combat and rear-echelon, right- and left-wing, working- and middle-class. In quoting from these interviews I decided to use pseudonyms, a decision I shared with veterans before we began our talks. I believed some veterans would feel freer to speak openly knowing that their identities would not be revealed.

In addition to individual interviews, I attended a weekly Vietnam veterans' rap group from 1981 to 1988. I am very thankful to Marie Cassella of the Dorchester House and to the veterans who attended her group for generously allowing me to participate. Those discussions were an invaluable part of my education.

My work also draws heavily on the extraordinary body of published work about the Vietnam War. Anyone who writes about the war finds the size of this collection both inspiring and daunting. I have not been able to read or cite all the authors who have made important contributions to this flourishing field. However, my largest intellectual debts will, I trust, be obvious in the pages that follow.

A dissertation fellowship from the Marine Corps History and Museums Division helped to provide financial support for a year of research and an opportunity to use the resources of the Marine Corps Historical Center. Two summer research grants from the Committee on Higher Degrees in the History of American Civilization were also greatly appreciated. While doing research in Washington I had the pleasure of staying with my sister, Karen, and Steve Baumann. I have long depended on their encouragement and friendship.

My good friend Michael Williams deserves special thanks for helping me arrange interviews with veterans in Alabama and for offering many useful suggestions on early drafts. Other friends and colleagues who have provided important aid and advice on this project include Tom Barber, Alan Brinkley, Walter Capps, Steve Foell, John Foran, Gary Gerstle, Alec Green, Mark Hirsch, David Jaffee, Malcolm Jensen, Chris Keller, Jeffrey Kimball, Dugan Mahoney, Fred Marchant, Barry O'Connell, Arthur Samuelson, Joyce Seltzer, Richard Sennett, Jack Shulimson, Ron Spector, and Patsy Yaeger.

At the University of North Carolina Press I have been blessed with excellent editors: Kate Douglas Torrey, Ron Maner, and Stephanie Wenzel.

I also want to acknowledge my mother, Shirley Appy, and my late father, Gerard Appy. Their love and support have far exceeded the context of this book, but their keen interest in my work was extremely bolstering.

My gratitude to my wife, Meri, and my children, Henry and Nathan, is immeasurable. For their patience, love, and enormous high spirits I am forever indebted. I am especially thankful to Meri for her good faith in this book and in me. I have also been sustained and inspired by the commitment and high standards she brings to her own work. The dedication of this book seems like paltry recompense for all she has given me.

Working-Class War

Introduction

Facing the Wall

We face the wall, beholding the names of the dead. We see ourselves on the smooth surface, our clothes rippled by the breeze, shading a space of chiseled names. Our reflections seem small at first—pale and fleeting against the granite's dark permanence. This is a memorial, however, not a monument. Silence, sadness, a kind of timid wonder may fall upon us, but not because they are exacted by monumental size or grandeur or pretense. With time, in fact, we are enlarged, not diminished, in the presence of the wall. It draws us closer. Our reflections deepen. We feel an almost irresistible need to touch the letters cut in the gleaming, black granite. Offerings are placed along the base of the wall: a flower, a faded photograph, a poem scrawled on lined paper and secured by a rock, a pair of old jungle boots, a small statue of St. Francis, a figure of Buddha, a frayed shoulder patch of the First Infantry Division. Thousands of gifts are left at the wall, items ordinary and bizarre, some so obscure only the dead could know their meaning: a childhood toy, perhaps, or a lost bet made good; an inside joke about a certain long patrol in the A Shau Valley, a hated officer, or an R&R in Bangkok.

The Vietnam Memorial was built in 1982 to honor the 58,152 Americans in the armed forces who died in Southeast Asia from 1959 to 1975. Of course, it is more than that. It is also a site of profound cultural communication, a symbol of the war, and a repository of our nation's history. Yet the memorial thwarts those who would precisely define what the wall communicates, who insist on an exact meaning of what it symbolizes, or who try neatly to summarize the history it represents. By displaying the names of the dead, without comment or context, the wall resists easy formulation, and it is well that this is so. War memorials should not lend themselves to clichés. When war is reduced to slogans, its savagery is either masked or trivialized. Having experienced World War I, Frederic Henry, the hero of Hemingway's *A Farewell to Arms*, could no longer tolerate words such as *sacred, glory,* and *sacrifice.* "I had seen nothing sacred, and the things that were glorious had no glory and the sacrifices were like the stockyards at Chicago if nothing was done with the meat except to bury it." For Henry, abstract conceptions of war had become obscene. The only words that retained meaning and dignity were "the concrete names of villages, the numbers of roads, the names of rivers, the numbers of regiments and the dates."[1]

The names and concrete details of war are important. They challenge empty generalizations and are crucial to the process of remembering. Gloria Emerson, a writer careful with details, insists we get the names right, and not just the American ones. Recalling a visit with a Vietnamese woman, a prisoner, in Cao Lanh in Kien Phuong province, she writes, "It is important to remember, to spell the names correctly, to know the provinces, before we are persuaded that none of it happened, that none of us were in such places."[2] When we face the wall, we should be conscious of the irreducible complexity of each life the war touched and the multiplicity of experiences the war comprised, but it is not enough simply to acknowledge the names and details of history. To say, along with Frederic Henry, that only the concrete reality of war has meaning or dignity can be as politically dangerous as the patriotic slogans he found so obscene. Unless we risk some generalizations about particular wars, we cannot take clear positions on the most crucial events of our time. To reject all generalizations is itself a generalization, one that implies all wars are equally meaningless and therefore beyond moral distinction or judgment. The competing views essential to a democratic society require not only a recovery of historical names but an ongoing debate about their significance. To acknowledge the dead and to grieve for them are difficult and important acts, but they are not sufficient. To acknowledge and to grieve are not necessarily to question and to know.

At its best, the Vietnam Memorial can move us beyond necessary reconciliations and endings and toward renewed efforts of critical understanding. That movement is the intention of this book. More specifically, we will explore the lives and experiences of people like those whose names are listed on the black granite. What sort of people were they? How did they come to fight in Vietnam? What was the nature of the war they waged? How did they respond? What were the commonalities of their experiences and perceptions?

Such basic questions remain largely unexamined in spite of the fact that American veterans have been the focus of most public imagery of the Vietnam War since the early 1980s. Long ignored, they have become the subject of dozens of films, books, magazine articles, television shows, and even cartoon strips. A key source of growing public awareness of Vietnam veterans was the opening in 1980 of some ninety walk-in counseling centers where vets could seek the help of peers (the centers were staffed by Vietnam veterans), participate in rap groups, and locate—in many cases for the first time—a community of fellow veterans. This federal program, Operation Outreach, was the culmination of years of lobbying by Vietnam veterans and represented the first significant national recognition that hundreds of thousands of veterans continued to be plagued by war-related problems.[3]

Shortly after the storefront vet centers began opening in American cities, the fifty-two Americans held hostage in Iran returned home (January 1981). The hero's welcome given the former hostages dramatized by contrast the point expressed by a growing number of veterans—that they returned from Vietnam in virtual isolation, received no national homecoming ceremonies, and lacked adequate medical and psychological care, educational benefits, and job training.[4] The hostage return, I believe, tapped feelings that had much of their origin in the final years of Vietnam. At some level, perhaps mostly unconscious, Americans greeted the hostages so enthusiastically because their return marked precisely the sort of formal, collective, and ritual ending the Vietnam War lacked. This absence was felt most intensely by veterans, but not by them alone. The hostage homecoming also provided a model of celebratory nationalism (tending toward xenophobia) that required no searching examination of the events giving rise to the crisis (for example, the Iranian revolution and U.S. support of the shah). A yellow ribbon would do. The attention directed at Vietnam veterans in the 1980s represented, in part, an effort to find an equally easy ending to the Vietnam War.

It was crucial that veterans be central to this process, for they were among the Americans who could raise the worst memories and the most troubling questions about the war. By honoring Vietnam veterans, no matter how superficially, the culture seemed to be struggling to find a way to both accept and contain the very people who had the potential to reopen the pain of the war most fully. Accordingly, veterans were typically presented in ways akin to the hostages, as survivor-heroes. Indeed, throughout the Reagan years people who suffered terrible ordeals at the hands of foreigners or in the name of the United States were accorded the status of heroes. Victims and survivors of disasters, not champions of popular causes, became the dominant models of heroism. Hostages, prisoners of war (real or imagined), the 241 marines in Lebanon killed by car bomb, and the victims of the *Challenger* explosion were all treated as heroes by the media and by national politicians.[5] By focusing on what people suffered or endured in foreign lands (or in space), you need not examine what they were doing there in the first place. By this standard, Vietnam veterans seemed the ultimate survivor-heroes. After all, as the typical treatment went, these were men who had endured jungle rot, malaria, poisonous snakes, booby traps, invisible enemies, spitting war protesters, and other, unimaginable horrors.

By 1983 or 1984, the crowds at Veterans Day parades commonly gave the biggest ovation to the contingent of Vietnam veterans. What did the applause signify? Was it genuine support, gratitude, guilt, the "new patriotism"? All of these were factors, no doubt, but the acclaim also expressed, I believe, a desire to end or suppress the negative emotions and controversies still associated with the war—who fought and who did not, whether the war was just or unjust, why it was fought at all, and why it was such an utter failure.

Yet there is another equally important dimension to the improved public image of Vietnam veterans. The newly ascendant far right of the early 1980s had long sought to portray Vietnam as a just war that the left wing did not have the will or courage to win. Their historical interpretation of the war gained to the extent that they could persuade the public that Vietnam veterans were patriotic heroes who had been betrayed by left-wing criticism and cowardice. Thus, conservative politicians, filmmakers, and writers insisted that Vietnam veterans had fought, in Ronald Reagan's words, on behalf of a "noble cause" that could have triumphed had it not been sabotaged by irresolute liberal politicians, the antiwar movement, and a near-treasonous media. Because of a lack of domestic will, Reagan argued, American soldiers in Vietnam were "denied permission to win." President Bush made the same claim repeatedly during the Persian

Gulf War, insisting that the soldiers of Desert Storm, unlike those in Vietnam, would not have to fight "with one hand tied behind their backs."[6]

For Reagan and Bush, the central lesson of Vietnam was not that foreign policy had to be more democratic, but the opposite: it had to become ever more the province of national security managers who operated without the close scrutiny of the media, the oversight of Congress, or accountability to an involved public. Yet this response was founded, in part, on two dubious propositions: first, that democratic politics, public protest, and media attention had greatly constrained the military in Vietnam; and second, that the war in Vietnam could have been won. Even granting that not every possible military action was taken—no nuclear bombs were dropped, there was no major ground invasion of North Vietnam, and troop levels did not rise as high as the military wanted—the violence wreaked on Southeast Asia was in many ways unprecedented. In bomb tonnage alone, the United States dropped three times more explosives than were dropped by all sides in World War II. Efforts to imagine a victorious outcome in Vietnam avoid the question of whether the means required to "win," assuming victory were possible or desirable, would have justified the end. Preoccupied by what we might have done differently in Vietnam, we have made too little effort to understand exactly what the military did do. Constructing fallacious images of Vietnam veterans held back from sure victory substitutes for serious attention to the actualities of their wartime experience.

Liberals, too, have largely evaded close scrutiny of American soldiers in Vietnam. Many have focused on the ill treatment received by veterans since the war, their difficulties adjusting to civilian life, and their painful memories. The desire to offer veterans nonjudgmental acceptance has led many writers to avoid challenging these men to answer difficult questions about Vietnam, believing such inquiries might elicit further pain and grief. In much of this writing, veterans appear as victims and the writers as opinionless confessors. Like the title of *Newsweek*'s special feature on Vietnam veterans, the accent is on "What Vietnam Did to Us."[7] A more complete understanding of these men, however, requires that we examine not only what Vietnam did to them but what they were sent to do in and to Vietnam.

Throughout American culture Vietnam veterans have been presented in ways that remove them from their own history. In 1985, for example, on the tenth anniversary of the war's end, United Technologies ran an editorial advertisement called "Remembering Vietnam." This advertorial epitomizes the cautious approach many Americans have taken toward the war. Avoiding controversy at every turn, it seeks "only to draw attention to those who served." Superficial acknowledgment of the sacrifices and service of veterans is offered as a sufficient response to our longest and most divisive war. According to United Technologies, Vietnam and the war fought on its soil exist merely in the "part of the mind inhabited solely by memories." "Whatever acrimony lingers in our consciousness . . . let us not forget the Vietnam veteran." Token gestures like this, however, are true forgetfulness. Abstracted from history, veterans cannot be remembered or even honored; they can only be exploited.[8]

Even the Vietnam films, though usually centered on the experiences of American soldiers, generally fail to locate their subjects in historical or political context. We see terrifying firefights, occasional atrocities, traumatized peasants, and U.S. troops who range from the well-intentioned but tormented to the sadistically flipped-out, but we rarely learn why people were placed in such circumstances and how these events could take place as they did. Films such as *Platoon*, *Full Metal Jacket*, and *Born on the Fourth of July* often provide vivid and visceral representations of American GIs, but they leave us as baffled as ever about the nature of the war, about the relationship of events to American policies and objectives, and about almost everything having to do with the Vietnamese and their responses to American intervention. Without that context, our understanding of the principal subject, American soldiers, remains shallow.[9]

This book attempts to provide that context as it explores the war-related experiences and attitudes of the 2.5 million young American enlisted men who served in Vietnam. Drawn from the largest generation in U.S. history, from the 27 million men who came of draft age during the war, American troops represented a distinct and relatively small subset of those born during the post–World War II baby boom. However, this subset was not representative of the generation as a whole. Roughly 80 percent came from working-class and poor backgrounds. Vietnam, more than any other American war in the twentieth century, perhaps in our history, was a working-class war. The institutions most responsible for channeling men into the military—the draft, the schools, and the job market—directed working-class children to the armed forces and their wealthier peers toward college. Most young men from prosperous families were able to avoid the draft, and very few volunteered. Thus, America's most unpopular war was fought primarily by the nineteen-year-old children of waitresses, factory workers, truck drivers, secretaries, firefighters, carpenters, custodians, police officers, salespeople, clerks, mechanics, miners, and farmworkers: people whose work lives are not only physically demanding but in many cases physically dangerous. From 1961 to 1972, an average of 14,000 American workers died every year from industrial accidents; the same number of soldiers died in Vietnam during 1968, the year of highest U.S. casualties. Throughout the war, moreover, at least 100,000 people died each year from work-related diseases. Combat may be more harrowing and dangerous than even the toughest civilian jobs, but in class terms there were important commonalities between the two. In both cases soldiers and workers did the nation's "dirty work"—one group abroad and the other at home—and did it under strict orders with little compensation. While working-class veterans have often found pride in their participation in America's tradition of military victory, Vietnam veterans lack even that reward and have had to draw what pride they can from other aspects of their experience. Soldiers in Vietnam, like workers at home, believed the nation as a whole had little, if any, appreciation for their sacrifices. If that perception was not always accurate, there is little doubt that many well-to-do Americans would have been more concerned about U.S. casualties had their own children been the ones doing the fighting.[10]

In Vietnam, American soldiers encountered a reality utterly at odds with the official justifications of the war presented by American policymakers. Though many men arrived in Vietnam believing they had been sent to stop communism and to help the people of South Vietnam preserve democracy, their experience fundamentally contradicted those explanations. Told they were in Vietnam to help the people, soldiers found widespread antagonism to their presence. Told they were there to protect villagers from aggression, they carried out military orders that destroyed villages and brought terror to civilians. Told they were fighting to prevent the spread of communism, they discovered that support for revolution already flourished throughout the country and could not be contained behind fixed boundaries.

The demoralization caused by the contradictions in American policy was exacerbated by the fact that U.S. troops fought at a tactical and strategic disadvantage. Despite the much-vaunted superiority of American technology—our greater firepower and mobility—the Vietnamese opposition clearly established the terms of battle. American soldiers spent much of their time in fruitless searches for an enemy who almost always determined the time and place of battle. The majority of American infantrymen who lost their lives in Vietnam were killed by enemy ambushes, by enemy booby traps and mines, or by their own side's bombs, shells, or bullets ("friendly fire"). Pitted against such an elusive enemy, American search-and-destroy missions were essentially efforts to attract enemy fire. American soldiers were used as bait to draw the enemy into identifiable targets so the full weight of American firepower—bombs, rockets, napalm—could be dropped on the Vietnamese. As American troops soon learned, the central aim of U.S. policy in Vietnam was to maximize the enemy body count. In executing that policy, soldiers also learned that the high command was rarely particular about determining if dead Vietnamese were combatants or civilians.

In the face of this experience most soldiers came to perceive the war as meaningless, as a war for nothing, but they responded to that common perception in various ways. Some took the war on its own terms and found exhilaration in its danger and violence. Others thought of the war as a specialized job and blocked from their minds questions about the purpose or value of that job. Others gave as little of themselves to the war as possible by avoiding or resisting combat, shirking duties, or withdrawing into drugs or alcohol.

Vietnam veterans have carried the heaviest sense of responsibility for the conduct and outcome of the war. They have felt blamed on all sides—by conservatives for losing the war and by liberals for having participated in its immorality. Veterans rightly want other Americans to assume a share of responsibility for the war. Those most responsible, the major policy-makers and military commanders, have never owned up to the deceptions of their wartime claims and decisions: their portrayal of South Vietnamese dictatorships as democratic, their lies about the Gulf of Tonkin incident, their claims of progress based on false body counts and undercounted enemy forces, or their insistence that civilian casualties were unfortunate accidents rather than an inevitable result of American military strategy responsible for the deaths of at least a half-million civilians. American soldiers on the ground were placed in deep moral jeopardy. Even those who sought to act as humanely as possible often feel tainted by their role in carrying out such destructive policies. They have felt all the more tainted by the failure of American leaders to take responsibility for the worst of the war and by the efforts of those leaders to seek moral immunity from their own decisions. Nothing symbolizes the moral safety of the powerful more dramatically than the massacre at My Lai. While American GIs killed hundreds of unarmed villagers on the ground, the commanding officers, including a general and two colonels, circled 2,000 feet above the village in helicopters. None of these airborne officers was indicted for the crimes committed under their command.[11]

Many veterans still struggle to free themselves from a paralyzing fixation on the history they lived so long ago, desperately wishing that somehow it might have turned out differently. That way of thinking often leads veterans to rage against the various people and groups they believe were responsible for sending them to fight an unwinnable war, for not finding a way to win, or for the deep divisions at home that widened as the war continued. All too often, however, veterans have internalized such anger, turning it on themselves. No one knows how many veterans have committed suicide as a result of their wartime experiences, but most specialists who have worked closely with veterans believe the number of suicides far exceeds the number of men who died in the war itself.[12]

The stories of those veterans will never be heard, nor will those of the men whose names appear on the Vietnam Memorial. That thought occurred to one veteran in 1984, recently back from a visit to the wall. Asked for his response to the memorial, he said, "It was really overpowering. I saw the names of some guys I knew. . . . Cried real hard. But, you know, I think it's a lot easier for Americans to feel bad about the guys that died than it is for them to think about those of us who are still around. Those guys who died, their stories died with them. I'm not sure people really want to hear the kind of stories they could tell. I think a lot of people just want to bury the war."[13]

On 20 January 1981 President Reagan spoke a word that no American president had ever used in an inaugural address: Vietnam. It came at the end of a tribute to Americans who died in war, at "Belleau Wood, The Argonne, Omaha Beach, . . . Guadalcanal, . . . the Chosin Reservoir, and in a hundred rice paddies and jungles of a place called Vietnam." Reagan's battlefield litany seeks to incorporate Vietnam into a vision of American history as an unsullied continuum of virtue, heroism, and national unity. Rhetoric alone, however, could not erase Vietnam's persistent challenge to Reagan's vision. Eight years later, when George Bush also mentioned Vietnam in his inaugural, he was still trying to rid the nation of its troubling memory: "That war cleaves us still. But, friends, that war began in earnest a quarter century ago; and surely the statute of limitations has been reached. This is a fact: The final lesson of Vietnam is that no great nation can long afford to be sundered by a memory."[14]

Vietnam is not, as George Bush and United Technologies would have us believe, merely a memory; it is a fundamental part of our history and, therefore, a fundamental part of who and what we are. In the face of such willful denials of history, the experiences and stories of veterans represent what Michel Foucault has described as "disqualified" or "illegitimate" forms of knowledge. The task ahead is to recover and interpret that knowledge.[15]

Working-Class War

MAPPING THE LOSSES

Where were the sons of all the big shots who supported the war? Not in my platoon. Our guys' people were workers. . . . If the war was so important, why didn't our leaders put everyone's son in there, why only us?
– Steve Harper
   (1971)

"We all ended up going into the service about the same time—the whole crowd." I had asked Dan Shaw about himself, why *he* had joined the Marine Corps; but Dan ignored the personal thrust of the question. Military service seemed less an individual choice than a collective rite of passage, a natural phase of life for "the whole crowd" of boys in his neighborhood, so his response encompassed a circle of over twenty childhood friends who lived near the corner of Train and King streets in Dorchester, Massachusetts—a white, working-class section of Boston.[1]

Thinking back to 1968 and his streetcorner buddies, Dan sorted them into groups, wanting to get the facts straight about each one. It did not take him long to come up with some figures. "Four of the guys didn't go into the military at all. Four got drafted by the army. Fourteen or fifteen of us went in the Marine Corps. Out of them fourteen or fifteen"— here he paused to count by naming—"Eddie, Brian, Tommy, Dennis, Steve: six of us went to Nam." They were all still teenagers. Three of the six were wounded in combat, including Dan.

His tone was calm, almost dismissive. The fact

that nearly all his friends entered the military and half a dozen fought in Vietnam did not strike Dan as unusual or remarkable. In working-class neighborhoods like his, military service after high school was as commonplace among young men as college was for the youth of upper-middle-class suburbs—not welcomed by everyone but rarely questioned or avoided. In fact, when Dan thinks of the losses suffered in other parts of Dorchester, he regards his own streetcorner as relatively lucky. "Jeez, it wasn't bad. I mean some corners around here really got wiped out. Over off Norfolk street ten guys got blown away the same year."

Focusing on the world of working-class Boston, Dan has a quiet, low-key manner with few traces of bitterness. But when he speaks of the disparities in military service throughout American society, his voice fills with anger, scorn, and hurt. He compares the sacrifices of poor and working-class neighborhoods with the rarity of wartime casualties in the "fancy suburbs" beyond the city limits, in places such as Milton, Lexington, and Wellesley. If three wounded veterans "wasn't bad" for a streetcorner in Dorchester, such concentrated pain was, Dan insists, unimaginable in a wealthy subdivision. "You'd be lucky to find three Vietnam veterans in one of those rich neighborhoods, never mind three who got wounded."

Dan's point is indisputable: those who fought and died in Vietnam were overwhelmingly drawn from the bottom half of the American social structure. The comparison he suggests bears out the claim. The three affluent towns of Milton, Lexington, and Wellesley had a combined wartime population of about 100,000, roughly equal to that of Dorchester. However, while those suburbs suffered a total of eleven war deaths, Dorchester lost forty-two. There was almost exactly the same disparity in casualties between Dorchester and another sample of prosperous Massachusetts towns—Andover, Lincoln, Sudbury, Weston, Dover, Amherst, and Longmeadow. These towns lost ten men from a combined population of 100,000. In other words, boys who grew up in Dorchester were four times more likely to die in Vietnam than those raised in the fancy suburbs. An extensive study of wartime casualties from Illinois reached a similar conclusion. In that state, men from neighborhoods with median family incomes under $5,000 (about $15,000 in 1990 dollars) were four times more likely to die in Vietnam than men from places with median family incomes above $15,000 ($45,000 in 1990 dollars).[2]

Dorchester, East Los Angeles, the South Side of Chicago—major urban centers such as these sent thousands of men to Vietnam. So, too, did lesser known, midsize industrial cities with large working-class populations, such as Saginaw, Michigan; Fort Wayne, Indiana; Stockton, California; Chattanooga, Tennessee; Youngstown, Ohio; Bethlehem, Pennsylvania; and Utica, New York. There was also an enormous rise in working-class suburbanization in the 1950s and 1960s. The post–World War II boom in modestly priced, uniformly designed, tract housing, along with the vast construction of new highways, allowed many workers their first opportunity to purchase homes and to live a considerable distance from their jobs. As a result, many new suburbs became predominantly working class.

Long Island, New York, became the site of numerous working-class suburbs, including the original Levittown, the first mass-produced town in American history. Built by the Levitt and Sons construction firm in the late 1940s, it was initially a middle-class town. By 1960, however, as in many other postwar suburbs, the first owners had moved on, often to larger homes in wealthier suburbs, and a majority of the newcomers were working class.[3] Ron Kovic, author of one of the best-known Vietnam memoirs and films, *Born on the Fourth of July*, grew up near Levittown in Massapequa. His parents, like so many others in both towns, were working people willing to make great sacrifices to own a small home with a little land and to live in a town they regarded as a safe and decent place to raise their families, in hope that their children would enjoy greater opportunity. Many commentators viewed the suburbanization of blue-collar workers as a sign that the working class was vanishing and that almost everyone was becoming middle class. In fact, however, though many workers owned more than ever before, their relative social position remained largely unchanged. The Kovics, for example, lived in the suburbs but had to raise five children on the wages of a supermarket checker and clearly did not match middle-class levels in terms of economic security, education, or social status.

Ron Kovic volunteered for the marines after graduating from high school. He was paralyzed from the chest down in a 1968 firefight during his second tour of duty in Vietnam. Upon returning home, after treatment in a decrepit, rat-infested VA hospital, Kovic was asked to be grand marshal in Massapequa's Memorial Day parade. His drivers were American Legion veterans of World War II who tried unsuccessfully to engage him in a conversation about the many local boys who had died in Vietnam:

"Remember Clasternack? . . . They got a street over in the park named after him . . . he was the first of you kids to get it. . . There was the Peters family too . . . both brothers . . . Both of them killed in the same week. And Alan Grady. . . Did you know Alan Grady? . . .

"We've lost a lot of good boys. . . . We've been hit pretty bad. The whole town's changed."[4]

A community of only 27,000, Massapequa lost 14 men in Vietnam. In 1969, *Newsday* traced the family backgrounds of 400 men from Long Island who had been killed in Vietnam. "As a group," the newspaper concluded, "Long Island's war dead have been overwhelmingly white, working-class men. Their parents were typically blue collar or clerical workers, mailmen, factory workers, building tradesmen, and so on."[5]

Rural and small-town America may have lost more men in Vietnam, proportionately, than did even central cities and working-class suburbs. You get a hint of this simply by flipping through the pages of the Vietnam Memorial directory. As thick as a big-city phone book, the directory lists the names and hometowns of Americans who died in Vietnam. An average page contains the names of five or six men from towns such as Alma, West Virginia (pop. 296), Lost Hills, California (pop. 200), Bryant Pond, Maine (pop. 350), Tonalea, Arizona (pop. 125), Storden, Minnesota (pop. 364), Pioneer, Louisiana (pop. 188), Wartburg, Tennessee (pop. 541), Hillisburg, Indiana (pop. 225), Boring, Oregon (pop. 150), Racine, Missouri (pop. 274), Hygiene, Colorado (pop. 400), Clayton, Kansas (pop. 127), and Almond, Wisconsin (pop. 440). In the 1960s only about 2 percent of Americans lived in towns with fewer than 1,000 people. Among those who died in Vietnam, however, roughly four times that portion, 8 percent, came from American hamlets of that size. It is not hard to find small towns that lost more than one man in Vietnam. Empire, Alabama, for example, had four men out of a population of only 400 die in Vietnam—four men from a town in which only a few dozen boys came of draft age during the entire war.[6]

There were also soldiers who came from neither cities, suburbs, nor small towns but from the hundreds of places in between, average towns of 15,000 to 30,000 people whose economic life, however precarious, had local roots. Some of these towns paid a high cost in Vietnam. In the foothills of eastern Alabama, for example, is the town of Talladega, with a population of approximately 17,500 (about one-quarter black), a town of small farmers and textile workers. Only one-third of Talladega's men had completed high school. Fifteen of their children died in Vietnam, a death rate three times the national average. Compare Talladega to Mountain Brook, a rich suburb outside Birmingham. Mountain Brook's population was somewhat higher than Talladega's, about 19,500 (with no black residents of draft age). More than 90 percent of its men were high school graduates. No one from Mountain Brook is listed among the Vietnam War dead.[7]

I have described a social map of American war casualties to suggest not simply the geographic origins of U.S. soldiers but their class origins—not simply where they came from but the kinds of places as well. Class, not geography, was the crucial factor in determining which Americans fought in Vietnam. Geography reveals discrepancies in military service primarily because it often reflects class distinctions. Many men went to Vietnam from places such as Dorchester, Massapequa, Empire, and Talladega because those were the sorts of places where most poor and working-class people lived. The wealthiest youth in those towns, like those in richer communities, were far less likely either to enlist or to be drafted.

Mike Clodfelter, for example, grew up in Plainville, Kansas. In 1964 he enlisted in the army, and the following year he was sent to Vietnam. In his 1976 memoir, Clodfelter recalled, "From my own small home town . . . all but two of a dozen high school buddies would eventually serve in Vietnam and all were of working class families, while I knew of not a single middle class son of the town's businessmen, lawyers, doctors, or ranchers from my high school graduating class who experienced the Armageddon of our generation."[8]

However, even a sketchy map of American casualties must go farther afield, beyond the conventional boundaries of the United States. Although this fact is not well known, the military took draftees and volunteers from the American territories: Puerto Rico, Guam, the U.S. Virgin Islands, American Samoa, and the Canal Zone. These territories lost a total of 436 men in Vietnam, several dozen more than the state of Nebraska. Some 48,000 Puerto Ricans served in Vietnam, many of whom could speak only a smattering of English. Of these, 345 died. This figure does not include men who were born in Puerto Rico and emigrated to the United States (or whose parents were born in Puerto Rico). We do not know these numbers because the military did not make a separate count of Hispanic-American casualties either as an inclusive category or by country of origin.[9]

Guam drew little attention on the American mainland during the war. It was only heard of at all because American B-52s took off from there to make bombing runs over Vietnam (a twelve-hour round-trip flight requiring midair refueling) or because a conference between President Johnson and some of his top military leaders was held there in 1967. Yet the United States sent several thousand Guamanians to fight with American forces in Vietnam. Seventy of them died. Drawn from a population of only 111,000, Guam's death rate was considerably higher even than that of Dorchester, Massachusetts.

This still does not exhaust the range of places we might look for "American" casualties. There were, of course, the "Free World forces" recruited by and, in most cases, financed by the United States. These "third country forces" from South Korea, Australia, New Zealand, Thailand, and the Philippines reached a peak of about 60,000 troops (U.S. forces rose to 550,000). The U.S. government pointed to them as evidence of a united, multinational, free-world effort to resist communist aggression. But only Australia and New Zealand paid to send their troops to Vietnam. They had a force of 7,000 men and lost 469 in combat. The other nations received so much money in return for their military intervention that their forces were essentially mercenary. The Philippine government of Ferdinand Marcos, for example, received the equivalent of $26,000 for each of the 2,000 men it sent to Vietnam to carry out noncombat, civic action programs. South Korea's participation was by far the largest among the U.S.-sponsored third countries. It deployed a force of 50,000 men. In return, the Korean government enjoyed substantial increases in aid, and its soldiers were paid roughly 20 times what they earned at home. More than 4,000 of them lost their lives.[10]

The South Vietnamese military was also essentially the product of American intervention. For twenty-one years the United States committed billions of dollars to the creation of an anticommunist government in southern Vietnam and to the recruitment, training, and arming of a military to support it. Throughout the long war against southern guerrillas and North Vietnamese regulars, about 250,000 South Vietnamese government forces were killed. The United States bears responsibility for these lives and for those of third country forces because their military participation was almost wholly dependent on American initiatives.

In this sense, perhaps we need to take another step. Perhaps all Vietnamese deaths, enemy and ally, civilian and combatant, should be considered American as well as Vietnamese casualties. To do so is simply to acknowledge that their fates were largely determined by American intervention. After all, without American intervention (according to almost all intelligence reports at the time and historians since), Vietnamese unification under Ho Chi Minh would have occurred with little resistance.[11]

However one measures American responsibility for Indochinese casualties, every effort should be made to grasp the enormity of those losses. From 1961 to 1975 1.5 to 2 million Vietnamese were killed. Estimates of Cambodian and Laotian deaths are even less precise, but certainly the figure is in the hundreds of thousands. Imagine a memorial to the Indochinese who died in what they call the American, not the Vietnam, War. If similar to the Vietnam Memorial, with every name etched in granite, it would have to be forty times larger than the wall in Washington. Even such an enormous list of names would not put into perspective the scale of loss in Indochina. These are small countries with a combined wartime population of about 50 million people. Had the United States lost the same portion of its population, the Vietnam Memorial would list the names of 8 million Americans.

To insist that we recognize the disparity in casualties between the United States and Indochina is not to diminish the tragedy or significance of American losses, nor does it deflect attention from our effort to understand American soldiers. Without some awareness of the war's full destructiveness we cannot begin to understand their experience. As one veteran put it: "That's what I can't get out of my head—the bodies . . . all those bodies. Back then we didn't give a shit about the dead Vietnamese. It was like: 'Hey, they're just gooks, don't mean nothin'.' You got so cold you didn't even blink. You could even joke about it, mess around with the bodies like they was rag dolls. And after awhile we could even stack up our own KIAs [killed in action] without feeling much of anything. It's not like that now. You can't just put it out of your mind. Now I carry those bodies around every fucking day. It's a heavy load, man, a heavy fucking load."[12]

THE VIETNAM GENERATION'S MILITARY MINORITY: A STATISTICAL PROFILE

Presidents Kennedy, Johnson, and Nixon sent 3 million American soldiers to South Vietnam, a country of 17 million. In the early 1960s they went by the hundreds—helicopter units, Green Beret teams, counterinsurgency hotshots, ambitious young officers, and ordinary infantrymen—all of them labeled military advisers by the American command. They fought a distant, "brushfire war" on the edge of American consciousness. Beyond the secret inner circles of government, few predicted that hundreds of thousands would follow in a massive buildup that took the American presence in Vietnam from 15,000 troops in 1964 to 550,000 in 1968.[13] In late 1969 the gradual withdrawal of ground forces began, inching its way to the final U.S. pullout in January 1973. The bell curve of escalation and withdrawal spread the commitment of men into a decade-long chain of one-year tours of duty.

In the years of escalation, as draft calls mounted to 30,000 and 40,000 a month, many young people believed the entire generation might be mobilized for war. There were, of course, many ways to avoid the draft, and millions of men did just that. Very few, however, felt completely confident that they would never be ordered to fight. Perhaps the war would escalate to such a degree or go on so long that all exemptions and deferments would be eliminated. No one could be sure what would happen. Only in retrospect is it clear that the odds of serving in Vietnam were, for many people, really quite small. The forces that fought in Vietnam were drawn from the largest generation of young people in the nation's history. During the years 1964 to 1973, from the Gulf of Tonkin Resolution to the final withdrawal of American troops from Vietnam, 27 million men came of draft age. The 2.5 million men of that generation who went to Vietnam represent less than 10 percent of America's male baby boomers.[14]

The parents of the Vietnam generation had an utterly different experience of war. During World War II virtually all young, able-bodied men entered the service—some 12 million. Personal connections to the military permeated society regardless of class, race, or gender. Almost every family had a close relative overseas—a husband fighting in France, a son in the South Pacific, or at least an uncle with the Seabees, a niece in the WAVES, or a cousin in the Air Corps. These connections continued well into the 1950s. Throughout the Korean War years and for several years after, roughly 70 percent of the draft-age population of men served in the military; but from the 1950s to the 1960s, military service became less and less universal. During the Vietnam years, the portion had dropped to 40 percent: 10 percent were in Vietnam, and 30 percent served in Germany, South Korea, and the dozens of other duty stations in the United States and abroad. What had been, in the 1940s, an experience shared by the vast majority gradually became the experience of a distinct minority.[15]

What kind of minority was it? In modern American culture, *minority* usually serves as a code word for nonwhite races, especially African Americans. To speak of American forces in Vietnam as a minority invites the assumption that blacks, Hispanics, Asian Americans, and Native Americans fought and died in numbers grossly disproportionate to their percentage of the total U.S. population. It is a common assumption, but not one that has been sufficiently examined. For that matter, the whole experience of racial minorities in Vietnam has been woefully ignored by the media and academics. For Hispanics, Asian Americans, and Native Americans, even the most basic statistical information about their role in Vietnam remains either unknown or inadequately examined.

We know how many black soldiers served and died in Vietnam, but the more important task is to interpret those figures in historical context. Without that context, racial disproportions can be either exaggerated or denied. To simplify: At the beginning of the war blacks comprised more than 20 percent of American combat deaths, about twice their portion of the U.S. population. However, the portion of black casualties declined over time so that, for the war as a whole, black casualties were only slightly disproportionate (12.5 percent from a civilian population of 11 percent). The total percentage of blacks who served in Vietnam was roughly 10 percent throughout the war.[16]

African Americans clearly faced more than their fair share of the risks in Vietnam from 1965 to 1967. That fact might well have failed to gain any public notice had the civil rights and antiwar movements not called attention to it. Martin Luther King was probably the most effective in generating concern about the number of black casualties in Vietnam. King had refrained from frequent public criticism of the war until 1967, persuaded by moderates that outspoken opposition to the war might divert energy from the cause of civil rights and alienate prowar politicians whose support the movement sought (President Johnson, for example). By early 1967, however, King believed the time had come to break his silence. As for diverting energy and resources from domestic social reform, King argued, the war itself had already done as much. More importantly, he could not in good conscience remain silent in the face of a war he believed unjust.

King's critique of the war was wide ranging, based on a historical understanding of the long struggle in Vietnam for national independence, on a commitment to nonviolence, and on outrage over the violence the United States was inflicting on the land and people of Indochina. Always central in King's criticism of the war, however, was its effect on America's poor, both black and white. "The promises of the Great Society," he said, "have been shot down on the battlefield of Vietnam." The expense of the war was taking money and support that could be spent to solve problems at home. The war on poverty was being supplanted by the war on Vietnam. Beyond that, King stressed, the poor themselves were doing much of the fighting overseas. As he put it in his famous speech at Riverside Church in New York City (April 1967), the war was not only "devastating the hopes of the poor at home," it was also "sending their sons and their brothers and their husbands to fight and to die in extraordinarily high proportions relative to the rest of the population."[17]

While King focused attention on the economic condition of white and black soldiers, he emphasized the additional burden on blacks of fighting overseas in disproportionate numbers while being denied full citizenship at home: "We have been repeatedly faced with the cruel irony of watching Negro and white boys on TV screens as they kill and die together for a nation that has been unable to seat them together in the same schools. So we watch them in brutal solidarity burning the huts of a poor village, but we realize that they would never live on the same block in Detroit." In another speech he added, "We are willing to make the Negro 100 percent of a citizen in warfare, but reduce him to 50 percent of a citizen on American soil. Half of all Negroes live in substandard housing and he has half the income of white. There is twice as much unemployment and infant mortality among Negroes. [Yet] at the beginning of 1967 twice as many died in action—20.6 percent—in proportion to their numbers in the population as a whole."[18]

In his postwar apologia for U.S. intervention, *America in Vietnam*, Guenter Lewy accused King of heightening racial tension by making false allegations about black casualties in Vietnam. After all, Lewy argued, black casualties for the whole war were 12.5 percent, no higher than the portion of draft-age black males in the total U.S. population. Lewy's charge falls apart, however, as soon as one points out that black casualties did not drop to the overall figure of 12.5 until well after King was assassinated. During the period King and others were articulating their criticisms of the war, the disproportions were quite significant. To attack the antiwar movement for failing to use postwar statistics is not only unfair, it is ahistorical. Moreover, King was by no means the first prominent black to criticize the war or the disproportionate loss of black soldiers. Malcolm X, Muhammad Ali, Adam Clayton Powell, Dick Gregory, John Lewis, and Julian Bond were among those who spoke out repeatedly well before 1967. In fact, had the civil rights movement not brought attention to racial disproportions in Vietnam casualties, those disproportions almost certainly would have continued. According to Commander George L. Jackson, "In response to this criticism the Department of Defense took steps to readjust force levels in order to achieve an equitable proportion and employment of Negroes in Vietnam." A detailed analysis of exactly what steps were taken has yet to be written. It is clear, however, that by late 1967, black casualties had fallen to 13 percent and then to below 10 percent in 1970–72.[19]

Blacks were by no means united in opposition to the war or the military. For generations blacks had been struggling for equal participation in all American institutions, the military included. In World War II the struggle had focused on integration and the "right to fight." Aside from some all-black combat units, most blacks were assigned to segregated, rear-area duty. The military was officially desegregated in 1948, and most blacks served in integrated units in the Korean War. It was the Vietnam War, though, that was hailed in the mass media as America's first truly integrated war. In 1967 and 1968 several magazines and newspapers ran major stories on "the Negro in Vietnam." While disproportionate casualties were mentioned, they were not the target of criticism. Instead, these articles—including a cover story in *Ebony* (August 1968)—emphasized the contributions of black soldiers, their courageous service, and the new opportunities ostensibly provided by wartime duty in an integrated army. The point was often made that blacks had more civil rights in the military than at home. In *Harper's* magazine (June 1967) Whitney Young of the Urban League wrote, "In this war there is a degree of integration among black and white Americans far exceeding that of any other war in our history as well as any other time or place in our domestic life." As Thomas Johnson put it in *Ebony*, giving the point an ironic turn, "The Negro has found in his nation's most totalitarian society—the military—the greatest degree of functional democracy that this nation has granted to black people."[20]

Whitney Young justified disproportionate black casualties as the result not of discrimination but of "the simple fact that a higher proportion of Negroes volunteer for hazardous duty." There was some truth to this. In airborne units—the training for which is voluntary—blacks were reported to comprise as much as 30 percent of the combat troops. Moreover, blacks had a reenlistment rate three times higher than whites. It fell dramatically as the war went on, but it was always much higher than that of white soldiers. These points surely suggest that many blacks were highly motivated, enthusiastic troops.[21]

That enthusiasm itself does not prove that the military had equal opportunities for blacks or an absence of discrimination. After all, presumably the same blacks who volunteered for airborne (for which they received additional pay) might just as eagerly have volunteered for officer candidate school had they been offered the chance. Only 2 percent of the officers in Vietnam were black. Blacks might have taken advantage of opportunities to fill higher-paying, noncombat positions, had they been offered. The military's response was that blacks were disproportionately enlisted combat soldiers because they were simply not qualified to fill other jobs. Of course, qualifications are determined by the crudest measurement—standardized tests—and black soldiers scored significantly lower than whites. In 1965, for example, 41 percent of black soldiers scored in the lowest levels of the Armed Forces Qualification Test (categories IV and V), compared to 10 percent of the white soldiers.[22]

These scores account for much of the disproportion. To that extent they reflect the relationship of race and class in civilian society. Poor and working-class soldiers, whether black or white, were more likely to be trained for combat than were soldiers economically and educationally more advantaged. While enlisted men of both races were primarily from the bottom half of the social structure, blacks were considerably poorer. One study found that 90 percent of black soldiers in Vietnam were from working-class and poor backgrounds. This is a large part of the reason why more blacks reenlisted. Men who reenlisted were given bonuses of $900 to $1,400, equivalent to one-third of the median family income for black families in the mid-1960s. However, the military's assignment of blacks to low-ranking positions was not simply a reflection of the economic and racial inequalities of civilian society. The military contributed its own discrimination. In the first years of American escalation, even those blacks who scored in the highest test category were placed in combat units at a level 75 percent higher than that of whites in the same category.[23]

Though racial discrimination and racist attitudes surely persisted in the military, class was far more important than race in determining the overall social composition of American forces. Precisely when the enlisted ranks were becoming increasingly integrated by race, they were becoming ever more segregated by class. The military may never have been truly representative of the general male population, but in the 1960s it was overwhelmingly the domain of the working class.

No thorough statistical study has yet been conducted on the class origins of the men who served in Vietnam. Though the military made endless, mind-numbing efforts to quantify virtually every aspect of its venture in Vietnam, it did not make (so far as anyone has discovered) a single

Table I. Occupations of Fathers of Enlisted Men, by Service, 1964 (Percent)

Father's Occupation	Army	Navy	Air Force	Marines
White-collar	17.0	19.8	20.9	20.4
Blue-collar	52.8	54.5	52.0	57.2
Farmer	14.8	10.7	13.3	9.1
Military	1.8	2.1	1.8	2.0
Father absent	13.6	12.9	12.0	11.3
(Approx. N)	(28,000)	(17,500)	(28,000)	(5,000)

Source: 1964 NORC survey, in Moskos, *American Enlisted Man*, p. 195.

study of the social backgrounds of its fighting men. Quantitative evidence must be gathered from a variety of disparate studies. Probably the most ambitious effort to gather statistical information about the backgrounds of Vietnam-era soldiers was conducted just prior to the large-scale American escalation. In 1964 the National Opinion Research Center (NORC) surveyed 5 percent of all active-duty enlisted men.

According to NORC's occupational survey (table 1) roughly 20 percent of American enlisted men had fathers with white-collar jobs. Among the male population as a whole more than twice that portion, 44 percent, were white-collar workers. Of course, not all white-collar jobs are necessarily middle class in the income, power, and status they confer. Many low-paying clerical and sales jobs—typically listed as white collar—are more accurately understood as working-class occupations. While the white-collar label exaggerates the size of the middle class, it nonetheless encompasses almost all privileged Americans in the labor force. Thus, the fact that only 20 percent of U.S. soldiers came from white-collar families represents a striking class difference between the military and the general population.[24]

The high portion of farmers in the sample is a further indication of the disproportionate number of soldiers from rural small towns. In the 1960s only about 5 percent of the American labor force was engaged in agriculture. In the NORC survey, more than twice as many, 12 percent, came from farm families. Though the survey does not reveal the economic standing of this group, we should avoid an American tendency to picture all farmers as independent proprietors. At the time of the survey about two-thirds of the workers engaged in agricultural labor were wage earners (farm laborers or migrant farmworkers) with family incomes less than $1,000 per year.[25]

There is also good reason to believe that most of the men with absent fathers grew up in hard-pressed circumstances. In 1965, almost two-thirds of the children in female-headed families lived below the census bureau's low-income level.[26] All told, the NORC survey suggests that on the brink of the Vietnam escalation at least three-quarters of American enlisted men were working class or poor.

Although this book focuses on enlisted men, the inclusion of officers would not dramatically raise the overall class backgrounds of the Vietnam military. Officers comprised 11 percent of the total number of men in Vietnam, so even if many of them were from privileged families, the statistical impact would be limited. Furthermore, though we need further studies of the social backgrounds of the Vietnam-era officer corps, it may well have been the least privileged officer corps of the twentieth century. For example, in his study of the West Point class of 1966, Rick Atkinson found a striking historical decline in the class backgrounds of cadets. "Before World War I, the academy had drawn nearly a third of the corps from the families of doctors, lawyers, and other professionals. But by the mid 1950s, sons of professionals made up only 10 percent of the cadets, and links to the upper class had been almost severed. West Point increasingly attracted military brats and sons of the working class."[27] Also, as the war dragged on, the officer corps was depleted of service school and ROTC graduates and had to rely increasingly on enlisted men who were given temporary field commissions or sent to officer candidate school. These officers, too, probably lowered the class background of the officer corps.[28]

Class inequality is also strikingly revealed in the most important post-war statistical study of Vietnam veterans, *Legacies of Vietnam*. Commissioned by the Veterans' Administration in 1978, about two-thirds of the *Legacies* sample of Vietnam veterans was working class or below. That figure is remarkable because the survey used sampling techniques designed to produce the widest possible class spectrum; that is, in choosing people for the study it sought a "maximum variation in socioeconomic context." Even so, the sample of Vietnam veterans was well below the general population in its class composition. When measured against backgrounds of nonveterans of the same generation, Vietnam veterans came out on the bottom in income, occupation, and education.[29]

The key here is disproportion. The point is not that *all* working-class men went to Vietnam while everyone better off stayed home. Given the enormous size of the generation, millions of working-class men simply were not needed by the military. Many were exempted because they failed to meet the minimum physical or mental standards of the armed forces. However, the odds of working-class men going into the military and on to Vietnam were far higher than they were for the middle class and the privileged.

The *Legacies* study also suggests an important distinction between black and white soldiers. The black veterans, at least in this sample, were significantly more representative of the entire black population than white veterans were of the white population. This reflects the fact that whites and blacks have different class distributions, with blacks having a much larger portion of poor and working people and a much smaller middle class and elite. In the *Legacies* sample, 82 percent of black nonveterans were working class and below, compared with 47 percent of the white non-veterans. In other words, while black soldiers were still, as a group, poorer than white soldiers, in relationship to the class structure of their respective races, blacks were not as disproportionately poor and working class as whites. This is, I think, one reason why black veterans seem to have less class-based resentment than white veterans toward the men of their race who did not serve in Vietnam.[30]

Education, along with occupation and income, is a key measure of class position. Eighty percent of the men who went to Vietnam had no more than a high school education (table 2). This figure would compare well to statistics of some previous wars. After all, at the time of the Civil War and well into the twentieth century, only a small minority of Americans had high school educations. However, if considered in historical context, the low portion of college educated among American soldiers is yet another indication of the disproportionately working-class composition of the military. The 1960s was a boomtime for American education, a time when opportunities for higher education were more widespread than ever before. By 1965, 45 percent of Americans between eighteen and twenty-one had some college education. By 1970 that figure was more than 50 percent. Compared with national standards, American forces were well below average in formal education. Studies matching school enrollments to age and class show that the educational levels of American soldiers in Vietnam correspond roughly to those of draft-age, blue-collar males in the general population (table 3). Of course, many veterans took college courses after

Table 2. *Educational Attainment of Vietnam Veterans at Time of Separation from the Armed Forces, 1966–1971 (Percent)*

Fiscal year	Less than 12 Years of School	12 Years of School	1 to 3 Years of College	4 or More Years of College
1966	22.9	62.5	8.3	6.3
1967	23.6	61.8	9.0	5.6
1968	19.6	65.5	9.7	6.2
1969	18.3	60.0	15.9	5.8
1970	17.5	56.9	17.0	8.6
1971	14.7	55.4	19.4	10.5
Total, 1966–71	19.4	60.3	13.2	7.2

Source: Reports and Statistics Service, Office of Controller, Veterans' Administration, 11 April 1972, in Helmer, *Bringing the War Home*, p. 303.

their military service. However, the *Legacies* study found that by 1981 only 22 percent of veterans had completed college compared with 46 percent of nonveterans.[31]

The portion of soldiers with at least some college education increased significantly in the late 1960s as draft calls increased and most graduate school deferments ended. By 1970 roughly 25 percent of American forces in Vietnam had some college education. Impressive as this increase was, it still fell well below the 50 percent for the age group as a whole, and it came as American troop levels in Vietnam were beginning to drop. Moreover, college education per se was no longer so clear a mark of privilege as it had been prior to World War II. Higher education in the post–World War II era expanded enormously, especially among junior and state colleges, the kinds of schools that enrolled the greatest number of working-class students. Between 1962 and 1972, enrollments in two-year colleges tripled. College students who went to Vietnam were far more likely to come from these institutions than from elite, four-year, private colleges. A survey of Harvard's class of 1970, for example, found only two men who served in Vietnam. College students who did go to Vietnam usually secured non-combat assignments. Among soldiers in Vietnam, high school dropouts were three times more likely to experience heavy combat than were college graduates.[32]

Table 3. Percentage of Males Enrolled in School, 1965–1970

Age	Blue-Collar	White-Collar
16–17	80	92
18–19	49	73
20–24	20	43

Source: Levison, *Working-Class Majority*, p. 121.

Young men have fought in all wars, but U.S. forces in Vietnam were probably, on average, the youngest in our history. In previous wars many men in their twenties were drafted for military service, and men of that age and older often volunteered. During the Vietnam War most of the volunteers and draftees were teenagers; the average age was nineteen. In World War II, by contrast, the average American soldier was twenty-six years old. At age eighteen young men could join or be drafted into the army. At seventeen, with the consent of a guardian, boys could enlist in the Marine Corps. Early in the war, hundreds of seventeen-year-old marines served in Vietnam. In November 1965 the Pentagon ordered that all American troops must be eighteen before being deployed in the war zone. Even so, the average age remained low. Twenty-two-year-old soldiers were often kidded about their advanced age ("hey, old man") by the younger men in their units. Most American troops were not even old enough to vote. The voting age did not drop from twenty-one to eighteen until 1971. Thus, most of the Americans who fought in Vietnam were powerless, working-class teenagers sent to fight an undeclared war by presidents for whom they were not even eligible to vote.[33]

No statistical profile can do justice to the complexity of individual experience, but without these broad outlines our understanding would be hopelessly fragmented. A class breakdown of American forces cannot be absolutely precise, but I believe the following is a reasonable estimate: enlisted ranks in Vietnam were comprised of about 25 percent poor, 55 percent working class, and 20 percent middle class, with a statistically negligible number of wealthy. Most Americans in Vietnam were nineteen-year-old high school graduates. They grew up in the white, working-class enclaves of South Boston and Cleveland's West Side; in the black ghettos of Detroit and Birmingham; in the small rural towns of Oklahoma and Iowa; and in the housing developments of working-class suburbs. They came by the thousands from every state and every U.S. territory, but few were from places of wealth and privilege.

THE DRAFT AND THE MAKING OF A
WORKING-CLASS MILITARY

The Selective Service System was the most important institutional mechanism in the creation of a working-class army. It directly inducted more than 2 million men into the military, and just as important, the threat or likelihood of the draft indirectly induced millions more to enlist. These "draft-motivated" volunteers enlisted because they had already received their induction notices or believed they soon would, and thus they enlisted in order, they hoped, to have more choice as to the nature and location of their service. Even studies conducted by the military suggest that as many as half of the men who enlisted were motivated primarily by the pressure of the draft (table 4). Draft pressure became the most important cause of enlistments as the war lengthened.

The soldiers sent to Vietnam can be divided into three categories of roughly equal size: one-third draftees, one-third draft-motivated volunteers, and one-third true volunteers. In the first years of the American buildup most of the fighting was done by men who volunteered for military service. That does not mean they volunteered to fight in Vietnam. Few did. Even among West Point's class of 1966 only one-sixth volunteered for service in Vietnam (though many more eventually ended up there). As the war continued, the number of volunteers steadily declined. From 1966 to 1969 the percentage of draftees who died in the war doubled from 21 to 40 (table 5). Almost half of the army troops were draftees, and in combat units the portion was commonly as high as two-thirds; late in the war it was even higher. The overall number of draftees was lower because the Marine Corps—the other service branch that did the bulk of fighting in Vietnam—was ordinarily limited to volunteers (though it did draft about 20,000 men during the Vietnam War).[34]

The draft determined the social character of the armed forces by whom it exempted from service as well as by whom it actually conscripted or induced to enlist. Because the generation that came of age during the 1960s was so large, the Selective Service exempted far more men than it drafted. From 1964 to 1973, 2.2 million men were drafted, 8.7 million enlisted, and 16 million did not serve. Of course, the millions of exemptions

Table 4. Percentage of Draft-Motivated Enlistments

Year	Enlistees	Officers	Reservists
1964	38	41	71
1968	54	60	80

Source: U.S. House Committee on Armed Services, 1966, 100038; 1970, 12638. Cited in Useem, *Conscription, Protest, and Social Conflict*, p. 78.

Table 5. American Draftees Killed in the Vietnam War

Year	Total American Deaths, All Services	Draftees (Percent) All Services	Army
1965	1,369	16	28
1966	5,008	21	34
1967	9,378	34	57
1968	14,592	34	58
1969	9,414	40	62
1970	4,221	43	57

Source: Columns 1 and 2 from U.S. Bureau of the Census, 1971, 253; column 3 from U.S. House Committee on Armed Services, 1971, 172. Cited in Useem, *Conscription, Protest, and Social Conflict*, p. 107.

could have been granted in a manner designed to produce a military that mirrored the social composition of society at large. A step in that direction was made with the institution of a draft lottery in late 1969, a method that can produce a representative cross-section of draftees. However, this reform did little to democratize the forces that fought in Vietnam because student deferments were continued until 1971, troop withdrawals late in the war lowered draft calls, and physical exemptions remained relatively easy for the privileged to attain.

Prior to the draft lottery, the Selective Service did not even profess the ideal of a socially and economically balanced military. Instead, it was devoted to a form of "human resource planning" designed to serve the "national interest" by sending some men into the military and encouraging others to stay in school and seek occupational deferments. At the heart of this conscious effort at social engineering was the concept of "channeling." The basic idea was to use the threat of the draft and the lure of educational and professional deferments to channel men into nonmilitary occupations that the Selective Service believed vital to the "national health, safety and interest." The primary architect of this system was Gen. Lewis B. Hershey, director of the Selective Service from 1941 to 1968. According to his biographer, George Flynn, Hershey was at first ambivalent, if not hostile, toward student deferments, unsure of their value or fairness. However, this master bureaucrat, determined to build and maintain a permanent draft, was soon persuaded otherwise. The six advisory committees he appointed in 1948, during the creation of the first peacetime draft, all supported student deferments. They argued that virtually every academic field had contributed to victory in World War II and that the draft should protect at least the most successful college and graduate students. Many advisers were especially concerned that potential scientists be protected. As the nuclear age advanced, influential policymakers were increasingly persuaded that the outcome of future wars—whether hot or cold—might be determined not by masses of muddy combat soldiers but by teams of high-powered, white-jacketed scientists and engineers. Hershey quickly embraced student deferments, and by the mid-1950s he became their most important advocate.[35]

Most of the class-biased draft policies of the 1960s were in place by the early 1950s. Still, the Korean War was not quite as class skewed as the Vietnam War, for two reasons. First, though there were student deferments during the Korean War, college graduates enlisted in rough proportion to their numbers (they did not do so during the Vietnam War). Second, for Korea, unlike Vietnam, the reserves were mobilized. Reserve units usually have a more balanced class composition than the regular army. During the period between Korea and Vietnam, draft calls were so low the military could afford to raise its admission standards and place more draftees in electronic and technical fields. These factors raised the class level of inductees. In fact, throughout the late 1950s and early 1960s, the Selective Service System was commonly criticized not because it offered too many deferments to the privileged but because "the underprivileged were too often barred from the benefits of military service by unrealistically high mental and physical standards."[36]

In 1963 Daniel P. Moynihan, assistant secretary of labor for policy planning, learned that one-half of the men called by their draft boards for physical and mental examinations failed one or both of the tests and were thus disqualified for military service. Moynihan was particularly disturbed that poor boys were the most likely to be rejected. They were most commonly rejected for failing the intelligence test, the Armed Forces Qualification Test. In the early 1960s almost half of the men who failed this test came from families with six or more children and annual incomes of less than $4,000. Moynihan described this high rejection rate as a form of "de facto job discrimination" against "the least mobile, least educated young men."[37]

Moynihan organized a presidential task force to examine conscription policies and to explore proposals by which the military might take responsibility for training men who initially failed to meet the military's mental standards. The task force study, *One Third of a Nation* (1964), called for the military to lower its entrance requirements and provide special training to those with mental or social handicaps. For Moynihan, the military seemed like a vast, untapped agent of social uplift with the potential to train the unskilled, to put unemployed youth to work, and to instill confidence and pride in the psychologically defeated. More than that, he believed the military could help solve the problem he claimed was at the heart of black poverty—broken, fatherless families. The military, Moynihan argued, would serve as a surrogate black family: "Given the strains of disorganized and matrifocal family life in which so many Negro youth come of age, the armed forces are a dramatic and desperately needed change; a world away from women, a world run by strong men and unquestioned authority."[38]

In 1964, in response to Moynihan's proposal, the military began a series of pilot programs to admit a small number of draft rejects who agreed to voluntary rehabilitation as part of their military training, but these programs had little impact on the social composition of the military. In 1965, however, as draft calls jumped to fill the troop buildup in South Vietnam, the military began to lower its admission standards quite radically. With no intention of engaging in any social uplift, the military simply accepted more and more men with terribly low scores on the mental examination. During the 1950s and early 1960s, men who had scored in the two lowest categories (IV and V) were rarely accepted into the military. Beginning in 1965, however, hundreds of thousands of category IV men were drafted. Most were from poor and broken families, 80 percent were high school dropouts, and half had IQs of less than eighty-five. Prior to American escalation in Vietnam such men were routinely rejected, but with a war on, these "new standards" men were suddenly declared fit to fight. Rejection rates plummeted. Between 1965 and 1966 the overall rejection rate fell from 50 to 34 percent, and by 1967 mental rejections were cut in half.[39]

The new-standards men were offered no special training to raise their intellectual skills. Most were simply trained for war. Yet, in 1966 Moynihan was still calling for lower military standards. That year Secretary of Defense Robert McNamara instituted a program that promised to carry out many of Moynihan's proposals. Called Project 100,000, McNamara's program was designed to admit 100,000 men into the military each year who failed the qualifying exam even at the lower standards of 1965. This program, McNamara claimed, would offer valuable training and opportunity to America's "subterranean poor." As McNamara put it, "The poor of America . . . have not had the opportunity to earn their fair share of this nation's abundance, but they can be given an opportunity to serve in their country's defense and they can be given an opportunity to return to civilian life with skills and aptitudes which for them and their families will reverse the downward spiral of decay."[40] Never well known, Project 100,000 has virtually disappeared from histories of the Johnson presidency. It was conceived, in fact, as a significant component of the administration's "war on poverty," part of the Great Society, a liberal effort to uplift the poor, and it was instituted with high-minded rhetoric about offering the poor an opportunity to serve. Its result, however, was to send many poor, terribly confused, and woefully uneducated boys to risk death in Vietnam. There is an important analogy here to the way American officials explained the war itself. It was not, they claimed, a unilateral military intervention to bolster a weak, corrupt, and unpopular government in South Vietnam against revolutionary nationalism, but a generous effort to help the people of South Vietnam determine their own fate. But if governments were judged by their professed intentions alone, and not by the consequences of their actions as well, every state would bask in glory. Graham Greene might have said about Project 100,000 what he said about the well-intentioned Alden Pyle in his novel *The Quiet American*: "I never knew a man who had better motives for all the trouble he caused."[41]

The effect of Project 100,000 was dire. The promised training was never carried out. Of the 240,000 men inducted by Project 100,000 from 1966 to 1968, only 6 percent received additional training, and this amounted to little more than an effort to raise reading skills to a fifth grade level. Forty percent were trained for combat, compared with only 25 percent for all enlisted men. Also, while blacks comprised 10 percent of the entire military, they represented about 40 percent of the Project 100,000 soldiers. A 1970 Defense Department study estimates that roughly half of the almost 400,000 men who entered the military under Project 100,000 were sent to Vietnam. These men had a death rate twice as high as American forces as a whole. This was a Great Society program that was quite literally shot down on the battlefields of Vietnam.[42]

Project 100,000 and the abandonment of all but the most minimal mental requirements for military service were crucial institutional mechanisms in lowering the class composition of the American military. Had the prewar mental standards continued, almost 3 million men would have been exempted from military service on the basis of intelligence. Under the lowered standards, 1.36 million were mentally disqualified.

Almost three times as many men, 3.5 million, were exempted because of their physical condition. One might expect men from disadvantaged backgrounds, with poorer nutrition and less access to decent health care, to receive most of these exemptions. In practice, however, most physical exemptions were assigned to men who had the knowledge and resources to claim an exemption. Poor and working-class men ordinarily allowed military doctors to determine their physical fitness. Induction center examinations were often perfunctory exercises in which all but the most obvious disabilities were overlooked. According to the best study of the subject, Baskir and Strauss's *Chance and Circumstance*, men who arrived at their induction physical with professional documentation of a disqualifying ailment had the best chance of gaining a medical exemption. Induction centers usually did not have the time or desire to challenge an outside opinion. The case of an induction center in Seattle, Washington, may be an extreme example, but it underlines the significance of this point. At that center, the registrants were divided into two groups: "Those who had letters from doctors or psychiatrists, and those who did not. Everyone with a letter received an exemption, regardless of what the letter said."[43]

Even very minor disabilities were grounds for medical disqualification. Skin rashes, flat feet, asthma, trick knees—such ailments were easily missed or ignored by military doctors, but they were legal exemptions that were frequently granted when attested to by a family physician. Even dental braces provided a means of avoiding the military. "In the Los

Angeles area alone, ten dentists willingly performed orthodontic work for anyone who could pay a $1000–2000 fee. Wearing braces was a common last-minute tactic for registrants who faced immediate call-up."[44]

According to Baskir and Strauss, men who were knowledgeable about the system and had the means to press a claim had a 90 percent chance of receiving a physical or psychological exemption even if they were in good health. Draft lore such as Arlo Guthrie's "Alice's Restaurant" has made famous some of the more bizarre efforts at draft avoidance—loading up on drugs before the physical, fasting or gorging to get outside the weight requirements, feigning insanity or homosexuality, or aggravating an old knee injury. There is no telling how many men tried such things, but the majority who received medical exemptions through their own efforts probably did so in a far less dramatic fashion by simply finding a professional to support their claim.[45]

That the men who were most able and likely to seek professional help in avoiding the draft were white and middle class is not surprising. On many college campuses students could find political and psychological support for draft resistance along with concrete advice on how to get an exemption. In working-class neighborhoods, the myriad ways to avoid the draft were not only less well known, they had little, if any, community support. Avoiding the draft was more likely to be viewed as an act of cowardice than as a principled unwillingness to participate in an immoral war.

The onus of responsibility for claiming exemptions fell, except in obvious cases, on the individual registrant. Even those exemptions that were especially aimed at the poor, such as those for "hardship," were often ineffectual for men who were unaware of them or lacked the wherewithal to demonstrate their claim to the Selective Service. Much depended on the discretion of local draft boards. Though the national headquarters of the Selective Service provided the general framework of guidelines and regulations, the system was designed to be highly decentralized, with authority largely delegated to the 4,000 local boards across the country.

Draft boards were comprised of volunteers who typically met only once a month. With hundreds of cases to decide, board members could give careful attention to only the most difficult. The rest were reviewed by a full-time civil service clerk whose decisions were usually rubber-stamped by the board. One study found that the civil servant determined the outcome of 85 percent of the cases. Under this system, the advantage went to those registrants who were able to document their claims clearly and convincingly. What was persuasive to one board, however, might not be to another. There were, in fact, significant variations in the way different boards operated. Occupational deferments, for example, often depended simply on what local boards determined to be "in the national health, safety, or interest."[46]

While local discretionary power produced a number of anomalies,[47] most local boards administered the system in ways that reinforced the class inequalities underlying the broad national system of manpower channeling. In fact, the decentralized system probably gave an added advantage to registrants with economic clout and social connections. Draft boards were overwhelmingly controlled by conservative, white, prosperous men in their fifties or sixties. A 1966 study of the 16,638 draft board members around the nation found that only 9 percent had blue-collar occupations, while more than 70 percent were professionals, managers, proprietors, public officials, or white-collar workers over the age of fifty. Only 1.3 percent were black.[48] Until 1967, when Congress revoked the prohibition, women were forbidden from serving on local draft boards because General Hershey "feared they would be embarrassed when a physical question emerged."[49]

The student deferment was the most overtly class-biased feature of the Vietnam era draft system. Census records show that youth from families earning $7,500 to $10,000 were almost two and a half times more likely to attend college than those from families earning under $5,000.[50] Also, working-class boys who did go to college were far more likely to attend part time while working. This distinction is crucial because deferments were only offered to full-time students, thus excluding those trying to earn a degree by working their way through school a few courses at a time. These students were subject to the draft.

In addition, unsuccessful students with low class ranks could lose their deferments. The grades required to keep a student deferment varied according to the practice of local draft boards, but in 1966 and 1967 the Selective Service sought to weed out poor students systematically by giving almost a million students the Selective Service Qualifying Test. Many who scored poorly were reclassified and drafted. The irony, of course, is that the draft grabbed those students who were among the least qualified according to its own test.[51]

While unsuccessful and part-time students were "draft-bait," successful full-time students could preserve their draft immunity by going on to graduate school. Those who were trained as engineers, scientists, or teachers could then acquire occupational deferments. Though graduate students in every field received deferments, the primary intention of the inducement, according to General Hershey, was to bolster the ranks of scientists and technicians, many of whom would serve defense-related industries. In 1965 Hershey wrote, "The process of channeling manpower by deferment is entitled to much credit for the large number of graduate students in technical fields and for the fact that there is not a greater shortage of teachers, engineers and scientists working in activities which are essential to the national interest."[52]

The campus-based antiwar and draft resistance movements deserve much of the credit for exposing the class-biased system of channeling to public scrutiny. The antiwar critique of channeling is often neglected by those who glibly accuse movement participants of hiding behind their student deferments. As one draft resistance manifesto put it: "Most of us now have deferments. . . . But all these individual outs can have no effect on the draft, the war, or the consciousness of this country. . . . To cooperate with conscription is to perpetuate its existence. . . . We will renounce all deferments." Though most young men in the antiwar movement kept their deferments or found other ways of evading the draft (a small group did accept prison sentences for resisting the draft), the major thrust of their effort was to keep *all* Americans from fighting in Vietnam. By drawing attention to the inequalities in the system, they helped generate support for the draft reforms of 1967 and the draft lottery of 1969. The 1967 reforms included the elimination of deferments for graduate school. (Those who had already begun graduate school were, however, usually allowed to keep their deferments.) This reduction in deferments was a key factor in raising the portion of college graduates who served in Vietnam from about 6 percent in 1966 to 10 percent in 1970.[53]

Still, there were many ways to avoid Vietnam after graduating from college. In addition to seeking medical exemptions, one of the most common was to enlist in the National Guard or the reserves. In 1968, fully 80 percent of American reservists described themselves as draft-motivated enlistees (see table 4). The reserves required six years of part-time duty, but many men who joined believed correctly there was little chance they would be mobilized to fight in Vietnam. President Johnson rejected the military's frequent request for a major mobilization of the reserves and the National Guard. He feared that activating these units would draw unwanted attention to the war and exacerbate antiwar sentiment. Since these men were drawn from specific towns and urban neighborhoods, their mobilization would have a dramatic impact on concentrated populations. Johnson also realized that reservists and guardsmen were generally older than regular army troops and were, as a group, socially and economically more prominent. By relying on the draft and the active-duty military to fight the war, Johnson hoped to diffuse the impact of casualties among widely scattered, young, and powerless individuals. He wanted, as David Halberstam put it, a "silent, politically invisible war."[54]

During the war over a million men served in the reserves and National Guard. Of these, some 37,000 were mobilized and 15,000 were sent to Vietnam. As the war continued, thousands of men tried to enlist in this relatively safe form of military service. By 1968 the National Guard alone had a waiting list of 100,000. Throughout the country the reserves and the guard were notorious for restrictive, "old-boy" admissions policies. In many places a man simply had to have connections to get in. For the poor and working class it was particularly difficult to gain admission. In the army reserves, for example, the percentage of college graduates among the enlisted men was three times higher than in the regular army.[55]

For blacks, whatever their economic standing, to become a reservist or guardsman was nearly impossible. In 1964 only 1.45 percent of the Army National Guard was black. By 1968 this tiny percentage had actually decreased to 1.26. Exclusion of blacks was especially egregious in the South. In Mississippi, for example, where blacks comprised 42 percent of the population, only 1 black man was admitted to the National Guard of 10,365 men. In the North, the guard was only slightly more open. In Michigan, for example, only 1.34 percent of the National Guard was black, compared with 9.2 percent of the population. Thus, the safest form of military service almost entirely excluded blacks and was most open to middle-class whites.[56]

The Selective Service System's class-biased channeling, the military's wartime slashing of admissions standards, Project 100,000, medical exemptions that favored the well-informed and privileged, student deferments, the safe haven of the National Guard and the reserves—these were the key institutional factors in the creation of a working-class military. But these are not the only factors that encouraged working-class boys to serve so disproportionately. In many respects our whole culture served to channel the working class toward the military and the middle and upper classes toward college. We can understand some of the more complex influences by exploring the consciousness of young men who fought in Vietnam—specifically, their prewar understanding of their place and purpose in American society and how they perceived the prospect of military service and war. That is the subject of chapter 2. However, before proceeding we need a brief account of common, middle-class assumptions about how working people thought about the Vietnam War, for these images and stereotypes still distort much of the thinking about our subject.

WARTIME IMAGES OF A HAWKISH WORKING CLASS

That the Vietnam War was a working-class war may not be surprising news, but it has never been widely and publicly acknowledged or discussed. For that matter, class issues of any kind have rarely been a focus of common, explicit debate in American public life. Indeed, the very existence of class has been denied, diminished, or distorted by the institutions most responsible for establishing the terms of public discourse: the large corporations (including, of course, the major media), the schools, and the two major political parties.

During the war, the mass media gave little serious attention to the relationship of the working class to Vietnam. Instead, the subject was presented in an indirect and distorted way that reduced workers to a grossly misleading stereotype. Rather than documenting the class inequalities of military service and the complex feelings soldiers and their families had about their society and the war in Vietnam, the media more commonly contributed to the construction of an image of workers as the war's strongest supporters, as superpatriotic hawks whose political views could be understood simply by reading the bumper stickers on some of their cars and pickups: "America: Love it or Leave it." These "hard-hats" or "rednecks" were frequently portrayed as "Joe six-pack," a flag-waving, blue-collar, anti-intellectual who, on top of everything else, was assumed to be a bigot.

This caricature really began to crystallize in 1968 during the presidential campaign of George Wallace. The segregationist, prowar governor of Alabama surprised experts by winning 8 million votes for his third-party candidacy, many of them coming not only from white southerners, but also from white working-class voters in the North. Yet, this support was too easily taken as evidence that the working class was the most racist and prowar segment of American society. While those characteristics certainly drew many voters to Wallace, his success also reflected a deeply felt anger and disillusionment that had as much to do with class position as it did with race and war. Wallace appealed to the fear many working-class families had that their values—love of country, respect for law and order, religious faith, and hard work—were being ridiculed and threatened from above and below, by privileged campus protesters, ghetto rioters, and Great Society liberals who seemed always to talk about helping the poor without regard for the millions of working-class people just one rung up the economic ladder.

Wallace mobilized this anger, in both 1968 and 1972, by lashing out at "limousine liberals," "pointy-headed intellectuals," and "dirty hippies and protesters." Those were the people, Wallace claimed, who were running America, and who, in so doing, were always "looking down their noses at the average man on the street—the glass workers, the steel workers, the auto workers, the textile workers, the farm workers, the policeman, the beautician and the barber and the little businessman."[57]

President Nixon courted these same "average" Americans when he called on the "forgotten Americans" to rally in support of his Vietnam policies. These people, he claimed, comprised "the great silent majority." The idea that workers formed the vanguard of this supposed majority and would break their silence to support Nixon became a media commonplace during the tumultuous month of May 1970. The month began with Nixon's announcement that American troops would invade Cambodia. Coming in the wake of reassurances that U.S. troops were being withdrawn, that the war was winding down for America, and that the South Vietnamese were taking over the fighting, Nixon's sudden expansion of the war generated an enormous new wave of antiwar protest. Students at more than 500 college campuses went on strike. At one of them, Kent State, four students were killed by national guardsmen. To Pentagon officials, Nixon described the student protesters as bums.

A few days later, on 8 May, antiwar demonstrators—most of them from New York University and Hunter College—held a rally in the financial district of New York City. Construction workers at several large building sites in lower Manhattan had heard about the rally a day or two in advance and planned, as one of them put it, to stage a counterdemonstration and "bust some heads." At noontime on the day of the rally, about 200 construction workers, wearing their yellow hard hats, carrying American flags, and chanting "All The Way USA" shoved through police lines and began beating the antiwar demonstrators with their fists and helmets.

Some used tools. At least a few police were seen standing by as the attack continued.[58]

From Wall Street the workers, their ranks enlarged to 500, marched to city hall, where the American flag was flying at half-mast, on Mayor John Lindsay's orders, in memory of the four students killed at Kent State. The workers demanded that the flag be raised. When it was, the men cheered and sang "The Star-Spangled Banner." Then, observing an antiwar banner at nearby Pace College, the workers broke down the glass doors of a Pace building and beat more students. Throughout the day, dubbed "Bloody Friday" by the media, about seventy victims were injured badly enough to require treatment.

Some workers reported that the attack was far from spontaneous and that it had been orchestrated by union leaders in the Building and Trades Council of Greater New York. Even so, the leaders seemed to have no trouble finding volunteers. Two weeks later the council, perhaps hoping to offset the violent imagery of Bloody Friday, organized a peaceful march to demonstrate their "love of country and love and respect for our country's flag." *Time* magazine described it this way: "Callused hands gripped tiny flags. Weathered faces shone with sweat. . . . For three hours, 100,000 members of New York's brawniest unions marched and shouted . . . in a massive display of gleeful patriotism and muscular pride . . . a kind of workers' Woodstock."[59] These events were crucial in shaping an idea that came to dominate middle-class thought about the war—that the "hawks" were workers and the "doves" were privileged. As the *New York Times* put it, "The typical worker—from construction craftsman to shoe clerk—has become probably the most reactionary political force in the country."[60]

This stereotype received perhaps its most significant dramatization a few months later in the form of Archie Bunker, hero of the situation comedy "All in the Family." Archie could be counted on for mindless verbal swipes at blacks, Jews, feminists, and peace activists ("coloreds," "kikes," "libbers," and "pinkos"). But rail as he would against his long list of enemies and the liberal views of his "meathead" son-in-law, Archie's hostility was cushioned by a larger family devotion. While the nation came apart at the seams, the Bunkers kept their conflicts "all in the family." Part of the show's liberal condescension was to suggest that the working class, however retrograde in its views, does not really act out its hostilities and is therefore essentially harmless.

Of course, the image of the hawkish worker (be it Archie Bunker or the hard-hats of Bloody Friday) had enough surface familiarity to serve for many as a sufficient model of a whole class. After all, many working-class people certainly did support the war. But was the working class as a whole really more prowar than the rest of society? (Or more racist?) Not so. In fact, virtually every survey of public opinion on the war found little or no difference between the responses of the working class and those of the middle and upper classes. There were, in other words, at least as many hawks in corporate office buildings as there were in factories. Part of the problem with the hard-hat stereotype is that it made white, Christian males the symbol of the entire working class. The working class, of course, includes women, blacks, Hispanics, Jews—an enormous variety. Polls suggest that the three groups most consistently opposed to the war over time were blacks, women, and the very poor. Yet, even white, working-class men were far less conservative as a group than Archie Bunker. One survey, taken in the same year the media invented the term *hard-hats* (1970), found that 48 percent of the northern white working class was in favor of immediate withdrawal of American troops from Vietnam, while only 40 percent of the white middle class took this dove position. More-over, while the New York construction unions continued to be prowar, members of the Teamsters and the United Auto Workers had turned against it. In 1972, a higher percentage of blue-collar workers voted for peace candidate George McGovern than did white-collar professionals.[61]

There was, however, one very telling difference between the war-related attitudes of workers and the middle class. More workers were openly opposed to antiwar demonstrators. One study found that even one-half of those workers who favored immediate and total withdrawal from Vietnam were nevertheless opposed to antiwar demonstrators. This, I think, indicates that working-class anger at the antiwar movement—primarily a middle-class movement—often represented class conflict, not conflict over the legitimacy of the war. The union men who marched in the New York City parade carried signs that said "Support our boys in Vietnam." The sign can be read quite literally. Many of their sons were in Vietnam. Working-class people opposed college protesters largely be-cause they saw the antiwar movement as an elitist attack on American troops by people who could avoid the war. At its best, the antiwar move-ment tried to correct that perception by focusing its criticism on the people in Washington who planned the war and kept it going. But class division—inflamed by the politicians and institutions that ran the war—continued to muddy the ideological water. A significant segment of the student antiwar movement explicitly denounced the unequal distribution of power and privilege in American society, but to many workers the demonstrators seemed at once to flaunt and deny their own privileges. How, they wondered, could college students possibly claim to be victims (of police brutality, of bureaucratic university administrators, of an inhuman corporate rat race that provided meaningless work) when they were so obviously better off than workers who endured far more daily indignity and mind-numbing labor? A firefighter who lost his son Ralph in Vietnam told Robert Coles:

> I'm bitter. You bet your goddamn dollar I'm bitter. It's people like us who give up our sons for the country. The business people, they run the country and make money from it. The college types, the professors, they go to Washington and tell the government what to do. . . . But their sons, they don't end up in the swamps over there, in Vietnam. No sir. They're deferred, because they're in school. Or they get sent to safe places. Or they get out with all those letters they have from their doctors. Ralph told me. He told me what went on at his physical. He said most of the kids were from average homes; and the few rich kids there were, they all had big-deal letters saying they weren't eligible. . . . Let's face it: if you have a lot of money, or if you have the right connections, you don't end up on a firing line in the jungle over there, not unless you *want* to. Ralph had no choice. He didn't want to die. He wanted to live. They just took him—to "defend democracy," that's what they keep on saying. Hell, I wonder.
>
> I think we ought to win that war or pull out. What the hell else should we do—sit and bleed ourselves to death, year after year? I hate those peace demonstrators. Why don't they go to Vietnam and demonstrate in front of the North Vietnamese? . . . The whole thing is a mess. The sooner we get the hell out of there the better. But what bothers me about the peace crowd is that you can tell from their attitude, the way they look and what they say, that they don't really love this country. Some of them almost seem *glad* to have a chance to criticize us. . . . To hell with them! Let them get out, leave, if they don't like it here! My son didn't die so they can look filthy and talk filthy and insult everything we believe in and everyone in the country—me and my wife and people here on the street, and the next street, and all over.

This man is not, by any thoughtful definition, a hawk. He wants the war ended, if not in victory, then by immediate withdrawal. He has serious doubts about the purpose of the war. As his wife says, "I think my husband and I can't help but thinking that our son gave his life for nothing, nothing at all." But they can't abide "the peace crowd." The husband believed the demonstrators cared more about the Vietnamese than they did about ordinary Americans. His wife responded:

I told him I thought they want the war to end, so no more Ralphs will die, but he says no, they never stop and think about Ralph and his kind of people, and I'm inclined to agree. They *say* they do, but I listen to them, I watch them; since Ralph died I listen and I watch as carefully as I can. Their hearts are with other people, not their own American people, the ordinary kind of person in this country. . . . Those people, a lot of them are rich women from the suburbs, the rich suburbs. Those kids, they are in college. . . . I'm against this war, too—the way a mother is, whose sons are in the army, who has lost a son fighting in it. The world hears those demonstrators making their noise. The world doesn't hear me, and it doesn't hear a single person I know.[62]

Since the Vietnam War, the world continues to hear very little from or about such women. In the Reagan era, however, it also stopped hearing about the experiences of people of any class who opposed the war. Lost in the silence was the awareness that a significant number of American troops themselves turned against the war in its final years. By the late 1960s, some soldiers in Vietnam began to write UUUU on their helmet liners, meaning the unwilling, led by the unqualified, doing the unnecessary for the ungrateful.[63]

Life before the Nam

"Boy, you sure get offered some shitty choices," a Marine once said to me, and I couldn't help but feel that what he really meant was that you didn't get offered any at all. Specifically, he was talking about a couple of C-ration cans, "dinner," but considering his young life you couldn't blame him for thinking that if he knew one thing for sure, it was that there was no one anywhere who cared less about what he wanted.

– Michael Herr,

Dispatches

A draftee: "It was either go to Canada, go to prison, or go in the army. What choice did I have?"

A volunteer: "It was either college, a job, or the military. College was out of the question. We couldn't afford it. And I couldn't get a good job. So I enlisted."[1]

These cryptic explanations hardly exhaust the range of attitudes among Americans who entered the military during the Vietnam War, but they do suggest the narrow boundaries of choice within which these men faced the prospect of military service. Whether draftees or volunteers, the great majority believed they had no real or attractive alternative. Even many who eagerly enlisted were drawn to the military as much by the pressures and constraints of their civilian lives as they were by the call of patriotism or the promised attractions of military life.

"It's not just a job. It's an adventure." So reads the recruiting slogan. But what other jobs were available? The economy as a whole in the 1960s did remarkably well. It was the final decade of the extraordinary postwar economic boom. Between 1960 and 1972, median family income nearly doubled and the GNP advanced even more. For most of the war years, national unemployment was below 5 percent. With such growth one might expect working-class youth to have better options in the civilian economy than in the military. The working class, however, did not share equally in the economic boom of the 1960s. In fact, during the major years of the American war in Vietnam, 1965–69, the real wages of working people remained constant and in some cases dropped. Even more significantly, the unemployment rate among young men was far above the national level. In 1965–70, unemployment among males aged sixteen to nineteen averaged 12.5 percent (12 percent among whites, 27 percent among blacks).[2]

Poor and working-class youth—those most likely to be drafted—were least able to secure stable, well-paying jobs. Even when good blue-collar jobs were open, many employers were reluctant to hire draft-vulnerable men. Such jobs often required a period of training, and employers did not want to invest in young men who might be drafted. For working-class draft-bait in search of nonmilitary labor, all but the most menial jobs were nearly impossible to land. In Glens Falls, New York, for example, the *New York Times* (July 1967) found draft-age men unable to get decent jobs at the local lumber mills and manufacturing plants. "You try to get a job," reported eighteen-year-old Jerry Reynolds, "and the first thing they ask is if you fulfilled your military service." The only jobs available were those paying $50 to $75 a week with no hope of advancement.[3]

John Picciano, a working-class high school graduate from Lodi, New Jersey, began looking for work in 1966. "He tried employer after employer, applying for jobs in stores, factories, offices. It was the same everywhere. As soon as they found out he was 'draft bait,' the interview ended abruptly with the explanation that the company wanted someone on a permanent basis. 'Come back and see us when you get this draft thing out of the way,' was the usual reply."[4] The job market in Alabama was no different: "Needless to say, with Vietnam going and the draft popping about like popcorn, I couldn't get a job. They knew I was goin'. I managed to land one job, general flunky in a nitwit little book company."[5]

College was not a realistic option for most working-class men. Those who started college often interrupted their education to earn the money to continue; others went to school part time. In either case, they were draft-vulnerable. Chris Debeau was a student at the University of Hartford when he received his draft notice. "I was in school. But I was only carrying a course load of nine credits. You had to have 12 or 15 back then [to receive a deferment]. But I was working two jobs so I didn't have time for another three credits."[6]

In the face of these constraints, many men decided to enlist. With the prospect of a dead-end job, little if any chance for college, and the draft looming on the horizon, many saw enlistment as a way of "getting over" the unavoidable. Military recruiters often tailored their pitch to the draft-vulnerable. Sign up, and you can pick your branch of the service and the kind of training you want—so went the standard spiel. An army recruiting slogan added the key threat: "Make your choice now—join, or we'll make the choice for you."[7] Some recruits were won over with smiling assurances that, by volunteering, their odds of going to Vietnam (or at least fighting in combat) were almost nil. These come-ons were rarely backed by guarantees.

Raymond Wilson, from a working-class suburb of Birmingham, Alabama, described his situation:

It was a white working-class community. Everybody is living virtually hand-to-mouth. We're not poor but the wolf's at the door and we're standing a half step ahead of him all the time. My mother was an RN, so she could get a decent job. But my father was laid off from his job [desk clerk at a car rental agency] when I was in high school. I could not go to college knowing my parents would have to borrow so much money. What happens if something happens to one of them? They'd lose their house.

You knew damn well you were going to get drafted. And you're young and naive so you figure that by enlisting you might get an easy out. The next thing you know you end up in Vietnam.[8]

Ken Lombardi, another draft-motivated volunteer, grew up in an Italian-American neighborhood of Brockton, Massachusetts. "Before the Nam I was in high school and I was a jock. But I didn't have the so-called qualifications by the standard aptitude test to be, quote-unquote, 'college material.' So I didn't go [to college]. I graduated from high school in June and got my draft notice in September. I didn't want to get drafted so I enlisted in the army because they gave me the old scam that if you enlist you can pick your career and you may not go to Vietnam." In 1968 Ken was sent to Vietnam as an infantryman.[9]

The high percentage of draft-motivated volunteers was confirmed by two large-scale surveys of 1964 and 1968 (table 6). Subjects were asked to

Table 6. Entry Motivations of Enlisted Volunteers

Most Important Reason[a]	1964	1968
Draft-motivated	37.6	47.2
Personal	28.8	20.1
Self-advancement	22.3	20.1
Patriotism	11.2	6.1
None of the above	—	6.6

Sources: The 1964 figures are from a NORC survey and can be found in Albert D. Klassen, Jr., *Military Service in American Life* (Chicago: National Opinion Research Center, 1966). The 1968 figures are from a Department of Defense survey and can be found in Helmer, *Bringing the War Home*, p. 34.
[a]These categories are composites of several choices: to increase options in choice of service or time of entry (Draft-motivated); to become more mature and self-reliant; for travel, excitement, and new experiences; to leave some personal problems behind me (Personal); to learn a trade; opportunity for advanced education, professional training; career opportunities (Self-advancement); to serve my country (Patriotism).

choose their reason for volunteering from a list of possibilities stated in positive terms—"My choice . . . ," "To fulfill . . . ," "A chance . . . ," "To become . . . ," "To learn . . . ," "To serve . . . ," "Opportunity for. . . ." This language invited people to define their enlistment as a constructive, individual choice. (With the choices framed in this manner, only 4 percent selected the response with the most negative tone: "Wanted to leave some personal problems behind me.") In spite of the upbeat language, most men attributed their enlistment to a rather lackluster motive: the pressure of the draft. According to these surveys, the greatest attraction of enlistment was its presumed advantage to being drafted. In 1968, 30 percent of the subjects checked the response "Wanted my choice of service rather than be drafted." Another 17 percent picked "To fulfill my military obligation at the time of my choice." (The military considers both responses draft-motivated.) The third most common response, "To learn a trade that would be valuable in civilian life," comprised only 11 percent. Patriotism was not a decisive factor for many. In 1964, well before the war had become an issue of widespread national debate, patriotism was chosen by only 11 percent of the volunteers as their main reason for enlisting. Not surprisingly, by 1968, as more Americans began to question the morality of military intervention in Vietnam, that portion dropped to 6 percent.

Responses to open-ended surveys and in-depth interviews provide an even more negative view of the circumstances and motives responsible for military enlistments. In his study of white, working-class veterans, John Helmer found that volunteers enlisted primarily because they felt they had no other alternative. At best, it struck them as a way to get away from a familiar and often troubled world. Helmer had his subjects offer their own major reason for enlisting. The seventy-six volunteers in the sample gave the following responses:[10]

Nothing else to do	14
Draft-motivated	13
To avoid trouble, police	11
To get away from home/family	9
No stated reason	9
To do duty like friends	8
To prove manliness, self	6
Sick of school, hassles	4
For the security of a job	2

These white, working-class men did not regard military service as an opportunity so much as a necessity (nothing else to do, draft pressure, duty, job security) or an escape (to avoid trouble, get away, leave school). Some who volunteered to "avoid trouble" were doing so because the only alternative was prison. It was not uncommon for judges to present young offenders with a Hobson's choice between going to jail or enlisting in the service. Bruce Springsteen may well be alluding to this phenomenon in his popular song about Vietnam veterans, "Born in the U.S.A.":

> Got in a little hometown jam,
> So they put a rifle in my hand.
> Sent me off to a foreign land,
> To go and kill the yellow man.

Some superficial listeners (including the Reagan advisers who tried unsuccessfully to recruit Springsteen's support for the 1984 election) heard the song as a sign of the rebirth of patriotism in the 1980s. However, even casual attention to the lyrics reveals the song to be a sharp critique of American society, the war, and the pain and hardship suffered by Vietnam veterans.

The "hometown jams" that resulted in a prison-or-military sentence have not been counted, but however small the portion of men who went to

Vietnam under these circumstances, the judge's choice provides an apt metaphor for the way many others regarded the options before them. There was simply "nothing else to do," was how some put it to Helmer. The draft was on their necks, school was a boring hassle, jobs all seemed dead-end, family life was becoming unbearable, conflicts with authorities were turning serious and dangerous—in this context the military, for many men, seemed like the only option.

Economic hardship was an important aspect of that belief. It limited the boundaries of choice, both real and imagined. It also played a major role in generating the family tension and juvenile delinquency from which many men hoped to escape through enlistment. While few white, working-class men claimed that the basic need for a job was paramount in explaining their enlistment, the absence of clear avenues of economic opportunity elsewhere surely influenced many enlistments.

For black volunteers, economic and social improvement were often decisive motivations. The 1964 NORC survey found that almost twice as many blacks as whites gave self-advancement as their primary motive for enlisting, 37 percent to 21 percent, respectively.[11] Such men no doubt had real hope that military training and veterans' benefits might someday bring them significant upward mobility, but even the rudimentary economic security provided in the service was, for a considerable number, black and white, a marked improvement over civilian life. For some men, the military was their first experience of secure housing, steady wages, and the opportunity to eat as much as they wanted.

Many draft-vulnerable men saw no advantage to enlisting. The air force and the navy—the service branches with the best opportunities for specialized training and the least likely to expose their troops to ground combat in Vietnam—each required four-year commitments. They also had the highest admission standards, thereby excluding many men routinely accepted by the army and the marines. Because of their relative popularity, the air force and the navy tended to fill their personnel quotas quickly, leaving few openings for otherwise qualified candidates who wanted to avoid the army.

Even to enlist in the army required a three-year commitment as compared with the two years demanded of draftees. The Marine Corps allowed a minimum enlistment of two years, but the marines sent a higher proportion of men to Vietnam than did any other branch. With those limited options, many men decided to take their chances with the draft. Perhaps, they hoped, it might somehow pass them by. If not, at least it was the shortest form of military service. As one draftee said, speaking for thousands, "I hoped I'd just be able to last out two years and get back. I wanted to get the damn thing over with and get back to my life."[12]

Countless men also clung to the hope that somehow the war would end by the time they were inducted and trained. After all, American generals and policymakers were always claiming steady progress. Maybe they were right, or maybe the peace movement would gain enough strength to force the government to pull out immediately. From 1968 on, the news of peace talks and gradual troop withdrawals continued to feed the hopes of potential draftees that they might avoid Vietnam altogether. In any case, two years with the gamble of Vietnam seemed better to many than a three- or four-year commitment with the odds against going to war perhaps only slightly improved.

Wishful thinking aside, many draftees never gave much thought to possible evasions of hazardous duty. Those from poor and working-class backgrounds were the least likely to know about or exercise the dozens of actions that could be taken to avoid Vietnam. Many believed the only real alternatives were the extreme steps of foreign exile, imprisonment, or conscientious objection. Furthermore, military service was such a pervasive reality in working-class communities the draft seemed irresistible. As one veteran recalled, "Everybody was going in—the draft notices were coming out like *Newsweeks*. You knew they were going to catch up with you sooner or later."[13] The fact that everybody seemed to be in the same boat made the idea of avoiding military service seem, to many men, not only remote, but self-centered. "I mean, even if *you* escaped it, they were just going to take your buddies. Suppose I had found a way out. How could I face my friends who were drafted or joining up? And how would I feel walking around town, seeing their parents, and knowing that they were over in Nam getting shot at while I'm home partying? I'd feel like a chickenshit."[14]

MIDDLE-CLASS DILEMMAS:
AN EXPANDED SENSE OF CHOICE

A middle-class draftee from a small town in Missouri expressed his reservation about draft avoidance: "I knew they didn't want Mike Dowling, they wanted a body. And if I wrangled a medical-out for *my* body, they'd just take another in my place."[15] But Mike and other middle-class men faced the draft from a fundamentally different vantage point than working-class men. For them, the other body that might go in their place was usually an anonymous abstraction. For working-class men, it could very well be a next-door neighbor. Men such as Mike wrestled with the moral dilemma of whether or not to avoid the draft, but most working-class draftees did not see the matter as open to debate. For them, the draft notice represented an order, not a dilemma.

In middle-class circles, especially on many college campuses, the effort to avoid the draft was commonly accepted as legitimate and normal, if not always ethically consistent (as in the case of Dan Quayle, who supported the war but avoided fighting it). Techniques of avoidance were openly discussed, shared, and supported. Opponents of the war tended to promote every effort of young people to avoid serving in the Vietnam era military, be it draft resistance, conscientious objection, exile in a foreign country, or the pursuit of exemptions. Serious hope was invested in the idea that if enough people refused to fight, the war could be brought to an end. That aim, often dismissed as absurdly naive, was clearly not realized in one very concrete way: the military had little problem finding enough bodies to field an army. Yet the merit of the idea was at least partially vindicated late in the war when the military did indeed have trouble getting its troops to fight.

The problem, though, was that most working-class men had to learn about the war the hard way, by fighting it. Few of them went to the colleges where they were most likely to encounter complete or thoughtful criticism of the war. Those who did resist the draft typically developed their opposition to the war largely on their own initiative and in the face of the censure of their communities. One such man, a conscientious objector from a working-class family in Dorchester, recalls what it was like at Boston Technical High School, from which he graduated in 1967. Despite his repeated efforts to raise questions about the war in government class, the teacher refused to allow any debate or discussion. "You couldn't talk about the war in school but they still marched us into the auditorium to listen to military recruiters give their spiel."[16] From settings like this, most working-class men saw their draft notice as a fait accompli allowing no individual choice. Middle-class men were more likely to regard it as a personal and moral crisis demanding some decision. Even those who made no effort to avoid the military tended to believe that they had somehow allowed themselves to be drafted. As one middle-class draftee stated, "Making no choice was a choice."[17]

Novelist Tim O'Brien, the son of a middle-class insurance salesman, was raised in a small Minnesota farm community. After graduating from college in 1968 he was drafted and sent to Vietnam as an infantryman in the Americal Division. In his postwar memoir, *If I Die in a Combat Zone*, O'Brien describes his conflicting feelings about entering the military. At college, he had read and thought a good deal about the war in Vietnam. "I was persuaded then, and I remain persuaded now, that the war was wrong. And since it was wrong and since people were dying as a result of it, it was evil."[18] Tim wrote an editorial against the war in his college newspaper, supported Eugene McCarthy for president, and believed the United States should immediately withdraw from Vietnam. He recognized that to submit to the draft would betray those convictions. Bad as the alternatives were—seeking exile abroad or resisting the draft at home and risking imprisonment—Tim saw them as clear and plausible options that might be far more courageous and moral than the decision to participate in a war he opposed.

He felt isolated by his dilemma. His family did not raise the subject, nor did he find much support among his friends. "Most of my college friends found easy paths away from the problem, all to their credit. Deferments for this or that. Letters from doctors or chaplains. It was hard to find people who had to think much about the problem."[19]

As Tim persuaded himself to accept induction, he did what many people do when confronted with the power of state policy: he questioned his own knowledge. He worried that he lacked "expertise" about the "specifics of the conflict" and that the knowledge he needed to make an unqualified stand against the war was part of an "irretrievable history" that was "hidden away." "Perhaps I was mistaken, and who really knew, anyway?"[20]

These doubts were fueled by a feeling of indebtedness to his family, town, and country. It had been a happy and comfortable childhood, and Tim felt that he "owed something" in return. "I'd lived under its laws, accepted its education, eaten its food, . . . and wallowed in its luxuries." Though he resented the form of service demanded of him and was angered by the town's "lethargic acceptance" of the war, he feared the consequences of resistance. To fight the draft would, he believed, embarrass his family and sever his connection to the traditions of the community. However, to submit to a war he believed unjust also posed the threat of radical loss; it would "extinguish" all his "books and beliefs and learning." He wrestled with the dilemma throughout his military training and at one point came so close to deserting that he purchased a plane ticket to Sweden where he intended to live in exile. O'Brien went to war, however, feeling that he had failed to determine his own fate, that he had abandoned his principles by allowing the military to decide his fate.[21]

One of the most striking aspects of this account is O'Brien's sense of being alone with his dilemma. His friends having found easy draft evasions, he felt like the only one he knew who really had to face the draft and the moral questions it raised. This sense of social isolation is common in the accounts of middle-class draftees and volunteers and represents a sharp contrast to the accounts of working-class men like Dan Shaw, who said that his decision to enlist had really been a collective one and that a "whole crowd" of his friends had joined up.

The minority of middle-class men who fought in Vietnam were usually struck by how exceptional their experience was, how unlike that of most of their friends. While working-class men saw military service as a natural, essentially unavoidable part of life, one they believed would at least maintain their social and economic standing and perhaps, with luck, raise it a notch or two, men from wealthier families were likely to view the military as an agent of downward social mobility, an unnatural, dislocating move across a social frontier—like moving from a college campus to a factory floor. Even middle-class men who volunteered for adventure ordinarily thought of the military as an interruption to the making of a career rather than a necessary credential to gain along the way.

Stewart Bushnell was drafted in 1967 because he lost his college deferment while on academic probation from the University of Alabama ("I was partying more than I was going to school"). Both of his parents were university professors. "I was involved in the university environment and most of my circle of friends at least got master's degrees in business or went on to get degrees in medicine, or dentistry, or law. I'm the *only* one that went to Vietnam. I'm the *only* one that only has a bachelor's degree. So I feel like my background was probably different than a lot of Vietnam veterans which were drawn for the most part from the lower economical, sociological backgrounds."[22] Bushnell felt alienated both from his middle-class friends and from the working-class soldiers he met in the military. Taken away from one group, he was unable to identify with the other. He felt displaced and cheated ("I'm the only one"). On the other hand, some middle-class men enlisted precisely because they wanted to be different from their friends. A volunteer from San Jose, California, put it this way:

I lived on the last block of a new development surrounded on three sides by apricot orchards and vineyards. The high school was typically middle class. There were very few blacks. We had warm weather and cars. Most of the kids' dads were engineers at Lockheed or they worked at IBM.

I was the perfect age to participate in Vietnam and I didn't want to miss it, good or bad. I wanted to be part of it, to understand what it was.

Why should I take the Goddamn SATs and go off to college? Everybody was going to San Jose State College right there in town. And who wants to do what everybody else does anyway?[23]

Nick Green grew up in Canton, Massachusetts, a middle-class suburb south of Boston. He enlisted in 1971, volunteered for jump school, and went to Vietnam as a "Pathfinder." He, too, was curious about the war and saw himself as an adventure seeker. He was one of two boys from his graduating class at a Catholic prep school to go to Vietnam.

Most of the people I hung around with were middle-class people. They could afford to go to a private school. And all my friends from Canton were, you know, it's just a middle-class town. It's not a wealthy town, it's not a poor town. But when you get into the army you realize that most of the people were poorly educated. I was amazed at how stupid some people were. And then when I went to Fort Polk, Louisiana, it was about 50 percent black and the other 50 percent were poor whites. Well, not 50 percent. You had a smattering—like some of the guys that were drafted were—one guy had a master's degree in chemistry. But, for the most part, you get these boys from Tennessee and Texas. I never had anything to do with people like that. Really poor people. You don't like to think that because, well, if I'm with all these guys that are just from the lower classes then how the fuck did I get here.[24]

Nick was enthusiastic about enlisting, but once in the military he felt estranged from most of the men he encountered. He began to wonder if the experience would erase the distance he initially perceived between himself and the other men. Maybe he was not so different. After all, if he were so much smarter, he wondered, why had he joined an institution filled by the poor and ill-educated? Unlike many of the men he saw at Fort Polk, for whom military service seemed unavoidable, Nick was anxious because he believed that he had made a choice, perhaps the wrong one.

Common to almost all who entered the military, draftees and volunteers, working and middle class, was an effort to find a measure of affirmation and hopefulness upon entry into the military. The *Legacies* study found that while only 21 percent of veterans claimed they entered the military because of its attractions, twice as many arrived at boot camp with the faith that the experience would have a positive effect on their lives.[25] Even men who were deeply reluctant or who felt they had no choice in the matter struggled to believe they were doing the right thing, that the military, even war itself, might prove to be a valuable experience.

AFFIRMING THE UNAVOIDABLE

In the 1960s, students at Boston's Dorchester High School were primarily white and working class. For the 1967 yearbook, seniors were asked to state their "ambition." These personal goals appear below each student's photograph, along with the usual list of sports, clubs, and other school activities. Of the eighty-six boys who listed an ambition (several did not), forty put down either working-class occupations—most of them skilled trades—or military service. Among this portion of the class, the most popular choices were cabinetmaker and military service (eight boys each). The others aspired to such jobs as electrician, pattern maker, construction worker, and police officer. Among the other forty-six boys some listed professional occupations (teacher, 4; lawyer, 3; musician, 2; architect, 1). Most of the responses, however, were of a more general nature: college (10), to succeed (10), to own my own business (4), to be a millionaire (4), to be happy (4).[26]

Many Dorchester students undoubtedly dreamed of the kind of success that would move them out of the working class. In fact, a 1969 study of Boston's high school seniors from low-income families found that 60 percent hoped to attend college,[27] but those ambitions were expressed in private to survey takers. In the public forum of the yearbook, most students expressed more modest aspirations. Significantly, those students who were most specific about their ambition were generally those who aimed at essentially working-class jobs. These were the jobs that could be named most readily, the ones most within reach. Those who seemed to express hope for a future of nonmanual work tended to offer vague responses. They wanted to "succeed," go to college, own their own business, or become wealthy, but how they would pursue those ends simply was not (or could not) be named.

Ed Johnson was one of the Dorchester students who listed military service as his ambition. He remembers talking with classmates about postgraduation plans. They weighed the advantages of each branch of the military against the prospects of various jobs. A few spoke of college. Ed sensed, however, that these discussions were largely irrelevant. However much they sought to believe that their future was contingent upon individual choice, as graduation approached, military service looked increasingly inevitable. "You could see it. They knew. When they got out of high school there was no college. The families couldn't afford it. There was no jobs. And the service looked good. You knew you were going in. You knew. There was a few of us that would say, 'Hey, I ain't going in no matter what. I ain't going to go over there [to Vietnam] and get shot.' But I felt like it was my duty. Cause once you get out of high school, it's better than just hanging around. Might as well get paid—go in the military and get some money."[28]

The shifts in Ed's account are extremely important. He moves back and forth between a view of military service as unavoidable ("you knew you were going in") and efforts to explain his enlistment as a product of his own volition ("the service looked good," "it was my duty"). However circumscribed their choices, people want to feel they are exercising some control over their lives. After all, to attribute one's course in life to external forces is an admission of powerlessness, a painful acknowledgment that one's humanity has been severely restricted. Instead, people often describe as matters of choice the actions they also perceive as unavoidable. As Richard Sennett and Jonathan Cobb found in their study of working-class consciousness, "They were resolved to shape actions open to them so that, in their own minds, they felt as though they acted from choice rather than necessity."[29] By claiming responsibility for their lives, they were claiming a sense of dignity and self-worth. Even so, notice how strained this tension can become, how reduced the affirmations. Ed says the service "looked good" but only in comparison to "hanging around" without work. While his sense of duty might involve some hope of attaching himself to a larger, patriotic purpose, he quickly moves the discussion back to work and money.

Todd Dasher had a strong personal motivation to enlist. In 1964 his brother, a helicopter pilot in Vietnam, was shot down and killed. Todd was in high school when his brother was killed. He dropped out to enlist, fully intending to go to Vietnam and somehow avenge the loss of his brother. "I wanted to go kill some gooks. I was all joined up and ready to go when I turned seventeen. I would have left on my seventeenth birthday except it was a Sunday. So I went on Monday morning." His brother's death is crucial in understanding the personal intensity of Todd's desire to fight in Vietnam. In fact, once in the military Todd could have requested non-Vietnam duty, since the military offered exemptions from war-zone duty to men whose brothers had served in Vietnam. But Todd was determined to fight, and as he tells his story, it begins to sound like he might have made the same decision regardless of his brother's death. Todd grew up in a small, working-class suburb on Long Island, New York.

Our little town had a Legion Post and a VFW Post and a DAV [Disabled American Veterans] Post and this kind of post and that kind of post. We were just swamped with it all our adolescent years. My father was in the service with all his brothers. His father and all his uncles were in the service. I kind of grew up around the older fellows. My father and his peer group talked about World War II and Korea and how "this one was there" and "that one was there" and [pause] it was the right thing to do.

There wasn't any question as to whether you were going to do it or not. It's part of life. There'd be something wrong with you if you didn't go in.[30]

Talk of former wars established links between families and generations and informed the dreams and expectations of the young. If, in retrospect, it seemed like a military "swamp," as a young man Todd believed it was simply the way the world worked. The war stories about "this or that" battle were enthralling, and many Vietnam veterans testify to the importance of hearing older men tell their war stories, how it inculcated a fascination with military life. The older men also conveyed the view that military service and even war were central to the lives of men. It was the experience that most clearly divided male adulthood from adolescence. Like Ed Johnson, Todd viewed military service as a natural and unquestioned part of life.

"It was the right thing to do." For Todd, that belief had little to do with considerations of the rightness or wrongness of U.S. foreign policy. He simply assumed that America was always on the right side of international conflicts. "It never occurred to me that America would go to war without a good reason." The moral or ideological legitimacy of America's wars was rarely an issue for discussion among the older veterans who so influenced Todd's childhood. Military service was right primarily because it was normative, because it was understood to be an integral part of growing up, a rite of passage to manhood, and the responsibility of each successive generation. As Dan Shaw put it, "I thought I was doing the right thing. I mean, my grandfather went in 1917, my father went in 1942. It was my turn."[31]

All kinds of men were profoundly affected by World War II, and even some who became very prosperous in the postwar years look back on wartime experiences as the most significant in their lives. Yet, most middle- and upper-class veterans developed postwar career identities that largely replaced and reduced their wartime associations. For working-class veterans, the rewards of their civilian work lives are not usually as great. For them, wartime memories are more likely to play an active and ongoing role in shaping their identities. During the Vietnam War, journalist Jimmy Breslin visited a union hall in a working-class Long Island community like Todd Dasher's. He believed that most of the men supported the war in Vietnam and did so primarily because their own experience in the military had been the most extraordinary of their lives:

> Most of these fellows have had only one thing in their lives. They went into the military service, and they went away and got into a war like Korea or World War Two and they saw things they never thought they'd see. They experienced every range of human emotion, from exhilaration to absolute terror to complete sadism to manly togetherness. . . . They went from A to Z on the scale of life, and it is the greatest thing and only thing ever to happen to them in their lives. Everything that happened before and everything that happened after is nothing. It's just one day going in to another.[32]

Though overstated, Breslin's comments touch on a key issue: the way the emotional extremes of warfare can stand out above all other experience, perhaps especially for men whose lives are most routine. What he misses, though, is the economic significance of World War II. For millions of working-class men, World War II marked a clear-cut break from the hardships of the Great Depression. The war brought new forms of suffering and sacrifice, but it decisively ended the years of vast unemployment, economic stagnation, and starvation wages. In the postwar years as well the scale of fundamental economic insecurity was vastly reduced. Of course, working people did not share equally in postwar prosperity, and changes in the industrial workplace made many working-class jobs ever more routine, divided, fast paced, and expendable. Still, many working-class families made modest gains, established homes, and developed a new hopefulness about the American dream: it might be realizable after all, if not by them, perhaps by their children. Millions believed the war had been good for America, that it had brought them out of the Depression, and that their military service had been rewarded. As Billy Cizinski, the son of a laborer, said, "In World War II everybody fought that was able-bodied. That included guys that ended up in civilian life in the working class. But what was life like for them before that?—the Depression! So anything above that Depression level was like a castle. So they trained us. They told us America does work, it does do things for you. They made us very patriotic, very aggressive."[33]

Of course, these attitudes did not always translate into parental injunctions to serve in the military. Some fathers discouraged their sons from enlisting. However, what a father says about the military can be less important than how much he says. Whether the father characterizes the experience as good or bad, if the son perceives the military as a major experience in his father's life, he is more likely to consider it for himself.

Though the generational pull to military service influenced some middle-class men, they were more likely to see it as an option rather than as an inevitable rite of passage.

One way or another in every generation when there was a war, some male in the family on my father's side went to it. I had never had it drilled into me, but there was a lot of attention paid to the past, a lot of not-so-subtle "This is what a man does with his life" stuff when I was growing up. . . .

I got drafted at the end of the summer [1968]. I went into a state of total panic for days. What the fuck am I going to do? I went running off to recruiters to see if I could get into the Coast Guard or the Navy or the Air Force. No way.

There were probably some strings that I could have pulled. One of the things that is curious to me, as I look back on it, is that I had all the information, all the education and all the opportunity that a good, middle-class, college-educated person could have to get out of it . . .

and I didn't make a single choice that put it anywhere but breathing down my neck. Even in the midst of the terror after the induction notice came, there was a part of me that would lie in bed at night and fantasize about what it would be like if I went. . . .

With all my terror of going into the Army . . . there was something seductive about it, too. I was seduced by World War II and John Wayne movies. When I was in high school, I dreamed of going to Annapolis.[34]

He was so unconvinced by American justifications for the war, he spent "six solid months of really examining my feelings . . . to determine whether or not I was a conscientious objector." Yet, so powerful was the lure and fascination of war, he accepted the draft.

It is hard to exaggerate the extent to which young boys growing up in the 1950s and early 1960s were captivated by fantasies of warfare. Boys who would be sent to fight a war of counterinsurgency in Vietnam grew up fighting an imaginary version of World War II. Tim O'Brien related his childhood adventures: "In patches of weed and clouds of imagination, I learned to play army games. Friends introduced me to the Army Surplus Store off main street. We bought dented relics of our fathers' history, rusted canteens and olive-scented, scarred helmet liners. Then we were our fathers, taking on the Japs and Krauts along the shores of Lake Okabena . . . writhing insensible under barrages of shore batteries positioned under camouflage across the lake. I rubbed my fingers across my father's war decorations, stole a tiny battle star off one of them and carried it in my pocket."[35]

Even boys who lacked this personal connection to World War II found it celebrated in movies, magazines, television, comic books, and war toys. American popular culture was suffused with romantic images of warfare. Again and again Vietnam veterans attest to the importance of those images, especially the war movies, in shaping childhood conceptions of combat as grandly heroic. Ron Kovic's memoir, *Born on the Fourth of July*, provides evocative testimony of the pervasiveness of military culture and its strong emotional impact:

> Every Saturday afternoon we'd all go down to the movies in the shopping center and watch gigantic prehistoric birds breathe fire, and war movies with John Wayne and Audie Murphy. . . . I'll never forget Audie Murphy in "To Hell and Back." At the end he jumps on top of a flaming tank that's just about to explode and grabs the machine gun

blasting it into the German lines. He was so brave I had chills running up and down my back, wishing it were me up there. There were gasoline flames roaring around his legs, but he just kept firing that machine gun. It was the greatest movie I ever saw in my life. . . .

The army had a show on Channel 2 called "The Big Picture," and after it was over Castiglia and I crawled all over the back yard playing guns and army, making commando raids all summer into Ackerman's housing project blasting away at the imaginary enemy[,] . . . throwing dirt bombs and rocks into the windows, making loud explosions like hand grenades with our voices then charging in with our Matty Mattel machine guns blazing. I bandaged up the German who was still alive and had Castiglia question him as I threw a couple more grenades.[36]

The boys of the 1950s refought World War II. They took on the "Japs" and the "Krauts" but rarely, if ever, the "Commies." The Korean War had lacked a decisive victory, and no one knew how to make a believable imitation of a nuclear bomb, so playing World War III was out of the question. Nor did children of the 1950s imagine themselves fighting Third World revolutionaries. The closest anyone came to that were some left-over counterguerrilla campaigns against Native Americans—"cowboys and Indians." Perhaps the main point, though, is that these young war gamers never cast the Americans as the losers or questioned the righteousness of their cause. That would have been utter blasphemy.

The celebrations of military culture so central to many World War II movies and enacted in childhood games undoubtedly played an important role in shaping a glorified view of war among many young boys of the Vietnam generation. With many other aspects of American culture in the early years of the Cold War, the glorification of war surely contributed to the proliferation of uncritical patriotism and self-righteous nationalism. It is true that childhood fantasies of war stayed with some boys throughout their adolescence, but John Wayne, toy guns, and overheated patriotism were rarely the decisive factors that moved people to enlist. After all, most boys of that generation grew up liking John Wayne, playing war, and believing their country was always virtuous in its relations with other nations. The fact that working-class boys were far more likely to fight in Vietnam is not an indication that they, above all others, were seduced by Hollywood war stories. Rather, I argue, the fundamental factors moving people into the military were economic and institutional. Even Ron Kovic, who gives so much breathless attention to his childhood romance with war, is careful to point out the social and economic foundations behind his decision to enlist. His father worked long hours as a grocery store checker to support a large family. Thinking about the burdens of his father's life was crucial to Kovic's decision to enlist. Joining the marines, he hoped, would be a way to escape the onerous work world of his father. "I didn't want to be like my Dad, coming home from the A&P every night. He was a strong man, a good man, but it made him so tired, it took all the energy out of him. I didn't want to be like that, working in that stinking A&P, six days a week, twelve hours a day. I wanted to be somebody. I wanted to make something of my life."[37] War fictions presented strong men overcoming fatigue and boredom, "blasting . . . into the German lines," liberating towns and villages, becoming heroes. Ron Kovic was not sure what he wanted to make of his life in the long run, but the marines seemed the best immediate means of becoming somebody.

Blacks who faced military service, voluntarily or not, were even more likely—especially in the early years of the war—to be hopeful that the military might improve their social standing and provide more racial justice than they found in civilian society. Reginald Edwards from Louisiana explained that he went into the military because it was "the only thing left to do," but he also brought an enormous reservoir of hopefulness to the enterprise, a hopefulness largely stirred by the generally positive image the military enjoyed in American culture during the twenty-year period after World War II:

> I was the first person in my family to finish high school. This was 1963. I knew I couldn't go to college because my folks couldn't afford it. I only weighed 117 pounds, and nobody's gonna hire me to work for them. So the only thing left to do was go into the service. I didn't want to go into the Army, 'cause everybody went into the Army. The Navy I did not like 'cause of the uniforms. The Air Force, too. But the Marines was "bad." The Marine Corps built men. Plus just before I went in, they had all these John Wayne movies on every night.
>
> In them days we never hang with white people. You didn't have white friends. White people was the aliens to me. You don't have integration really in the South. You expected them to treat you bad. But somehow in the Marine Corps you hoping all that's gonna change.[38]

Even men more reluctant than Reginald Edwards often looked for ways to affirm what seemed like the "only thing left to do"; then, adolescent war fantasies could play a vital role. One draftee who had considered seeking exile in Canada (and later deserted from the military) described the transformation in his thinking once he decided to submit to the draft: "I had lost the battle with my wits and my mind—I wasn't able to say no, I'm not going to go. . . . So I gave in to it [the draft] and almost with a maniacal twist of wit, I just said, aw fuck it, I'll go in and . . . ah . . . just enjoy it, you know; I'll play the game and see what they're doing; I'll see what the army's like. Then I had these flashbacks of when I was eleven, twelve, thirteen years old, and I used to be the commando . . . [and] my friends and I would run around playing jungle fighter."[39] Adolescent war fantasies, dreams of battlefield glory, hopes for social advancement, and a world of greater racial equality—these were rarely the decisive factors in moving men into the military, but they were crucial to men trying to reconcile themselves to a largely unavoidable and uncertain fate.

AT A VERY EARLY AGE

Billy Cizinski could not wait to join the marines. In 1965, at age fifteen, he doctored his records and convinced a recruiter that he was two years older. After serving in the Mediterranean and the Caribbean he was sent to Vietnam as an infantryman in 1967. He fought his first firefight when he was sixteen and a half. After his return from war, Billy spent a long time trying to figure out why he enlisted. In 1981 he began his explanation with these words:

I come from European parents. My mother was German, my father was Polish. They experienced World War II. After the war they married and came here to get away from war-torn Europe, depressed Europe. They both hated communism. I grew up in an environment where communism was a taboo, better red than dead. Went to a Polish school—same thing. And you can go back into the '50s and see how the country trained kids—the pledge of allegiance to the flag, a lot of militarism. Every Christmas you find guns under the tree and you went out and played war all the time. So that was your way of being militarily indoctrinated at a very early age. And then you had Kennedy—"ask not what your country can do for you—ask what you can do for your country." That was the philosophy all the way into the middle '60s even though there was a counter-culture growing.[40]

This is Billy's shorthand explanation of why he enlisted. He covers the subject quickly and routinely. Notice that he accidentally reverses the slogan "better dead than red." The slip of tongue is consistent with the general tone of the passage, a tone that suggests the irrelevance of rendering the pervasive anticommunism with much precision. After all, the message was everywhere and always amounted to the "same thing"—"a lot of militarism." Billy speaks this history with a detached voice. The world he recalls now seems remote, and its slogans and "philosophy" were something that "you" simply absorbed "at a very early age." The pledge of allegiance, toy guns, Kennedy's words—the entire culture is sketched as a seamless whole, each component contributing to the training and indoctrination of youth for war.

Billy's statement is useful as an elliptical cultural collage of military socialization, and the economy of his explanation helps to recapture the superficiality and naivete with which many young recruits perceived the prospects of war. Yet we need to press beyond the distanced and critical edge of Billy's retrospective analysis for a fuller understanding of his outlook on life in 1965. If the patriotism and anticommunism of the 1950s and early 1960s were absorbed as unquestioned verities, they were nevertheless deeply felt.

John Kennedy's famous call for service to the nation has lost much of its resonance through repetition and because the history that followed demoralized so many of those once inspired by his words, but some of its appeal can be recovered by examining the complete inaugural address that formed the context of the famous quotation. Out of context, "Ask not . . ." has a rather dull and pedantic ring, like a civics class lesson on the duties of citizenship, but Kennedy's address is the opposite of dull. He articulates a vision of national service calling for heroic sacrifices on behalf of the highest ideals. Explicitly addressing the young—a "new generation"—Kennedy summons America to nothing less than a global struggle against "tyranny, poverty, disease, and war itself."

> Since this country was founded, each generation of Americans has been summoned to give testimony to its national loyalty. The graves of young Americans who answered the call to service surround the globe.
>
> Now the trumpet summons us again—not as a call to bear arms, though arms we need—not as a call to battle, though embattled we are—but a call to bear the burden of a long twilight struggle, year in

and year out, "rejoicing in hope, patient in tribulation"—a struggle against the common enemies of man: tyranny, poverty, disease and war itself. . . .

. . . Will you join in that historic effort?

In the long history of the world, only a few generations have been granted the role of defending freedom in its hour of maximum danger. I do not shrink from this responsibility—I welcome it. I do not believe that any of us would exchange places with any other people or any other generation. The energy, the faith, the devotion, which we bring to this endeavor, will light our country and all who serve it—and the glow from that fire can truly light the world.

And so, my fellow Americans: ask not what your country can do for you—ask what you can do for your country.[41]

Much of the forcefulness of Kennedy's summons depends on its peculiar blend of utopian and apocalyptic visions. He gives voice to the greatest dreams and the worst nightmares. This duality appears at the very outset of the address and establishes the keynote: "Man holds in his mortal hands the power to abolish all forms of human poverty and all forms of human life." Throughout the address there is a persistent combination of the ominous and the hopeful, darkness and light, danger and possibility. By pairing these contrasts, Kennedy's call to service attains a dramatic urgency. To "shrink from this responsibility," he suggests, would imperil freedom at a moment of "maximum danger."

Kennedy is not precise about the form of national service Americans should offer. Indeed, one of his most impressive qualities was an ability to inspire people of widely divergent backgrounds and ideologies. The inaugural speech itself sounded to some like a progressive call for human rights, economic justice, and an end to the Cold War. Others took it as an essentially aggressive manifesto of anticommunism. Was he calling for peacemakers or warriors? He seemed to be calling for both; although he used the language of negotiation and "peaceful revolution," Kennedy made it clear that he considered the "iron tyranny" of communism the greatest threat to human freedom and one to be opposed throughout the world. He pledged America to "pay any price, bear any burden, meet any hardship, support any friend, oppose any foe, to assure the survival and success of liberty." Thus it was by no means clear whether the "long twilight struggle" to be waged "year in and year out" would be a peaceful attack on "the common enemies of man" or a real and bloody war against

Third World revolutionaries. Of course, Kennedy saw no inconsistency. For him, the Peace Corps and the Green Berets were inspired by the same vision and devoted to the same end—an anticommunist crusade to be waged, using both carrot and stick, throughout the world.

Though the Green Berets (officially known as the Special Forces) had a formal existence dating from 1952, they were rescued from institutional obscurity in the early 1960s by President Kennedy. Convinced that the United States had to improve its capacity to fight small counterinsurgency operations anywhere in the world, Kennedy looked to the Green Berets as the ideal troops for such missions and began beefing up their budget and personnel. His enthusiasm for this elite force (he displayed a green beret in his office) made them a frequent focus of media attention. Indeed, throughout the early 1960s the Special Forces were perhaps the most significant symbol of the American military, and it was an extremely positive symbol. Green Berets were typically characterized as dashing (the jaunty beret with the yellow flash), intelligent (every man had to master a foreign language), intrepid (small teams of men who would jump into danger anywhere in the world), and possessed of the most sophisticated training in unconventional warfare. In fact, the popularity of the Green Berets did not peak until 1965 and early 1966. In that period Robin Moore's fictional paean to the Special Forces in Vietnam, *The Green Berets*, was a number one best-seller; Barry Sadler's "The Ballad of the Green Berets" reached number one on the Top 40 charts; work began on the high-budget motion picture *The Green Berets*, starring John Wayne (1968); and there were many commercial spin-offs—Green Beret dolls, toy weapons, bubble gum, and clothing.[42]

For Billy Cizinski, who enlisted in 1965 at age fifteen, Kennedy's call to service seemed to echo throughout the land. True, he knew there was a small antiwar movement and that some young men were burning their draft cards. In his neighborhood, though, and indeed throughout American society at the time, this dissent was widely abhorred. Moreover, the glorification of war he saw in movies, the anticommunism that was a part of his daily education in Catholic school, and Kennedy's warnings about a long twilight struggle all resonated, for Billy, in a deeply personal way. Cold War anticommunism was not, for him, a political abstraction. He saw a direct link to his family history. Billy's father served with the Polish army at the outset of World War II and was eventually pressed into the Soviet military, and his grandfather had fought with the White Russians at the time of the Russian Revolution. Both men hated Soviet communism and made a point of passing along to Billy a vivid impression of Soviet treachery. "They were always talking about how the Russians manipulated and back-stabbed. I hated the Reds. I wanted to fight those nasty bastards." When Presidents Kennedy and Johnson claimed that the enemy in Vietnam was not indigenous, revolutionary nationalism but Soviet- and Chinese-dominated communism—part of a global threat that had to be contained—most Americans were slow to ask questions; but Billy required less persuasion than most. He had grown up believing the Soviets were responsible for almost all the world's ills.

Upon reflection, however, Billy has his doubts about the significance of anticommunism and patriotism as explanations for his premature enlistment. The longer he talks, the less convinced he becomes. There were other factors, he insists, perhaps even more important ones: "My conscious motivation to go in [to the marines] was all patriotism and communism. But there are deep-seated motives for anyone that goes into the military and especially anyone that goes to war. There's a motive. I mean, going to war to kill or be killed is totally illogical, totally irrational. You have to have subconscious motivations that push you into it."

Explaining these motivations is much more difficult. Where Billy had raced through his descriptions of "better red than dead," toy guns, and Kennedy, here the words came slowly. He offered a halting, painful, intimate account of his early family life in South Boston. "Well, I had a lot of problems at home. There was a lot of turmoil there. My parents split up when I was really young." Billy's father was an unskilled laborer. Though he often worked two or three jobs, the pay was low and the work unsteady. Money was a constant source of tension. Billy thinks another major problem between his parents was an inability to reconcile their different nationalities.

Billy's mother was a German who met Billy's father in the last days of World War II. She had lost several relatives in the war against the Russians on the eastern front. They were drawn together, in part, because of their mutual loathing of the communists. Billy believes their relationship was always troubled and tenuous. For one thing, Mr. Cizinski's Polish-American friends used to bait him about marrying a German. "Down at the Polish-American club they were always asking, 'Why'd you marry a German? She's no good.' So my father ended up in a lot of fights with his friends, which he didn't want to do, but he had to protect his wife. Then he felt guilty and when he got drunk he'd take it out on her." Billy believes that, deep inside, his father shared his friends' prejudice against Germans. He had lost an eye while fighting against them in World War II, and though his father would not admit it, Billy thinks he somehow held that loss against his wife.

This is Billy's adult interpretation of his parents' problems, however. As a young boy, Billy was far more confused. When his parents fought, he felt guilty and worried that he was the cause of their troubles. Weren't they always blaming each other for failing Billy, their only child? And when they fought about money, wasn't he just an added expense? Though he felt this pain, he could not express it. His mother told him, "You gotta be a man, you gotta be strong, you gotta hold things in. Don't tell the neighbors what's happening in your house because what we have is our business. Don't let them know that we're fighting."

Billy's mother left home when he was nine or ten, and Billy stayed with his father. He perceived his mother's absence as a personal abandonment. After she left, Billy told new friends that his mother had died. "I was too embarrassed to say she just left me behind." Billy soon moved with his father to an apartment on D Street in South Boston. It was not far from their old neighborhood near Andrew Square, but once again he had to endure the struggle of being a Polish kid in a predominantly Irish neighborhood. "I was constantly fighting with the Irish kids in the neighborhood." At home Billy grew up speaking German and Polish. His English was the last language to develop, and kids made fun of the way he spoke. "I was trilingual but that didn't matter." To the Irish kids on the corner, "I was just a dumb Polack."

Billy fought hard to gain acceptance, though. He wanted to become a member of the Black Hawks, a streetcorner gang. Gaining approval was difficult not only because he was non-Irish but because he was small. "Being the smallest one out of the group I was always doing things to prove myself." After stealing a few cars Billy won acceptance in the gang.

The Black Hawks were a tougher, more violent gang than the one Billy had associated with in Andrew Square. "It was very violent, especially if anybody strange was in the area. We did wild things at a very early age." Billy accounts for the gang's behavior by pointing out the hardships its members encountered at home; most of the boys came from poor and broken families. These conditions help to explain the gang members' violence toward outsiders and their loyalty to each other. The gang became for Billy and for many of the other Black Hawks a surrogate family: "This was our new family and no one was going to interfere with it."

When Billy was fifteen, several older members began to talk about joining the marines. Billy wanted to go with them. In part he hoped to find in the marines a continuation of the sense of belonging he had found in the gang. He also clung to the hope that his parents might reunite. Perhaps by going to war he could make his parents happy and give them something to be proud of, a pride that might bring them back together. "German-Slavics admired war heroes and I figured that would get them together and get them off my back." But what if he got killed? Then it would be a way to "pay them back—make them feel guilty for pushing me into it."

Bob Foley went to the University of Montevallo in Alabama for a year and a half. In 1967 he was put on academic probation, and several weeks later he received a draft notice.

Most people don't really understand what it was like to go to college and be a male in 1966, or '67, or '68 when the draft was real heavy and the teachers all made jokes of it. They knew if you didn't make good grades your ass was going in the army. And they thought it was funny, they really did. It was a joke. They held it over your head all the time. I went to college for a year and a half and I just wasn't much of a student. I had girl friend problems just like most every young male. This one particular girl that I was deathly in love with, she was from the rich side of town, and I was from the poor side, so that just wouldn't cut it. Social structure wouldn't allow that to happen, I'm sure. And then, she really wouldn't have been very happy with me because there's no way in hell I could ever afford for her to live the way that she lived. There ain't no way. Anyway, it doesn't much matter. I just wasn't much of a student. I didn't figure that college had that much to teach me. If I was going to be a lawyer or a doctor or something like that, it would be a different situation. But so many times when I would ask my mother about accounting homework it was so below what she was doing [as a bookkeeper]. She says, "well we don't do it that way in the real world."[43]

College reminded Bob of high school. It was like "learning something for nothing." It seemed to hold little promise of a better future. Even a practical course like accounting was taught in a way that seemed useless in the "real world." His criticisms of school are grounded in a profound sense of social constraint. For those not destined to be professionals, college had little to teach, and "social structure wouldn't allow" a relationship with a wealthy classmate. These criticisms, however, do not relieve Bob of self-blame. Understanding the obstacles he encountered has not removed the belief that personal inadequacy was as decisive as any factor: "I just wasn't much of a student."

Bob did not want to enter the military. Faced with the draft, however, he noticed that his anxiety was mixed with a slight feeling of relief. In part, Bob was glad simply to know he was drafted; it put an end to the uncertainty. As another draftee put it, "It was kind of a relief getting drafted. It's like you're a little kid waiting to get a shot in the arm. The waiting can be worse than the shot. You're glad to get it over with."[44] For Bob, college had been a great disappointment. Perhaps, he hoped, the military would provide better opportunities, a greater chance for success. For almost two years, until he received orders to go to Vietnam, his hopes were realized:

> A lot of people really enjoyed the military. Like me. I was a good troop. I made E-5 sergeant in under two years and I liked the army. I thought about going to Officer Candidate School and making a career of it. Because it was real organized. You know what's expected and it's a real easy job. Why do you think people are lifers? There's not much demanded of you. I mean someone higher up makes a decision and it all trickles down and eventually, if you're an NCO, you have a bunch of flunkies out there to do it for you—all them Spec 4s and PFCs. You got all these people to direct and a lot of responsibility. It's really neat. It's so organized and so well put together. And if you do good, oh wow man, you do *real* good. You're just outstanding. "Outstanding" was the word. I mean, you could go take a shit and that was "OUTSTANDING!" It gets you so hyped up.

The military was organized. You knew what was expected. There was a clear chain of command. If you were a "good troop," you would be rewarded. It was not that demanding. You simply had to carry out the routine. Praise was easily won. In fact, as Bob describes it, the praise was like the reinforcement offered by a parent toilet training a child.

In many respects, the military posed a striking contrast to Bob's early life. The order and organization of military life attracted Bob, in large measure because of the awful disorder and disorganization of his childhood.

> Mom and Dad had definite marital problems ever since I can remember. My father was an alcoholic. He wasn't drunk all the time.

There were periods up to two or three years where he would not drink at all. I guess that's what was so difficult to deal with—things would be great and then the next day he would be fucked up totally. Never knew when, or if, or how you could bring people home. I never brought any of my friends to my home because I never knew how my father would be. Some of my most embarrassing times was when he came to school to get me and he was drunk. He would scare me to death 'cause he drove fast and he always made me go with him to bars.

Life was always uncertain. There was nothing you could really count on. Bob's early life was a long series of ups and downs. Sometimes his parents were together, then they were apart. Sometimes his father worked well and steadily, and then there would be unemployment, drinking, and indebtedness. Bob recalls one transitional moment in particular: "My father sold shoes and he worked well for a while. But one time at Christmas he was working for the Sampler Shoe Center and they were having a Christmas party and the boss said, 'Everybody here can have a drink but Foley.' And my father walked over to him and handed him his shoehorn and said, 'Have my check ready at six o'clock.' The boss says, 'Where you going?' And he says, 'To get a drink.' So that was one Christmas that my father got drunk."

Bob struggles to be fair to his father. "Whatever he tried to do for me, he tried his best to do good and everything." While childhood "wasn't real pleasant," "it wasn't as bad probably as a lot of people had." Still, "My father was the kind of person who had to have that up and down. When he wasn't drinking he gambled a lot. One weekend he lost $800. We'd get in very bad financial problems. He'd hock a lot of things—my stereo, the TV, his clothes, my mother's wedding ring, anything. And he would drink anything—rubbing alcohol, Aqua Velva, bay rum, sell his blood, anything to get a drink. Anything." During the bad times, Bob's father became very violent. "One time I was standing on a gas meter looking in the window outside our apartment and my father picked up a smoking stand and swung it at my mother and knocked a hole in the wall about a foot wide. He would have crushed her head if he had hit her."

Given these experiences, Bob found stateside military service a welcome source of stability. Vietnam ended his thoughts of making the military a career, but prior to experiencing the war firsthand, Bob had few serious misgivings about it. "I had to learn at a very early age the realities of life. But, then, all the things about the country, I didn't learn until Vietnam. I felt like, well, your parents will fuck you over, but your *country* won't do you wrong. It [the war] must be a good cause if we're sending people over there. I felt like maybe it was a good cause. I really didn't have much of an opinion about it actually. I knew I didn't much want to go, but there was really no choice. So I went."

At a very early age Bob Foley learned about alcoholism, divorce, violence, unemployment, loss, and fear: the realities of life. He associated these realities with family life. Somehow "the country" seemed unconnected to these realities. Bob believed the nation as a whole—as represented by the government and the military—possessed the very traits his family had lacked: wealth, power, predictability, and organization. That very contrast contributed to Bob's assumption that the government could be trusted to have a good reason for sending its boys to war.

SOMETHING TO PROVE

Frank Mathews grew up in Holt, Alabama, a working-class factory town five miles east of Tuscaloosa. After graduation from high school at age seventeen he tried to join the marines; but parental permission was required, and Frank's parents would not give it. His father had been severely wounded in World War II and then worked for more than twenty years as a guard at the VA hospital where each day he watched the casualties of war come and go. "My parents didn't care much for the service. My Daddy got shot up real bad in World War II in the navy and he didn't have much for the service because of that. But I figured that the only way to get ahead was to be in the service, and being a marine was the only thing. I couldn't see army or air force or anything else that was good enough. And I'd been told how rough it would be and all of this and I was psyched-up. I was all gung-ho for it and going to war was part of it. I expected it, I wanted to go."[45]

It is curious that Frank describes the service as "the only way to get ahead." Unlike many working-class recruits, he had a strong opportunity to attend college. His skill as a trumpet player had earned him offers of music scholarships to both Walker College and the University of Alabama. "I thought about going to college and I really wanted to be a pediatrician. I really had those thoughts. But I just had to prove to me and most everybody else I guess, what I was made of." Frank turned down the scholarships and, after turning eighteen, enlisted in the marines despite the protests of his parents. "Daddy is still raising hell about my giving up the scholarships."

Somehow college did not seem like sufficient proof of Frank's substance. He wanted to demonstrate his physical courage and toughness and discover how much punishment he could take and how much he could give out. "When I joined and thought about going to war it was sort of like . . . always being like . . . well . . . with my size. I'm always seemingly smaller than anybody else, so I had to do a lot of extra fighting to catch up."

Frank is about five feet, five inches tall. Much of the extra fighting came in Frank's senior year of high school. After years of playing trumpet in the marching band, "I decided I'd quit and play football one year. I'd already made up my mind to join the Marine Corps. So that whole year I had to fight everybody because I was going into the Marine Corps so that made everything a little bit rough."

The football players ridiculed Frank's talk of becoming a marine, and that made him all the more eager to fight back. "They laughed or thought it was crazy to join the service then [1966]. But most of them were drafted so the laugh turned around. They thought it was a little bit stupid to jump right out there in the fire. But, I don't know, it's sort of like playing football. You take the risk when you play football. I figured I was taking the same risk only this time with the real toys."

At times, Frank's explanation for enlisting sounds pragmatic—not so much a need to prove his toughness as a practical calculation: "My reasoning then was that if you didn't finish service first, they were going to get you anyway. But I wanted to get mine over with so I could do anything else I wanted to do." Nevertheless, Frank did not view the military as simply an inevitable burden that had to be endured. He invited the risks of war. He felt he had to "jump right out there in the fire" in order to prove himself. Much of this attitude was shaped by Frank's relationship with his father.

My daddy had a real bad way. There was fourteen brothers and sisters in his family. He had a real cruel daddy, and his mother wasn't much better, and he seemed to take that out a good bit on me and my brother. And I didn't ever let him forget it for a minute. I guess that's what made me more hardheaded about everything and trying that much harder to make sure I achieved. Just like joining the Marine Corps. I was going to go ahead and do it anyway [against his father's opposition]. It always seemed like I was getting back at him. Being little has always been an aggravating predicament to me and it's always been the same thing. I had to be an overachiever to feel like I had achieved at all.

In the Marine Corps, Frank was trained in reconnaissance and demolitions. When his overseas orders came, he was outraged. Instead of Vietnam, he was ordered to Guantanamo Bay in Cuba, a routine assignment involving few risks. Frank wrote his congressman, complaining that he had volunteered for Vietnam. "I told them to change my orders because I was trained to kill and there is a war going on so that's what I should be doing." The orders were changed, and Frank was sent to Vietnam to serve in the Third Reconnaissance Battalion. On his last mission he was shot in four places, the only survivor of the eight men in his team.

I asked Frank if he would have joined the service if there had not been a war. He said yes. "Would you have been wishing for a war?" "Yeah," he responded, "that just seemed like part of growing up or part of a life span. You had to do that part in order to be equal to anybody else. That's what I felt like." Frank gave little consideration to the political or ideological significance of the Vietnam War. The meaning or justice of America's role in Vietnam played no discernible part in shaping his desire to fight. Open-ended questions about his motives never elicited talk of patriotism or anticommunism. When I pressed him about his prewar opinions on the politics of the war and what he thought we were fighting for, he said simply, "I felt like going to Vietnam was helping some little guy fight a big guy."

Richard Deegan gave this explanation for enlisting: "I didn't really think too much about it. I kind of ran headlong into it. A lot of my buddies were doing it. It was the thing to do at the time [1966]. I went down to the recruiting station and talked with the recruiter. I wanted to go in for two years at first and he said: 'No, why don't you make it four years. By the time they train you and everything most of your time will almost be up.' So, I didn't really care one way or the other. I said, 'I don't care. I'll go in for four years.'"[46]

For Richard, going into the service did not feel like a life and death decision, one requiring careful thought and planning. Even a few extra years did not seem very significant. It was simply "the thing to do." Nevertheless, however headlong the enlistment, it was grounded in a strong set of feelings. Richard expressed those feelings in response to a question he described as "tough, and really kind of corny." "When you were growing up," I asked, "did you ever have hopes of becoming a war hero?"

A war hero. What is a war hero? A guy that goes out and kills ten million people? I don't know. [Pause.] When I was a little kid the Old Man used to have on the [television], you know—World War II shit. And I got all that crap from watching that shit. I watched John Wayne movies—*The Sands of Iwo Jima* and *Flying Leatherneck*. You go for this shit and you start thinking, well, I want to be like my Old Man. I want to be a war hero, whatever the hell a war hero is. And then Vietnam came along. Everybody was going in the service so I figured I'd go. I get into a lot of things because my Old Man said I didn't have the balls to do it when I was a little kid: "You're a coward. You'll never be this, you'll never be that." So I went in to basically prove something to myself. Maybe show that bastard, too, you know?

But when I got over there, let's face facts—war ain't like you see in John Wayne. You'll be there and *you're* dead and *I'm* still talking to you. Somebody you know one minute and then he's dead the next and he's gone. I don't know if I wanted to be a war hero. I just wanted to see if I could prove something to myself. I didn't go over and pull a Lt. Calley. I cried when people got killed over there. Because I cried doesn't make me less of a man.

While Richard was in Vietnam, his father never wrote to him. "My father was very into his alcoholism at the time," and "he never really acknowledged" the fact that Richard had fought in a war. One time after the war, Richard came home on leave all decked out in his dress greens and wearing his combat ribbons. His father was silent, but Richard hoped the uniform would convey this message: "Hey motherfucker, you may have been there, but I been there too. You may have been in World War II, but people were dying in Vietnam too. So I got nothing to prove to you."

Then, in a soft, sad, quiet voice, Richard confides, "You know, I hate my father in a way. I don't think beating him up would prove anything but I still hold a lot of resentments." He tries to understand the difficult circumstances of his father's life: "I know now that he was a sick man. It was all he could do to keep food on the table and I don't think he really hated us." But Richard cannot forget the times his father came home drunk and angry, beat the children, and told them, "You'll never amount to anything."

Talking about his periodic desire to beat up his father makes Richard remember that, as a youth, he had always avoided fights. "I was certainly not a fighter." Though many of the other kids in the neighborhood belonged to gangs, Richard kept to himself. This leads to a further, more profound reflection: "You know, it's funny, if I wasn't a fighter, why did I join the marines and go to Vietnam? It was the worst thing I could have done!"

OFF THE STREET

In the mid-1960s Dwight Williams was a member of the Blackstone Rangers, a notorious Chicago street gang. "I was with the Blackstone Rangers for five years." Adding up those years from the perspective of his mid-thirties, Dwight sounded a bit nostalgic, almost like an aging athlete trying to recall how long he had played for a particular club. It made him laugh to remember that he was only eleven years old when he entered the gang. Asked why he had joined the gang, the hint of nostalgia vanished, and his voice took on a steely edge. "I didn't join them. They had what the government got—a draft. I was drafted. Like you walk down the street and five or six guys walk up to you and they ask you to 'represent,' and you say you don't belong to no gangs, you don't want to be in no gangs, and they tell you: 'Well, you *will* be at club meeting at such and such a day and you will have to pay dues.' And if you didn't go, you get jumped on when you get out of school or something."[47]

Dwight did not want to belong to a gang, but he knew it would be nearly impossible to avoid the gang draft. To stay independent of the gangs, he would have to fight, and he knew he could not do it alone. Dwight had two brothers; but the oldest was not much of a fighter, and the other was too young to be of any help. "So I just decided, well, I didn't have no help. If I go to a show or something and a gang of boys jump on me, I ain't got no help. So yeah, why not? I'll join the gang and then, in the event a gang of boys jump on me, I got *my* gang with me."

As a member of the Blackstone Rangers, Dwight went around the streets representing the gang by drafting recruits and collecting protection fees. There were many forms of protection. At the lowest levels it was a way of extorting lunch money from children ("we get your lunch money and we won't let nobody bother you"). Higher stakes were involved in the protection fees demanded of storekeepers and landlords.

"After you've been in so long, it's like the military, you develop rank, and you move up from a member until you get a position like warlord, or council chief." Dwight continued his account for some time, a complicated story of initiations, parties with the "Rangerettes," "gang-banging" against the Disciples, and the formation of new "chains" of members to expand territory. What is crucial here is Dwight's growing awareness of the perils of street life. Though he eventually embraced the gang and most of its activities—its violence as well as simply "being with the fellas"—he kept a certain distance from the most involved members, "the guys who stayed out all night." He spent a lot of time playing sports and always tried to conceal his membership in the Rangers from his guardian aunt. By the time he was seventeen, he wanted to leave. Though "being on the street" had always had its dangers, an important change occurred in the wake of Martin Luther King's assassination. "Mayor Daley decided that he was tired of this gang-banging stuff and decided to put the order out to shoot to kill. He put lights up in the alleys and told the police to shoot to kill. That's what helped me change my mind about staying on the street."

Before the assassination most of the Rangers' battles had been against other black gangs, not the police. Daley's crackdown and the heightened militance of blacks, however, brought the Rangers into more frequent confrontation with white authority. "Martin Luther King had been dead almost a year and we was back to gang-banging and everything. But mostly now it wasn't just between ourselves, like the Blackstone Rangers and the Disciples. It was anybody that would push us around and I see myself getting into trouble. I was a junior in high school and I just decided that the best thing to keep me from going to the penitentiary is to go to the service. I'll be incarcerated, but I'll still have my freedom. That's what led me to go to the service."

In the spring of 1969 Dwight went to a Marine Corps recruiter and asked to enlist. Marines were dying by the hundreds in Vietnam, but Dwight did not think much about the war; he did not consider the likelihood that he would be sent there or that its dangers might be greater than the ones he had faced in Chicago. "When you're young you don't really think ahead like that. You just figure, well, you don't like what's going on at home and now you finally got a chance to *get away*."

Dwight had few illusions about the military. He did not fantasize about exotic, foreign ports of call. He did not have much confidence that the military would provide him with valuable job training, nor did he feel much need to prove something about himself. In fact, he viewed the military as a form of incarceration, but it would, he hoped, leave him a fuller measure of freedom than the kind of imprisonment that seemed inevitable if he were to stay on the street.

But why the marines? "My father was a marine. I never knew my Dad. He didn't raise me. But I was hearing things about him growing up and I always said I wanted to be a marine too."

Carlos Martinez was drafted in 1967. He begins a description of himself thus: "I've had a complicated life so I don't like to put it into little capsules. But if I had to capsulize my life, I would describe it as three wars: the war of growing up on the streets and in the orphanages of Bronx and Brooklyn, the war in Vietnam, and the war of life in Boston after Vietnam."[48]

Carlos calls himself a Latin American black man or a black Latin. His mother was West Indian and his father a Sephardic Jew. Carlos was born with dark skin and grew up believing that his color caused his father to leave home when Carlos was born. His mother put Carlos in St. Dominic's orphanage where he spent most of his first six years. When Carlos was six, his mother took him out of the orphanage. For the next three years he lived at home with his older brother and his mother. He spent most of his time on the street. "Me and my brother used to be really good hustlers. We used to steal everything. We got a baby carriage, put in a false bottom and used it to hustle the A&P. And we'd steal milk crates from school and sell it cheap to a shopkeeper. We were doing stuff that was really crazy. We were already making guns and breaking into stores. See, in New York being six to nine is like being twelve to fifteen almost anyplace else."

Though he remembers himself as a young, street-tough hustler, Carlos also recalls the pain and fearfulness of his life. "We were very, very poor. I used to drink water out of the toilet because it was the cleanest and coldest water we had. The water that came out of the faucets was always brown with rust." He remembers lying in bed at night hearing the junkies walking around overhead on the roofs, terrified they would break in. Life in the orphanage had its own bad memories, but compared to the poverty and danger of life on the outside, he sometimes thought of it as a kind of sanctuary. When he was nine, Carlos was placed in another orphanage, where he stayed until age seventeen.

When I was seventeen I was on the streets of Brooklyn and I had just got thrown out of the orphanage. Me and six other guys were living on the street and doing a lot of anti-social stuff—like burglaries. And I had just started to shoot heroin. My best friend had joined the marines so I went right after him and I tried to join. It was mainly because of him and to get off the street. I was willing to do anything to get out of Brooklyn at that time. I had already gotten arrested once and we're dealing with a lot of guns and we had six people get shot in a gang fight.

As a kid I was brought up mostly in orphanages but for the three years that I lived with my mother, from the ages of six to nine, I was in and out of children's courts. I was making guns already at six years old in the Bronx. So I was kind of around all that. But going back into the orphanage from age nine till seventeen was a whole toning down of that kind of life. When I got back into it [life on the street, crime, gang violence], well, I started to miss the orphanage. I just really wanted to get off the streets because I saw myself going nowhere.

Things started getting serious. Right? Everything wasn't a joke anymore. So I just sort of wanted to get away from the whole thing and everybody else. But I ended up failing the military exams [in 1964]. So I ended up going to the Job Corps program.

In the Job Corps, Carlos was sent to a small town in New Mexico, went through a high school equivalency program, and worked on local projects, "like the WPA." He did extremely well. He became head of his dorm and captain of the basketball team and formed a "corps patrol" among the other men in the Job Corps center to help reduce friction with the local community. Eventually he was asked to join the staff as a counselor. At first Carlos liked the job. He took pride in his ability to help a wide variety of Job Corps workers—blacks, whites, Chicanos, Hispanics, and gays. Gradually, however, he realized that the staff was using him as a troubleshooter. They always put him in the dorms with the worst racial tension or the greatest discipline problems. He was expected to placate or punish those who voiced dissent, but Carlos increasingly found that he was opposed to many of the regulations he was asked to enforce. After a year or so, he resigned and returned to New York. He was immediately drafted by the army. "When I worked for the Job Corps I had an occupational deferment through the Department of Agriculture. But within two weeks of returning to New York I was drafted. When I left the Job Corps they didn't want me to leave. So I have to presume that they just went down the hall and said, 'Here's Martinez's records, he's on his way back to New York.' Because when I got back to the orphanage, the after-care office, my draft papers were waiting for me."

In 1964 Carlos had been rejected by the military and classified I-Y. Though not as extreme a disqualification as IV-F, I-Y designated men who were considered unfit for service except in times of national emergency. In 1966, however, under Project 100,000, most I-Y men were reclassified as I-A—fit for service.[49] Thus, thousands of men who, like Carlos, had been rejected before the major American escalation in Vietnam, suddenly found themselves drafted. "We were the bottom of the barrel. We were the people that had failed the military tests before—the I-Y's. I was almost legally blind. But when we got down to the induction station in 1967 it really wasn't even about physicals, man, it was like you were being taken. The assumption was already made that you were available. Everybody was taken. The only way you don't pass is if you don't have a leg. They ain't going for it if you attack somebody. I don't remember anyone being disqualified."

In 1964 Carlos had tried to enlist in every branch of the service, thinking it was the best way to escape the streets. He was turned down by all of them. But in 1967, with the American ground war reaching a peak, Carlos was simply taken. This time, however, he was far more ambivalent about entering the military.

I knew we were going to be dealing with some serious shit. I knew the war wasn't no "conflict." And I had a taste of some political stuff because I had been reading Malcolm X. But I didn't have a real intent political consciousness. I didn't want to go in, but I didn't really think about not going. I didn't really see any options.

I didn't want to go, and yet, I remember something beginning to stir up in me because my best friend had gotten killed in Vietnam four months before I went in. I didn't want to go in, but when I thought about Marcus, then I really wanted to go in and I wanted to kill. I wanted to avenge. So it was this two-sided thing.

If I would have had any real political awareness I would have never went to that fucking war.

STREETWISE INNOCENTS

A young, innocent boy with fuzz on his face and patriotic fervor in his heart marches off to war, as excited and proud as a young colt. He returns a hardened man—tough, troubled, disillusioned. This rudimentary story is commonplace in the mythology of war. It is one of the major paradigms structuring the way we think about the experience and meaning of war. In *The Great War and Modern Memory* (1975), Paul Fussell argues that the perception of "innocence savaged and destroyed" by war was especially typical of the way people experienced and responded to World War I. After that war, he suggests, people would never again anticipate war with such innocence.[50]

However, judging by many of the Vietnam films, novels, and memoirs, it appears that the paradigm of innocence savaged continues to have a powerful hold on America's cultural response to war. For example, in *Born on the Fourth of July*—both film and memoir—the prewar Ron Kovic seems utterly unaware of human evil or of his own capacity for wrongdoing. Nor does he seem to have any presentiment of war's destructiveness and moral complexity. His naivete seems little different than that of Fussell's World War I subjects.

Ideas about prewar innocence warrant a more subtle reading, however. Perhaps most soldiers have never been so innocent as many artistic narratives suggest. In fact, the story of innocence savaged might be more persuasive as a literary convention than as a historical explanation. Much of the power of the narrative resides, of course, in the transformative drama of its before-and-after structure. Moreover, at a superficial level at least, the paradigm can hardly be disputed. After all, the contrast of war to almost all civilian experience provides solid ground for depictions of war as a fundamental break from the past, what Eric Leed calls a liminal or threshold experience. Regardless of prewar experience, exposure to premature and violent death on a massive scale must make even the most hard-pressed childhood seem relatively tame. The "thousand-yard stare" attributed to combat veterans is not just a journalistic cliché. War does diminish the light and focus of youthful eyes.[51]

That said, what about the specific quality and range of prewar "innocence"? Surely innocence is not a static entity, the same throughout society and among all who go to war. Evocations of prewar life as a happy, carefree, idealistic time are most commonly found in novels, memoirs, and films—the narratives, in most cases, of middle- or upper-class artists. *The Deer Hunter* is one of the few films about the Vietnam War that even tries to explore the backgrounds of working-class characters. While its prewar portrayals are more extensive and convincing than those in many other Vietnam films, it too romanticizes many features of the civilian home front (the Alpslike mountains embracing the grimy steeltown, the male bonding, the community solidarity, Michael's hunting codes) in order to set a vivid contrast to an unremittingly demonic vision of Vietnam.

The stories of innocence savaged told in memoirs like *A Rumor of War* by Philip Caputo and films like *Platoon* focus our attention on innocent, idealistic, middle-class volunteers who are brutalized by the war. However, the oral histories of working-class veterans suggest a very different theme. According to these accounts, many American soldiers experienced considerable brutalization long before they put on a uniform. As one white, working-class Texan recalled, "I learned a lot of reality before I even got to Nam. I learned about ass-kicking when I was a kid and that wasn't any big thing."[52] In his vastly understated way, this veteran was looking back on a life that had involved, by age fifteen, parental beatings, knife fights, homelessness, thieving, pimping, juvenile courts, and finally Vietnam. These young men were hardly innocent in the same way or to the same degree as prosperous, middle-class, suburban children who have had little personal experience of hardship, violence, or humiliation. For the poor and the working class, adolescence was full of very adult concerns: money, jobs, and survival. Carlos Martinez remembers his life before Vietnam not as a time of innocence but simply as another kind of war. If you assembled a typical squad of infantrymen on their way to Vietnam, you could hardly find a group of young people who had encountered more of the grimmer actualities of American life—its poverty, racism, and violence. As a group they were among the least privileged and sheltered of their generation. The really striking point is not that Vietnam disillusioned the innocent but that it destroyed many of America's most streetwise and resilient.

Yet even the many soldiers who learned at a very early age a great deal about the hardships life had to offer still had a kind of innocence, a political innocence. Savvy as they often were about life in their own homes and neighborhoods—how things got done, who had power, where to go for help—they remained largely ignorant about the world of national and international politics and power. Like most Americans, they had little idea of how American economic and military power was used in countries throughout the world or how that power was perceived by the people of those countries. As Bob Foley put it, "I had to learn at a very early age the realities of life. But . . . things about the country, I didn't learn until Vietnam." Growing up he knew that his family and community could make life miserable, but he clung to the faith that "your country won't do you wrong." Men like Foley possessed a curious combination of skepticism and trust, guile and guilelessness, worldliness and parochialism, sophistication and naivete. They were at once streetwise and innocent.

This quality of innocence often took the form of an uncritical patriotism. Most young Americans grew up in the 1950s and early 1960s trusting their national leaders. However, few entered the military knowing or caring much about Vietnam or the ideological commitments that propelled American intervention. Convinced as many were that the United States was the greatest nation in the world, few enlisted men had the ideological fervor of Alden Pyle, the "Quiet American" of Graham Greene's extraordinary novel. Instead their innocence was largely based on the passive assumption that their government would not lie to them about matters of war and peace and that it would not send them to fight unless the cause were legitimate, the objective clear-cut, the chances for victory reasonable, and the war worth winning. Of course, these assumptions were deeply undermined by the experience of Vietnam, and as the war continued year after year, an increasing number of men entered the military with little faith in what the government was telling them about the war. Yet the remnants of trust that remained, combined with the narrow boundaries of choice within which most men entered the service, served to convince many that there was really no alternative but to hope that their doubts were needless and that military service—even war—might somehow reward their loyalty or at least return them to civilian life whole and undamaged.

Because war exposes people to some of the most extreme forms of violence and suffering, we might expect veterans to look back on their prewar experience with a certain nostalgia, as a time of relative innocence and security (regardless of its actual difficulties). Yet such accounts are not nearly as commonplace as one might expect. When they appear, they tend to be voiced by men from the most stable and economically secure families. For example, Paul Berlin, the main character of Tim O'Brien's novel, *Going after Cacciato*, has frequent reveries about his happy midwestern life before the war:

He'd played baseball in summer. He'd gone canoeing . . . A conscientious student: high marks in penmanship and history and geography. He had thrown rocks into the Des Moines River, pretending this would someday change its course . . . Pretending he might become rich and then travel the world . . . Spent a summer building houses with his father. Strong, solid houses. Hard work, the sun, the feel of wood in his hands . . . Cruising up Main Street in his father's Chevy, elbow out the window, smoking and watching girls, stopping for a root beer, then home.[53]

For some veterans, life before the war reminds them of something out of *American Graffiti*, a movie about California teenage nighttime car culture (set in 1962) in which anxieties about the future are checked by the current passion for a certain girl, a favorite Buddy Holly song, or a prized 1950s-era car.[54] While such associations may be more common among men from middle-class backgrounds, they are also expressed by working-class veterans. Yet when the latter emphasize the carefree innocence of prewar life, they tend to focus not on their entire childhood but on the months just before entering the service. "Man, those were *good* times," recalls Raymond Wilson, describing a nine-month period before he enlisted. "You could just lay back and not give a damn about anything or anybody."[55]

Some men feel so cut off from their prewar lives, they can only evoke it in the barest terms, as if they had been playing some bit part or scene that had no bearing on the movie's ending. It may even have been a good childhood, but compared with what came later, it seemed insignificant. According to Ken Lombardi, "I had a good childhood. It was going to school and living in the neighborhood and I did all the things you're supposed to do. Went to a nice Catholic Sunday School so I could learn my catechism and get confirmed. Did the whole bit and then went to high school and did the whole jock scene and had some close friends. From there, after that, the whole thing was a different ballgame—after '65 when I graduated and got drafted."[56]

Some men were drafted. Some volunteered. Some went burning for battle. Others entered with great reluctance, feeling dragged down by pressures both obvious and obscure. Some were torn by conflicting emotions, feeling at one moment like a dove, at other times like a hawk. Most entered the military with little reflection, however, believing it a natural and unavoidable part of life. Despite their different backgrounds, no one really knew what to expect. Even the most gung-ho volunteers had little specific desire to fight in Vietnam. Billy Cizinski wanted to fight communism, but his imagined enemies were Russians, not Vietnamese. Frank Mathews simply wanted to fight in a war, it did not really matter which one. It took a few months in Vietnam to make him wish that he had been sent to a "clean war" like the one against German Nazis.[57]

As Tim O'Brien suggests in *Going after Cacciato*, American soldiers may have been most united by their common lack of understanding, by "the things they didn't know" about the war they were sent to fight.

> With the war ended, history decided, he would explain to her why he had let himself go to war. Not because of strong convictions, but because he didn't know. He didn't know who was right, or what was right; he didn't know if it was a war of self-determination or self-destruction, outright aggression or national liberation; he didn't know who really started the war, or why, or when, or with what motives. . . . He went to the war because it was expected. Because not to go was to risk censure, and to bring embarrassment on his father and his town. Because, not knowing, he saw no reason to distrust those with more experience. Because he loved his country and, more than that, he trusted it.[58]

In the absence of knowledge about the war, and lacking strong convictions on any side, most acted like Paul Berlin and simply did what was expected or demanded by law: they left for basic training.

Basic Training

TEARING DOWN

They tore you down. They tore everything civilian out of your entire existence—your speech, your thoughts, your sights, your memory—anything that was civilian they tore out and then they re-built you and made you over. But they didn't build you from there up. First they made you drop down to a piece of grit on the floor. Then they built you back up to being a marine.

– Marine veteran Gene Holiday

A bus full of marine recruits pulls into boot camp. It is well past midnight, but a team of drill instructors (DIs) stands ready to pounce. As the bus rolls to a stop, one of the DIs jumps in and screams: "'YOU GOT THREE SECONDS TO GET OFF THIS BUS AND TWO OF 'EM ARE GONE.'"[1] The men scramble and shove their way off, ordered to stand on yellow footprints painted on the concrete parade deck. As the men line up, a second DI roars out of a nearby shed. He marches up to one of the recruits and comes so close their faces almost touch. The DI screams in the boy's ear: "'You no good fucking civilian maggot. . . . You're worthless, do you understand? And I'm gonna kill you.'" Several other men are singled out for similar abuse. Then the drill instructor addresses the whole group: "'There are eighty of you, eighty young warm bodies, eighty sweet little ladies, eighty sweetpeas, and I want you maggots to know today that you belong to me and you will belong to me until I have made you into marines.'"[2]

The DI proclaims his ownership of the recruits, his civilian maggots. Screaming his taunts and insults, the sergeant asserts his absolute control of their lives. The most ominous threats ("I'm gonna kill you") are meant to inspire terror, but they also express a quite literal intention to destroy everything civilian in the recruits. Nothing in their former lives is deemed worthy of preservation. Every civilian identity is worthless. New recruits are the lowest form of life. They do not deserve to live. If they are ever to become marines, they must acknowledge their total inadequacy. They must be torn down in order to be rebuilt, killed in order to be reborn.

Gustav Hasford, a combat journalist who served in Vietnam with the First Marine Division, writes about basic training in his novel *The Short-Timers* (the film *Full Metal Jacket* was based on this book). Hasford's drill instructor speaks these words to his new recruits: " '*If* you ladies leave my island, *if* you survive recruit training, you will be a weapon, you will be a minister of death, praying for war. And proud. Until that day you are pukes, you are scumbags, you are the lowest form of life on Earth. You are not even human. You people are nothing but a lot of little pieces of amphibian shit.' "[3]

After the initial hazing, according to Ron Kovic's account, the recruits are herded into a large building and lined up in front of long rows of empty boxes. " 'I want you to take your clothes off,' the sergeant shouted. 'I want you to take off everything that ever reminded you of being a civilian and put it in the box. . . . I want everything!' "[4] Naked now, the men are marched to a group of barbers. With fast, rough strokes, the barbers run electric razors over each man's head, shearing the hair down to the scalp in less than a minute. After the haircut the men are sent down long metal hallways, shoved along by drill instructors. The men get jammed up, the "young bodies tense and twisted together, grasping each other, holding on like children." They are run into a large shower room. A sergeant screams: " 'Wash all that scum off! I want you maggots to wash all that civilian scum off your bodies forever!' "[5]

Dripping and still naked, the men are moved to another room and are lined up in front of a row of boxes containing military uniforms. " 'Awright ladies! . . . We're going to begin today by learning how to dress. These are trousers . . . Not pants! Pants are for little girls! Trousers are for marines!' " An overweight recruit in Kovic's training platoon cannot fit into the trousers he is issued. The drill sergeants circle around him, screaming and taunting and punching him in the stomach. When the recruit breaks down and begins to cry, one of the sergeants yells for everyone in the building to look at the crybaby. " 'Cry Cry Cry you little baby! That's what we want, we want you people to cry like little babies because that's all you maggots are. You are nothing!' "[6]

The first days of basic training were indeed designed to reduce recruits to a psychological condition equivalent to early childhood. As Robert Flaherty recalls, "It was like you were a little baby and you were starting all over again." The drill instructors acted as surrogate parents, seeking, in several intense weeks, to replace seventeen or eighteen years of psychological and physical development with wholly reconditioned minds and bodies. Every detail of life was prescribed, regulated, and enforced. Every moment was accounted for. There was a method and time for every action. Even using the bathroom was limited to short, specified times or required special permission. "Head calls," like all boot camp "privileges," were especially infrequent at the outset. Some men went for a full week before they were able to defecate in the time allotted.[7]

Moreover, the regimen was carried out in an environment of strict impersonality, a kind of collective isolation. Recruits were denied both privacy and intimacy. They could not be alone, nor could they engage their fellow recruits in unofficial activities or conversations. During the first week, conversation was forbidden altogether. Every form of language or behavior that expressed individuality or fraternal resistance to boot camp regulations was, when observed by the drill instructors, immediately and severely punished. Punishments almost always involved some physical ordeal or debasement: men were exercised until they dropped (sometimes locked in the DI's metal locker, "the sweat box"), forced to eat garbage or unauthorized possessions found in their area (often inducing vomiting), made to put their heads into the urinals they had not sufficiently cleaned, and so on. While the DIs called the recruits every insulting pejorative they could think of, the recruits could only address their sergeants in the third person. A recruit never said *I* to a sergeant. *I*—the individual—was not acknowledged to exist.

Robert Flaherty is about six-foot-three, a big, strong ex-marine. His size and strength, however, did not protect him from the deep anxiety and fear induced by his drill instructors. "You get up in the morning at attention and you go to sleep at attention. You go to sleep from fright. Speak to the drill instructor in the third person only: 'Sir, Private Flaherty requests permission to speak to the drill instructor, sir.' Sir before, sir after. Look him straight in the face. Don't look any other way. Stand at attention at all times. Look straight ahead. You could get you head handed to you for looking another way."[8]

At the mess hall, recruits ate their meals in silence, looking straight ahead. Robert demonstrates the prescribed eating method: Keeping his head completely still, he uses his fork to probe the plate for food. Then he raises the fork straight up to a point about one foot in front of his face, brings it to his mouth, empties it, and returns it to the plate. "We called them 'square meals,'" he recalls, the term's extra meaning coming from the path of the fork from plate to mouth. If the drill instructor was on the other side of the room, men sometimes glanced at their food or at one of the other men, but it was a risky move. "If the drill instructor catches you sneaking a peak, he will just hop right up on the table and start walking through everybody's food. And you know what you do when he's walking through your food? You just keep eating your square meal. And the drill instructor will say: 'Motherfucker, you *better* not stab your sergeant with that fork.' And everybody at the table yells, 'NO, SIR!' It's that crazy. It's that intense."

In other words, much of boot camp was truly *basic* training. Recruits were told how to eat, how and when to speak, how to dress, when to go to the bathroom, how to walk, how to fold clothing and make beds, how to stand at attention and salute—how, in short, to perform the most elemental routine according to a rigid and standardized set of regulations. The drill instructors maintained this discipline with an iron hand. Though obedience was exacted by sheer intimidation, the physical stress of basic training also induced compliance.

Even well-trained athletes were taxed to the limit by the physical demands of Marine Corps boot camp. The day began between 4:00 and 5:00 in the morning, and between then and lights-out at 9:00 P.M. the recruits were continually subjected to torturous exercise. Aside from the regularly scheduled hours of physical training (PT), sergeants called for additional rounds of PT at any hour, for any reason. A speck of dust might send the entire platoon on a mile run or another hour of scrubbing down the barracks. A sloppy salute could bring fifty push-ups. "Man, the PT was constant. They PT'd you to death. At the drop of a hat the drill instructor would have you on the ground doing push-ups or sit-ups or squat thrusts. You wouldn't think you could sweat that much."[9]

Simple exhaustion was a key factor in explaining the willingness of recruits to follow orders. They soon learned that disobedience of any kind only brought more pain—more harassment, more cleaning, and more fatigue. If the standard forms of breaking down recruits to a level of unquestioning compliance were not effective, the DIs could always transfer inept or recalcitrant men to a special platoon. Drill instructors often reminded their men of the ordeal awaiting them if they were sent to a "Motivation Platoon" or, even worse, "Correctional Custody." (The army version of the motivation platoon was called the "Special Processing Detachment," and the equivalent of correctional custody was the army stockade.)

In these special platoons recruits underwent an excruciating round of forced marches, disciplinary labor, and even more constant verbal and physical abuse. Those recruits who proved themselves sufficiently motivated (that is, submissive to orders and able to perform the basic round of drills) were returned to their original platoons. Others had to repeat boot camp from the beginning with a new cycle of recruits. The rest were ultimately court-martialed and given dishonorable discharges.[10]

Given these circumstances, it is not surprising that most men followed orders and worked as hard as possible to avoid the wrath of their drill instructors. Gene Holiday speaks for many as he describes the series of responses that characterized his effort to adjust to boot camp. He moved from fear to self-doubt to absolute obedience. "I started out being real scared. And then I ended up feeling real worthless. I felt that I wasn't going to cut it and not because it was their fault for putting me through it, but because it was my own fault. And then I started to feel better by telling myself I'm just going to do everything these guys say. I'm going to do it so fast that if he says 'jump,' it's not even going to get out of his mouth and—BOOM—I'll be right there."[11]

Marine Corps basic training in the Vietnam years, conducted in only two places (Parris Island, South Carolina, and San Diego, California), was a highly standardized and predictable cycle. Accounts of the experience are so similar one can draw from them a fairly clear-cut model of its essential elements. The army, the service that trained the most men for Vietnam, had a similar system but was less brutal, and veterans report a variety of training experiences. The army operated about a dozen basic training camps throughout the country (for example, Fort Lewis, Washington; Fort Polk, Louisiana; Fort Dix, New Jersey; and Fort Jackson, South Carolina). While some army veterans report training experiences that sound virtually identical to marine basic, others indicate that the training was significantly less severe in both tone and substance. Nor does army basic seem to have left such an indelible mark on its trainees. While former marines almost always include boot camp anecdotes in their Vietnam stories, army veterans often skip their training experiences unless asked about them specifically.

Until the early 1960s the army used platoon sergeants and special instructors to train recruits. Drill sergeants were brought in to present men with a more dominant and ever-present authority. At least superficially, the drill sergeants were modeled on the Marine Corps drill instructors, even wearing the same forest ranger style hats ("Smoky-the-Bear hats"). In practice, however, the army drill sergeants were less omnipresent and less vicious. Even in the first days of boot camp, many organizational tasks were handled by squad leaders drawn from the ranks of the trainees. Although the drill sergeants subjected their men to demeaning verbal abuse, it was neither so constant nor so extreme as that of the marine DIs. Though they called their men "shitbirds" and other epithets, they also addressed the recruits as "troops" and "men." Marine DIs would have found such language unthinkably polite.[12]

In Bo Hathaway's novel, *A World of Hurt* (set in 1966), an army lieutenant addressed a group of trainees:

"I'm going to make soldiers out of you bunch of riffraff if I have to work you till you drop. And go ahead and write your congressmen. I think you'll find those congressmen on our side. They don't want a bunch of crybabies doing their fighting for them.

"Most of you know by now there was one coward in the company who couldn't take it anymore. He decided he didn't have an obligation to defend his country. All he wanted was to get out of the army and go back to his mommy. Last night this man put a couple of scratches on his wrist so we'd have to take pity on him and send him to the hospital. And let me tell you something, he's going to get his wish. He's getting out of the army, all right—with a dishonorable discharge that will follow him the rest of his life.

"I don't know if this fairy infected any of the rest of you, but if any of you punks out there don't want to become soldiers and men, just let me know, and we'll slap a dishonorable discharge on you, and you can run home, too. But just try to get a job."[13]

The substance of this statement is similar to that offered by marine DIs: trainees are punks and riffraff, and anyone who is unwilling or unable to become a soldier is simply a crybaby, a coward, and a fairy. But there is a defensive quality in this speech that is ordinarily absent in accounts of

Marine Corps training. If the lieutenant truly had absolute control, why should he even mention the existence of civilian authorities? This sense of constraint is made more explicit in Hathaway's novel by the response of a sergeant to a trainee who talked back: "If this was the old army—if things were the way they should be—I'd beat the shit out of you."[14]

There is a similar tone in the lieutenant's warnings about dishonorable discharges ("just try to get a job"). He sounds like a man charged with controlling a group of men who will do anything to get out of their situation, a group that has to be reminded at every turn of the dire consequences of resistance or escape. In fact, suicide attempts were common among military recruits. At Fort Dix alone, there was an average of more than 200 suicide attempts per year during the Vietnam War. Actual suicides, though not uncommon, were far fewer; for example, at Fort Dix in 1968, six trainees killed themselves. The high number of what the army called suicide gestures indicates that most men were not driven to kill themselves, but many were willing to take extreme risks to escape the military.[15]

Marine DIs revealed no doubts about their ability to keep their men in line. When a marine trainee "botched" a suicide in *Sand in the Wind*, a novel by Vietnam veteran Robert Roth, the DI told his platoon that the man would "get court-martialed for the destruction of government property." Then he proceeded to instruct his men on the proper way to commit suicide. "The civilian turd did it the wrong way. I'm gonna show you the *Marine Corps way*." He took a razor and moved the blade up and down his forearm. "*Remember*, up and down, not across—that way you get all the arteries."[16]

The Marine Corps relied primarily on verbal and physical abuse—behavioral conditioning—to indoctrinate its recruits. The army put additional emphasis on ideological indoctrination. In practical terms this distinction simply meant that army trainees had to sit through more films and lectures than did the marines. For example, in an effort to swell the spirit of anticommunism, the army ran films like *The Red Menace*, *The Anatomy of Aggression*, *Guardians at the Gate*, and *Night of the Dragon*. These films are packed with crude images of communist expansion—world maps inexorably covered by a tide of red ink and crowds of civilians apparently fleeing the advances of invading communists.[17]

Most army trainees also heard a series of lectures by an army chaplain on "character guidance." The central point of these lectures was to explain why soldiers ought to obey their commanders. Invoking God, honor, and prudence (that is, if you do not obey you will get into trouble), the chaplain followed a course outline called Character Guidance Discussion Topics provided in an army field manual. "The freest soldier," the manual argues, "is the soldier who willingly submits to authority. When you obey a lawful command you need not fear, nor worry. You can devote all your energies to getting the job done." What is omitted from the discussion, as Peter Barnes points out, is any clear definition of what the trainees should consider an *un*lawful order and how they are to respond in such a situation. Though the army modified its regulations, after the Nuremberg Trials, to hold individual soldiers responsible for their own actions, indoctrination stressed simpleminded obedience. There was no special training about the moral responsibilities and complexities encountered by soldiers fighting a counterguerrilla war among a civilian population.[18]

One of the most unusual and amusing accounts of army basic training during the Vietnam War is Peter Tauber's *The Sunshine Soldiers* (1971). A reservist from New York, Tauber writes about his experience of basic training at Fort Bliss, Texas, in the spring of 1969. His detailed and imaginative journal presents a view of army training at its most lax. Indeed, Tauber persuasively argues that most of the military authorities were more preoccupied with processing as many trainees as possible with the fewest hassles than they were with instilling military rigor or discipline. In Tauber's company, the trainees routinely ignored and openly defied their sergeants. They found dozens of ways to circumvent or undermine the routine. They slacked off, skipped drills, and opened a "clubhouse" in an abandoned barracks where they went to relax, smoke pot, and sleep. Even when drill sergeants were aware of the infractions, they did little, if anything, in response. So long as the trainees stayed on base, the authorities were content to tolerate repeated irregularities. (Some men even addressed their sergeants by their first names.)[19]

Lectures and films did not succeed in persuading the sunshine soldiers to toe the military line. Tauber describes his unit's response to a film designed to prevent trainees from using drugs:

> The Army's cinematic explanation of the drug scene seems to have replaced the traditional venereal-disease slides. No more full-color blowups of infected genitalia before lunch. No indeed. Sex is out, because drugs are farther out. *Trip to Where?*, a film about LSD, begins with a Russian roulette game which ends with a gun actually being fired at some poor acid head's head. . . . [Then] we settle down

to a half hour of freaky music and light-show effects, which the movie tries to imply are horrific. The fatigue-clad audience begins to groove on the welcome vibrations; the soldier next to me whispers that he has been stoned since he took the oath a week ago, and has three day's supply left. On the screen an LSD freak-out party leads to an obvious sexual liaison between Good Joe and Clean Suzie, bringing lusty cheers from the audience. The announcer, who has remained silent for a half hour, breaks in to tell us that "you are beginning to see the dangers of LSD—now let's look at the medical facts." The main danger he has in mind, it seems, is Sex. Someone is always forgetting to pass the word to the Pentagon.[20]

Tauber concedes that his company was not typical. While some of the men in his unit went to Vietnam, about 50 percent were reservists (none of whom was sent to Vietnam). Tauber found the reservists considerably more irreverent and disobedient than the regular army volunteers and draftees. The military may well have treated companies filled with reservists with greater leniency. Still, if Tauber's account does not reflect the majority experience of basic training for Vietnam-bound soldiers, it does help to define one end of the spectrum. It also reminds us that the military was not always successful in getting across its view of the world.

Army boot camp was hardly the all-encompassing, closed world of marine boot camp. While marines were completely isolated from civilian life throughout the basic training cycle, army trainees were usually allowed occasional off-base passes after four or five weeks of boot camp. These leaves gave trainees a chance to gain some psychological as well as physical distance from the military. And for the increasing number of men who were seeking a way out of the military and who opposed the war, they provided a chance to make contact with a community of supporters. By the late 1960s, antiwar groups had established GI coffee houses near most training bases; here, trainees could gather informally to talk, meet civilians with antiwar views, and get concrete information on seeking exile abroad or filing for conscientious objector status. There were also, by 1969, more than forty antiwar, underground GI newspapers that circulated secretly among trainees off and on base (for example, *Shakedown* at Fort Dix, *Left Face* at Fort McClellan, *The Fatigue Press* at Fort Hood, *Last Harass* at Fort Gordon, and *Short Times* at Fort Jackson). In-service applications for conscientious objector status rose from 829 in 1967 to 4,381 in 1971. Primarily due to some key federal and Supreme Court decisions, the Pentagon began accepting many more of these claims, and the approval rate rose from 28 percent in 1967 to 77 percent by 1972. Desertions also mounted steadily—40,227 in 1967, 73,121 in 1969, and 90,000 in 1971. While 20,000 men deserted after serving full tours in Vietnam, a far greater number left the military during the training process. There were roughly 500,000 deserters during the Vietnam War.[21]

The level of resistance within the military by the late 1960s was extraordinary. Nonetheless, even antiwar draftees were frequently struck by the capacity of basic training to inculcate military values. However skeptical and resistant they may have been to military indoctrination, however much they may have loathed the mindless routines, and however opposed they were to the effort to instill obedience and aggression, most men who went through the process felt that it had changed them, in many cases far more than they had believed possible.

Take the case of Peter Milord. He was an upper-middle-class graduate of the University of Connecticut when he was drafted in 1969. At first he thought military training was having no impact on him: "In my mind I was being a cynical, satirical wit. . . . I was able to laugh and stone [smoke marijuana] my way through basic, staying above it." But gradually he found himself changing. He had always enjoyed sports and physical competition, and the military training drills began to tap those emotions. Along with his enjoyment he noticed himself becoming increasingly aggressive. Though at first he had simply mouthed, without feeling, the violent slogans ("Kill! Kill! Kill! To kill without mercy is the spirit of the bayonet!"), he began to suspect he was absorbing, through repetition, the real meaning of the words. "I didn't become a robot, but you can get so close to being one it's frightening." In Milord's case, the changes he felt in himself were decisive in setting him on the course of action he had seriously considered when he first received his draft notice. A few weeks after basic training he deserted to Canada.[22]

Another former army trainee described basic training this way:

When you first go in, everybody realizes [basic training is] a lot of horse shit. They show you all those movies about the good guys getting wiped out by the dirty commies—that they're going to come over here and rape your mom, and eat your apple pie, and that kind of thing. Everybody realizes it's horse shit, but by the end of training, there were actually guys who started talking about killing the dirty commies—it works. Other people didn't believe it, but they had been through so much smoke that they outwardly accepted it because it had been impressed on them so much. They realized that in order to survive they had to conform.[23]

Stan Bodner, an army Vietnam veteran, described the effect of basic training in much stronger language:

A soldier lives a very, very low life in the service—highly regimented, highly mechanical. He is ingrained with the spirit of the corps, but his own personal self is sacrificed. His personal identity is put on ice. I mean he forgets totally about himself, he becomes a sacrificial human being, a person who is totally acquiesced to a system, to a body-regiment. Unless you've been through eight weeks of boot camp you have no idea of what I'm talking about. Because what's taught in basic training is a whole unquestionable obedience.[24]

Thus, even while army training was not usually as brutal or imprisoning as marine boot camp, it was certainly capable of tearing down many of its trainees, stripping them of a personal identity, and making them feel like unquestioning members of a body-regiment. Also, many of the army combat soldiers who fought in Vietnam went on to advanced training as paratroopers or Rangers, experiences comparable in intensity to marine basic. Moreover, army trainees who entered the military reluctantly may have found basic training more of an emotional jolt than marine recruits who went to boot camp expecting the worst. After all, some men enlisted in the marines precisely because they had heard it was "really bad," the toughest branch of the service.

Lt. Col. William E. Datel found extremely high levels of anxiety and stress among army trainees throughout the 1960s. As chief of the Mental Hygiene Unit at Ford Ord, California (a major army basic training center), Datel studied the stress levels of boot camp trainees for almost a decade. By the middle of basic training, Datel found, recruits became so intensely anxious and angry that their stress levels surpassed those of frontline soldiers. Producing and controlling that anger was, of course, not an unwanted by-product of basic training but one of its main goals.[25]

COMPLIANT AGGRESSION

Basic training was devoted to the tricky business of promoting two not always compatible traits: unswerving obedience and ruthless aggression.

Recruits were trained to be both compliant and violent. Therefore, drill instructors tore down their recruits not only to generate the kind of fear that elicits obedience but also to inflame the sort of anger that might be channeled into aggressive soldiering. Uncontrolled aggression was not, however, the final object. Unfocused, undisciplined rage is not usually an advantage in a firefight. Instead, the military hoped to turn out soldiers who would be "cool under fire," men able to return fire quickly, calmly, and mechanically. Thus, basic training combined discipline and aggression, obedience and anger. The final goal was to instill in recruits a focused hostility aimed at a prescribed enemy.

Before drill instructors attempted to focus aggression on a specific enemy, they wanted simply to generate as much rage as possible, whatever its source or object. In part this was accomplished through the standard boot camp training drills in which men were pitted against one another in various physical competitions. In bayonet training, for example, recruits fought one another with pugil sticks (five-foot poles with heavy padding on each end). These were tough, often ferocious battles in which drill instructors encouraged recruits to perceive their opponent as an absolute enemy warranting no mercy.

Sometimes, especially in the Marine Corps, drill instructors went beyond the traditional boot camp regimen with their own unofficial methods of heightening aggression. For example, Robert Flaherty's drill instructor periodically called for an "air-raid." In the middle of the night the DI burst into the barracks screaming at everyone to get into the showers and take everything with them—their clothes, their footlockers, even their mattresses ("every goddamn thing"). The DI yelled "AIR-RAID," and everyone pushed and kicked to find a place on the floor of the packed shower room. Then the sergeant screamed "FLOOD," and everyone jumped up to get to the shower handles and turn them on—"hot, cold, indifferent." The sergeant encouraged the wildest behavior. "He wanted us to go absolutely berserk. Screaming, pounding, pushing—it was a raging free-for-all. They made you inhuman, my man, inhuman."[26]

Drill instructors were careful, however, to maintain control of the violence they provoked. They wanted to use the growing aggression of their recruits to help enforce the discipline and conformity of basic training. The goal was to make their units essentially self-regulating and self-disciplining, enforcing among themselves the demands initially made by the drill instructors alone. The technique was simple. Whenever a trainee failed to perform according to the DI's standards, everyone in the unit was punished. While they did their extra push-ups, the drill instructor repeatedly denounced the slacker who had caused their collective pain. In fact, DIs sometimes ordered particularly inept or intractable recruits to sit and watch while the other men did extra PT—an especially effective way of producing unitwide anger against those who could not or would not keep pace and maintain discipline. "'I want you men to take a look at those cowards who have caused you to stay in this strain. You may think those men are your buddies, but they're cheaters and fuckoffs, and they're putting you in a world of hurt.'"[27]

Whatever initial sympathy a recruit might have for those unable or unwilling to conform was soon quelled by the additional suffering such lapses in discipline might bring to all. A single sloppy man could cause hours of extra scrubbing for everyone, so almost everyone scorned recruits who caused trouble. Some men bent or broke the rules without getting caught. That was a different matter. These men might be very popular indeed (especially in the army), doubly respected for their ability to do what was required without becoming "ass-kissers." Those who caused problems for everyone, however, became outcasts and pariahs. Sometimes, especially in the Marine Corps, such men were beaten by the other recruits during midnight "blanket parties": "If somebody fucks you up—if somebody talks, or somebody gets caught doing something they're not supposed to do, and the whole platoon suffers for it—that night a bunch of guys will get together and throw a blanket over this guy's head when he's sleeping and kick his ass real good."[28] The blanket was used to muffle the screams.

Individual behavior of any kind was risky in basic training. Even when recruits decided to break rather than enforce the standards of basic training, they tended to do so collectively. At Fort Jackson in 1967, draftee John Picciano recalled occasional nights when someone took out a hidden bottle of scotch and passed it around the barracks. He dreaded those times because he felt pressured to drink when he did not want to.

"Hey, we've got a bottle here. Have a drink," one of the guys would say.

"No, thanks, I don't drink much."

"You better drink. What's the matter with you, anyway?"

John believed that the military was making everyone a conformist and that "no one was allowed to be his own man even when the sergeants weren't around."[29] He also noticed a decided increase in the level of aggression. People were thinking and acting much more violently. "A perfectly regular guy could come into the Army, and before he knew it, he was doing things he'd never done before. Making fun of some poor fat guy after the sergeants had kicked him around. Talking about what it would be like to get a gang together and take the cafe waitress out in the alley."[30]

The verbal abuse hurled at recruits was crucial in fomenting these attitudes. Aside from the general terms of degradation DIs used to address their entire units ("scumbags," "hogs," "shitbirds"), individuals were commonly branded with their own particular derogatory name. Often these slurs were based on race, religion, class, region, or physical traits.

In *Sand in the Wind,* Robert Roth describes in detail the process by which the DIs labeled their men. Roth's fictional narrative, drawing on his own experience at Parris Island, is one of the most gripping and insightful accounts of marine basic training in the enormous body of literature about Vietnam.

> Hacker [the DI] stopped in front of a dark recruit. He slowly moved closer until his mouth was within an inch of the recruit's nose, then shouted, "YOU A SPLIB OR A SPIC?"
> "Splib."
> "SPLIB, WHAT?"
> "Splib, sir."
> "COCKSUCKER, if you want to live, the first word out of your mouth will be '*sir.*' . . . ARE YOU A SPLIB OR A SPIC?" . . .
> "SIR, THE PRIVATE IS A SPLIB."
> "Remember that, you high-yellow come bubble."[31]

Another recruit was branded "Red-Neck" after a drill sergeant found out he was from a Mississippi farm. At one point a DI told him, "You're going back to Mississippi where you're needed . . . to slop the hogs, clean the cow pies out of the barn, move the outhouse around. Isn't that right red-neck? . . . I'm not gonna waste any more time trying to make a Marine out of white trash like you."[32]

Aware that most recruits were from the bottom rungs of the American social order (as were most drill instructors), the DIs used class and racial epithets to aggravate the pain many recruits associated with their civilian status. They called their men "bums," "losers," "morons," "riffraff," and "trash." The DIs sought to persuade their recruits that, so long as they remained civilians, they amounted to nothing more than a lumpen proletariat, a class of "low-lifes," "dead-beats," "punks," and "scum." As soldiers, however, society's losers were offered the prospect of professional standing. This particular version of social mobility was trenchantly voiced by a drill instructor in Roth's novel: "'You ain't standing on no corner and you ain't sloppin' no hogs. You're professional men now, each and every one of you worthless cunts has a profession. YOU'RE PROFESSIONAL KILLERS *in the service of the United States government.'*"[33]

What about those recruits who were not poor or working class? How did drill instructors deal with the question of class among the minority of men from middle-class and privileged backgrounds? They, too, were singled out and subjected to ridicule. They were told that their civilian advantages were worthless in the military, that their class privileges were, in fact, a disability. Their comfort had made them even more soft and cowardly than the other recruits. They were "pussies," "faggots," and "candy-asses."

In *Sand in the Wind*, during one of the first formations, a sergeant said, "Any of you hogs that have been to college take one step forward." Of a platoon of eighty only five stepped forward. Only one had graduated from college, and he suffered particular abuse.

> "How many years did *you* waste, hog?" . . .
> "SIR, THE PRIVATE SPENT FOUR YEARS IN COLLEGE."
> "SPENT?" . . .
> "Sir, *the Private wasted four years in college.*" . . .
> "*I* DON'T *fucking believe it*! How could *anyone* with balls spend FOUR YEARS in college?"

Concluding the inquest, one of the sergeants said, "'COME BUBBLE, your education has *just* started.'" From that point on, the recruit was called "College Fag."[34]

Paradoxically, one of the functions of these epithets was not to divide the men but to unify them. So long as everyone was insulted—the "college fags" along with the "morons," the "rednecks" and "wops" along with the "spics" and "bean-bags" (Chicanos)—everyone was, in theory, equal. The insults generated a sense of mutual degradation, a kind of solidarity of the despised. Ex-marine Paul Atwood recalls his drill instructor saying, "There are no niggers in this platoon, there are no spics, there are no wops, there are no kikes, there are no poor white whatever. . . . You are all fucking maggots and maggots you will remain until you've earned the right to call yourself United States Marines."[35] Some recruits felt that the very abuse each man had to endure contributed to a sense of collective respect and helped to defuse potential conflicts among the men. "They figure if they put us through enough shit, we'll respect each other more."[36] But others noticed that despite talk about all marines being equal, many drill instructors still differentiated their men with racist epithets.

No doubt the experience of basic training did, for many, create a sense of unit solidarity across lines of race, class, and region. That was the point. The goal, however, was not to eliminate racist thought entirely or to promote tolerance of individual, ethnic, or national differences. The goal was to mold a rigid and intolerant conformity to military discipline and to mobilize hostility against a foreign enemy. If the drill instructors' use of racist language served to defuse internal hostilities among the trainees, it also served to legitimize racist stereotypes when projected onto external groups such as the Vietnamese. If racist language seemed to lose its venom when used to homogenize American soldiers, it preserved its poison when used to demonize a foreign enemy.

This point is underlined by the way drill instructors used the language of gender and sexuality. One of the most common forms of harassment was to call recruits "ladies," "girls," "cunts," or "pussies." Any evidence of weakness or fatigue (or simply failure to conform) was typically attributed to a lack of manhood. Failure as a soldier constituted failure as a man and left the recruit with the status of a woman. Describing that status, Tim O'Brien writes, "[In basic training] women are dinks. Women are villains. They are creatures akin to Communists and yellow-skinned people and hippies."[37] And, he might have added, they are akin to homosexuals. Women and gays were referred to interchangeably as the epitome of all that is cowardly, passive, untrustworthy, unclean, and undisciplined. Moreover, homosexuality was more than a negative reference. Homosexual relations are forbidden by military law, and even the suspicion of a homosexual affair usually results in severe punishment. Bob Foley recalls the brutal treatment given an army trainee at Fort Lewis, Washington, in 1968: "There was a kid that had been accused of being homosexual. So consequently he was followed around by a sergeant and called faggot and queer and everything you can call somebody. And he was kicked, and made to crawl on his hands and knees and police cigarette butts. And he was made to keep his eyes averted downward to the ground and was ridiculed in front of *everyone*. I saw that kid sitting in his bunk one afternoon and he was just rocking back and forth, banging his head against his pillow."[38]

The model of male sexuality offered as a military ideal in boot camp was directly linked to violence. Sexual talk permeated the distribution and handling of weapons. Recruits were instructed to call their weapons rifles, not guns. To emphasize the point, drill instructors might order their men to run around the barracks with their rifle in one hand, their penis in the other, chanting, "This is my rifle, this is my gun; one is for fighting, the other's for fun." The significance of this drill rests on the ironic linking of guns and penises. While the ostensible point is to distinguish between sex and violence, applying the language of weaponry to both does more to associate the two behaviors than to divide them. Rifles are for fighting and penis-"guns" are for fun, but the distinction is so slight (the drill mockingly implies) that most men need special training to understand the difference. Drill instructors repeatedly described war as a substitute for sex or as another form of sex. For example, the drill instructor in *The Short-Timers* ordered his recruits to give their rifles a proper female name (for example, "Charlene"). Then he made the following speech: "This is the only pussy you people are going to get. Your days of finger-banging ol' Mary Jane Rottencrotch through her pretty pink panties are over. You're married to *this* piece, this weapon of iron and wood, and you *will* be faithful."[39]

Thus, drill instructors used sexual, class, regional, and racial slurs not to render those categories irrelevant but to raise the level of aggression and to inculcate attitudes about each of these topics that conformed with dominant military ideology. DIs fostered a military sexual identity based on denunciations of women and homosexuality, demanded obedience to a military class system (trainees had to memorize the chain of command from the president on down), promoted dedication to the national interest (usually defined as militant nationalism), and sought to instill bitter animosity toward a foreign, nonwhite enemy. Directing men to these ends, military training served to legitimize bigotry and inequality founded on race, sex, nationality, and class.

In the first half of basic training, drill instructors fostered a general climate of aggression and anger. Much of it was focused internally. Trainees were encouraged to be angry at themselves, each other, and their drill instructors. As training progressed, however, drill sergeants increasingly sought to direct hostility outward. As American recruits were turned from "maggots" and "shitbirds"—worthless and subhuman—into "professional killers," "real men," "Marines," and "Soldiers," the foreign enemy became the central focus of animosity, the primary repository of all that was base and loathsome: "gooks."

BUILDING UP TO KILL

Midway through basic training you might find yourself near the end of a two-mile run. Just a few weeks ago, the same run brought you to the point of collapse, drenched in sweat and gasping for air; but today your legs feel strong, and you are breathing easily. Glancing around, you notice the other men are equally relaxed, bobbing along in the early morning light. For the first time you pay attention to the way the pine trees look against the sky. You hear birds singing and the echo of distant platoons calling cadence. You can't remember ever feeling so good, so full of energy. The thrill of your own new strength expands in recognition of the enormous collective power surging through the platoon. The others seem to feel it too. Running the final half-mile with no sergeant in sight, the group quickens its pace. Then, spontaneously, someone sings out an opening line of cadence, and everyone joins in, shouting the now familiar words with gusto:

> I wanna be an Airborne Ranger
> I wanna live a life of danger
> I wanna be a fighting man
> I wanna go to Vietnam
>
> I wanna jump out of the sky
> I wanna make the VC die.[40]

The once motley and uncoordinated collection of trainees has begun to think and act as organized units. Platoons that once were unable to keep a straight line or count off in sequence now march with precision, barking their cadences in crisp unison. At this point, the drill instructors began a subtle but crucial shift in their relationship to the men. Of course they still screamed and carried on, ranting, threatening, and punishing; but somehow the harassment lost some of its sting. Underneath, there seemed to be signs of genuine concern, perhaps even a grudging affection. The DIs actually seemed to want their men to succeed. Along with all the put-downs, they began offering some encouragement. Some of the drill instructors even stopped calling the men hogs and maggots. They had become "troopers" (army) or "my herd" (marines).

These changes were crucial to the second stage of training, the effort to produce strong, confident fighters. Having been broken down to nothing—their identities stripped, their compliance won, and their aggression heightened—recruits were gradually rebuilt into soldiers. The transition was gradual, but the key turning point, a moment of great significance, came when the trainees began weapons training. Peter Barnes describes the moment well in his book *Pawns*.

> This rebuilding process begins in earnest at about the fourth week, when the platoon moves to the rifle range. Here, for the first time, the recruit feels that he is being given something useful to do, that he is acquiring a skill that is of some interest and value. The anxiety and rage that develop during the first weeks of training now have an outlet. The recruit no longer merely absorbs punishment; he has an opportunity to perform. . . . He is tested on his proficiency with the rifle and he passes the test. Suddenly, he is no longer a worthless human being; he has a worthwhile skill for which he is rewarded by a lessening of harassment.[41]

On the rifle range, trainees were ordinarily taught by marksmanship instructors rather than their regular drill instructors. "The sergeants out on the range weren't hard like the drill instructors." They helped the men spot their rounds and adjust their sights. Even the hard drill instructors began to sound like potential allies—stubborn and tough but devoted to making everyone combat-ready. They began to talk about the importance of teamwork and unity, how in combat each man's life depended on everyone in the unit. A failure by one man could result in the death of all. The warning gained extra impact as the recruits began firing live ammunition. Suddenly the prospect of combat felt much more tangible. Of course, the DIs still regarded their men as incompetent, untrustworthy, and untested, and during training drills it was not uncommon for DIs to scream: "YOU'RE DEAD, BIRDBRAIN." "YOU'RE GONNA DIE." "YOU WON'T LAST ONE WEEK IN VIETNAM." Recruits began to listen to their DIs with new ears. After all, many of the sergeants were combat veterans, men who might very well possess lifesaving information.[42]

With these changes came an easing of restrictions. More conversation was allowed among the men. Recruits began to get to know one another, and the drill instructors encouraged them to take pride in their platoon. Harassment of individuals was less frequent and less brutal. Recruits were increasingly addressed as a group. Competitions within the training unit were gradually replaced by competitions against other units. Recruits were still encouraged to enforce conformity within their own units, to put pressure on slackers, but the focus was primarily on unit pride and solidarity. Most men embraced the change, some because they were developing a genuine sense of unity and purpose, others simply because it was such a relief from the torment of the first weeks. One army trainee put it this way:

> The first four weeks, they work your ass off, they abuse you, they run you from 4:30 in the morning until ten at night. You are so tired, you're so afraid you are going to get abused, that you'll do anything. Then they start to lay off. They'll joke with you, they'll talk to you when you're having smoke breaks, and they tell you, "Now if you work hard there will be less smoke on everybody." And they encourage you to put smoke on the guy who is lagging behind in your unit. The thing is, "We are going to have the best platoon so we won't have to do as much work." Everybody falls in because they are so willing to get out from under this shit that they have been catching. By the end of training they're all gung-ho.[43]

Some men really enjoyed the second half of basic training. For marine veteran Gene Holiday, the first weeks of basic were deeply traumatic. He felt scared and worthless. A few weeks later, however, his attitude completely changed: "After rifle range I just ate it up. I was having a hell of a lot of fun. I saw such improvement. When they weren't picking on you all the time and you got over that initial fear, it was nice seeing the improvement. Man, you're marching *nice*, you're looking *good*, you're working as a *team*, you really feel that unity, that camaraderie."[44]

As recruits began to feel more confident and less abused, they began to internalize the attitudes of the drill sergeants. Just as rifle training gave recruits an outlet for the intense anxiety and rage that came to a boil in the initial weeks, drill instructors also increasingly aimed their recruits' hostility at external enemies. The most obvious current enemy, of course, was the Viet Cong. Many DIs, however, also directed hostility at a variety of civilian targets. Recruits learned in their first minutes of basic training that civilians were scum and that to become soldiers they would have to eradicate their identities as civilians. As training proceeded, many began to share their instructors' hostility toward civilians. Drill instructors especially denounced "hippies," "draft-dodgers," and "demonstrators." These figures were portrayed as pampered cowards who were simply trying to escape the danger and difficulty of military service. On the other hand, such people were not to be taken lightly. They were "traitors" who posed a threat to the nation and the soldiers themselves. Recruits were encouraged to believe that all protesters supported the Viet Cong and that the antiwar movement cheered when American troops got wiped out in Vietnam. Sometimes DIs embellished the civilian threat by introducing the specter of the hometown "Jody." A legendary figure in military culture, Jody is a civilian who steals girlfriends and wives while soldiers are away fighting wars. Promoting animosity toward draft evaders and Jodies (sometimes presented as the same figure) was a backhanded way to build support for the war in Vietnam. Somehow fighting in Vietnam would be a way to get back at those who had managed to escape the draft, those who had not shared the abuse of basic training, those who could sit home and criticize the war (and steal girlfriends).[45]

Being trained to suspect civilians has an even darker side in the context of the Vietnam War. The official American mission was to save South Vietnamese civilians from Viet Cong insurgents. However, most civilians either supported the Viet Cong, were themselves part of a local Viet Cong self-defense cadre, or were reluctant to act in opposition to the Viet Cong. How could civilians be saved when so many sided with the enemy? While this dilemma posed a fundamental contradiction to American policy, military training ignored it altogether. Trainees were often told that all Vietnamese were potential enemies, but they received no special training designed to reduce civilian casualties. Of course, given the American military effort to destroy the Viet Cong in heavily populated areas, perhaps no form of training could have done much to protect civilian lives. Yet, if anything, the training received promoted hostility toward noncombatants.

The foreign enemy was variously called Viet Cong,* VC, Victor Char-

---

*"Viet Cong" means "Vietnamese communists." The term was invented by the United States Information Service. It refers to the revolutionaries of *South* Vietnam and was intended to brand all of them communists. The "Viet Cong" called themselves the People's Liberation Armed Forces (PLAF) and called their political leadership the National Liberation Front (NLF). While the leadership of both groups was dominated by communists, the rank and file included many noncommunist members. Also, many Americans mistakenly used the term *Viet Cong* to refer to *all* anti-American forces, whether members of the North Vietnamese Army or South Vietnamese guerrillas. The North Vietnamese Army was referred to by the American command as the NVA. They called themselves the People's Army of Vietnam (PAVN). Sheehan, *Bright Shining Lie*, p. 189.

lie, Charlie, Mr. Charles, Charlie Cong, the Cong, Communists, commies, dinks, slopes, zipperheads, zips, and gooks. The variety of names was telling. After all, the point was not to know the enemy but simply to despise him. At Fort Polk, Louisiana, one of the major training posts for Vietnam-bound infantrymen, billboards were put up around the camp to bolster morale. One billboard featured a painting of an American soldier using the butt of his rifle to knock down a man holding a rifle and wearing black "pajamas" (military slang for the traditional peasant garb that was worn by civilians and Viet Cong alike). Written under the picture in bold letters were the words BONG THE CONG. Another sign showed a man wearing black pajamas and a bamboo hat crouching down in a rice paddy. He is holding a large knife across his chest. This knife provides sufficient evidence that the man is a guerrilla, for above his head is printed, THE ENEMY, and below the picture, VIET CONG. At Fort Dix, one of the signs said, VIET CONG—BREAKFAST OF CHAMPIONS.[46]

Beyond these portrayals of the enemy, trainees learned little more about the Vietnamese revolutionaries and why they were fighting so hard against American forces. As one veteran recalls, "The only thing they told us about the Viet Cong was they were gooks. They were to be killed. Nobody sits around and gives you their historical and cultural background. They're the enemy. Kill, kill, kill. That's what we got in practice. Kill, kill, kill."[47]

RESPONSES BY CLASS

No single factor of a recruit's personality or family background provides a certain measure of how he would respond to military training, but class differences do indicate some rough commonalities of attitude. Middle-class trainees tended to feel socially isolated among the working-class majority. For some this was perceived as a great opportunity: "I loved that part of it. It was great to make friends with people who grew up with such different experiences and outlooks. I probably learned more about life, and about myself, from John [the son of a Pittsburgh steelworker] than I ever learned in college."[48]

Other men, however, felt alienated and lost:

For a long time, I was lost in the shuffle. It was a shock. I never really got my bearings.

The people in the Army were not intellectuals. Most of them were from working class backgrounds. A lot of them were Southerners. It was my first contact with blacks and they tended to stick together. . . . Blue-collar kids and city kids adjusted very quickly to the Army. Most of the middle-class kids like me didn't fit into what was going on. We hadn't had to do much on our own before. We grew up in a secure environment where a lot of things were taken for granted.[49]

For this man, boot camp brought a keen feeling of lost privilege. He was also convinced that working-class kids adjusted much more easily to military life. Some middle-class men were scornful of the other trainees, thinking them mindless robots. Tim O'Brien expresses this view in his account of basic training at Fort Lewis, Washington.

The people were boors, a whole horde of boors—trainees and drill sergeants and officers, no difference in kind. In that jungle of robots there could be no hope of finding friendship; no one could understand the brutality of the place. . . . Laughing and talking of hometowns and drag races and twin-cammed engines—all this was for the others. I did not like them. . . . For the other trainees, it came too easy. They did more than adjust well; they thrived on basic training, thinking they were becoming men, joking at the bullyism, getting the drill sergeants to joke along with them. I held my own, not a whisper more. I hated my fellows. . . . I hated the trainees even more than the captors. I learned to march, but I learned alone. . . . I was superior. I made no apologies for believing it.

For O'Brien, the goal of basic training was to preserve himself from brutality and boorishness. He hoped to save some "remnants of conscience and consciousness," some individuality and privacy. But it was not simply the military as an institution that posed a threat to his sense of himself. Indeed, he reserved the greater share of disdain for his fellow trainees who, he believed, could not understand the brutality of the place.[50]

Peter Tauber was not so scathing about the other men in his unit. Like O'Brien, however, he wanted to withhold as much of himself as possible from the military, to do the minimum required and no more, aiming (as O'Brien put it) at a "tranquil mediocrity." Nevertheless, Tauber could not remain entirely distant from the challenges of military training. He began to compare his presence in boot camp to a life lived in material and social hardship. He wondered about his ability to survive without middle-class advantages. He asked himself, "Could I cut it in the world if I hadn't been born lucky? Could I pioneer, or could I even face a Harlem winter's morning? I may never know, so here is where I test myself."

So Tauber, despite his disdain for the military and his convictions against the war, worked hard to get himself in shape and to master the skills introduced during basic training. Though he poked fun at the mindless propaganda and found countless ways to avoid the most onerous aspects of basic training, he needed to prove to himself that he could do whatever the army required. "It is fine to be a sloppy soldier," Tauber writes, "but another thing not to be *able* to be good when you want to." He discovered, however, that this was a spurious distinction. He could not have it both ways; he could not remain unaffected by the military and still seek to fulfill its requirements. By testing himself on the army's terms, Tauber found himself changing. He noticed, for example, that he joined the others in ridiculing the few men who did not keep pace with army drills.[51]

Accounts like these suggest that we approach with some skepticism the claim that working-class men adjusted or acquiesced to basic training more readily than did wealthier trainees. There is certainly little evidence to suggest that middle-class trainees were more likely to fail or resist the basic training regimen, and oral histories suggest that almost everyone found the first weeks of training extremely stressful, bewildering, and dislocating. In fact, the recruits who had the most profound trouble adjusting to basic training were neither middle class nor from stable, working-class families. Rather, from the poorest segment of trainees came the largest portion of military misfits, men who deserted, attempted suicide, were sent to special processing or motivation platoons, or were in some other way unable or unwilling to conform to military standards. These men were commonly high school dropouts from poverty-stricken and broken families. Describing this group, Peter Barnes writes, "In civilian life, most of them have been losers many times over. In the military, this pattern is repeated." According to Baskir and Strauss, the prototypical army deserter of the Vietnam era "came from a low-income family, often with only one parent in the home. He had an IQ of 90, and dropped out of high school in the tenth grade."[52]

Although there is no clear indication of which social class tended to adjust most easily to basic training, it is probably true that working-class men were more likely to be enthusiastic about military life and more likely to find it a rewarding challenge that offered a genuine feeling of individual accomplishment and collective camaraderie. Mark Sampson, for example, found basic training gave him a fresh chance to succeed in an arena that struck him as more meaningful and egalitarian than school had ever been. He had found high school boring and worthless—"a big joke." In the middle of his senior year he was expelled for hitting one of his teachers. His mother, a factory worker, sent him to live with relatives in another town to finish high school (his father died when Mark was three). In the new high school the yearbook editors of 1966 put these words below Mark's photograph: "Comes new to us this year. Doesn't say much. Makes you wonder what he's thinking. Unexcited."

After high school Mark enlisted. "In basic [training] everybody blended in. No one gave a shit what you did before. No one cared what grades you made in high school or if you were a star athlete or if you belonged to the glee club. It was a whole new set of standards and it seemed like the drill instructors didn't play favorites as much as teachers do."[53]

For Mark, graduation from Marine Corps basic training was far more meaningful and moving than his high school graduation. During the ceremony tears filled his eyes. Afterward his drill instructor praised him, called him a marine, and offered him a shot of whiskey. Many shared his sense of pride and achievement—men like Richard Deegan who had worried growing up that he would "never amount to anything," or Gene Holiday, whose high school guidance counselor told him he was not "college material." On graduation they stood in full dress uniform, listened to military bands, and heard speeches celebrating their progress and the important contribution they would make to their nation's security. For many, it was the first time in their lives they had received public acknowledgment and praise.

For most trainees, whatever their background, the first weeks of boot camp were a rude shock. Practically everyone would lie in their bunks at night asking themselves over and over, "What the hell am I doing here?" or "What have I gotten myself into?" Still, it is among working-class recruits that one tends to hear the most upbeat accounts of basic training. For example, Todd Dasher, a working-class volunteer from Long Island, went to army basic training at Fort Jackson, South Carolina. "I graduated really high in my [basic training] class. Basic training was pretty easy I thought. I had a good time. It was the first time I'd ever been away from home, really. I was meeting all kinds of cross-matches of people—Spanish, black, white, American Indian. I thought it was just great."[54]

Few accounts of basic training are as enthusiastic as Todd's, but it is not unusual, especially among working-class men, to hear a similar discounting of the difficulty or brutality of boot camp. For men who grew up in hard-pressed or dangerous circumstances—be it a tough family life, economic hardship, or survival on city streets—boot camp might not seem such a radical break from civilian life. Frank Mathews, the marine volunteer from Holt, Alabama, described boot camp as "just normal." "I had heard how bad [the marines] mistreated their troops and I was prepared for the worst. But hell, my Daddy had treated me worse than some of those drill sergeants. Boot camp was just normal. The sergeants were rough. I saw a lot of beatings and I took a few. But I got to where I could give out as much as I took and I felt like I toughened up into the Marine Corps attitude."[55]

VIETNAM: THE ORDERS COME DOWN

At the end of basic training, recruits were assigned Military Occupational Specialties (MOS). A man's MOS determined what sort of Advanced Individual Training (AIT) he would undergo for the two months following basic training. There were dozens of military specialties: transportation, mechanics, clerical work, administration, cooking, communications, artillery, infantry, and so on. It was not until the final weeks of AIT that men learned where they would be sent for their tour of duty. In fact, most of the men who were sent to Vietnam in 1965—the first year of the major buildup of American ground forces—did not receive word of their orders until just before leaving the United States or their overseas bases. With the rapid escalation of 1965–67, however, when American forces rose from 20,000 to over 500,000, recruits entered basic training well aware that the prospect of service in Vietnam loomed as a distinct possibility. In some units DIs invoked the war as a warning or threat, as if they had personal control over exactly who would go to Vietnam. The DIs would tell disobedient recruits that if they did not shape up, they would certainly be among those sent to Vietnam. (Beginning in 1965 most tour of duty assignments were made by computer, and the DI's power to affect such orders was probably quite limited.) Yet, there were still plenty of soldiers sent to Germany, Korea, and elsewhere around the world, assignments many recruits longed for as a last chance to avoid Vietnam.[56]

Those entering AIT in combat specialties were often warned from the beginning that the chances for a non-Vietnam assignment were slim. As one AIT drill sergeant said in 1968, "'I don't want you to mope around thinking about Germany or London. . . . Don't even think about it, 'cause there ain't no way. You're leg men now, and we don't need no infantry in Piccadilly or Southampton. . . . Every swingin' dick is going to Nam, every big fat swingin' dick.'"[57]

As the war continued, however, the military began to downplay the likelihood of service in Vietnam. By 1969 and 1970 it was not unusual for trainees to be told there was only a remote chance of being sent to Vietnam. As troop levels were gradually reduced beginning in 1969, the chances of fighting in Vietnam were somewhat lessened. But false assurances also reflected a desire to placate reluctant and increasingly antiwar trainees and to stem the ever growing tide of desertions. As one veteran recalls: "To discourage us from going AWOL and deserting, all the new draftees were told that only 17 percent of us were going to Vietnam. And of that small percentage, only 11 percent would actually be combat troops. That eased my mind a great deal. Hey, there's still a chance that I won't have to go and get my guts blown out. Terrific.

"At the end of our training, with only three exceptions . . . every single one of us went to Vietnam—200 guys."[58]

In 1965, the desertion rate was only 15 men per thousand (a lower rate than Korea or World War II). By 1969, the rate had climbed to 50 per thousand, and by 1972 it was up to 70—the highest rate of desertion in modern American military history. By the end of the war, more than 500,000 men had deserted.[59]

The military has always been concerned about desertion, but in the late 1960s and early 1970s it had become a major preoccupation. The effort to reduce desertions was no doubt a factor in the moderation of army training suggested in some accounts from the latter years of the war. Peter Tauber argues this point in his description of basic training at Fort Bliss in 1969. Tauber's company was given the option of skipping the final three weeks of physical training, and even after sixty-eight men failed at least one of the two final proficiency tests, no one was required to repeat basic training. As Tauber reports: "The word has been sent down from Colonel Treandley's office that no one from our battalion was to be recycled.

"The secret is out: the Army doesn't care. No matter what you do, it'll pass you—lie, prostitute itself, betray itself—if you promise not to go AWOL. That's all." On graduation day, Tauber's company was given a special award for having the fewest AWOLs.[60]

When soldiers did receive orders for Vietnam, many were struck with the realization that, for all their military training, they knew practically nothing about Vietnam. That nation's history, geography, culture, politics—such topics were covered, at best, with a few lectures and a film at the end of AIT. According to John Sack, a journalist who followed "M" Company through its AIT training cycle in 1966, the two Vietnam orientations received by "M" Company (an infantry unit) were primarily devoted to presentations on "environmental dangers" such as venereal disease, malaria, dysentery, punji pits, and poisonous snakes.[61]

Perhaps it is not surprising that American soldiers were taught nothing, for example, about the Vietnamese overthrow of French colonialism. What is astonishing, however, is how little preparation most soldiers had for the actual conditions they would experience in Vietnam, both in combat and in rear areas. Even veterans who believe they were well trained tend to confine their praise to such things as the physical endurance and toughness they developed in training, the confidence and pride they gained, or the general military skills they learned (firing weapons, reading maps, throwing grenades, etc.). It is rare, however, to find veterans who believe they were prepared for the specific challenges they would face in Vietnam: the hostility of many Vietnamese civilians; the dangers, anxieties, and moral pressure of conducting a counterrevolutionary war amidst a civilian population largely supportive of the Viet Cong; the uncertainties of service in rear areas; and the nature of battle once the enemy was engaged.

Probably the one aspect of training best designed to introduce American soldiers to the particular conditions of warfare in Vietnam, and the one most widely received (at least by combat soldiers), was the training conducted in mock Vietnamese villages. However, only men trained for combat were likely to participate in these exercises, and few men found the experience memorable or significant enough to describe in oral histories or literary accounts.

Though little has been written about this form of training, one fascinating document indicates that the efforts of the American military to replicate the conditions of warfare in the heavily populated regions of Vietnam were, even after years of U.S. intervention, a ludicrous failure. The document is a memo sent from Marine Col. Edwin H. Simmons to the chief of staff in August 1966. Simmons had served a full tour in Vietnam and wrote the memo to offer his recommendations after witnessing a demonstration of a helicopter assault on a mock Vietnamese village at Officer

Basic School. The demonstration was intended to showcase one of the military's most sophisticated new training devices. Simmons began his memo by offering a summary of the exercise.

The demonstration follows a simple and predictable scenario: the village of XA Viet THANG ("Village of Vietnamese Victory") is under oppressive VC domination. As the day begins, a Marine force encircles the village, forming the cordon for the cordon and search operation to come. A helicopter flies overhead, making a loudspeaker broadcast and dropping leaflets, informing the populace of the impending arrival of the Americans and their intentions. The Viet Cong in the village, uniformed soldiers from North Vietnam, meanwhile take cover in the hamlet. An "assault" element, consisting of a Marine platoon accompanied by the GVN [government of South Vietnam] district chief, then enters the village. As the search begins, the platoon commander and district chief confer with the village chief. Then follows a series of incidents as the "assault" force uncovers the hidden VC and their arms caches. Several booby traps are encountered. There are two Marine casualties. One by one the VC are eliminated. The remnant attempts to break out of the cordon and is destroyed by a combination of ground fire and armed helicopter action.[62]

Even this brief description of the mock battle reveals fundamental misrepresentations of the reality encountered by American soldiers in Vietnam. The most obvious falsehood is the assumption that the VC are uniformed soldiers of North Vietnam. In fact, the Viet Cong rarely wore uniforms. They tended, instead, to wear traditional peasant garb. Moreover, the Viet Cong were not North Vietnamese soldiers but *South* Vietnamese guerrillas, and the uniformed soldiers of the NVA were rarely encountered by American troops in Vietnamese villages. Such engagements tended to occur in sparsely populated areas.

The misrepresentation of the Vietnamese opposition is far from merely semantic. It utterly obfuscates one of the most crucial aspects of the war: the Viet Cong were often indistinguishable from noncombatant civilians. By filling the mock village with clearly identifiable enemies, the marines were given an advantage they simply did not have in Vietnam. In recommendation "d," Colonel Simmons offered an understated critique: "It is somewhat unrealistic, or at least unusual, to encounter uniformed North Vietnamese in a hamlet. The more usual enemy would be the local guerrilla [the real Viet Cong]. . . . More emphasis should be given to the purpose of the cordon and search operation as being to eradicate the VC infrastructure rather than the driving out Main Force elements."

The latter part of this recommendation obliquely suggests another major flaw in the exercise. In the real warfare of Vietnam, no anti-American force (whether Viet Cong or NVA) was likely to wait around in a village while American helicopters announced the arrival of marines, while the various dignitaries conferred, and while a military cordon was established. Ordinarily they would be long gone by the time the American troops started searching the village. That fact probably explains why Simmons recommended that such exercises focus on an effort to "eradicate the VC infrastructure." By "infrastructure" he means the local villagers who supported the Viet Cong with food, shelter, and information and by helping manufacture and set out booby traps and mines. Identifying this infrastructure, much less eradicating it, often proved impossible in Vietnam.

Simmons's other recommendations provide additional hints of a reality far more complex and disturbing than any envisioned or reproduced in American training camps. For example, Simmons found the American marines who participated in the demonstration "much too starched and well-shined to be very convincing." As for the mock village (more properly, as Simmons points out, called a hamlet because of its small size), it was too "antiseptic" to be realistic.

Within limits of necessary sanitation, more mud, more odors, and more livestock would add to the realism of the setting. While a water buffalo might be difficult to arrange, it should be possible to add some pigs and chickens, and perhaps a goat or two. . . . The interiors of the buildings should be well-blackened with the smoke of wood and charcoal cooking fires. Some dried fish should be hung from the rafters along with some dried tobacco leaf. There should be numerous blackened cooking pots giving off the characteristic smell of boiled rice.

Simmons also recommended the addition of the thorny hedgerows that subdivided hamlets in Vietnam and created "such a problem" by restricting the mobility and visibility of American soldiers.

As we shall see, no military training program, however "realistic," could have successfully prepared American soldiers for the war they were to fight. The fundamental obstacles to fighting a counterrevolutionary war among a people so largely supportive of the anti-American cause would have remained no matter how many more soldiers learned the Vietnamese language or confronted, from the outset of training, the difficulties of determining the political affiliations of the Vietnamese people. Indeed, had they confronted such complexities early on, their anxiety might have been even higher. As it was, when American troops landed in Vietnam, they stepped into a reality unlike anything they had ever imagined.

Ominous Beginnings

SURREAL ARRIVALS

It didn't take long to see that something was seriously wrong. There we were, flying into Nam on a fancy commercial jet, sipping drinks like a bunch of goddamn businessmen, and as far as we knew the VC were going to start shooting us up as soon as we touched down! And we didn't even have our weapons yet! I don't think there was a single rifle on the whole damn plane. It was crazy.

– Luke Jensen

No one knew what to expect, but what they found was more bizarre and unnerving than anything they had ever imagined. From their first moments in-country, American soldiers were confronted with the war's most troubling questions: Where are we? What are we doing here? Where is the enemy? Whom can we trust? Where is it safe? What is our mission? The answers received provided little comfort or clarity. Instead, the green troops faced a series of confusing and incongruous experiences— ominous portents of a yearlong tour of duty against enemies they could not identify, among allies who did not welcome their presence, and on behalf of a policy that was neither meaningful nor realizable.

In the beginning they arrived by ship. The First and Third Marine divisions, the 173d Airborne Brigade, the First Cavalry Division, the First Infantry Division, the 101st Airborne Division, the Twenty-fifth, Fourth, and Ninth Infantry divisions: most of the major American combat units made their initial arrival in Vietnam by sea, thousands of men carried on large troop transports. In August 1965, for example, 13,500 men of the First Cavalry Division left on seventeen ships from Charleston, Savannah,

Jacksonville, and Mobile.[1] These ocean crossings had a familiar look, like something out of World War II newsreels. It was a very black-and-white image—creaky old ships packed to the gills with smelly soldiers suffering from seasickness, frayed nerves, bad food, and petty shipboard duties. The crossing took several weeks and produced nothing more exciting than endless card games.

Though some ships pulled up at dockside in Danang or Cam Ranh Bay and unloaded like ordinary passenger ships, many men (especially those in infantry units) were transferred to landing craft to be unloaded on beaches. This, too, evoked images from World War II—American marines and soldiers, in full combat gear, charging into the surf from their open-mouthed landing craft. They stormed the beaches, expecting the worst. As it turned out, however, the similarity to World War II newsreels soon evaporated. The beaches were almost always quiet. There was no enemy fire, and the enemy himself was nowhere to be seen. Most Americans were undoubtedly relieved. However, for those whose heads were full of romantic visions of the D-day landing at Normandy, the absence of resistance was a bit disappointing. After all, the combat units that made the beach landings in 1965 and 1966 contained the largest portion of enthusiastic volunteers of any time in the war. Eager for battle or not, most found it a strangely surreal beginning, like falling asleep during an old war movie, only to wake up and find oneself flailing in the sand of a tropical beach resort.

The sense of incongruity was perhaps most acute in the arrival of the first major American combat unit on 8 March 1965. The marines waded ashore on Red Beach, ready for bloody combat, and found, instead, a well-orchestrated welcoming committee set up by American and Vietnamese officials. As Philip Caputo describes the moment in *A Rumor of War*, the marines "charged up the beach and were met, not by machine guns and shells, but by the mayor of Danang and a crowd of schoolgirls. The mayor made a brief welcoming speech and the girls placed flowered wreaths around the marines' necks."[2] One month later, the Second Battalion, Third Marines, made a similar landing. In his memoir *Green Knight, Red Mourning*, Richard Ogden recalled that his unit had been told to expect a "hot beach." When no one fired on them, he felt like "the victim of an unfunny hoax." But suddenly a platoon-size group appeared on the horizon. "It must be a Bonsai attack!" Though the American troops were shaking with tension, they were ordered to hold fire. A few seconds later someone yelled, "It's the press corps!" A reporter and cameraman walked right up to Ogden and put a microphone to his mouth: "How do you like the Vietnam war so far, son?"[3]

During the early stages of the big American buildup of 1965 few of the arriving soldiers anticipated that the war would drag on for years. In fact, the most eager men worried that they might get to Vietnam too late and that the war would be over before they had a chance to fight. Matthew Brennan went to Vietnam in December 1965, among a gung-ho group of paratroopers, to join the First Cavalry Division. "Most of us didn't understand what was really happening in Vietnam. We believed that the war had reached its final stages and that we might arrive after the last big battles were won. . . . We were too naive to be afraid."[4]

Robert Flaherty landed in Vietnam with the Third Battalion, Ninth Marines, in the summer of 1965. After boot camp in the fall of 1964 he was scheduled to receive advanced training as a helicopter mechanic. In early 1965, however, "they started changing a lot of people's orders. All of a sudden they made me a machine gunner. We knew something was wrong when they started changing the MOS's."[5]

When Flaherty boarded a ship for Vietnam, he found the mood a peculiar mixture of intense anxiety and lighthearted bravado. "We were afraid and we weren't afraid. It was bullshit and it wasn't. We didn't know what to expect." One inclination was to dismiss the danger awaiting them in Vietnam. "We had heard about Vietnam in boot camp, but we thought it was just some little rinky-dink thing—a skirmish." Aboard ship, however, stories and rumors began to circulate. There was talk of massive enemy wave attacks, invisible booby traps, and Viet Cong sneaking up in the middle of the night and slitting throats. "By the time these stories got around it was Tarawa all over again." (In World War II more than 1,000 U.S. Marines were killed during the three days it took to defeat the Japanese who occupied Tarawa, a tiny but heavily fortified Pacific island.)[6] "Everybody was getting really jittery, but part of the time we thought the stories were exaggerated, that it couldn't be that bad. We wanted to make-believe that this war was just going to be some month-long gig, some two-month thing that was going to be like Santo Domingo—a few shots fired and everybody goes home."

Flaherty's landing was uncontested. Yet the anxiety and uncertainty of the landing held an important clue about the war: "You never knew when they were going to hit. We'd be expecting a huge firefight and end up picking our nose. And then one day we'd be walking along day-dreaming and—BOOM—they'd spring an ambush. We almost never caught *them* by surprise." It only took a few weeks for Flaherty's unit to realize that Vietnam would hardly be a one-month gig.

Raymond Wilson joined the air force in 1963. He had no idea he would end up in Vietnam. By 1965 the war was daily news, but Wilson still thought the odds of going were slight. He was stationed in Florida, working as a mechanic on air force jets, and generally enjoying himself.

It's November, 1965. Everything is cool. It's a Sunday and I'm laying out in the sun, having a great time. But that day they put up notes in all the barracks: "Be at Hanger 5 tomorrow morning at 7:00 o'clock." I just figured it was some big United Appeal bullshit. But when we show up everybody notices that the pilots are there too. So we say, "Shit, something's fixing to happen." And then this commander walks out: "I got a telegram from the Pentagon." Nobody said a word, boy, you talk quiet—it was like a damn funeral home. Cause you knew what was coming next. And this big macho idiot gets up there and starts this shit about how he's been to war before and he's going again, and how he's gonna take all of us with him.

Then he says, "You won't go home, you won't tell anybody, you won't even tell your wife where you're going, if you're married." But the news hit the Tampa paper two days later. The air force denied it: "Nobody's going anywhere. Nobody's leaving this base." But they ain't fooling nobody. Officers are selling their houses, wives are moving back with their folks. You didn't have to be Einstein to figure some shit's happening.[7]

Wilson's unit was flown to Cam Ranh Bay, Vietnam, in January 1966 aboard a C-130, an enormous military cargo plane.

The closer we got the more serious it became. There was no more laughing and carrying on. We're about two hours out and this loadmaster starts handing out rifles and ammo and you start getting this feeling: "Hey what the hell's going on here? I didn't sign up for this shit. Are we gonna have to fight our way in here?"

They made a pass and then took back off over the ocean. "Why don't we just go in? What's this fooling around jive? We never played this game before." And this guy comes back and says, "Look, there's a little action, so we're going to have to wait a while."

So finally we come in, and they bring that sucker in at about a 90 degree angle, nose straight down. We get down there and they drop the door down and all we see is sand and concertina wire. I'm thinking: "This ain't good. They're gonna kill us as soon as we step off the airplane. They're just gonna be standing there and they're gonna blow our ass away." Now we'd seen TV, we'd seen this damn war going on, we'd seen them stacking bodies up, we'd seen them shooting rockets and mortars into bases, and all of a sudden you're right in the middle of this shit. "Hey this is not right." *But you don't say it.* You don't cry and you don't moan and whatever you do you don't say "Hey, there's something wrong with this war." It just isn't done at this point in time.

They knew they were going to a war zone war—they had seen it on TV—but they had no idea what was expected of them. They were not marine infantrymen, only a bunch of jet mechanics, and here they were with rifles and ammunition thinking they were about to fly into the middle of an ambush. Meanwhile, the authorities—the president and the air force commanders—were doing their best to disguise the escalation, acting as if there really was not an enormous movement of American troops into Vietnam. At precisely the time Wilson's unit arrived in Vietnam (January 1966), President Johnson approved Gen. William Westmoreland's request for an increase in the number of U.S. troops from 235,000 to 459,000. Yet, a month later at a press conference (26 February 1966), Johnson failed to mention either Westmoreland's request or his own approval of the escalation. Rather, he withheld the truth by saying, "We do not have on my desk any unfilled requests from General Westmoreland," thereby leaving the American public to believe that the number of U.S. troops in Vietnam was holding steady at 235,000.[8]

By the end of 1966 most of the major American units had arrived in Vietnam. Once established in-country, brigades and divisions typically brought in additional troops and replacements not by ship or military cargo planes but by commercial jetliner. In 1966, arrival by commercial jet was commonplace. By 1967 it was routine. Throughout the war, most men returned from their tours on commercial planes. The military command called for these "government contract" flights as the only way of handling the rapid movement of troops to and from the war; at the peak of the U.S. ground war, about 1 million Americans were either entering or leaving Vietnam each year. Indeed, in the late 1960s, Tan Son Nhut was the second-busiest airport in the world (after Chicago's O'Hare). The military had neither the ships nor the planes to accommodate such a large and rapid transportation of men while still maintaining their other global movements. The use of commercial flights may have helped to disguise the scale of the U.S. buildup by dispersing and sanitizing it. An enormous fleet of troop-carrying transports continually crossing the Pacific would surely have given a more striking visual representation of the size of American involvement. Chartering commercial jets may not have been calculated by policymakers to conceal the escalation, but it was certainly consistent with Johnson's other efforts to soften the domestic impact of the war.[9]

Soldiers flying to Vietnam on civilian jets had to keep looking at their uniforms to remind themselves they were on their way to a war. Braniff Airlines ran a line from Okinawa to Vietnam for the marines. The planes were "all painted in their designer colors, puce and canary yellow," one veteran recalled. "You would think we were going to Phoenix or something." In his novel *Free Fire Zone*, Rob Riggan writes: "We might have been over Gary, Indiana. . . . Stewardesses with polished legs and miniskirts took our pillows away from us. As we trooped out the door [they] said 'Good luck! See you in 365 days.'"[10]

Charles Anderson went to Vietnam in 1969 aboard a World Airways jet. In his valuable memoir, *The Grunts*, Anderson evokes the initial greeting received by a group of war-bound marines from the head flight attendant:

> Hi, fellas, where you going?
>
> Boo . . . Hiss . . . Oh, wow! Look at the set on her . . . Jesus Christ, lady . . .
>
> Please keep your seats as I introduce the girls. . . . Way in . . . the back is Carol, from Detroit. A little farther up is Dianne, from New Orleans. Behind me here is Suzie. She used to work at the Playboy Club in San Francisco—how about that one, men! In the galley is Janie, from Kansas City; and I'm Shirley from beautiful downtown Burbank. . . . If there is anything at all we can do for you, just let us know. Well, almost anything! Come on now, be nice. Oh, you're all so sweet, you sure don't look like killers! Now, Dianne and I will demonstrate the life jacket.

After stops in Atsugi, Japan, and in Okinawa, the plane approached Vietnam. The captain offered this farewell message: "Gentlemen, we'll be touching down in Da Nang, Vietnam in about ten minutes. The local time is now two in the afternoon on the twelfth, and the ground temperature is ninety-six degrees with a clear sky. Please extinguish all cigarettes and fasten your seat belts, please. On behalf of the entire crew and staff, I'd

like to say we've enjoyed having you with us on World Airways government contract flight Hotel Twenty-Nine, and we hope to see all of you
again next year on your way home. Good-bye and good luck."[11]

Imagine flying to war on an air-conditioned jet, listening to the casual
banter of the airline crew, and being reminded to buckle your seat belt. If
some men were able to pretend they were aboard an ordinary civilian
flight, the fantasy quickly ended upon approach to Vietnam. No planeload
of new soldiers was ever shot down, but they sometimes received ground
fire. To reduce this risk, pilots made fast, steep, stomach-churning de-
scents.[12] The surreal juxtaposition of the jet's commercial comfort alongside the real and imagined dangers of the landing brought anxiety to a
peak. The soldiers were flooded with troubling questions: If we are landing in a dangerous place, why haven't they issued weapons? Will we have
to fight our way off? Who's in charge—the civilian jet captain?

Jim Barrett arrived at Cam Ranh Bay in May 1967, after his plane was
diverted from Bien Hoa: "We were supposed to land at Bien Hoa, a big
military base just north of Saigon about thirty miles. But the pilot came on
and told us we couldn't land there. Bien Hoa base was being shelled. You
could cut the fear on that plane with a knife. You could smell it. The guy
sitting next to me was married. I'm sure he was worried sick about his
family back home. The stewardess came by and gave us sandwiches after
they made this big announcement, and he started crying. He couldn't eat
his sandwich. He just sat there and cried."[13]

Debarking from their planes, new troops often crossed paths with other
American soldiers, men who were going in the opposite direction: home to
the United States. The same planes that brought new troops to the war
served as "Freedom Birds" for the departing soldiers. Crossing paths was
a significant and upsetting moment for both groups. It gave the new men a
vision of what they might become; to the veterans it presented a vision of
what they had been. The contrast was startling. To the new men, the
returning veterans looked old, dirty, dull-eyed, jaded, cynical, and smug.
To the seasoned veterans, new men seemed ridiculously clean, innocent,
awkward, and doomed. There was a strong measure of envy-fed resentment between the two groups. Many new men wished it was their turn to
go home on the Freedom Bird. Others envied the veterans' war-tested
looks, the disdainful air which seemed to say, "I've seen more shit than
you can even imagine." For their part, the veterans envied what they
perceived as the newcomers' fresh, open naivete and their youthful,
bright eyes. The new men were too scared and nervous to approach the

nasty-looking veterans, and the latter were too preoccupied with getting out of Vietnam to waste time with the newcomers. According to the many accounts of these path crossings in the Vietnam literature, however, there was a deeper significance to these moments, and a deeper tension. Archetypal reports have homebound men shouting insults and derogatory warnings at the new soldiers. Richard Deegan landed in Danang in 1966:

> We were walking by and this crowd of marines waiting to get on the plane to go back to "The World" [the United States], started telling us all this shit: "You guys ain't gonna make it home"; "They'll kill every fucking one of you"; "The gooks are better than you guys." Yeah! They were really fucking with your mind. They even said, "Hope you die, you bastards!" We didn't pay no attention. We knew they were just fucking with us. And what are you gonna do, start a fight with these guys? We were scared out of our wits. The biggest, bad-ass guy that we had with us was shaking in his socks.[14]

These insults and warnings are among the most extreme reported, but the general form of Deegan's arrival story is commonplace. In *The Killing Zone*, Frederick Downs describes his 1967 arrival in Vietnam:

> We exited the aircraft in a long khaki line to stand apprehensively under a series of large open-sided tents. . . . The oppressive heat and humidity was filled with the smells of dust, machinery, and rotting vegetation. . . .
>
> The plane was being refueled for takeoff. Opposite our naive line stood another line of soldiers, waiting to go home. The soldiers hooted disparagingly at us.
>
> "It's a lick, motherfucker!"
>
> "You'll be sorrrryyy!"
>
> "New cannon fodder!"
>
> "You guys short yet? Only 365 days to go? Shiiiit!"
>
> We had no comeback to those veterans. . . . We suffered our ignominy in silence.[15]

Jim Barrett recalls his departure from Vietnam, waiting for the new soldiers to debark the plane that would take him home. From the group of returning soldiers a single voice cried out: "FRESH BLOOD!" Jim added, "I didn't say anything but I agreed—that's just what they looked like."[16]

Popular Hollywood movies about World War II were crucial in shaping the images of war held by many young men prior to military service. Soldiers in Vietnam found from the outset a reality radically different from that portrayed on the screen. World War II movies ordinarily depicted whole units of fresh troops moving into war together, sometimes trained and led by battle-tested veterans (like Sergeant Stryker—John Wayne— in *The Sands of Iwo Jima*). As the unit entered combat, men from the rear might be brought in to replace the dead and wounded, and battle-weary units were sometimes relieved. But the movies underscored the fact that American forces were committed "for the duration."

In Vietnam, however, individual tours lasted for one year. Some of the first ship-transported units had trained together and would fight together in Vietnam. Most men arrived in Vietnam as individual replacements, however, and often the other men on the plane were complete strangers. Even when coherent training units flew over together, they were typically divided up and sent as individuals to separate units throughout Vietnam.

In World War II movies, experienced soldiers greeted replacements with attitudes ranging from comradely gratefulness to sardonic bemusement, but they were rarely hostile or insulting to the new men; there was nothing like the hazing reported by Vietnam veterans in which the departing soldiers stood at the gates of war like birds of ill omen. At the end of *Darby's Rangers* (1958), for example, Darby (James Garner) returns to a beachhead after heavy fighting inland. New troops are wading ashore from landing craft. A few of them point to the Ranger insignia on Darby's uniform and stare at him in awe. He snaps them a jaunty salute and strides off into the surf to board the landing craft that will take him back to the rear.

A scene from Michael Cimino's film *The Deer Hunter* (1978) poses an instructive counterpoint. Three young steelworkers are about to enter the military and fight in Vietnam. One of them has just married, and the three friends are celebrating at the reception, held at a local VFW hall. They notice a Special Forces sergeant, recently returned from Vietnam, sitting at the bar. The three future soldiers approach the veteran respectfully, eager to talk. One of them says, "Hi. We, uh, we're going Airborne." The veteran's only response is "Fuckit!" Pursuing the conversation, the young steelworker says, "Well, maybe you could tell us how it is over there [in Vietnam]." Again the veteran answers with a tight-lipped "Fuckit." Another contrasting example, the opening scene in Oliver Stone's *Platoon*, features a planeload of American troops arriving in Vietnam, eyeing a heap of body bags, and passing a group of homebound grunts. "New meat!" one of the veterans calls out. "You gonna love the Nam, man, for-fucking-ever."[17]

Upon first landing in Vietnam, many soldiers were struck by the extraordinary size and impact of the American presence: the rows of military aircraft, the constant buzz of helicopters overhead, the roar of powerful jet bombers landing and taking off, and the military buildings everywhere in sight. Some men drew a measure of comfort from the display of American power and hoped they might spend their entire tours inside one of these enormous American bases; certainly, they assured themselves, no Viet Cong would pose a serious threat to such a place. Other newcomers were unnerved. Amid the hundreds of men and machines moving here and there, they had a piercing sensation of their own insignificance, of how small a part of the whole war they really were, and how little anyone cared about their own well-being. This new world had a life of its own—strange, complicated, and forbidding. Eric Stevens, from Texas, arrived in Vietnam in March 1969:

> We landed in Danang and it's hard to explain the impact: There's Phantoms landing and taking off: SSSHHHUUUGGG, SSSHHHUUUGGG, SSSHHHUUUGGG!!! And there were some people walking around with beards, looking as grungy as can be, and other people walking around looking just as sharp as any military person you ever saw—I mean *slick*. There was a real contrast there: some guys all spit-shined and polished and other guys just back from the field looking rugged and hard-eyed. And you had guys walking around with pump shot-guns they were using to guard the supplies: mostly guarding them from other Americans who stole stuff to sell on the black market. But I couldn't figure any of that out at the time. It was just a very weird scene. I was safe, but I had no idea how safe. I had no idea what was going on or how I would fit in.[18]

Stevens's first order was to escort some supplies from Danang to Phu Bai. Assuming someone in Phu Bai was expecting his arrival and would be there to meet him, Stevens got on a cargo plane with the two large pallets of equipment he was supposed to deliver. It was nighttime. The plane aborted its first landing attempt. The crew chief explained:

> "They took a few mortar rounds down there so we're gonna circle around for awhile." I'm really getting nervous because I don't know

what's down there. Phu Bai doesn't mean nothing to me. I never heard of it in my whole life. So we landed in pitch dark, only a few lights at the end of the runway. Out of nowhere comes a humungus forklift. It unloads the two pallets I'm with and sets them down right next to the runway and then disappears. Then the crew chief said, "See you later," and then the plane's gone. I'm standing there by myself. There ain't nobody to check in with. Where am I? I see the outline of a building and I get over there and it's the old [abandoned] terminal building that's got holes all shot in it and concertina wire everywhere. I stayed up all night, of course. I laid up on top of the pallets, and I listened to all the night sounds. When the sun come up in the morning, I'm on an airport in Phu Bai and I'm safe as a baby. There wasn't nobody safer than I was that night. But I learned a lot that night. Everything hit home. Dealing with the apprehension of the unknown.

There is more to this statement than the predictable fear we might associate with entering a war zone. There is also a profound feeling of abandonment and isolated vulnerability. The apprehension of the unknown is so terrible because it is so complete and because it is suffered alone. Underlying all of these emotions is the jarring, disorienting recognition that one cannot even trust one's emotions; the war poses such surreal and unpredictable environments and experiences that one might feel most threatened precisely when one is "safe as a baby" and (as soldiers would soon learn) most secure at times of greatest danger.

A POISONED WORLD

The first smell of Vietnam: "When we finally touched down at Bien Hoa at midnight and they opened the door of the cabin, it was a summer like no summer I had ever known. The air rushed in like poison, hot and choking. I caught a whiff of the jungles, something dead there. I was not prepared for the heat and smell."[19]

It was, veterans say, an awful, unforgettable smell. They attribute the foul odor to a variety of sources and have different ways of evoking its quality, but an extraordinary number of veterans describe their first impression of Vietnam as an overpowering sensation of physical revulsion. Along with the odor, veterans commonly describe an intense and shocking heat: "like stepping into a sauna" or "walking into a blast furnace"—"The sweat just popped."[20]

Stepping into this world, American soldiers felt, from the outset, defiled and unclean. The emphasis many veterans give to these impressions may reflect, in part, a retrospective view that the war as a whole was a contaminating experience. Indeed, for many it was. We need refer only briefly to the severe health and environmental problems caused by the chemical defoliants sprayed by U.S. forces in Vietnam and the hundreds of thousands of veterans who have suffered from posttraumatic stress disorder (delayed stress) to suggest how truly poisonous the war was, both physically and psychologically.

It is no surprise, however, that Americans would be struck by the heat and smell of Vietnam. Southern Vietnam is a tropical environment, lying just ten to twenty degrees north of the equator, on about the same latitude as Central America and central Africa. It is not uncommon for temperatures to soar well above 100 degrees, with high humidity. Moreover, high temperatures—especially the sort of humid heat found in Vietnam—greatly intensify odors. Many American veterans identified Vietnam with the smell of excrement. Jim Barrett remembers: "The first thing I noticed when we got off the plane at Cam Ranh Bay was the smell. It smelled like—the whole country smelled like—well, it smelled like shit. Like you just walked into a bathroom that hadn't been cleaned properly."[21]

Barrett does not identify the source of the odor; he simply implies that the land itself is mysteriously and innately fetid. W. D. Ehrhart, in his memoir *Vietnam-Perkasie*, offers a more specific catalogue of odors: "The first thing that struck me about Vietnam was the smell: a sharp, pungent odor compounded of cooking fires, fish sauce, rice fields fertilized with human and animal excrement, water buffalo, chickens, unwashed bodies, and I don't know what all else, but it clawed violently at my nose and caught fire in my lungs. It was awful. It permeated everything. I kept thinking, 'Jesus Christ, these people don't even smell like human beings.' "[22]

Ehrhart's description reflects an understanding that cultural differences may account for odors offensive to foreign senses. For example, the fish sauce called *nuoc mam* commonly used in Vietnam is made from decaying fish, and most Americans find it intolerably pungent.[23] Ehrhart also implies, however, that these awful odors represent more than mere cultural or economic differences (such as an absence of modern plumbing) and reflect racial inferiority.

Soldiers with this perception saw the Vietnamese as primitive people who lived like animals. Describing how the Vietnamese defecate in the fields, one veteran concluded: "It's like they're pigmies or Africans or something. They're very ignorant. They shit and wipe their ass with their finger. They smell. The villages stink. Stink!" Some Americans were more appalled by an apparent lack of shame about elimination than by the act itself. Said one veteran, "Those people were disgusting; they'd take a crap anywhere, and they didn't give a damn who was watching."[24]

Other veterans believe the United States was mostly to blame for fouling the Vietnamese air. The smell of feces, they claim, was produced primarily by the U.S. military burning its soldiers' waste. "The doors [of the airplane] opened up and I got my first whiff of Nam. What do you do if you've got 500,000 men and no plumbing facilities? What do you do with all the human shit? The Army's answer . . . was to collect it in barrels . . . and set it on fire."[25]

The smell of burning excrement did indeed pervade the air, especially around the large American bases where Americans most commonly landed by jet. The waste was collected in fifty-five-gallon drums that sat under American outhouses. When the drums began to fill, rear-echelon enlisted men drenched them with kerosene and torched them. The air was even more poisoned by the millions of gallons of petrochemicals required to keep the U.S. military machine—planes, helicopters, ships, boats, trucks, jeeps, tanks, and personnel carriers—on the move. The gravest pollution was caused by the 18 million gallons of poisonous chemical defoliants the military sprayed in South Vietnam from 1961 to 1971. The most poisonous, Agent Orange, contained TCDD-dioxin, perhaps the most toxic known substance. In addition to the untold number of human illnesses, deaths, and birth defects caused by the use of such chemicals, the defoliants damaged the land and wildlife of nearly 6 million acres of South Vietnam. In *Free Fire Zone*, Rob Riggan writes, "The land reeks of oil, of burned fuel, pesticides, feces."[26]

Most veterans describe the smell of Vietnam as a strange combination of odors, some brought from America, others indigenous to Vietnam. "It was like sweat, shit, jet fuel, and fish sauce all mixed together."[27] In the very odors, Americans confronted one of the most fundamental facts about the war: the conflict between the advanced technology of the wealthiest nation on earth and the largely preindustrial and agricultural world of the revolutionary Third World. It produced a fetid odor indeed. As John Ketwig writes, "The humidity was oppressive; and there was a sweet stink that suggested fruits and tires burning together."[28]

In much of the veterans' talk about Vietnam's odors one can hear an allegory not only about the clash of cultures but about the effort to attribute responsibility for the moral and political taint and defilement of the war. Where some would attach all or most of the blame to the "primitive" Vietnamese for tainting the United States, others would emphasize America's responsibility for poisoning Vietnam. Those seeking to avoid such a judgment are likely to attribute the "evil smell" of the war to a tragic mix of two cultures.

WIRE MESH AND BAD OMENS

After landing by commercial jet, most soldiers were taken by bus to large U.S. bases where they would wait for assignment to specific units. One detail about the bus ride particularly captured the attention of new men: the wire mesh over the windows.

> I arrived in-country at Cam Ranh Bay. It's hot. The kind of hot that Texas is hot. It takes your breath away as you step out of the airplane. We were loaded on an olive-drab school bus for the short ride from the airstrip over to the compound. There was wire mesh over the windows. I said to somebody, "What the hell is the wire for?"
>
> "It's the gooks, man, the gooks. . . . The gooks will throw grenades through the windows. See those gooks out there?" I look out and I see shriveled, little old men squatting beside the road in the fashion of the Vietnamese, filling sandbags. They looked up at me with real contempt on their faces.
>
> Here we are at one of the largest military installations in the world and we have to cover the windows to protect ourselves from little old men. I didn't put it all together at the time, but intuitively I knew something was wrong.[29]

Such experiences provoked a range of questions and anxieties: Why did Americans require protection from Vietnamese civilians? After all, weren't the Americans in Vietnam to help those people? Weren't those people our allies? Why don't they welcome our arrival? Why the expressions of contempt? And why does this other soldier refer to these civilians as "gooks"? Are we supposed to consider every Vietnamese a gook? And, if so, does that mean they are all enemies, or all potential grenade throwers? And if everyone is to be suspected and guarded against, why are we sitting on this bus without weapons?

The bus ride to the "replacement depots" caused confusion and tension, but it also evoked wonder, curiosity, and excitement. Rob Riggan explains:

> They loaded us onto buses. The windows are covered with wire mesh to protect us from hurled objects. Beyond the diamond screening I watch the first day break. . . . The landscape that unfolds with the rising sun is a snarl of barbed wire and shattered trees.
>
> We roar through a large town. Among the buildings of substance are hovels of plywood and tin. There's a freshness and vibrancy to the early morning streets with their crammed stalls and shops. People . . . zap by on scooters and pile into curious three-wheeled minibuses called lambros.[30]

Notice the variety in these observations. Along with the signs of war (the barbed wire) and poverty (the makeshift hovels) Riggan has a curiosity about the new culture that allows him to see the vibrancy and energy of Vietnamese life. But this openness, as John Ketwig writes, could soon be overshadowed by bad omens:

> I admit it. There was a certain fascination with the curious culture. Tiny people in cone-shaped bamboo sun hats, bicycle-powered rickshaws, cluttered hovels built of flotsam and jetsam, and naked children with large almond eyes all seemed to be pages of *National Geographic* come to life. But there was no escaping the omens of danger: olive-drab jeeps with machine guns mounted upon a pivot, . . . ARVN (Army of the Republic of Vietnam) soldiers, sandbag walls, and twisted strands of barbed wire lining the duty road to separate it from the tranquil-looking paddies. Viewed through a screen of quarter-inch wire mesh, it seemed too alien to be attractive.[31]

One of the most troubling of these omens was found in the reactions of Vietnamese civilians to the newly arrived Americans. Sometimes the signs looked good—children running to the roadside, laughing and waving. It was soon evident, however, that these responses were not the warm welcomes of grateful civilians cheering their liberators. Rather, they were the enthusiastic, sometimes desperate, expressions of people whose very existence depended on hustling the Americans. On his first day in Vietnam, David Parks wrote in his diary: "The villages we passed through were really poverty-stricken. People go to the bathroom in the streets, and the kids ran alongside the convoy. They held up two fingers for victory and a thumb for good luck; at least that's what we thought."[32] But the new American soldiers soon realized that the children were not celebrating the war effort; they were pimping. The two fingers did not mean victory; they meant that the price of "boom-boom" was two dollars. The children signified boom-boom by striking a fist (with the thumb up) into the open palm of the other hand.

The Vietnamese who lined the road calling for handouts or hustling the Americans were the ones most likely to be smiling and waving. But there were others—usually, veterans say, among the old people—who looked at the Americans with blank, silent stares full of unknowable but seemingly contemptuous scorn. Sometimes Americans encountered obvious acts of hostility in their first moments in-country. While John Ketwig's bus traveled from Tan Son Nhut to Long Binh, a group of Vietnamese approached the bus yelling at the Americans. "A chorus of 'Go home, GI' and 'Fuck you, GI' was accompanied by a barrage of assorted garbage and trash bouncing off the wire mesh that covered the windows. Somebody in the back of the bus hollered, 'Hey, you fuckin' gooks. We're supposed to be here to save your fuckin' puny asses!'"[33]

Some Americans arrived in Vietnam convinced that no Vietnamese were to be trusted, that all were potential enemies, and that all of them were "gooks." After all, this view had been hammered home in basic training by many drill instructors. But soldiers had also been told that America was in Vietnam to help our allies, to help the ordinary people of South Vietnam fight off communism, develop a democracy, and live a better life. The conflict between these attitudes was present from the beginning, and it did not take much prompting to draw out the contradiction. It was, in fact, exactly stated by the soldier who screamed "We're supposed to be here to save your fuckin' puny asses."

Larry Hughes arrived in Vietnam in 1966 and heard two conflicting briefings on this subject. A colonel told a group of fresh American replacements to give themselves time to adjust to the new environment, time to "understand the Vietnamese and their way of life." Hughes was encouraged by the briefing. It made him think that "perhaps there was a purpose or a deeper significance to the American involvement than I'd been able to comprehend." The colonel made Hughes feel that he was "a good guy far from home helping this tiny neighbor in a nasty neighborhood of nations. . . . It was the first time I'd had the feeling of purpose since entering the Army." But a sergeant's briefing hastily contradicted the colonel's: "Be alert from this moment and don't trust nobody with slanted eyes!"[34]

Dick Boyer arrived in Bien Hoa at the end of 1968. Soon after Dick disembarked from the TWA jet, a Vietnamese shoeshine boy approached him. The boy persuaded Dick to have his boots shined. Afterward, the boy said the shine cost one dollar. Dick was incredulous. Growing up in Boston, Dick had been a "shine boy" himself and never remembered charging more than twenty-five cents. He thought the Vietnamese kid was asking a "totally unreasonable price." Dick gave the boy about fifty cents and walked away, but the boy followed after insisting on a full dollar. Dick could not manage to shake the persistent boy, even after trying to shove him away. An American sergeant, a man who had been in Vietnam well before Dick arrived, witnessed the scene and brutally intervened. "The sergeant walked right up to the Vietnamese kid and started slapping him in the face. I mean he just whaled the piss out of him. Then he turned to me and said, 'That's the only way to treat these gooks. If you don't get tough with them, they'll walk all over you.'"[35]

Dick went away feeling edgy, angry, and confused. "Right there from the start I had this terrible feeling that something was really wrong here. Everything was totally screwed up." He had no clear preconceptions of what he would find in Vietnam, but like most new men, he at least expected the children to like him. "I guess I had this image in my mind of the big American GI handing out candy-bars to little smiling kids and that they would, you know, respect you and look up to you." But the shoeshine boy seemed interested only in his money. "I thought we were supposed to be over there to help these people and right off the bat I feel like a total idiot, like a tourist in some country where everyone hates the rich Americans." The sergeant's brutality was even harder to understand. "I was really pissed at the kid, but I couldn't believe the sergeant started beating him up. He blew the whole thing way out of proportion."

In Winston Groom's novel, *Better Times Than These*, a large contingent of American soldiers arrives at Cam Ranh Bay in 1966. (Groom served in Vietnam that same year as a lieutenant in the Fourth Infantry Division.) Waiting for a convoy to take them to an inland firebase, the soldiers gathered on the edge of the American compound. Outside the compound, on the other side of the barbed-wire fence, across from the neat and symmetrical American base, was a Vietnamese settlement. Unlike the best Vietnamese hamlets in rural areas that had neat hedgerows and carefully thatched dwellings, this was purely a patchwork shantytown. Like most of the settlements that bordered American bases, it was largely peopled by Vietnamese who had become economically dependent on the American military presence. The dwellings were mostly constructed from American garbage—flattened beer cans, scrap metal, and empty C-ration boxes. To the men of Groom's novel the Vietnamese shantytown looked "like some giant seething reptile." There were hundreds of people going about their business, but to American eyes, "it was impossible to tell what they were doing."[36]

A group of Vietnamese children gathered on the opposite side of the barbed wire. The American words and phrases they used offered a pointed and telling history of the war. Many of the children were begging. "You give me C ration?" they asked. Amidst the pleas for food or cigarettes, more puzzling expressions were heard. "You VC?" some children asked, throwing back at the Americans the question U.S. troops were always asking of the Vietnamese. In the background, "a small naked boy kept repeating over and over again, 'Fuck you, fuck you.'"

A lieutenant named Brill was especially annoyed by the children. They reminded him of monkeys at a zoo. He watched as a private handed out pieces of a Hershey candy bar. The "jabbering" subsided, but when the candy was gone the children "broke into a wild, furious cacophony." Brill approached the fence.

"Hey—that's enough—see—all gone—no more—okay?" he said harshly.

"Okay, okay," they repeated, saying it over and over again until Brill began to get the impression he was being mocked.

"All right—get out of here," he scowled. "Go on—beat it!" He gestured down the rutted track toward the shack town.

"Okay, okay, okay—Ahmerican, numba ten," they cried frantically, still holding out their hands, obviously with no intentions of leaving.

Brill stooped for a flat gray seashell at his feet and drew back with it in a threatening gesture. "GET OUT OF HERE, GODDAMN IT," he roared.[37]

Brill threw the shell, and some of the older children responded in kind. A full-fledged rock fight broke out across the barbed wire between the Americans and the Vietnamese. The fight was broken up by an American sergeant and a lieutenant. While the lieutenant took Brill aside, the sergeant interrogated the enlisted men.

"Can *you* tell me what the hell went on here?" Trunk said threateningly.

"Them little gooks was throwing stones at us so we started to throw them back," Muntz said weakly. "They started to throw them at Lieutenant Brill, anyway, and they was hitting us too," he said.

"Well let me tell you something, soldier," Trunk said. "You don't throw stones at kids—ever; do you hear that?—*ever*. The United States Army don't throw rocks at children."

"Aw, Sarge, they was probably VC kids anyway," Muntz said defensively. "They coulda had grenades or something."

The others agreed. "Yeah, Sarge, you heard about the kids throwing grenades over here, haven't you? Spate's brother got killed by a kid throwing a grenade—didn't he, Spate?"

"Shut your ass up," Trunk said.[38]

The hostility between the American soldiers and the Vietnamese children erupted so quickly, it was as if both sides had anticipated trouble; each had such negative preconceptions of the other that a conflict was almost inevitable. Even though these soldiers were new to Vietnam, the children responded in a way that had evolved in many prior encounters with Americans. If the Americans offered handouts, the children were all smiles and the GIs were "Number One"; if no treats were forthcoming, the children cursed the Americans and called them "Number Ten." The Americans, though seeing Vietnamese children for the first time, had their own preconceptions. Many arrived in Vietnam already convinced that the children were just "little gooks." Just about everyone had been warned to regard all Vietnamese as potential enemies; even the children could be Viet Cong guerrillas fully capable of throwing grenades. In Groom's story the men automatically used their suspicions to justify their participation in the rock fight.

Groom's story also dramatizes the inability of officers and NCOs to provide clear or consistent instructions about how to behave toward the Vietnamese. A lieutenant started the rock fight. Another lieutenant, along with Sergeant Trunk, opposed the fight, but they could neither prevent the conflict nor provide helpful responses to the doubts and anxieties expressed by the men. The sergeant could not tell them that children never throw grenades in Vietnam, nor could he tell them how to predict which children might, or when, or how to guard against the possibility without resorting to preemptive and random violence. Instead, the sergeant simply says, "Shut your ass up."

Anxiety about the political loyalties of the Vietnamese people contributed to a flood of GI folklore, rumors, and horror stories about American soldiers victimized by civilians who turned out to be ruthless agents of the Viet Cong. Everyone heard stories about Vietnamese barbers who slit American throats, prostitutes who put razor blades in their vaginas to cut American soldiers, children who walked onto American bases with explosives strapped to their stomachs, and soft drinks and beer that the VC adulterated with tiny pieces of glass to sell to thirsty Americans. The point was always the same: no Vietnamese could be trusted; all were dangerous. Recalling his first purchase of a beer in Vietnam, Micheal Clodfelter writes: "I was a little apprehensive. . . . We had been warned of instances where the Viet Cong sympathizers had dropped slivers of glass or battery acid into the beer and coke."[39]

In his novel *Fragments*, Vietnam veteran Jack Fuller suggests that the pervasive horror stories of civilian sabotage and betrayal reflected an "expectation of deceit." The Americans expected Vietnamese civilians to prove themselves, in the end, loyal to the Viet Cong. That expectation, Fuller believes, had a corrupting influence and contributed to the atrocities committed against Vietnamese civilians by American forces.

> "My brother was here. . . . He told me about these villages. They may look peaceful. People will bow, children smile. But they'll blow you away in a minute if you give them a chance.
>
> "My brother said the VC are always watching. They see through the eyes of the little kids peering from doorways, the old ladies doing their wash. You can feel the blood against your throat as you pass a young girl slicing fruit."
>
> "He must be some storyteller," said Neumann.
>
> "They weren't just stories. He told us all about it in his letters. Then he was killed."
>
> In a way that I did not appreciate at the time . . . I recognized for just an instant a hint of what would happen to us in Xuan The [where an American soldier killed three Vietnamese civilians]. And sometimes I wonder whether it wasn't our expectation of deceit more than deceit itself that proved so corrupting.[40]

Some Americans believed that if no Vietnamese could be trusted, the safest response was for America to eliminate as many Vietnamese as possible, indiscriminately. By this logic, the more Vietnamese killed, the better the odds of survival for Americans. This was the message heard by Gary Battles during his week of in-country training. One of his instructors told the new American soldiers, "The only good gook is a dead gook, and the more gooks you can kill, the more slant-eyes you can kill in Vietnam, that is the less you will have to worry about them killing you at night."[41]

FNGS

As American soldiers moved from replacement depots to their units throughout Vietnam, they felt isolated, anxious, and out of context. They were entering a war in progress, and they wondered what their own role in the ongoing struggle might be, what effect they could possibly have on such a long and complicated history. Traveling by truck, helicopter, or plane to join their assigned unit, they saw evidence of the long war's wreckage: bomb craters, refugee camps, pockmarked Buddhist temples, destroyed hamlets, and devastated terrain. Along Highway 19, for example, which ran inland from the coast toward the large American base at An Khe, the roadside was littered with "the twisted skeletons of burned and rusting vehicles": "Automobiles, jeeps, trucks, personnel carriers, an occasional tank, some dismembered beyond recognition. A few were unmistakably American, others appeared to be French and the older, battered ones looked as if they might have been Japanese."[42]

Looking at the physical evidence of the war's long and complex history made new American soldiers deeply uneasy. Many felt insignificant and powerless. How was their involvement going to make a difference? In *Fields of Fire*, James Webb develops this theme as one of his characters moves by convoy from Danang to join a combat unit at An Hoi. The year is 1969:

> Strings of American bases and well-kept villages gave way to wide, ruptured fields, saturated with little ponds, permanent bomb craters from the years of war. The multitude of gravestones and pagodas beginning just outside DaNang bore chips and divots from a hundred thousand bullets. Hodges could make out old fighting holes along many of the ridges, where units had dug into their night perimeters

months and years before. He felt young, even more naive, a stranger to an on-going game that did not demand or need his presence.[43]

The new soldiers were not just entering an unfamiliar place with foreign names and an unknown geography. They were confronting the sites of countless battles. Just how long had these people been fighting and what was behind it all? That sense of historical confusion and displacement was one of the most isolating and terrifying experiences of the initial days in Vietnam.

When these strangers joined their assigned units, they looked to the other Americans for support, community, and a sense of belonging and purpose. But these moments rarely felt like homecomings. The new men were put wherever there was an opening, usually replacing a man who had finished his tour and gone home or someone who had been wounded or killed. When Sam Warren was dropped off at his unit, a lieutenant greeted him this way: "Oh, an FNG, huh? Well, let's see. Hey Sarge! [he yelled] Who got hit last night?"[44]

To men who had been in Vietnam for awhile—even just a month or so— the FNGs (fuckin' new guys) were easily identifiable. It was more than just their clean boots and fresh utilities. Everything about them looked new: a certain sparkle in their eyes, an awkwardness in their gait, an uncertainty about where to go or what to do or how to hold their bodies. Their inexperience was apparent in the questions they asked and their incomprehension of the most basic Vietnam slang. The seasoned soldiers called the new men "twinks," "greenies," "cherries," "boots," "new-bees," and FNGs. On the surface, at least, these new men were scorned, ignored, belittled, and reminded at every opportunity of their inexperi- ence and stupidity. Underneath this surface coolness, though, the more experienced men kept careful eyes on the replacements who joined their units, and the care they did take, however minimal, had an enormous impact on the new men. One veteran recalls his first night at Phuoc Vinh. The base was mortared, and someone directed him to a bunker.

It was pitch black in the bunker and nobody was saying anything for a while. Out of the silence and the darkness, somebody said, "Where's the new guy?"

"I'm here," I said.

That was that, but there was something about that little exchange in the dark that I will never forget. . . . [It] was authentically . . . generous . . . that somebody even bothered to think about me. Who the hell was I? This rather quiet, slightly older FNG in clean fatigues, whose boots weren't even red yet. I was amazed.[45]

For soldiers thrown into such a world, even small gestures of concern had a profound impact. Generosity surprised the new men. To the FNGs, the seasoned soldiers usually appeared crude, brutal, and indifferent to death and danger. When Frank Mathews arrived with his unit, he had the unusual experience of reuniting with a boot camp buddy, but it was not a pleasant reunion. The friend had been in Vietnam for a few months and began telling Frank about the terrible things that had happened to mutual acquaintances: "You remember so-and-so?" he asked. "He got it through the throat." Someone else had "got it right through the head." The man told Frank all of these horrible stories with a perfectly straight face. His voice was calm, his eyes were steady, and he "didn't show any feelings at all." Frank was bothered as much by the apparent indifference to death as by the deaths themselves. He said to himself in those first days, "Ah shit, what have I gotten into, man? These people don't care if you live or die over here."[46]

Tim O'Brien first saw the men of his infantry unit when they came into camp after an operation in the "boonies." "They were dirty, loud, coarse, intent on getting drunk, happy, curt, and not interested in saying much to me." During O'Brien's first night at LZ Gator, the Viet Cong mortared the base. The experienced grunts (infantrymen), just back from their operation, seemed utterly unconcerned by the mortar attack. Many of them continued to sleep. Gradually a few of them "ambled" out of their barracks holding beer cans. "They sat on some sandbags in their underwear, drinking the beer and laughing, pointing out at the paddies and watching our mortar rounds land." When a lieutenant scrambled around trying to organize the company along the perimeter of the base, the grunts just ignored him. Were they so inured to danger they were not going to defend the base? No, but they did so in their own way, at their own pace. Instead of moving out to the perimeter as the lieutenant had ordered, they set up a machine gun in the middle of the base near the barracks. They had noticed the distant flash of a Viet Cong mortar tube and began to fire rounds "over the heads of everyone in the firebase" toward the enemy mortar. During the night ten people were killed: two Americans and eight Viet Cong. The next day one of the seasoned grunts said to O'Brien, "Look, FNG, I don't want to scare you—nobody's trying to scare you— but that stuff last night wasn't *shit*! Last night was a lark. Wait'll you see some really *bad* shit. That was a picnic last night. I almost slept through it."[47]

He was, of course, trying to scare O'Brien. Some men took great pleasure in shocking new guys with stories about all "the shit" they had "seen." But this was not mere bravado. He was also trying to make O'Brien aware that they were the men with real experience, the people to look to for leadership. Experienced soldiers also wanted to humble new men who might have cinematic fantasies about combat heroics. Seasoned grunts were at least as worried by new guys hell-bent for action as they were by those who expressed the most fear. Perhaps the most common words of advice given to new men were "Don't try to be John Wayne."[48]

In *A Few Good Men*, a novel by marine veteran Tom Suddick, one character offers this definition of "newguy":

> "Newguy—some dumbass boot, fresh from the States who doesn't know shit and will get at least four of us killed before he catches on." . . .
>
> "Newguy—a gung-ho asshole, just itchin' to get into action."[49]

"Breaking in" new soldiers was considered a crucial aspect of survival in Vietnam. Experienced enlisted men took upon themselves the responsibility of instructing new men on the laws of survival: when to be wary, what to watch out for, when and how to be aggressive, when to ignore orders, who to look to for help, which officers to trust and which to avoid. Ordinarily, new men were told to follow the example set by squad leaders. Squad leaders were usually enlisted men who had won field promotions to lance corporal or corporal (or sometimes sergeant) after five or six months in-country. Typically, these men had more combat experience than anyone in the unit (other than one or two crusty NCOs who might have fought in Vietnam on a previous tour). Officers, however, typically served only six months (a half-tour) in "line companies" (combat units). After that, they were given rear-area assignments. The common view among enlisted men was that officers were just beginning to learn how to lead men in combat when they were sent to the rear. Combat soldiers also deeply resented the obvious inequality between their twelve months in the field and their officers' six months. In addition, new men were often warned about those career officers—"lifers"—who were thought to put their own ambition for higher rank over the safety of their men.[50]

The use of drugs also played a crucial role in the way many seasoned soldiers established relations with the FNGs. Soldiers who smoked marijuana were curious to learn if the new men were also smokers. They might ask indirect questions to find out if the new men liked to "party." Often, especially from 1968 to 1972, new men were simply offered the grass as a standard part of the Vietnam initiation rite. A 1969 study among a thousand enlisted men about to leave Vietnam found that 31 percent had smoked marijuana before going to Vietnam. In Vietnam the portion of users rose to 51 percent.[51] When Sam Warren was assigned to a marine squad on Foxtrot Ridge, he found the men passing around a "bone." The first thing anyone said to him was "Want a hit, man?" Sam had never smoked marijuana before and responded, "Nah, I don't do it." The other man rejoined, "You will." Before the day ended, Sam had begun to smoke grass, and he smoked it regularly for the rest of his tour.[52]

John Lafite arrived in Vietnam as an army medic just a few days before Tet of 1968. On the night of the huge Viet Cong attack on American bases throughout Vietnam, John was sitting in a bunker. The other men were smoking pot, and John did not know what it was.

Until this point I had never even smoked a cigarette. So I just figured they were smoking some weird-smelling cigarettes. Maybe they were gook cigarettes. So when they offered it to me, I said, "What the hell, maybe I'll just take a few drags."

"Now this was Tet. First night of Tet. I was sitting in this bunker feeling very happy—completely stoned, and all of a sudden something exploded. There I am watching the opening of the Tet Offensive and I think I'm watching some kind of fireworks display. Then, when they grabbed me and told me we were under attack my mind started to race—"Oh God no, I'm going to die. The first time in my life I get stoned and I'm going to die."[53]

Some men had at least a few days of in-country orientation and training before being assigned to their permanent units, but just as often the need for replacements was so pressing that new men were dispatched almost immediately. Carl Shepard arrived in Vietnam during the siege of Khe Sanh (1967–68).[54] In the winter of 1967–68 the isolated jungle base in the northwestern corner of South Vietnam was occupied by 6,000 U.S. Marines. The hills and mountains surrounding the base were filled with two divisions of NVA soldiers (about 20,000 troops). From these hillside strongholds the NVA subjected the marines to daily rocket attacks. The need for American replacements at Khe Sanh was so urgent, Shepard received no in-country training and was moved quickly from Danang to

Quang Tri to Phu Bai to LZ Stud and then on to Khe Sanh. "Don't the new guys get broken in?" Shepard asked. "Yeah," he was told, "OJT" (on the job training). Reporting his experience to Mark Baker, he says:

> For the first time the reality of where I was and where I was going slapped me back worse than a nightmare. Now I'm in a war. Oh, God, I could really die out here. Up until that point I never took it seriously. It was happening, but it wasn't real. It was TV. . . . We landed and they ran us off the choppers.
>
> "Company. What company?" sombody yells at me.
>
> "Fox Trot."
>
> "Fox Trot that way, Fox Trot that way." Pointing and waving . . .
>
> Who the hell are these guys? I didn't see no rank on nobody's shoulders or helmets. Everybody looked like privates to me. They're all yelling at me like I don't got no sense, but I'm running anyway.[55]

The memory has such a hold on Shepard's mind that even ten years later he describes the events as if they are happening right now. He slips from the past tense to the present. In rear areas like Danang and Quang Tri, he had noticed that uniforms were crisply pressed and that some men even wore ribbons and medals. At Khe Sanh, however, as in most combat areas, rank was not flaunted. Officers used brown or green cloth insignia rather than the standard gold or silver metal. One explanation was obvious: they did not want to give enemy snipers a shiny target; but equally significant was the fact that enlisted men had little respect or tolerance for officers who paraded their authority out in the bush. For new men like Shepard, however, it was difficult to determine who was in charge.

Joining his company, Shepard learned he would be leaving on a patrol in a manner of minutes. First, however, he had to be outfitted in jungle fatigues and boots that were better camouflaged and lighter than the all-green utilities and black boots found in rear areas. A lieutenant told him to grab a pair of fatigues from a nearby pile. When Shepard joined his squad, the squad leader (an enlisted man) was furious: "Where did you get that shit from?" Unknown to Shepard, the fatigues had been worn by an American killed in action. "We don't touch that shit," the squad leader explained. When Shepard said that the lieutenant had told him to take the used clothes, the squad leader responded, "That boot's only been here two weeks." The lieutenant was as much an FNG as Shepard, and his order was ignored.

The enlisted men found another uniform for Shepard to wear. Then they gave him a few minutes to eat something before going on patrol. They also offered him some marijuana.

What blew my head was what they did to calm me down. The whole team got together and they're sitting around, laughing and bullshitting. My squad leader lit up a joint. He said, "Here, puff. You smoke, right? Well, go ahead. Light up. Relax. You got plenty of time to be scared later. Just relax."

My hand was still shaking, but I'm smoking. They was laughing and telling these weird stories. . . . Their jokes is about this kill and that kill and what this one clown does when there is incoming [enemy rockets]. He gets his chair, sits in front of his bunker and writes his letter. The only time he writes home is during incoming. . . . I wasn't too enthused about their jokes. . . .

That first patrol we went to where some Marines had ambushed a bunch of Viet Cong. They had me moving dead bodies, VC and NVA. Push this body here out of the way. Flip a body over. See people's guts and heads half blown off. I was throwing up all over the place.

"Keep doing it. Drag this body over there."

"For what?"

"You're going to get used to death before you get in a firefight and get us all killed. You're a [machine] gunner and gunners can't panic on us."

I moved some more bodies and after a while I stopped throwing up. . . .

[Then] they gave me about a ten-minute rest. They're laughing and joking.

Next, I had to kick one dead body in the side of the head until part of his brain started coming out of the other side. I said, "I just moved a dead body. What are y'all telling me?" The logic, I didn't see it then. I understood it later. At the time I thought, "These fuckers been up here too long. They are all insane." I'm going through my changes and the rest of these guys are laughing.

"Kick it," they said. "You are starting to feel what it is like to kill. That man is dead, but in your mind you're killing him again. Man, it ain't no big thing. Look-a-here." And they threw some bodies off the cliff. . . .

"So . . . Kick." They meant it. The chant started, "Kick. . . . Kick. . . . Kick. . . ."

I'm kicking now. I'm kicking and I'm kicking and all of a sudden, the brains start coming out the other side. Oh shit. I thought I was going to die when I saw what I was actually doing. I thought I was going to die. I started throwing up again, but there was nothing left to bring up. I'm dry heaving. God, it was killing me.

It was a traumatic initiation. Shepard felt he was going to die, and, in fact, the forced exposure to death and mutilation did involve a figurative death, the stifling of his natural revulsion to carnage. Gradually, after Shepard went through his changes, he began to accept the logic behind the ritual. He began to think of it as a sensible safeguard. The other marines no longer seemed insane, just serious. "They were serious men, dedicated to what they were doing. [They were] teaching me . . . not to fall apart. I saw it happen. I saw guys get themselves killed and almost get an entire platoon wiped out, because they panicked or because they gave up or because they got wounded and couldn't deal with their own blood. They had this thing about teaching a boot exactly what he's got to deal with and how to accept the fact of where he really is."

Americans who served in noncombat positions were not usually exposed to death so directly or so brutally as were these marines. But death was everywhere in Vietnam; it intruded on every sense. Soldiers did not have to be in combat to feel surrounded by death, to be obsessed with the fear of it, tainted or exhilarated by its presence, and complicit in its execution. They could see Phantom jets dropping 250-pound bombs a few kilometers away; from dozens of hillside bases, soldiers sat on sandbags to watch helicopter gunships spray thousands of machine-gun rounds into nearby villages; and they saw the body bags containing the remains of dead Americans stacked on the airstrips. Even when soldiers managed to avoid seeing, hearing, or smelling death, it was ever-present in the talk. The death tallies were constantly monitored and updated. In rear areas, command posts listed "box scores" on large chalk boards. These scores were the number of people who had been killed on either side: the body count. Indeed, killing was the central focus of American policy, the heart of America's strategy of attrition. Every man had to find some way to explain, accept, deflect, or escape the presence of that death. But to understand these various responses, we need to know more about the reality American soldiers confronted, the terms of battle.

The Terms of Battle

We could not defeat a people who carried ammunition on poles and who build bridges by hand. . . . The nation which put men on the moon was defeated by a nation where deputy ministers use outdoor privies.
– William Broyles, Jr.,
Brothers in Arms

"We're fighting Charlie in his own backyard." This was how American soldiers summarized the difficulty of warring against Vietnamese revolutionaries. How can you defeat an enemy who knows the land intimately, who has every reason to regard it as his own backyard, and who has fought for decades, even centuries, to rid it of foreign invaders—the Chinese, the French, the Japanese, and finally the Americans? U.S. troops were haunted by this question. Few were aware of the long history that shaped Vietnamese aspirations for a unified nation free of foreign domination, but the daily realities of warfare continually raised the nagging prospect that perhaps no military effort, however bloody or sustained, could remove "Charlie" from the land, dampen the fervor of his struggle, or undermine the support he received throughout the country.

Yet a conflicting voice posed a different question: how could the United States possibly lose? It had never happened before. Yes, the South did lose the Civil War, and there was the ambiguous stalemate of Korea, but never an outright national defeat. What is more, this tradition of victory enshrined a military ethic that made it intolerable even to imagine that some wars might be unwinnable. As George C. Scott proclaimed at the beginning of *Patton,*

President Nixon's favorite movie, "America loves a winner and will not tolerate a loser." Many Americans surely perceived the Vietnamese as little different from those colonial and nineteenth-century foes who had resisted U.S. forces—Native Americans, Mexicans, and Filipinos. They had been unable to block the road to continental and global preeminence when the United States was just a rising power. How, in the 1960s, at the zenith of U.S. wealth and power, could a small, Third World nation like Vietnam (a "raggedy-ass little fourth-rate country," Lyndon Johnson called it) defeat such a superpower? After all, the Vietnamese revolutionaries had no B-52 bombers, no Phantom jets, no Cobra gunships, no helicopters or flak jackets or napalm or chemical defoliants. True, they had automatic weapons, rockets, and an enormous array of land mines and booby traps. But how could that compete with the extraordinary technological sophistication, the devastating firepower, of the American military?

American soldiers were torn by the conflict between these two perspectives. On one hand they recognized the formidable skill and dedication of the Vietnamese opposition. They knew how hard it was even to locate the enemy, much less to determine the time and place and form of battle. They also quickly realized that the Revolutionary Forces* had support throughout the country, from the South Vietnamese villagers who planted booby traps and gave the enemy crucial information, to the southerners who joined the Viet Cong to become active guerrilla fighters, to the North Vietnamese soldiers who traveled hundreds of miles on foot down the Ho Chi Minh Trail to fight in the south. Yet, alongside these discouraging realities, American soldiers heard from their commanders what they had heard throughout their lives: America is the strongest nation in the world; America has never lost a war; no one can prevail against the courage of our soldiers and the power of our weapons. The two views could not be reconciled. In Vietnam, American soldiers came face-to-face with the

---

*I refer to the Viet Cong (the guerrillas of South Vietnam) and the North Vietnamese Army collectively as the Revolutionary Forces. This designation avoids the awkwardness of such usages as VC/NVA and conveys a truer sense of the nature of the war. The war against the South Vietnamese government and its American defenders was fought and supported by millions of Vietnamese from all parts of Vietnam and is best understood as the final stage of a long-term struggle of revolutionary nationalism. The Communist Party was the decisive leader of the revolution and the ultimate victor. However, not all participants in the revolution were communists, and it could not have been successful without the mobilization and inclusion of large numbers of noncommunists. For that reason, *Revolutionary Forces* is preferable to *Communist Forces.*

shocking fact that in spite of (and in some measure because of) the massive destructive force unleashed by the United States, the Vietnamese Revolutionary Forces maintained both tactical and strategic control of the war. They engaged the Americans at times and places of their own choosing. Whether they initiated combat or avoided it, almost always they controlled the terms of battle.

THE BATTLEGROUND

Vietnamese often liken the shape of their country to a long carrying pole with rice baskets attached at each end—a wonderfully apt simile. The carrying pole, placed across the shoulders, has been used for centuries by Vietnamese peasants to carry rice and other heavy loads. And the two "baskets" of Vietnam—the Red River Delta in the far north and the Mekong Delta in the south—are quite literally filled with rice. Joining the two low-lying deltas is a long "pole"—the narrow, curving stretch of mountains and plateaus that extends for almost 800 miles between north and south.[1]

The simile of the carrying pole reminds us that the Vietnamese conceive of their nation as whole, not divided. This sense of national unity, however, has been slow to develop and was much threatened along the way. Indeed, we might think of the length and thinness of the carrying pole (in one place only forty-five miles wide) as symbolic of the long and tenuous development of Vietnamese nationalism. A sense of nationhood grew out of centuries of struggle to win independence from foreign domination. China ruled Vietnam for a millennium, and France controlled Vietnam for a century. Geographically, the major thrust of Vietnamese nationalism has emanated from central and northern Vietnam. These regions have the longest national history. Southern Vietnam was, until the sixteenth century, the kingdom of Champa, a Hindu state dominated by people of Indian descent. Vietnam conquered Champa in the sixteenth and seventeenth centuries. This southward expansion established roughly the same geographic boundaries of present-day Vietnam, and by the early nineteenth century, Vietnam had become, by global standards of the time, a reasonably integrated nation-state. Southern Vietnam did have a regional history significantly distinct from that of the north. However, it had never formed a coherent or separate political identity of its own. Its social and political histories were far more fragmented than those of the northern regions of Vietnam, a condition exacerbated by the French imperial policy of divide and conquer. The strongest force for unity in the south came not from groups calling for regional or sectarian separatism but from those struggling for national independence from French colonial rule, the Viet Minh in particular.[2]

Thus, in 1945, when Vietnam achieved a short-lived independence, the Viet Minh had the potential to consolidate its leadership nationwide. It had widespread support in the northern two-thirds of the country and was the strongest, if contested, force in the deep south. This period also represented the best historical opportunity for the United States to avoid its disastrous thirty-year intervention. During World War II, American OSS officers (predecessors to the CIA) supported the Viet Minh, under the leadership of Ho Chi Minh, in their fight against the Japanese occupiers. Ho looked to the United States as an ally in his bid for postwar independence, basing his declaration of independence on the American model and drawing hope from the Atlantic Charter's promise of self-determination for all nations. He made repeated appeals to the U.S. government to recognize Vietnamese independence. The American government did not even respond.[3]

Instead, the United States supported the French reconquest of Vietnam. As George McT. Kahin has brilliantly documented, Vietnam was a trivial concern of U.S. policymakers in the first postwar years. Had France accepted Vietnamese independence, in all likelihood the U.S. would have followed suit and regarded Ho Chi Minh's leadership as a fait accompli. France wanted Vietnam back, however, and the United States did not want to offend the French. The top U.S. priority was building a strong, anti-Soviet alliance in Western Europe, and support for French recolonization in Indochina was primarily intended to shore up French support for this alliance. The secondary motive was the desire that France crush an independence movement the U.S. policymakers regarded as dangerously left wing. By 1950, with the recent communist victory in China and the outbreak of the Korean War, concern about communism in Vietnam became the driving force of U.S. policy toward Indochina. Aid to France was defended as an essential element in the global effort to contain communism. (Prior to 1950 the U.S. had simply denied aiding the French effort to hold on to its rebellious colony.) In the early 1950s, U.S. support for the war against the Viet Minh escalated so dramatically that French forces could fairly be regarded as American-backed mercenaries. By 1953, the United States was bankrolling 78 percent of the French war.[4]

In 1954 the Viet Minh defeated French imperial forces at Dienbienphu, and the two sides joined the major world powers at Geneva to formulate the terms of peace. Despite their victory, the Viet Minh accepted a temporary partition of Vietnam at the seventeenth parallel. The country was divided into two "regroupment zones," with military forces supportive of the Viet Minh to move north and those backing the French to move south. The "provisional military demarcation line" between north and south was intended to last two years, whereupon elections would be held to reunify Vietnam under a single, national government. The Viet Minh accepted these terms because they believed the provisions would allow them time to consolidate power in the north and still offer them an excellent chance to unify the nation under the promised elections of 1956. Also, the Soviet Union and China pressured Ho to accept the compromise, fearing that a push for immediate unification might lead the United States to intervene militarily.[5]

Had nationwide elections been held in 1956, as stipulated at Geneva, Ho Chi Minh would almost certainly have won a landslide victory. American intelligence officers estimated that Ho would win 80 percent of the vote. For that reason, the United States never supported the provision for national elections, nor did it sign the Geneva Accords. It did, however, pledge to honor the terms of the agreement. Betraying its pledge, the United States launched a campaign to create a strong, stable, permanent, anticommunist, pro-American South Vietnam. That aim became the foundation of American policy for the next twenty years. From the outset, the odds for success in that venture were poor. By 1954, as Frances Fitzgerald writes, "the south had become a political jungle of warlords, sects, bandits, partisan troops, and secret societies. . . . There seemed to be small chance for the establishment of an administration, much less a nation-state, in the midst of this chaos."[6]

Shortly after the Geneva conference, American-backed Ngo Dinh Diem became prime minister of South Vietnam, and France finally withdrew from Vietnam. Diem, who had been in America during the French war, was promoted by an influential group of supporters including Cardinal Francis Spellman, Justice William O. Douglas, Senator John Kennedy, and CIA agent Edward Lansdale. In Vietnam, Diem was hardly so popular. Yet, with enormous military and economic aid, he began to assert his power with a massive campaign of imprisonment, torture, and execution against his political opponents, especially the Viet Minh and Buddhists. Neither Diem nor his American supporters had any intention of honoring the 1956 reunification elections unless they were convinced that Diem would win, a probability even the most optimistic of his backers soon found utterly unlikely.[7]

Instead, for nine years the United States sought to build and bolster Diem's government, a regime founded on American aid, nepotism, corruption, and repression. The latter reached its highest expression in Law 10/59, under which the government claimed the right to execute anyone found guilty of "infringing upon the security of the State." The crime was interpreted so loosely ("whoever commits or attempts to commit"), anyone suspected of political dissent might be arrested or executed. Under the provisions of Law 10/59 thousands of South Vietnamese lost their lives. In the short term, this campaign of state terrorism severely depleted the ranks of every dissident group. That very repression, however, ultimately backfired by stirring the embers of revolutionary nationalism throughout the south.[8]

In 1960 the Vietnamese Communist Party set up the NLF, through which it directed the bourgeoning guerrilla movement being waged in the South by some 10,000 rebels who were inspired to fight by the promise of land reform, national unification and independence, and an end to the tyranny of Diem's corrupt regime. America's role in creating and sustaining a partitioned Vietnam, and its desire to consolidate the power of a pro-American, anticommunist regime, had the effect of snapping the carrying pole of Vietnam into two pieces. The Revolutionary Forces under Ho Chi Minh spent the next fifteen years and sacrificed hundreds of thousands of lives trying to piece it together.[9]

Knowing how South Vietnam was created is crucial to our understanding of even the most basic facts about the American war in Vietnam. It was there in the south, in the land below the seventeenth parallel, that the war was primarily fought. The war is best understood not as a civil war between North and South Vietnam but as a revolutionary war fought in the south over two different visions of Vietnam. The Americans fought for a divided nation, for a south that would serve as a noncommunist buffer against the communist north. On the other side were southern guerrillas and northern troops fighting together for national unification through the revolutionary overthrow of the American-backed regime in Saigon.

Though most of the fighting on the ground took place within South Vietnam, U.S. and South Vietnamese forces conducted hundreds of small, clandestine, across-the-border operations in Cambodia, Laos, and North Vietnam. Indeed, raids against the north were the provocation that led North Vietnamese patrol boats to fire at an American destroyer on 2

August 1964. President Johnson claimed this attack and another on 4 August (which did not, in fact, take place) were unprovoked acts of aggression, and he ordered air strikes on North Vietnam in response. More importantly, he used the incident to win congressional approval of the Gulf of Tonkin Resolution, a resolution drafted months earlier giving LBJ the power to "take all necessary measures to repel any armed attack against the forces of the United States and to prevent further aggression." Johnson viewed the resolution as sufficient congressional authorization for the enormous escalation that followed in 1965.[10]

The battleground was also extended beyond South Vietnam by two major ground offensives: the invasion of Cambodia in May 1970 and the invasion of Laos in March 1971. However, most of the fighting took place in South Vietnam. The military boundaries of the war were extended primarily through bombing. In 1965 the United States began the systematic bombing of North Vietnam; months earlier, in 1964, it had begun the clandestine bombing of Laos; and in 1969 the United States began the secret bombing of Cambodia. Many Americans have always assumed that North Vietnam was the most heavily bombed part of Indochina. Severe as this bombing was (1 million tons), it was exceeded by the bombing of Laos (1.5 million tons). Cambodia was hit by 500,000 tons. South Vietnam was, by far, the primary target of U.S. bombing, receiving more bombs (4 million tons) than the other three countries combined. The bombing of South Vietnam was a constant feature of the war from the early 1960s until the end of the war in 1975. The intermittent and much publicized American "bombing halts" applied only to North Vietnam above the twentieth parallel. During each of those halts the United States intensified the bombing of Laos and South Vietnam.[11]

Thus, while the war encompassed most of Indochina, the major battleground was South Vietnam. It was an ideal battleground for the Revolutionary Forces. Guerrillas drawn from the rural peasantry could move with relative ease among the heavily populated lowlands, and regular troops from the north found abundant cover in the dense and lightly populated jungle highlands. About 60 percent of South Vietnam consists of uplands—hills, plateaus, and mountains that stretch from the northernmost point at the seventeenth parallel to within about fifty miles of Saigon in the south. These highlands are thickly vegetated and very thinly populated. Fewer than 5 percent of South Vietnam's 17 million people lived in these mountainous jungles. The remaining 95 percent inhabited the densely populated lowlands that comprise 40 percent of South Vietnam.[12]

The American literature of the war is full of testimony about the extraordinary heat of South Vietnam. In *A Rumor of War*, for example, Philip Caputo writes: "The mercury level might be 98 degrees one day, 110 the next, 105 the day after that; but these numbers can no more express the intensity of that heat than the reading on a barometer can express the destructive power of a typhoon." In fact, the temperatures he offers as typical were well above the yearly average: about 80 degrees along the coast and in the southern lowlands, and a few degrees cooler in the highlands. The average, however, is greatly lowered by the rainy season. During the dry season, temperatures above 100 were by no means unusual. While many accounts of the war rightly emphasize the sweltering heat of Vietnam, rainy seasons could be shockingly cold. Sometimes, up in the highlands during monsoon, it got so cold, Michael Herr reported, "we were freezing, you could barely piss on those hilltop firebases."[13]

The seasonal winds—the monsoons—have a profound impact on the Vietnamese climate. The summer monsoon, lasting roughly from April to October, brings heavy rain throughout most of South Vietnam. In some of the northern sections of South Vietnam, however, the rainy season comes during the winter monsoon—November to March—when the wind drives rain into the land from the South China Sea. The rainy season varies, but throughout Vietnam the year is divided into two extremes of wet and dry. Annual rainfall ranges between 70 and 120 inches (78 inches in Saigon, 115 in Hue, for example). Compare these numbers with average rainfall in some American cities—New York (41 inches), Chicago (34), Miami (60), Denver (12), and Portland (43). The contrast is all the more striking considering that most of the rain in Vietnam falls during only half the year. The seasonal rain and cloud cover posed enormous obstacles to the American military with its heavy reliance on helicopter mobility and close air support.[14]

South Vietnam was, then, the geopolitical battleground. Vietnamese revolutionaries viewed it as an artificial puppet state held in place by American imperialism. The American government characterized South Vietnam as a free and independent nation struggling for democracy. Never fully understanding—or at least never publicly acknowledging—the depth of indigenous hostility toward the South Vietnamese government and U.S. intervention, American policymakers always attributed communism in the south to northern aggression. The figurative maps they carried in their heads were full of red arrows slashing from north to south, an utter contrast to the Vietnamese image of their nation as a long, but unbroken, carrying pole. One of those American maps is vividly described in Stephen Wright's novel, *Meditations in Green*. Wright, who served with an intelligence unit in Vietnam, has an army captain brief American troops about to fight in Vietnam. The captain replaces the usual red tide metaphor with an explicitly sexual one:

> Gentlemen, a map of Southeast Asia. This stub of land (Tap) hanging like a cock off the belly of China is the Indochinese peninsula. . . . The Republic of Vietnam [South Vietnam] occupies the area roughly equivalent to the foreskin, from the DMZ at the seventeenth parallel down along the coast of the South China Sea to the Mekong River in the delta. Today this tiny nation suffers from a bad case of VD or, if you will, VC. . . . What we are witnessing, of course, is a flagrant attempt on the part of the communist dictatorship of Hanoi [North Vietnam] to overthrow, by means of armed aggression, the democratic regime in Saigon [South Vietnam]. . . . Now I know the majority of you could give a good goddamn about the welfare of these people. . . . Believe me, this is a rather narrow shortsighted view. Consider the human body. What happens if an infection is allowed to go untreated? The bacteria spread, feeding on healthy tissue. . . . A sore on the skin of even a single democracy threatens the health of all. . . . Certainly we seek no personal gain; we're just pumping in the penicillin, gentlemen, just pumping in the penicillin.[15]

WAR BY NUMBERS

Attrition was the central American strategy; search and destroy was the principle tactic; and the enemy body count was the primary measure of progress. American soldiers were sent into the villages, rice paddies, and jungles of South Vietnam as hunters. The object of the hunt was to kill Vietnamese communists, as many as possible. That was the overwhelming, even obsessive, focus of the American mission. Every other pursuit paled in comparison with the effort to "find, fix, and finish" the enemy. The strategy was rudimentary attrition, the gradual, systematic grinding down of enemy forces. America sought to prevent communism in South Vietnam by killing communists. There was no concerted effort to gain and hold territory or to protect civilian populations, nor was the "other war"—the campaign to win the political support of the people—ever more than a secondary and largely ineffective feature of American intervention. Rather, the foundation of American policy was the premise that communism would fade away in direct proportion to the number of communist soldiers killed.

Attrition, however, was actually a strategy by default. The initial goal of U.S. military policy in Vietnam was not to wear away the enemy gradually but to annihilate it as fast as possible. Strategies designed to annihilate enemy forces had been the main thrust of American military thinking since the Civil War. Beginning in the mid-1950s, American advisers trained South Vietnamese troops for offensive combat. As historian Ronald Spector has well documented, most of the army training was conventional rather than antiguerrilla and gave no heed to the social and political sources of revolution. According to the official Marine Corps history of the Vietnam War from 1954 to 1964, the primary American mission in those years was to inject an aggressive spirit into the Vietnamese troops. Americans believed the Vietnamese had become passive under the heavy-handed domination of the French military.

From the outset of their experience with the Vietnamese Marine Corps, the Marine advisors perceived that a strong defensive orientation seemed to pervade every echelon of the small service. Most Americans, including U.S. Army advisors who were encountering similar difficulties with the Vietnamese Army, agreed that this "defensive psychology" was a by-product of the long subordination of the Vietnamese National forces to the French High Command. . . . the French tended to frustrate the development of the Vietnamese military forces by assigning them static security tasks rather than offensive missions. . . .

[From 1955 to 1959] The Marine advisors . . . undertook to adjust the orientation of the entire Vietnamese Marine Corps . . . through continuous emphasis on offensive training.[16]

Even in the early 1960s, when civilian and military leaders talked a great deal about counterinsurgency and "special warfare," implying that the United States would defeat the communists at their own game, the actual tactics were most often conventional efforts to engage the enemy in open, set-piece battles. However, neither South Vietnamese nor American forces proved capable of getting the Revolutionary Forces to fight on their terms. The results were endless, often fruitless patrols in search of the ever elusive guerrillas. The Americans often attributed the South Vietnamese failures to engage the enemy to factors like poor leadership, low morale, high desertion rates, cowardice, corrupt officers, or bad (French) training. Yet, the Americans, even at their most aggressive, often had just as hard a time initiating firefights. The enemy could not be annihilated if it could not be found.

The term *search and destroy* was coined in 1965 to describe missions aimed at flushing the Viet Cong out of hiding. Yet such operations had been a staple of American advisers and South Vietnamese troops from 1959 to 1964. The only fundamental differences between the American military approach of 1954–64 and 1965–70 were in the identities of the soldiers and the intensity of the warfare. In the early years most operations were carried out by South Vietnamese troops (with a few thousand American troops and advisers, mounting to 23,000 by 1964). The engagements were less frequent and the casualties lighter than in later years, but the terms of battle were established in embryo. From 1965 to 1970, U.S. troops carried out the lion's share of the offensive combat, with South Vietnamese forces primarily acting in a defensive capacity. During the period of "Vietnamization" (1970–75) there was a gradual return to the first stage, with Americans primarily directing the action from backstage and the South Vietnamese most involved in combat. The actors changed, but the script remained fundamentally the same.[17]

Gen. William Westmoreland, commander of American forces from 1964 to 1968, was the most important architect of U.S. military strategy during the crucial years of American escalation. By saturating the Vietnamese countryside with patrols of American ground troops on search-and-destroy missions, he believed the United States could force the communists out of hiding. Once flushed into the open, the enemy could be engaged by U.S. forces in big-unit, set-piece battles in which superior American firepower could be "brought to bear" with devastating impact. By 1966, if not sooner, even Westmoreland began to realize that a strategy of annihilation was not possible in Vietnam. The enemy simply would not agree to fight in the open, at least not often enough to hope for a rapid deterioration of their forces. Attrition was, Westmoreland concluded, the next best option, and in the absence of a full-scale invasion of North Vietnam or the use of atomic weapons, he thought it the only option. The United States, he argued, would have to grind down the enemy over time, gradually wearing away at their resources and their will to fight.[18]

According to Westmoreland and major American policymakers, this approach would "attrite" enough communists to produce at least one of the following results: (1) The Revolutionary Forces would lose more people than they could replace, and their war-making capacity would be crippled; (2) High death tolls would so demoralize the enemy that he would sue for peace on terms favorable to the United States; (3) Aggressive warfare would at least buy time for the South Vietnamese government to consolidate its power and improve its own capacity to resist communism.[19]

Though Westmoreland embraced attrition as the next best thing to annihilation, the tactics remained unchanged. In 1968, however, West-moreland tried to put an end to the phrase *search and destroy*. John Daly of Voice of America had alerted Westmoreland that the term had become "distorted" by critics of the war. *Search and destroy* was giving the wrong impression, Daly argued. It made the American policy sound brutal and without a higher purpose than killing. This news came as a shock to Westmoreland: "Since it is always the basic objective of military opera-tions to seek and destroy the enemy and his military resources, I saw nothing contradictory or brutal about the term, yet as the months passed, many people, to my surprise, came to associate it with aimless searches in the jungle and the random destroying of villages and other property."[20] Therefore, Westmoreland decided to keep the tactic but to polish up its associations by changing the name. He ordered military personnel to stop using the term *search and destroy* to describe American combat missions. Instead, they were to be called *sweeping operations* or *reconnaissance in force* or *search and clear*. The name changed, but the tactic remained the same.[21]

No measure of success was as important to the military command as the enemy body count. Competitions were held between American units to produce the highest "box score" of enemy KIAs or the best "kill ratio" (the most enemy killed in relation to American casualties). Some units even awarded a few days of R&R to soldiers who had an exceptional number of "confirmed kills," and infantry officers knew their opportuni-ties for advancement were largely dependent on the size of the body counts they reported. The pressures and incentives produced wild infla-tions of the statistics. One of the most thorough studies of this subject found that American commanders exaggerated enemy body counts by 100 percent.[22]

To the military command the body count was the most important statis-tic, but the effort to quantify the war pervaded every aspect of the American military presence in Vietnam. David Halberstam captures this emphasis in a description of a military briefing given to Secretary of Defense Robert McNamara:

One particular visit seemed to sum it up: McNamara looking for the war to fit his criteria, his definitions. He went to Danang in 1965 to check on the Marine progress there. A Marine colonel in I Corps had a sand table showing the terrain and patiently gave the briefing: friendly situation, enemy situation, main problem. McNamara watched it, not really taking it in, his hands folded, frowning a little, finally interrupting. "Now, let me see," McNamara said, "if I have it right, this is your situation," and then he spouted his own version, all in numbers and statistics. The colonel, who was very bright, read him immediately . . . and without changing stride, went on with the briefing, simply switching his terms, quantifying everything in numbers and percentages, percentages up, percentages down, so blatant a performance that it was like a satire.[23]

The statistical evidence upon which the American military measured its progress in Vietnam was indeed the appropriate subject of satire. Though McNamara did as much as anyone to promote a narrowly technocratic approach to the war, most policymakers shared his faith that the complexities of the war could be reduced to simple statistics, that victory was merely a matter of improving the numbers. Thus, every act or event deemed relevant to the American cause was quantified and duly recorded, or to put it differently, if an event could not be quantified, it was simply not considered relevant. But virtually everything that could be counted was— the number of bombs dropped, sorties flown, tunnels destroyed, rounds fired, propaganda leaflets dispersed, pounds of rice confiscated, equipment lost, bars of soap distributed, and so on. The command chronologies and after-action reports are filled with long lists of these figures. The numbers appear without comment or emphasis, statistics on candy bars and ponchos appearing alongside numbers of refugees "generated" or wounded soldiers evacuated.

There was in all of the quantification a laughable pretense of precision. Could, for example, a battalion really know that it had lost exactly fifty-two tent pins on an operation? Even if such figures were accurate, which of them is truly important, and in what larger context might we understand their significance? Such questions were hardly, if ever, asked.[24]

Even the other war, the war to "win the hearts and minds" of the Vietnamese people, was evaluated according to the crudest measurements. Complicated questions about political loyalties and beliefs were reduced to questions about the number of schoolhouses built or toothbrushes distributed. The numbers issued by those involved in the other war (variously known as "pacification," or "civil affairs," or "revolutionary development") always implied that the political affiliations of civilians could be measured simply by how many goods or services were supplied to them by the Americans or the South Vietnamese government. As William Gibson has argued persuasively, while the U.S. military effort was focused entirely on the "production of death," the "other war" was devoted to the "production and distribution of commodities." Neither approach addressed the fundamental social, economic, and political problems that underlay the Vietnamese revolution.[25]

Of course, for all the rhetorical emphasis given to the other war or pacification, it always took a back seat to the shooting war. A study of the last five months of 1966, for example, found that 95 percent of all combat battalions were devoted to search-and-destroy operations. The task of generating political support for the government of South Vietnam fell largely to the ARVN—an institution notorious for producing just the opposite through its routine abuse of the peasantry and its pervasive corruption. The American pacification program grew vastly in size and expense as the war continued, but the major thrust of its activities was limited to the distribution of billions of propaganda leaflets and massive amounts of various goods (soap, towels, bandages, TV sets—500,000 of them). Another major pacification program was devoted not to winning hearts and minds but to eliminating those identified as belonging to the enemy. This was the Phoenix program, an operation to create a network of spies and informers to identify members of the Viet Cong "infrastructure" (the U.S. term for villagers who offered vital support to the Revolutionary Forces). Once members of this infrastructure were fingered, they were captured, interrogated, and/or assassinated. Phoenix, according to many accounts, was responsible for some 20,000 assassinations.[26]

In fighting the other war, the United States spent an enormous amount of its time and resources seeking to quantify the political affiliations of the Vietnamese people. In 1966 Robert Kromer, chief of Civil Operations and Revolutionary Development, instituted a statistical survey called the Hamlet Evaluation System (HES), claiming to offer a sophisticated measurement of the political control asserted by both the South Vietnamese government and the Revolutionary Forces. The very complexity of the system gave it respectability among American leaders. The evaluations were based on eighteen criteria and were broken down into five categories (A-E) of governmental control of the population. Hamlets ranked A and B were deemed "secure," meaning that the South Vietnamese government was thought to have political control over the people of those hamlets. Category C was "relatively secure," and categories D and E were "contested." Hamlets in the final category were controlled by the Revolutionary Forces. Just as pressure for high body counts led to gross inflation of relevant statistics, so too the hamlet evaluations proved farcical. American district advisers supplied the data upon which the evaluations were made, and they quickly learned that their bosses at headquarters expected reports of progress. Also, included under "secure" population were millions of Vietnamese peasants who had been driven off their land by American military policy. These refugees moved from hamlets into large refugee camps, to shantytowns near big American bases, or into the cities. This forced urbanization did not reflect a growing control of the rural countryside by the GVN, and it certainly did not reflect a greater loyalty of the people toward the government. But according to HES, the United States and its GVN allies were winning the political war for the hearts and minds of the Vietnamese people.[27]

In truth, these statistics, like the body count, simply offered the illusion of progress and control. They were a surrogate for genuine understanding and mastery. To count the war, to break it down into quantifiable units, seemed to provide a sense of clarity and order about a war that was truly baffling and confusing. Rather than admit their lack of real control or understanding, Americans looked for new measurements or "improved" statistics. If the numbers did not fit, they could always be fudged. It was easier to change numbers than to change reality.

The effort to establish some nominal order and control over the war is suggested in the very names of American military operations. They evoke American history and American places: Operation Prairie, Operation New York, Operation Paul Revere, Enterprise, Apache Snow, Yellowstone, Kentucky. The names are different, but as you read through operational histories of the war, almost all of them sound alike. They have no distinct or memorable characteristics, no geographic order, no apparent connection to what came before or after, and no meaningful beginning and end. One soon learns that three, four, five, perhaps dozens of American operations were conducted *in the same area at different times*. The only differences between them might be the frequency and intensity of combat. If there was heavy fighting and high enemy casualties, the operation was proclaimed a success; operations resulting in little combat were downplayed. But whether or not a particular operation actually affected the political affiliations of the Vietnamese people or significantly altered the ability or willingness of the opposition to fight on were questions never seriously engaged.[28]

Twelve miles south of Danang, Go Noi island is locked between the serpentine branches of the Ky Lam River. This island, about five miles long and two miles wide, was the setting of at least nine marine operations between 1965 and 1969: Georgia, Macon, Stone, Newcastle, Shellbyville, Auburn, Allen Brook, Meade River, and Pipestone Canyon. The history of warfare on the island did not begin in 1965, however. Le Ly Hayslip grew up in Ky La, a village on Go Noi, from her birth in 1949 until 1965. As is clear from her extraordinary memoir, *When Heaven and Earth Changed Places*, Go Noi was the site of numerous battles dating back to the war against the French and continuing throughout the early 1960s. James Webb's novel, *Fields of Fire*, is also set largely on Go Noi, where he dramatizes intense hostility between the marines and the villagers in the late 1960s.[29]

In Operation Pipestone Canyon (1969), marine engineers leveled the island with plows and bulldozers. Similar efforts had been a part of previous operations, but none was so systematic. Having tried for years without success to rid the island of Revolutionary Forces (destroying many villages in the process), the marines decided finally to remove every person and knock down everything on the island. The after-action report emphasized the positive: the island was clear, the mission accomplished. Yet even amid the official optimism one finds an ominous note: "Go Noi Island had been converted from a densely populated, heavily wooded area to a barren wasteland; a plowed field. In that, the operation was a success. Continued defoliation of the island and continuous sweeping and use of Route 4 will be necessary to maintain denial of these areas to enemy forces." In other words, to keep Go Noi free of Revolutionary Forces would require, even in the wake of this massive destruction, permanent occupation by the Americans. On the last day of Pipestone Canyon, after months and years of patrolling, plowing, bombing, and defoliating, when at last the island was indeed a "barren wasteland," some marine vehicles hit two land mines. Three Americans were killed and seven more were "severely wounded."[30]

Far from asserting strategic control over the war, or revealing a clear strategic design, American military "operations" were often merely artificial labels attached to a set of patrols occurring in a given place and time. In fact, many operations were not planned or named until after a significant military engagement had begun. For example: The Viet Cong or the North Vietnamese Army ambush an American unit out on a nameless patrol in the countryside. Significant casualties occur on both sides. American commanders, hearing about the action over field radios, order the field officer to "maintain contact with the enemy" until additional troops and fire support can be brought to the area. Having thus engaged the enemy in battle, the command announces that the patrol that walked into the ambush was the beginning of an operation. Yet, as Marine Corps historian Jack Shulimson explains, the initial fighting often had nothing to do with American planning.

> The writing of the Macon operation plan, *like so many operations in Vietnam*, was completed 24 hours *after* initial contact had been made. The 3d Marine Division did not publish its [operational] order until 1545 on the 5th [of July 1966], but its mission statement read: "Commencing 4 July 1966 3d MarDiv conducts multi-bn S&D opn [multibattalion search-and-destroy operation] in An Hoa area. . . ." It was not until the early hours of 6 July, that the 9th Marines, the regiment responsible for the operation, issued orders to its subordinate battalions.[31]

By dating operations retroactively, firefights actually initiated by the enemy appeared to be the result of American design.

It is not surprising that this became a common procedure. After all, when the military command did plan big operations in advance of initial contact with the enemy, the enemy might simply leave the area, and thousands of American soldiers would spend weeks fruitlessly searching for them. A classic case of this sort was the army's Operation Thayer. In September 1966 almost two brigades of the First Cavalry Division were deployed in the rice-growing areas along the Soui Ca and Kim Son rivers in Binh Dinh province. Intelligence reports indicated that Viet Cong and perhaps even NVA troops would be in the area in large numbers during the fall harvest to recruit local support and resupply themselves with food. Accompanying the First Cav on Operation Thayer was the famous military historian S. L. A. "Slam" Marshall. He pronounced the operation a complete "bust." "The campaign was incredibly boring, wasteful, and exhausting. Rarely in warfare has so much artillery been brought up to shoot at clay pipes. . . . Either the enemy was not there or, if present, was so adroit and clever that American genius and aggressiveness must be rated as something less than we believe."[32]

Marshall decided not to publish the 20,000 words he wrote about the operation. The main reason seems clear enough. He did not want to provide material that might be used to support what he called the antiwar "kiddies' game." However, in his fairly lengthy effort to justify his exclusion of Operation Thayer from his book, *Vietnam: Three Battles*, Marshall himself touches on criticisms that might well be applied to the war as a whole: "Operation Thayer did not make sense to the soldiers who dealt with its stresses for almost one month. How then could others possibly get it in perspective. In the course of the operation, many men spent their energy in vain endeavor. A few died. Quite a few more were wounded. The Division's losses from malaria and accidental wounds became more grievous."[33]

Marshall avoided a fuller account not only because he was an enthusiastic supporter of the American war in Vietnam but because he did not know how to write about a war so apparently plotless and pointless. Not able or willing to see the fundamental futility of America's effort in Vietnam (never mind the question of its justice) nor to see the decided strategic advantage of the opposition, Marshall can only find in operations like Thayer a mass of boring details. "There is neither epic tragedy nor comic relief. Point is more lacking than plot. Hence it cannot be divided into acts and no one scene, taken by itself, stands serious examination."[34]

To his credit, Marshall does express his incredulity at the body count of 221 Viet Cong KIA claimed by the First Cavalry commanders for Operation Thayer. He knew from firsthand observation that the figure was a complete fabrication. Still, he leaves Thayer to devote most of his pages to Operation Irving. Unlike Thayer, Irving was not intended to generate any combat; it was simply a minor maneuver to secure a coastal strip of land. Yet, a "fluke shot" led to a major engagement. Marshall describes it as "an unexpected and spectacular success," basing his evaluation on the casualty figures: the Americans reported an enemy body count of 1,000. However, Marshall fails to perceive the significance of the fluke shot: Americans rarely held the strategic or tactical initiative.[35]

ON THEIR TERMS

There is no doubt that American forces in Vietnam managed to kill a great many South Vietnamese guerrillas and North Vietnamese soldiers. Even allowing for inflated body counts, Revolutionary Forces suffered at least

500,000 deaths. By contrast, American and South Vietnamese forces lost about 280,000 people (58,000 Americans). If victory were determined by this criteria alone, the outcome of the war would have been different.[36]

Revolutionary Forces, however, did not measure victory by the body count. They measured their success by the support they received from the South Vietnamese population and by the will of each side to continue fighting. The PLAF continued to draw replacements from South Vietnamese villages, and Hanoi sent a steady stream of well-trained soldiers from the north. Most significantly, the losses they sustained did not devastate morale. They were encouraged to fight on, in part, because they knew they controlled the terms of battle. They often took heavy losses, but they usually did so at times and places of their own choosing. This enhanced the morale of their forces and their stature among the civilian population. Conversely, as years passed and attrition failed to achieve its goals, the morale of American and South Vietnamese troops was severely undermined.

In 1972 the U.S. Joint Chiefs of Staff concluded that "three-fourths of the battles [in Vietnam] are at the enemy's choice of time, place, type, and duration." One of the earliest studies of the subject was done in 1966 by Assistant Secretary of Defense Alain Enthoven. Based on analysis of fifty-six firefights, Enthoven found that 79 percent of the engagements were initiated by the Revolutionary Forces (table 7). Another study found that the Viet Cong and NVA determined the time and place of battle in 88 percent of all combat engagements.[37]

American forces went on countless search-and-destroy patrols throughout the Vietnamese countryside, but most of the time the search proved futile. Even the extraordinary escalation in American forces from 23,000 in 1964 to almost 500,000 by the end of 1967 did not give the United States a tactical advantage. It did cause an increase in the total level of combat, and casualties went up on both sides; but it did not improve the ability of American forces to engage the enemy at will. In 1967–68, when U.S. ground offensives were at a peak, less than 1 percent of American combat patrols resulted in contact with the enemy. When such operations did produce a firefight, it was almost always because the Viet Cong or NVA decided to attack the Americans. As one American soldier told *Time* magazine in 1965 (after an enormous, 5,000-man operation around Ben Cat produced little combat), "You go out on patrol maybe twenty times or more and nothin', just nothin'. Then, the twenty-first time, zap, zap, zap, you get hit—and Victor Charlie fades into the jungle before you can close

Table 7. Types of Combat and Tactical Initiative, 1966

Type of Combat	Percentage of Total
Ambushes: surprise attacks on moving enemy unit from concealed positions	
VC/NVA ambush U.S. forces	49
U.S. forces ambush VC/NVA	9
Probes and wave assaults: organized attacks on known enemy static positions	
VC/NVA initiate	30
U.S. forces initiate	5
Chance engagement: both sides surprised	7
Totals: VC/NVA initiate combat	79
U.S. forces initiate combat	14
Neither side initiates	7

Source: Derived from Alain Enthoven, Memorandum for Secretary of Defense, 4 May 1967, in *The Pentagon Papers*, 4:462.

with him."[38] Thus, the most common forms of battle in Vietnam were ambushes and wave attacks initiated by the Revolutionary Forces.

What gave the Revolutionary Forces the ability to control the terms of battle so decisively? Was it a matter of troop levels? Were the American and South Vietnamese forces outnumbered? Also, how do you count the number of "enemy troops" in a revolutionary war in which thousands of peasants served as part-time guerrillas? These questions were raised in a 1982 CBS documentary, "The Uncounted Enemy," charging the American military command (Gen. William Westmoreland in particular) with intentionally lowering its estimates of enemy troop levels in order to show progress in meeting the goals of attrition. During the war, the U.S. military always insisted that enemy force levels were no higher than 300,000. The documentary pointed out, however, that CIA analyst Sam Adams had reported, as early as 1966, that a more accurate count was at least a half-million.[39] At first the CIA hierarchy supported Adams's estimate, but when Westmoreland rejected the higher figure, the CIA backed down, failing to press their dissent. Adams's reports were filed in dustbins, and the military command continued to announce enemy troop levels at under 300,000. In the fall of 1967 Westmoreland returned to the United States and announced that the U.S. military was making great progress in Vietnam: "The ranks of the Viet Cong are thinning. . . . The end begins to come into view." To support his optimistic appraisal, he claimed that enemy troop levels had actually declined from 285,000 in 1966 to 242,000 in 1967. At the same time Adams was finding evidence that made even 500,000 enemy troops look like a conservative estimate. By 1967 he estimated enemy strength at 600,000.[40]

The CBS documentary claimed Westmoreland was personally responsible for deceiving the nation about the war he commanded. Westmoreland sued CBS for libel. He dropped the suit well into the trial after two of his former top aides—Gen. Joseph McChristian and Col. Gains Hawkins—testified that it had been standard procedure under Westmoreland's command to reject any estimates of enemy strength that exceeded 300,000. Underlying the important issue of Westmoreland's responsibility for this gross deception is the equally important question of how enemy strength was determined. The debate over which Vietnamese were to be included among the enemy order of battle revealed fundamentally different conceptions about the nature of the war.[41]

Westmoreland rejected the higher estimates of enemy troop strength on the ground that they included "irregular" guerrillas—people who directly participated in the revolution but who did so in the context of their civilian lives. They might farm all day but plant booby traps at night. Westmoreland's figures excluded these "part-time guerrillas" and included only "main force" units. In part, the exclusion reflected wishful thinking, the desire to define the enemy as beatable. But it also reflected his conviction that the war was not fundamentally a "people's war" waged by ordinary Vietnamese civilians but a conventional, big-unit war that would be won by the side that brought the most power to bear in large, set-piece battles. To argue, as Sam Adams did, that irregular guerrillas ought to be included as part of the enemy order of battle was considered truly subversive within the American command, not only because it produced high numbers, but because it offered substantive evidence that the Viet Cong and NVA were fighting a "people's war," a revolution with wide popular support.[42]

During the libel trial, Westmoreland admitted that the figure of 500,000 was a closer reflection of real enemy strength than the lower estimates he insisted upon during the war. However, he continued to defend his exclusion of irregular guerrillas by insisting that their significance would have been exaggerated and misunderstood by politicians and the public. "The people in Washington are not sophisticated enough to understand and evaluate this thing, and neither was the media," he argued. Apparently the sophisticated way to understand the presence of several hundred thousand irregular guerrillas who were willing to sacrifice their lives to drive Americans out of their country was to think of them as a secondary consideration, a minor nuisance. In fact, however, the American military was continually thwarted by various levels of what it called the Viet Cong infrastructure (VCI). While these local supporters of the revolution were excluded from official counts of enemy forces, they were certainly a preoccupation of American combat missions. Countless operational assignments for search-and-destroy missions urged American soldiers to "root out the VCI" in village X or village Y. As much as the military command might deny its significance, the widespread local support for the full-time main forces of the NLF and NVA was the central disadvantage faced by American soldiers.[43]

The willful repression of efforts to measure the extent and variety of support for the revolution throughout South Vietnam was directly linked to the widespread belief among military strategists that successful efforts to suppress revolutions require that the government forces have an overwhelming troop advantage. Many thought the advantage should be 10 to 1, and even the most optimistic counterrevolutionaries believed the government required at least a 3 to 1 superiority in military forces. If the CIA estimates of an enemy force of 500,000 had been accepted, the American military command could claim no troop advantage at all unless it included the South Vietnamese forces. Of course these forces were routinely used in total counts of "Allied Forces," but there was always duplicity in American claims that their South Vietnamese allies represented a powerful fighting force. For much of the private rationale for American escalation in ground forces was the conviction among American military and political policymakers that the South Vietnamese forces were (however large in size) almost completely unreliable and ineffectual. Even if the United States included among its own allied forces every possible person (including the 400,000 members of the South Vietnamese "Popular" and "Regional" Forces who did not participate in offensive combat missions), the total force level for the years 1965–72 was never higher than 1.4 million. Thus, if it were admitted that opposition forces numbered a half-million or more, the U.S. and South Vietnamese governments could not even claim a 3 to 1 troop advantage. That is, they could not even match the minimum force ratio required by the most sanguine enthusiasts of military counterinsurgency.[44]

In fact, even if enemy strength were measured solely by the official estimates of its main force combat units (200,000 to 300,000), the U.S./GVN forces outnumbered the opposition only by the crudest calculation. If one counted the actual number of U.S./GVN troops who were involved in combat missions in comparison to Revolutionary Forces, the supposed advantage of the former would disappear. The allied forces had an enormous rear echelon. The ratio of supporting troops to combat troops has never been established precisely, but it was at least 5 to 1, and some sources put it at 10 to 1. In other words, for every American or GVN troop out on a combat mission there were at least five soldiers on a rear base working as mechanics, cooks, clerk-typists, truck drivers, and so on. The Revolutionary Forces, on the other hand, had a relatively small rear echelon. Living off the land and the people, most of the main force units of the PLAF and PAVN were actively engaged in combat.[45]

The discussion of troop strength and force levels is important because there has been so much deception and confusion surrounding it. This ambiguity invites an even greater misunderstanding, however—the idea that the war was lost by the United States simply because it did not commit enough combat troops (actual numbers of troops committed are shown in table 8). There is, of course, no way of knowing what might have been if the United States had acted differently. But there is persuasive evidence that the escalation of the U.S. military presence did far more to antagonize the Vietnamese people than it did to win their commitment to the South Vietnamese government.

The United States was indeed outnumbered in Vietnam, but not by troops so much as by the political opposition of millions of ordinary Vietnamese civilians. When American forces entered Vietnamese villages in search of communist guerrillas, the Americans were defeated not because they were met by overwhelming numbers of enemy forces armed to the teeth. Rather, they were defeated because they were met by villagers who rarely supported their effort to root out the guerrillas. We may never know precisely what portion of South Vietnamese supported the revolution, and to what extent, but even the South Vietnamese government conceded (in 1964) that 4 to 5 million people (of a population of about 17 million) supported the National Liberation Front.[46] Marine Col. William Corson, who served in Vietnam from 1965 to 1967, has written that "more

Table 8. United States Troop Levels in South Vietnam, 1960–1972

Year	Number of Troops
1960	900
1961	3,200
1962	11,300
1963	16,300
1964	23,300
1965	185,300
1966	385,300
1967	465,600
1968	536,000
1969	475,000
1970	334,600
1971	156,800
1972	24,200

Source: Terry, *Bloods*, pp. 302–7.
Note: These figures are from the end of each year.

often than not [the Vietnamese peasant] hopes the Vietcong will win because he imagines a Vietcong victory will eradicate the conditions he currently faces. Our experience showed that the Vietnamese peasant will help the Vietcong when there is not too much risk of doing so and that in the great majority of cases the peasant considers it unthinkable to betray the Vietcong to the enemy."[47] Lacking political support, American forces opted increasingly for military force, force that further alienated Vietnamese peasants from the U.S.-backed regime in Saigon.

One of the most important forms of support villagers offered Revolutionary Forces was in the manufacture and placement of land mines and booby traps. The successful use of these hidden explosives required the widespread knowledge and participation of the civilian population. Not everyone helped to make them or place them, but most villagers knew where they were. The Viet Cong did not want villagers to step on the mines, since that would erode their influence among the people, so they taught villagers to recognize special markings indicating where the mines were placed. Perhaps nothing so convinced American soldiers of the fundamental hostility of the Vietnamese people toward American intervention than the simple fact that civilians rarely stepped on land mines yet almost always claimed to lack any knowledge that mines had been set in and around their villages.

One astute observer who spent many months with a marine infantry unit in 1966 wrote of American soldiers: "The enemy they hated, the enemy they feared the most, the enemy they found hardest to combat, was not the VC; it was mines."[48] By most estimates, they accounted for between one-fifth and one-fourth of all U.S. casualties. Extraordinary as this statistic is, hidden explosives were as significant for the demoralization they caused among the survivors as they were for the sheer number of casualties they claimed. The losses would come instantly and unexpectedly. A unit moves along in silence. Boom!! Now a man (or two or three . . .) is lying along the trail. A leg is missing (or an arm or a hand . . .). The survivors feel utterly helpless. There is nothing to do but watch the medics slap pressure bandages on gaping wounds or help to clear a landing zone for the medevac chopper. But the demoralization goes deeper. There is no enemy in sight, no one clearly responsible for setting the trap. Yet the men know that the local population was at least aware that the mines were present.[49]

Many Vietnamese became demolition experts. They constructed mines and booby traps from every imaginable material: tin cans, bottles, scrap metal, nails, or whatever was available. Much of the material was culled from garbage dropped by the U.S. military. Even the explosives used in these homemade devices often came from the United States, taken from unexploded bombs and artillery shells. There were plenty of these duds lying around the countryside. Less than 5 percent of American ordnance turned out to be duds, but the huge volume of firepower produced an average of 800 tons of duds per month.[50]

The duds were recharged and planted underground, in trees, in gates and hedges—anywhere Americans might be expected to travel. Not all Americans in Vietnam were equally vulnerable to mines, however. In the thinly populated highlands of central and northern South Vietnam, American soldiers and marines encountered relatively few mines. Because the movements of American troops in those areas were less frequent and predictable, it made little tactical sense for the Vietnamese opposition to plant many mines there. More to the point, in areas where there was not a large population, there were fewer local guerrillas to chart the movements of American troops and to participate in the construction and planting of mines. In the thickly settled lowlands of South Vietnam, however, mines and booby traps were planted in great numbers. Those American units that conducted their operations in the densely populated lowlands often found that mines, rather than enemy soldiers, were the greatest danger. For example: In one five-week period in 1966, a marine infantry company of the Ninth Marine Regiment (about 175 men), running patrols in the rice paddy region southwest of Danang, lost 68 men to mines (10 killed and 58 wounded). The wounds were serious. Only 4 of the wounded were able to return to duty. In that same five-week period, the company had only 3 casualties that were not caused by mines.[51] Also, the percentage of American casualties killed by mines went up during periods of less intense combat. For example, in July of 1969, when there was little combat in I Corps (the four northernmost provinces of South Vietnam), mines accounted for 41 percent of U.S. KIAs. When American troops suffered a great many losses to mines and, at the same time, failed to make direct contact with opposition forces, they became all the more frustrated and all the more ready to wreak their vengeance on the local population.[52]

In places like the Batangan Peninsula, where mines were commonplace, American infantrymen were tormented by the prospect of triggering an explosion. Some American infantrymen became extraordinarily skilled at spotting booby traps. They developed a keen eye for the hidden trip wire, the signs of digging in the earth, or the bent twigs and rock formations often left to signal to local Vietnamese where the hidden explosives had been planted. For example, on one operation a unit of marines discovered that booby traps were marked by nearby elephant grass that had been tied in a knot with the loop end pointing toward the trap.[53] But even the most alert soldiers could not spot every mine or booby trap. Many devices were simply too well concealed, and long patrols sapped the energy and concentration needed to avoid those mines that were visible. The knowledge that every step was a gamble filled American soldiers with anxiety and dread. They could not just resign themselves to the inevitability that mines would explode despite their caution. After all, if they triggered a mine, it might kill their buddies as well as themselves; so they sought to master what could not be mastered. As Tim O'Brien recounts:

> You try to second-guess the mine. Should you put your foot to that flatrock or the clump of weed to its rear? Paddy dike or water[?] . . . The moment-to-moment, step-by-step decision-making preys on your mind. The effect sometimes is paralysis. . . .
> Once in a great while we would talk seriously about the mines. "It's

more than the fear of death that chews on your mind," one soldier, nineteen years old, eight months in the field, said. "It's an absurd combination of certainty and uncertainty: the certainty that you're walking in mine fields, walking past the things day after day; the uncertainty of your every movement, of which way to shift your weight, of where to sit down."[54]

The Americans thought about the guerrillas in much the same terms as the mines. They, too, were extraordinarily well concealed. Often they, too, dwelled underground, both literally and figuratively. To American soldiers, Frances Fitzgerald writes, "it must have appeared that in Vietnam the whole surface of the earth rested like a thin crust over a vast system of tunnels and underground rooms." It is not a terribly exaggerated image. In virtually every hamlet there were dozens of trenches and underground storage rooms, often used by the people as shelter from U.S. bombs. In the hamlets supportive of the revolution, the undergrounds were as complex as ant hills, with thin tunnels running to deep underground rooms and connecting with the underground systems of neighboring hamlets, and with offshoots to openings in the jungle providing escape routes for the guerrillas. The most famous and well documented system of tunnels were those of Cu Chi, about thirty miles northwest of Saigon. This enormous underground network is notorious because it lay beneath more than Vietnamese hamlets; it lay right below the surface of a huge American base, the headquarters of the Twenty-fifth Infantry Division. Periodically a sniper would emerge from a hole in this underground and fire at an American soldier, disappearing before anyone knew what had happened.[55]

Concealment was central to the tactical advantage of the NLF and the NVA. Even in the unpopulated areas of South Vietnam, far from the underground tunnel complexes of the villages, main force units dug spider holes, trenches, and fortified bunkers for use as ambush sites when American units ventured into the "boonies." Ambushes sprung by the Revolutionary Forces accounted for about 50 percent of all the firefights in Vietnam (see table 7). The Americans would hit the ground and return fire, but most of the time they could not see the enemy. They fired in the direction of the enemy fire, at muzzle flashes, or at glimpses of movement in the underbrush. A character in John Del Vecchio's *The 13th Valley* says: "The whole time I been over here I never've seen a live gook. That's no shit. I been in the boonies seven months and I never've seen a live one. . . . I've seen maybe a hundred dead ones. I don't know if I ever shot any.

There's a good chance I may have but I never had any in my sights. Ya know how it is during a firefight. You just fire into the brush with everybody else. When it's all over, maybe there'd be a body."[56]

Not seeing the enemy was particularly unnerving to American soldiers since so much of the combat took place at close range. One of the key tactics of the Revolutionary Forces was to allow the Americans to approach as close as possible before opening fire. Not having a bottomless supply of ammunition, the rebels became masters of "fire control." That is, they tried to make each shot count, and firing at close range raised the chances of hitting the enemy without wasting ammunition. They also learned to make timely retreats, before U.S. forces could effectively unleash their enormous firepower. This was particularly the case among Viet Cong snipers or small guerrilla units for whom hit and run was the standard tactic. In thick jungle terrain, snipers could strike as quickly and unexpectedly as booby traps. An account from a U.S. infantry unit's routine patrol in 1969 is representative of hundreds like it: "A VC sniper hidden in the bush put an AK-47 practically at their point man's ear, shot him dead and ran off without anyone having seen him."[57]

The Revolutionary Forces also engaged in close combat because it discouraged American troops from calling in air support—bombing strikes, helicopter gunships, artillery, or naval gunfire. If enemy positions were within 100 meters, U.S. commanders were usually hesitant to call in air strikes, fearing that the bombs might hit American positions as well. Even at close range, however, Americans would often try to "walk in" supporting fire, calling in coordinates that were a safe distance away and gradually directing the artillery and air strikes to move closer toward the enemy positions. Sometimes U.S. troops would try to maintain contact with the enemy until just before the air strikes were due to arrive and then make a hasty retreat before the bombs fell. But the Vietnamese became very skillful at predicting when supporting fire would come and often made a hasty retreat of their own before bombs and artillery landed on their positions.[58]

The Revolutionary Forces also maintained the tactical initiative by striking the Americans at night and in foul weather, when it was more difficult (sometimes impossible) for U.S. forces to use jets and helicopters. For example, during the first half of 1968 fully 60 percent of the fighting done by the 101st Airborne Division occurred at night. The divisional commander, Gen. O. M. Barsanti, reported these nighttime engagements as American victories. "The success of the division's operation at night was evidenced by the fact that of the 7,128 enemy killed by the division between January and June [1968], 18.8 percent were made at night." Leaving aside the dubious claim that mere body counts are an adequate measure of success, how could he consider operations successful when 60 percent of the fighting produced only 19 percent of enemy losses?[59]

Most American commanders never publicly conceded that the Revolutionary Forces had either a tactical or a strategic advantage. After all, they argued, how could a smaller army without helicopters and bombers succeed against the mightiest technological power in the world? All the evidence indicated that no matter how much firepower was used or how many enemy were killed, the opposition continued to fight on, continued to draw support from north and south, and showed no signs of wearing down or buckling under. Still U.S. commanders insisted that their power would prevail. Countless military briefings included the standard refrain: "Our overwhelming superiority in mobility and firepower gives us a decided advantage!" Mobility and firepower: it would be hard to exaggerate the resonance and promise these words had for the American command in Vietnam. When all else failed, these ostensible advantages were celebrated as the final guarantors of American success.[60]

Drawing Fire and Laying Waste

The American fighting man in Vietnam is supported by the best that his country can offer. . . . He is swiftly moved into and out of combat. . . . He has a camera, transistor, hot meals and regular mail. If he is hit, he can be hospitalized in 20 minutes; if he gets nervous, there are chaplains and psychiatrists on call. It is little wonder that he fights so well, and quite comprehensible that his main concern in off-duty hours is aiding Vietnamese civilians.

– Time, *6 June 1967*

In 1965, when the First Cavalry Division entered the war, the American mass media was dazzled by the prospect of helicopter warfare. It was as if the foot soldier had become a military anachronism. The First Cav arrived in Vietnam with an enormous fleet of fancy new helicopters and full of talk about "air mobility." They even added *Airmobile* to their name: First Cavalry Division, Airmobile. It was a cavalry not of horses but of flying "birds." Soldiers would mount the choppers and zip in and out of combat, apparently liberated from the ancient plight of the common soldier—the miles of sweated marching. *Time* magazine celebrated the First Cavalry's new image with a purple encomium to the "First Team" and its vaunted mobility. "Freed by their choppers from the tyranny of terrain, the First Team can roam at will over blasted bridges, roadblocks, swollen rivers and jungle mountains to hit the V.C. from the northern tip of the nation to the delta."[1]

The First Cav had the best new choppers. Unlike those huge, lumbering Choctaws the marines were stuck with, the latest birds were the light, fast, versatile Hueys (the nickname was derived from the formal nomenclature: UH-series helicopters). They were used as troop carriers and medical evacuation helicopters (medevacs), and they were outfitted with every combination of machine gun, rocket launcher, and minigun to serve as gunships. In addition to the Hueys there were Loaches (the tiny, insectlike observation helicopters), Chinooks (large, double-bladed cargo helicopters—the CH-47), Skycranes (long, latticed helicopters designed to carry huge loads from suspended cables), and many other varieties. By the end of 1967 there were a total of 3,000 American helicopters in Vietnam.[2]

The military used slick, technological images to describe helicopter warfare. Troops brought in by chopper were "inserted" into landing zones. When the soldiers were flown out, they were "extracted." Troops deployed by helicopter at points surrounding a particular AO (area of operation) were enacting a tactic called "vertical envelopment." All of this suggested a surgical precision; troops jump in, do the job, and are quickly removed, off to their next operation.

For all the hype, the helicopters simply did not provide the great advantage American commanders claimed. For one thing, they made too much noise. Men could be moved quickly, but when they arrived at a potential battleground, the enemy was rarely caught off guard. The raspy buzz of distant helicopters, followed by a rhythmic whup-whup-whup as the choppers approached, signaled their location for miles around. It gave the opposition time to find cover, prepare ambushes, or, if they chose, simply to flee the area.

Furthermore, helicopters could not always penetrate the thick jungle terrain. Vertical envelopment might work well in an empty parking lot, but in the jungle it often required the laborious clearing of landing zones, thereby eliminating the element of surprise. Nor did helicopters provide much help with the military's highest goal—locating the enemy. The Revolutionary Forces usually moved at night, underground, or in thick jungle terrain, invisible from the air.

So American ground troops were given the task of finding the enemy on their own. In fact, most soldiers spent very little time in helicopters. Even the paratroopers of the First Cav spent most of their time doing what foot soldiers have always done: they walked, endlessly and heavily burdened.

HUMPING THE BOONIES

Operations often began by helicopter. Once inserted, however, soldiers typically patrolled on foot for at least a few days. Sometimes they remained out for a month at a time. Indeed, perhaps the best single image with which to synthesize the physical experience of the American combat soldier in Vietnam would be that of a column of men spaced about five yards apart; burdened with eighty-pound packs; wearing thick armored vests called flak jackets; carrying rifles, mortars, hundreds of rounds of ammunition, and three or four canteens; and patrolling on foot through jungles, mountains, or rice paddies. Among the infantrymen, the "grunts," this was known as "humping the boonies."[3]

Sometimes patrols left directly from base camps. The grunts would simply leave the perimeter on foot. For most combat missions, however, soldiers were transported by truck or helicopter to a drop-off point. The first moments following the drop-off, or insertion, were among the worst. When men were flown in by helicopter, there was always the awful uncertainty about the landing zone (LZ). Would it be hot or cold? A hot LZ meant the enemy would be firing as soon as the Americans arrived. But as long as the men were on the helicopters, there was some feeling of power and protection. The choppers shot over hills and treetops like roller coasters, jolting, popping, and thundering. It was at once terrifying and exhilarating. Approaching the LZ, the area was sometimes "prepped" with a barrage of firepower. Jets made low passes over the LZ, dropping napalm and 250-pound bombs. Then fifty or sixty howitzer rounds from nearby firebases might pour in. Flying ahead of the fleet of troop-carrying choppers was a Cobra gunship or two—sleek, fast helicopters outfitted with miniguns, firing thousands of rounds into the nearby tree lines. The troops landed in haste, the choppers hovering above the ground for a mere second or two while the men jumped out. Then the choppers flew off. Whether the LZ was hot or cold, the departure of the helicopters was a profound moment. The grunts felt an awful sense of abandonment and vulnerability. The sense of power and security the choppers could provide was gone. They were alone, sometimes out in the open under direct fire. In cold LZs the moment was less obviously harrowing but held its own special dread. The movement from chopper to rice paddy or elephant grass represented the radical movement between two worlds, one dominated by technology and American power, the other a world of peasant agriculture or utter wilderness. When the LZs were cold, as they usually were, an eerie silence filled the vacuum left by the exploding bombs and thundering choppers. Though the land lay blasted and burnt, it seemed surprisingly resilient, already pushing back in on the stranded Americans.[4] "When the helicopters flew off, a feeling of abandonment came over us. Charley Company was now cut off from the outside world. . . . The helicopters had made it seem familiar. Being Americans, we were comfortable with machines, but with the aircraft gone we were struck by the utter strangeness of this rank and rotted wilderness."[5]

From first light until they established their "night defensive perimeters" just before sunset, American grunts humped their gear and weapons through, over, around, and under unimaginable obstacles. In the lowlands they faced mile after mile of rice paddy. Because the dikes were frequently booby trapped by local guerrillas, Americans often avoided them, walking instead through the paddies. In the flooded paddies the grunts walked in water that was sometimes waist deep. Their boots sank into the muck underfoot. Each step was labored, as feet and legs were pulled out of the sucking sludge and buried anew. The soldiers kept their pant legs unbloused (not tucked into their boots) so the water would run straight down their legs rather than collecting inside like heavy, bulging water balloons. But the open pant legs left openings for leeches. The bloodsucking leeches crawled up legs and burrowed into flesh. During rest periods soldiers examined themselves for leeches and burned them off with the tips of their cigarettes.[6]

At least the lowlands were relatively flat and open. The highlands presented the additional burdens of excruciating climbs and dense, sometimes impassable foliage. Patrolling the hills and mountains of the highlands, the grunts had to endure endless changes of altitude. Patrols rarely set out to climb one hill and stop. Usually they moved along ridge lines. As soon as a peak was reached, the patrol would move back into a valley—up and down, up and down, all the while on the lookout for enemy movements. Humping through dense jungles, the point man had to use a machete to cut a path for the rest of the men. Sometimes it got so bad, and movement was so slow, units had to call in supply choppers to drop chain saws to help clear trails. Even when a trail was cut, men were always getting hung up on "wait-a-minute vines" that reached out like invisible snakes to snag passersby. When humping the boonies in the highlands, a patrol could take all day to cover one or two kilometers.[7]

Though the upper branches of Vietnam's triple canopy jungles served to block out much of the direct sunlight, the dense foliage locked in the humid heat, making the air feel like a sauna. As Tom Mayer puts it in his story "Weary Falcon," it was "like living at the bottom of the ocean." The odor was "dank, stale, airless, like a cellar that hasn't been opened for years." In the jungle "everything rotted. Clothes, webbing, flesh. Thorn scratches festered within a few hours and were open running sores or boils within days."[8]

In uncultivated fields throughout Vietnam grew tall, thick, elephant grass. It could reach a height of ten feet or more. Humping through these fields, grunts often lost sight of the man in front of them. Worse than that, the grass had razor-sharp edges. Pushing aside the grass with their arms, they received dozens of tiny "paper" cuts. These cuts, like any wound received in the tropical heat of Vietnam and away from the possibility of thorough cleansing, were highly susceptible to infection. Grunts were constantly developing oozing, infected sores.[9]

Foot problems were endemic. During the rainy season, feet stayed wet for days and weeks at a time. It was simply impossible to keep them dry for longer than a few minutes. The skin blistered, bubbled, and decayed. Those who developed "immersion foot" had it the worst. Their feet swelled terribly, and sometimes boots could only be removed by cutting them off. When socks were removed, hunks of skin often came off as well.[10]

The psychological burdens of humping were every bit as onerous as the physical. Among the worst, of course, were the nearly constant anxieties of walking into an ambush or stepping on a land mine. But there was an even more basic strain on the minds of American grunts: the lack of knowledge about where one was going, the kind of terrain to be encountered, and the length of time it would take. Grunts were generally not privy to even such fundamental information. It was like running a race without knowing its length. However close to the limits of endurance, soldiers were nevertheless always aware of the need to hold back—if at all possible—some reserve of energy against the uncertainty of the finish. Patrols were often extended or rerouted in response to changing intelligence reports. Thus, even those field officers who tried to keep their men informed frequently had to pass along changes in orders that meant hours of additional humping, reversals of direction, and further uncertainty. These "word changes" that "came down" from above could crush morale. Grunts dreaded them. New orders always seemed to bring bad news. Anxiety about word changes was greatest at the end of long patrols as units settled into their night positions. With the ordeal of a day's hump apparently over, a sergeant might yell, "Saddle up! We got a word change." The grunts would then have to pull on all their heavy equipment and march off to another unknown destination.

"What do you mean we ain't staying here—what are you passing that bum word for?"

"You heard it—they changed the word again."

"Well, just how fucking far we gotta hump today, anyway?"[11]

"When are they gonna tell us where we are going?"

"Christ, I don't know! They never tell us. Just shut up and get ready."[12]

In all wars, perhaps, infantrymen are among the least informed, rarely consulted about the decisions and plans for which their lives are risked. But in Vietnam this exclusion was particularly demeaning because the grunts felt themselves to be the only ones left uninformed. Even the Vietnamese civilians always seemed to know in advance where the Americans would be going. For example, in 1968 grunts from a First Infantry Division combat unit were told by Vietnamese prostitutes in Lai Khe about a major operation the Americans would soon begin. The grunts received this quite precise information before their officers even mentioned the upcoming mission.[13]

For Jim Mead, a former infantryman in the Ninth Infantry Division, the endless humping was "the hardest thing about doing a year in Nam." In 1984, at the age of thirty-six, he completed a high school equivalency program at the University of Massachusetts (Boston) and started college at night (during the day he worked at the post office). He wrote about his experiences in Vietnam for an English class:

Our first mission was at night. We were scared stiff. We headed into the jungle without any idea where we were going, or what we were doing. We kept walking for a couple of hours in the dark, praying we wouldn't lose sight of the guy in front of us, and getting lost. . . . On all missions we would not be told anything about where we were going, why we were going, or when we would end the mission.

We very rarely got any free time to relax. The average operation lasted 30 days or so. And during that time we did nothing but walk. We would just walk—no rhyme, no reason—from the crack of dawn until dusk. We would stop occasionally during the day for 5 to 10 minutes, no more! We would splurge for lunch, 15 minutes! Couple this with the [lack of] sleep—one hour sleep, one hour on guard, all night long—and you can imagine what shape we were in.

If we didn't run across a river or stream within a day or two, that was another problem, a bad one. You can't walk for days and days in that heat, with all of the equipment and ammo we had to carry, and not get dehydrated. I never fully understood the value of water until I got to 'Nam.

We could not be resupplied because the choppers couldn't land in the jungle. And they would be sitting ducks if they hovered over us, plus they would be giving away our position to the V.C. There were times when I seriously considered drinking my own urine. If we did manage to run across some water, we were supposed to fill our canteens, then add two purification tablets, shake well, and wait 5 or 10 minutes. What we actually did was, fill our canteens, grit our teeth together (to filter out bugs and whatever) and drink, and drink, and drink some more. Around the third canteen I would start thinking about the bugs that slipped by my teeth and stop. And then I would add the purification tablets.[14]

Combat aside, the humping itself produced thousands of casualties. In the hottest weather, heat casualties often exceeded those of combat. Most men recovered after a few days in a rear hospital and would then rejoin their units. A man had to be seriously sick to warrant a medevac, however. Commanders did not want to call in a helicopter unless there was a true emergency. It would slow down the patrol and reveal their position. In order to be evacuated as a heat casualty, a man had to be utterly unable to go on—vomiting, cramping, fainting, or moving quickly from heat exhaustion to heat stroke, too dehydrated even to sweat, temperature soaring, close to death.

We lack statistics on heat casualties for the entire war, but the figures from specific combat operations demonstrate how devastating the heat could be. In May 1969, for example, some marine units were humping the hills near the Demilitarized Zone (DMZ) on Operation Virginia Ridge. Bravo Company, First Battalion of the Third Marine Regiment, began the operation with 147 men. Within the first three days of the operation 65 men had to be carried out of the field by helicopter because they had become incapacitated by the heat. During the first twenty days of the operation Bravo Company had no combat. They did not walk into an ambush, did not step on a booby trap, were not fired on by snipers, and did not see a single enemy soldier. The only enemies were the heat and the humping. The war was reduced to a long, forced march. There seemed to be no way to avoid dehydration. Even when the resupply choppers brought in enough water to fill the canteens, the grunts simply could not carry enough water to sustain themselves in the steaming jungle heat. During one day's hump the men of Bravo Company became so thirsty they drank their own sweat:

> They wiped their foreheads and licked their fingers. They raised a hand and ran the other up the hairless inside of the forearm, then drank the trickle of sweat that coursed down over the webbing of skin connecting thumb and forefinger. But . . . two and three hours after, it didn't seem like such a good idea. The urea, dirty salt and carbon dioxide they took in produced dizziness and nausea. . . . But there was damn little logic left in Bravo Company. . . . They kept drinking their sweat, some hoping they could get sick enough to get a medevac bird back to an air-conditioned hospital ward for a couple days of rest.[15]

Minds and bodies so dulled by exhaustion no longer felt the sharp anxiety of potential combat, and when companies went for days or weeks without a firefight, the prospect of combat began to seem remote and unlikely. Many men began to believe that nothing, not even a firefight, could be worse than the humping. Some even hoped for a firefight to break the monotony of the hump and to inject a shot of adrenalin into their sluggish bodies. But it would take a real firefight to do that. When grunts were really exhausted, the random shots of a distant sniper did not quicken their pulse. Often enough they just kept humping and hoped the commander would not order them to chase the sniper. It would be less exhausting just to keep slogging away in the same direction. Cpl. Robert McMann describes how snipers could predict when Americans were unlikely to attack them: "They'd wait until we went through, then open up on us from the rear and from the flank. They had sense enough to know that a bunch of tired Marines humping their packs weren't going to run out there and charge into them. [We were] just too tired."[16] Another grunt put it this way: "You go long periods of time just patrol after patrol after patrol for months and months and you don't run into any gooks or anything; no booby-traps, no nothing, just patrol after patrol—nothing. Then all of a sudden one day somebody gets killed or hits a booby-trap and gets real messed up. You learn then that you have to be alert at all times, but it's hard to do when you go long times with not running into any gooks or anything."[17]

Consider this soldier's language: "running into." The ostensible purpose of the endless humping ("patrol after patrol after patrol") was to search out the enemy. The point was not to "run into" the enemy but to flush him out of hiding, drive him into a corner like a fox, and surround him with a wall of ground fire. Or was it?

DRAWING FIRE

To the American military command the central dilemma of the war was how to engage the enemy, how to make contact with the Viet Cong or the NVA, how to bring them to battle. The alleged purpose of the search side of search-and-destroy missions was for Americans to find the enemy before they found the Americans. In practice, however, the Americans rarely initiated combat. Nevertheless, by sending troops out into the bush, day after day, on endless patrols throughout the Vietnamese countryside, firefights did result. American commanders came to realize that American troops could engage the enemy by acting as bait, by moving around the country saying in effect, "Here we are, come and get us." Thus, the covert purpose of the patrolling was to expose grunts to the Revolutionary Forces, hoping to lure them into combat. If the Americans, serving as bait, could draw fire from the enemy, the elusive goal of contact would be achieved.

Official descriptions of American military policy insisted that American units were carrying out aggressive tactics in an effort to go on the offensive. As Westmoreland explained, a commander "wins no battles by sitting back waiting for the enemy to come to him."[18] American troops were often aggressive indeed, and enormous operations were launched in hopes of doing battle. All this aggression was not usually successful at driving the enemy into the open, however. In his novel, *Fields of Fire*, James Webb describes the real function of U.S. operations: "Back in the villes again. Somebody said it was an operation with a name, but it had its own name: Dangling the Bait. Drifting from village to village, every other night digging deep new fighting holes, every day patrolling through other villes, along raw ridges. Inviting an enemy attack much as a worm seeks to attract a fish: mindlessly, at someone else's urging, for someone else's reason."[19] This view is echoed throughout the Vietnam literature, often in the bitter manner of a character in *Better Times Than These*: "We ain't nothing but bait . . . worms dangling on a hook."[20]

When PLAF guerrillas or PAVN forces decided to attack the bait,

American commanders pushed their field officers to maintain contact. If the Vietnamese managed to flee after a short hit-and-run firefight, the Americans lost an opportunity to destroy the enemy. From the command's perspective, combat opportunities were all too rare and had to be taken advantage of whenever they arose. If contact was broken and the enemy disappeared, there would be no chance to hit them with the full weight of American firepower. Field commanders needed time not only to respond effectively with ground fire but also to call in supporting fire. The exact location of the enemy had to be determined and coordinates called in, and even then it might take fifteen minutes or longer for the bombing or shelling to begin. As often happened, when the Revolutionary Forces withdrew after a short firefight, the Americans were ordered to chase after them to maintain contact.[21]

Supporting fire was really a misnomer. Bombs, napalm, and rockets were central to American military strategy. Grunts were used to draw the enemy into fixed and identifiable positions for the jets and gunships and artillery. The military command celebrated the massive use of these expensive, sophisticated weapons as the best way to kill the greatest number of enemy soldiers while keeping American casualties to a minimum. This "capital intensive technowar" has been brilliantly analyzed by James William Gibson. For the war managers, as Gibson has shown, the war was often conceived as a kind of high-tech assembly line for the production of enemy bodies. The goal of attrition—the steady and systematic depletion of enemy forces—translated into a pressure on combat units to produce regular body counts that was not unlike that felt by factory workers and their supervisors to meet production quotas.[22]

To the working-class grunts humping the boonies, however, Vietnam did not feel especially high-tech. For them, most of the time their work was the most labor intensive they had ever experienced. They did not feel like workers attending highly automated, computer-operated machinery. Much of the time their labor was more akin to the most brutal forms of outdoor labor. As one veteran described it, "Humping in the Nam was like being on a chain-gang, only the prisoners all got to hold rifles just like the guards."[23] Nor did the killing resemble a regular production schedule. Of course, periodically the sweated labor of patrolling was interrupted by a firefight, as if the routine work of soldiering were suddenly shifted inside the most dangerous mine or factory imaginable in the midst of some awful explosion; but the only thing truly systematic about grunt work in Vietnam was the humping. The killing came in brief spasms of violence. The production of bodies was routinized at the command level, but on the ground it was irregular and usually unexpected.

Grunts were skeptical about the high command's claim that supporting fire was used so extensively to reduce American casualties. If their lives were so important, why were they sent out as bait? Grunts were convinced that the main reason for all the air strikes was the most obvious one: to raise the enemy body count. Stanley Goff, a machine gunner who received the Distinguished Service Cross (the second-highest military decoration), believed American soldiers were used primarily as bait on most of their missions. He was especially critical of nighttime patrols:

> The purpose of [night movement] was for you to walk up on Charlie and for him to hit you, and then for our hardware to wipe them out. We were used as scapegoats to find out where they were. That was all we were—bait. They couldn't find Charlie any other way. They knew there was a regiment out there. They weren't looking for just a handful of VC. Actually, they'd love for us to run into a regiment which would just wipe us out. Then they could plaster the regiment [with air strikes and artillery] and they'd have a big body count. The general gets another damn medal. He gets promoted. "Oh, I only lost two hundred men, but I killed two thousand."[24]

Notice how Stanley Goff separates himself from the American command. "They" were the ones who wanted to find Charlie. "They" could only do it by using the grunts as bait; then "they" could bring in the hardware, plaster the enemy, and get a big body count. The ultimate objective was personal advancement—another damn medal. Goff carried out his assignments with great skill and distinction, but his language conveys a powerful rejection of the aims and motives that commanded his participation. Goff and other grunts were primarily concerned about their own survival, and that concern shaped their perception of bombs and artillery. Where the military command was preoccupied with plastering the enemy, the grunts looked to the skies for protection.

Among the grunts, supporting fire was perceived with deep ambivalence. It was both protector and destroyer, welcome ally and terrible threat. This ambivalence grew out of a profound dependence. Grunts depended on bombs and artillery to save their lives. In countless firefights, Americans were pinned down in enemy ambushes. The arrival of supporting fire commonly brought these firefights to an abrupt end. Even if the bombs and artillery were not successful in hitting enemy positions, their mere use (or the possibility of their use) often caused enemy units to withdraw. Thus, American soldiers looked to "air and arty" as their rescuer, their ace in the hole. Yet supporting fire was always risky. If the wrong coordinates were called in, if mistakes were made by pilots or artillerymen, or if equipment malfunctioned, the bombs could land on American positions. The grunts could be killed by "friendly fire."

Friendly fire killed an extraordinary number of American soldiers. A Pentagon study conducted by Col. David Hackworth in early 1968 concluded that 15 to 20 percent of all U.S. casualties were caused by friendly fire. Most Americans killed by their own side died from misdirected bombs, artillery, and strafing fire. Others died from accidentally discharged grenades or weapons on the ground. In the confusion of battle some men were shot by their own troops. The intentional murder or "fragging" of U.S. troops by other American soldiers may have accounted for 5 to 10 percent of friendly fire deaths. The frequency of friendly fire casualties added to the grunts' sense of vulnerability. They quickly learned to be on guard for booby traps and ambushes, but it was harder for grunts to accept the fact that even the skies could bring death and that the very firepower they depended on so greatly might endanger them as much as the enemy. Vietnam War literature is full of stories about friendly fire, and at least two novels by veterans conclude with the main American character being killed by a U.S. air strike (William Wilson's *The LBJ Brigade* and Thomas Taylor's *A Piece of This Country*).[25]

The grunts' dependence on supporting fire reminded them of their expendable status, their role as bait. They resented being placed in such vulnerable situations while pilots and artillerymen could fire from a distance. Many grunts wished supporting fire could completely replace their own. If jets and gunships could do so much damage at safe distances, why, they wondered, did they have to add their own firepower at such close range and at such risk? Why sacrifice *their* lives? "Why don't they just bring in the B-52s and cave the valley in?" asked a character in *The 13th Valley*.[26]

Not wanting to be used as bait to draw enemy fire, grunts pleaded with officers to call in "preparatory" fire on areas that looked dangerous. When walking across an open field toward a stand of thick foliage, troops wanted bombs dropped on the wood line, hoping they would destroy possible enemy positions or at least trigger enemy fire before the Americans got too close. From the perspective of many grunts, this kind of supporting fire could never be overused; so long as it did not fall on American positions, the more it was used the better. When air strikes arrived, grunts became cheerleaders. As Phantom jets roared in over their targets, GIs would yell, "GET SOME!" "Two Phantom jets were circling overhead. . . . The grunts let out a chorus of 'oo-get some, Sweetheart!'"[27]

Grunts cheered because air strikes could save their lives. They also cheered because the jets brought a feeling of power and control. Usually the Revolutionary Forces initiated firefights. Quite often the Americans were pinned down. But when the air strikes arrived, the earth trembled. The grunts took heart. The sheer volume of explosives injected a jolt of confidence. Suddenly the tide could turn, and the pressure fell on the other side. Such a moment is captured well in *Better Times Than These*. In a jungle ambush, an American unit was hugging the earth. Some of the grunts were so paralyzed by fear, they could not return fire, and those who could had no idea where to shoot. When American jets arrived and began dropping napalm on enemy positions, the mood of the grunts was radically transformed.

> "Napalm—they're napalming the bastards!" Muntz cried. . . .
> Suddenly a vigorous firing poured into the jungle in the direction of the enemy positions. . . .
> Muntz grabbed the machine gun and leaped up, his knees bent, and propped himself against the trunk of a tree. "*Keep me fed*," he bawled, and let loose a burst.[28]

Previously pinned down and ineffectual, the grunts suddenly became aggressive, adding their own fire to the napalm. The air strike had marked the target and inspired confidence.

Once again, however, there was always a dual and contradictory relationship to the supporting fire. Because the Revolutionary Forces usually chose to fight at close range, bombing strikes were frequently "walked in" dangerously close to American positions. Interviewed just a few days after his participation in Operation Allen Brook, PFC David Harmon reported that the bombs were landing only fifty to seventy-five meters from where his unit was pinned down by enemy fire. In an understated monotone Harmon added: "We were pretty close to impact. It was raising us up about eight inches off the ground."[29]

Sometimes the situation on the ground grew so desperate, with American troops under heavy, close-range fire or their positions completely overrun by the enemy, that field officers decided to call in air strikes or artillery on their own positions. The film *Platoon*, for example, concludes in precisely this way. To call in bombs on your own position was suicidal, of course, but there was always the hope that at least some men would survive the strike, men who otherwise would surely die. Another rationale went something like this: "If we're going to die, we might as well take Charlie along with us."[30]

Grunts who spent most of their tours humping the boonies were not the only soldiers who believed they were being used as bait. At a general level all Americans in Vietnam felt a bit like sitting ducks, acutely vulnerable to attacks by Vietnamese guerrillas. Of course, the military command did not deploy all its troops with that intention. Most large, rear-area American compounds, full of noncombat personnel and expensive equipment, were simply conceived of as supply and support bases. Some sizable American bases, however, especially those in remote areas, were indeed established for the express purpose of inviting enemy attack. Thus, American soldiers were used as bait not only while patrolling the countryside on search-and-destroy missions but also in static positions throughout Vietnam. Whenever these stationary bases were attacked, an opportunity arose to engage the enemy, and the military command welcomed virtually every such opportunity, even when American ground troops were threatened with being overrun.

Often enough, however, Revolutionary Forces chose to shell static U.S. positions from the relative safety of nearby jungle or mountains. The command justified keeping such outposts because even enemy rocket fire gave some indication of their location whereupon the United States could respond with firepower of its own. Yet, for the Americans stationed in such places, the experience could be devastating. In the fall of 1967, for example, 1,200 marines were stationed at Con Thien near the DMZ as part of a string of bases built to interdict North Vietnamese soldiers. The marines at Con Thien endured relentless North Vietnamese rocket attacks. To keep the American force above 1,000 required a constant stream of replacements. In September alone, 2,000 marines were wounded and 200 were killed.[31]

The most significant and well known instance of Americans placed in a fixed position to attract enemy fire was the huge buildup of marines at Khe Sanh in the northwestern corner of South Vietnam. By the end of 1967, 6,000 marines were dug in at Khe Sanh's jungle outpost. The base, and patrols run from the base, were designed to block the infiltration of North Vietnamese soldiers through that section of the country. Most of all, however, U.S. generals hoped the base itself would act as a magnet, drawing NVA soldiers into the area where they might be located and fired on from the air. By the winter of 1968 some 20,000 NVA troops were positioned in the hills surrounding Khe Sanh. The 6,000 American marines fell under a state of siege. For more than two months they were subjected to daily bombardment from NVA rockets.

The military command was almost uniformly sanguine about the situation at Khe Sanh. When Gen. Rathvon Tompkins, commander of the Third Marine Division, was asked what would happen if the huge NVA force surrounding Khe Sanh launched a massive ground attack on the marines, he responded, *"That . . .* is exactly *. . .* what we *. . . want* him to do."[32] Though the marines were outnumbered at least three to one (seven to one by some military estimates at the time), the American command saw Khe Sanh as a valuable chance to inflict heavy casualties on the enemy. As Westmoreland put it: "Our decision to defend [Khe Sanh] held the prospect of causing the enemy to concentrate his force and thereby provide us a singular opportunity to bring our firepower to bear on him."[33] The American buildup at Khe Sanh was, in other words, yet another way of dangling the bait. When, in the spring of 1968, the NVA moved out of their positions around the outpost, American forces evacuated Khe Sanh. The American bait no longer seemed to attract the enemy. In fact, the NVA was not lured to Khe Sanh by the American presence—just the opposite. The NVA placed two divisions around Khe Sanh to lure American attention and personnel away from the populated coastal areas where thousands of guerrillas were preparing to launch the Tet Offensive.[34]

Khe Sanh may have been the largest static position established by the U.S. military with the purpose of drawing enemy fire, but it was hardly the only base built for that reason. In October 1968, for example, an American battalion of the First Infantry Division was sent to Firebase Julie north of Tay Ninh near the Cambodian border. Army intelligence believed that perhaps 3,000 NVA troops were assembling just over the Cambodian border. Firebase Julie was established with the explicit purpose of tempting the NVA to engage in open battle with the American troops. Capt. Richard Rogers, a company commander, was quite frank in explaining the purpose of the mission to his lieutenants and NCOs: "We're going to use you for bait. . . . We're going to be bait for those guys [the NVA]. We want them to hit us." Rogers was not so forthright with the troops, however. He instructed the officers to hide the nature of the mission from their men.[35]

Firebase Julie was attacked several days after the battalion arrived. It was an enormous NVA wave attack begun in the middle of the night. A full division of NVA soldiers crashed into the American perimeter. The Americans were outnumbered, perhaps four or five to one, and it looked to many like they would be completely overrun. The Vietnamese "were coming at Julie like breakers on a beach," wave after wave approaching the perimeter and blasting holes in the coils of razor-sharp concertina wire looped around the base. Some NVA units broke through the perimeter and charged the American bunkers. In response the Americans poured out a huge barrage of ammunition. Machine gunners fired until their gun barrels began to turn red, and mortar teams loaded and fired with incredible speed and precision. Around the perimeter dead NVA bodies began to pile up, "so deep at points that Rogers had to order his men out of their bunkers to clear them so they could see more to kill."[36]

Most of the time in Vietnam, Americans never saw the enemy, but here the NVA was out in the open, completely exposed. They came one after another in face-to-face combat. For the Revolutionary Forces, these wave attacks often proved to be suicide missions. Unlike hit-and-run ambushes in which the Americans might be lucky to claim one or two confirmed kills, wave attacks usually resulted in dozens of enemy KIAs. At Firebase Julie, the Americans successfully beat back the assault. When the NVA withdrew at dawn, they left 128 dead soldiers. One American grunt likened the experience to "popping balloons with BBs on a carnival midway." Compared to the enemy body count, American casualties were low—eight men killed. The American command was ecstatic. Helicopters filled with soft drinks and ice cream were flown to the men. According to Peter Goldman and Tony Fuller, however, few of the soldiers felt like celebrating. "Most of the men . . . were too spent, and many were too full of grief and fury to share the pleasure of the generals."[37]

Even when American units outkilled the enemy or drove him back into the jungle, there was no clear sense of triumph or completion. The battle did not mark a movement toward a realizable objective, nor did it give the men a sense that they had gained control of the terms of battle. They had killed dozens of NVA only because the NVA had chosen to attack. Americans were not always able, as they had been at Julie, to defend their base. Stories about U.S. compounds completely overrun, with every American killed, circulated widely among the GIs in Vietnam. Many of these stories were no doubt exaggerated, but the fear they conveyed was not. Perhaps no experience in Vietnam was as terrifying as facing the onrushing attack of a wave assault in the middle of the night.

The fear of such attacks pervaded every American base and outpost. In many cases the fear was well founded. Wave assaults and sapper attacks (small units of commandos trained to penetrate compounds and detonate explosives) produced almost one-third of all U.S. firefights in Vietnam (see table 7). The fear was heightened by the accounts of American soldiers. According to most GI descriptions, the Vietnamese charged into American lines like crazed banzai attackers in a World War II B-movie, "screaming and laughing and all hopped up on dope."[38] It was drugs, some Americans claimed, that gave the Vietnamese the courage to attack and an ability to fight on even when seriously wounded. Frank Mathews describes a wave attack on a marine outpost in 1966: "When they tried to overrun the outpost the thing that made me scaredest was having them run straight into open machinegun fire and smile, or grin, or show their teeth, and not fall. I'd shoot 'em and shoot 'em again and they'd just stagger a little bit and keep on coming. . . . They were so screwed up on the dope and all."[39]

How could they keep coming, one after another? What was the motivation? Some Americans attributed it to drugs, some to "fanaticism" or "brainwashing"; others described it more positively—"incredible discipline" or "intense dedication." However they were explained, the wave attacks inspired fear and awe. The very willingness of Revolutionary Forces to suffer such high casualties helped them maintain a psychological advantage. As a result, though American soldiers often succeeded in gaining control of firefights after the first harrowing minutes and experienced the exhilarating rush of power that came when the full weight of the U.S. arsenal arrived on time and on target, overwhelming the enemy, most of the time American soldiers felt more like the hunted than hunters, more like reactors than initiators, and more like defenders than aggressors.

LAYING WASTE

An American soldier, nearly overcome by heat, fatigue, and anxiety, slogs through rice paddies, elephant grass, and jungle ravines. Or he edges his way through Vietnamese hamlets, on constant alert for signs of trouble. He has been sent out to find the enemy, but the enemy is not to be seen.

The grunt knows the enemy is most likely to appear when he—the American—is most vulnerable, most exposed, the choicest bait: moving down an open trail into an ambush or across an open field toward a wood line full of well-entrenched guerrillas. He begins to feel that the whole war is a booby trap waiting to explode at his feet.

What about another set of images: an American soldier uses his Zippo lighter to set a Vietnamese house on fire, beats up an old Vietnamese man during an "interrogation," throws a grenade into a bomb shelter full of unarmed women and children, or shoots a man running out of a village because "he wasn't supposed to run away."[40] What is the relationship between images of GIs abusing, even murdering, Vietnamese civilians and those depicting U.S. soldiers as beleaguered, defensive, and at the mercy of the land, the people, and the terms of battle? In truth, both sets of images are inextricably connected, and both are crucial to an understanding of the war. American soldiers were both passive and aggressive, victims and vanquishers. The forms and contexts of the former largely determined the nature of the latter. That is, the particular frustrations and terrors encountered by GIs are central to understanding, without necessarily justifying, the range of violent acts they committed.

The futility and frustration felt by American soldiers often peaked as they searched Vietnamese hamlets. These searches rarely uncovered an armed guerrilla. It was hard even to find young men. In hamlet after hamlet, U.S. troops encountered nothing but women, children, and old men. The Americans poked their rifles into the thatched walls and roofs of the dwellings looking for hidden caches of weapons, and they felt along the floors for trap doors leading to underground storage bins that might hold surpluses of rice to be used by the Viet Cong. Most searches produced nothing of significance. The soldiers interrogated the people but rarely received useful information. Aside from weapons and military supplies or unusually large amounts of food, they did not know what to look for or what to do with the things they found. In 1967 Jonathan Schell described the search of Vietnamese homes in Ben Suc during Operation Cedar Falls. One account, in its basic outline, is representative of thousands of searches conducted by American soldiers in Vietnam.

Stepping through the doorway of one house with his rifle in firing position at his hip, a solidly built six-foot-two Negro private came upon a young woman standing with a baby in one arm and a little girl of three or four holding her other hand. . . . She and her children intently watched each of the soldier's movements. In English, he asked, "Where's your husband?" Without taking her eyes off the soldier, the woman said something in Vietnamese, in an explanatory tone. The soldier looked around inside of the one-room house and, pointing to his rifle, asked, "You have same-same?" The woman shrugged and said something else in Vietnamese. The soldier shook his head and poked his hand into a basket of laundry. . . . She immediately took all the laundry out of the basket and shrugged again, with a hint of impatience, as though to say, "It's just laundry!" The soldier nodded and looked around, appearing unsure of what to do next. . . . Then, on a peg on one wall, he spotted a pair of men's pants and a shirt hanging up to dry. "Where's *he*?" he asked, pointing to the clothes. The woman spoke in Vietnamese. The soldier took the damp clothing down and, for some reason, carried it outside, where he laid it on the ground.[41]

Unable to find guerrillas in the hamlets, unable even to find young men, U.S. troops ransacked Vietnamese homes in search of physical evidence of the enemy's presence. There was a strong need to find such evidence. Somehow it promised to make the invisible visible, the intangible concrete. It seemed to offer some assurance that the enemy was, after all, a real being who lived in a specific place and wore specific clothes. Of course the villagers resented the intrusive searches and did as little as possible to cooperate with the soldiers. Even if the villagers understood English, their responses were evasive or incomprehensible to the Americans, very few of whom could speak Vietnamese. The "evidence" collected by Americans rarely offered any concrete conclusions. In this case it led to a shaky series of syllogisms quite commonplace among U.S. troops in Vietnam: there are no men in this village, but there is male clothing, so the men must be avoiding the American search; the Viet Cong usually fight in ordinary peasant clothing, the absent men are peasants avoiding the search, so the absent men must be Viet Cong guerrillas; the villagers are not cooperating with the Americans, so the whole village must be Viet Cong. There are certainly holes in this logic. For example, the absent men might be away (as villagers often claimed) fighting for government forces or working in a distant field or a nearby city. The Americans could never know for sure. In fact, often enough the absent men were guerrillas, and many villages did support the Revolutionary Forces. But what then? What was the next move? The Americans still had no clue where the guerrillas were at the moment or how to act toward the villagers. All this one soldier could think to do was lay out the male clothes as if they were Exhibit A and move on to search another house.

In the same year (1967) Daniel Ellsberg, on assignment for the State Department, spent two weeks with an army infantry battalion as they conducted search-and-destroy operations throughout Long An province in the Mekong Delta. While suffering many casualties from sniper fire, the American forces could not lure the Revolutionary Forces into a sustained or substantial firefight. For ten days the Americans could not claim a single enemy casualty. Taking losses themselves but unable to inflict harm on the Viet Cong, the American soldiers "grew increasingly angry." Their anger began to focus on the many villages and civilians they encountered. It was always hard to find armed guerrillas, but in the delta and the coastal lowlands, American soldiers saw a great many hamlets and civilians. To many GIs, these places and people came to represent the invisible guerrillas, and when soldiers grew embittered over the loss of friends to sniper fire and booby traps, it was not uncommon for them to seek revenge by attacking whatever or whoever was closest. While searching one hamlet the soldiers found an empty house containing a canteen and a picture of a Vietnamese man in an unfamiliar uniform. Believing the house belonged to a Viet Cong guerrilla, the commanding officer called headquarters to ask for permission to burn down the house. Permission was denied and the soldiers were infuriated. Along with "much swearing and stamping around" the soldiers took the canteen they had found and "furiously . . . punched it full of holes" with their bayonets. Ellsberg offers this explanation of their actions: "Their desire to burn the house was in part the result of frustration and in part reflected the fact that they honestly didn't know what might work. They had the feeling that at least if they burned the houses, something would happen; their presence would have been marked. Perhaps the Vietcong would be discouraged from operation in that area, though there were many houses, thousands in the area, and unless you burned them all, the Vietcong would still have shelter."[42]

A week later Ellsberg rejoined the same unit. On this patrol, the Americans burned down every single house they found. Ellsberg assumed the orders against such burnings had changed. After checking with battalion headquarters, however, he learned that no such permission had been granted. The field officers, it turned out, had ordered the burnings without formal authorization. In addition, when the operations officer at headquarters saw smoke rising in the distance and radioed a field commander to find out what was happening, the commander lied. He reported that the men were simply "burning the thatch off bunkers." "Within ten days," Ellsberg concluded, "this battalion had moved to a state of mind where lieutenants and captains were burning houses in violation of higher orders and lying about it."[43]

What Ellsberg ignores, in this example, is the question of whether or not the high command seriously intended to enforce its field regulations. The operations officer assured Ellsberg he "would do something about" the violation of orders. But why had he accepted the story about burning bunkers so uncritically? Did he understand the report to be a euphemistic way of describing the burning of houses? After all, it was common knowledge that bunkers were dug under almost every house, and the houses themselves were mostly made of thatch. One could not burn all the village bunkers without burning the houses as well.

Whether or not there was official sanction from the top commanders, burning villages was commonplace wherever the Viet Cong were suspected to have strong support. In some cases, the people were simply ordered out of the villages—driven from their land and homes where most people had lived for generations. Other times, U.S. forces rounded up the civilians, flew them off in choppers, and dumped them in refugee camps. By stripping the countryside of the civilian population, the U.S. military believed it would have a clearer shot at the enemy. In fact, despite the forced displacement of millions of peasants, the Revolutionary Forces proved as elusive as ever.

Matthew Brennan served with the "Blue platoon" of the First Cavalry Division in 1965. He spent part of his first tour clearing villagers out of the Kim Son region northeast of An Khe. After removing the villagers, some of whom had to be "forcibly dragged" from their homes, the First Cav declared the region a free-fire zone. "This would allow the Americans to kill the remaining rice with chemicals, to blanket everything with artillery fire, and to shoot on sight anything that moved." With the people gone, "the Blues would search deserted villages, many of which had beige stucco Catholic churches crowned by the one true cross, and burn every standing structure. Huts and haystacks were set aflame; rice caches were soaked with aviation fuel and burned. . . . The remaining livestock could not be left to feed the Communists, so the platoon shot pigs and chickens and machine-gunned water buffalo . . . Having been around farm animals for most of my life, I could never participate in the butchery."[44]

Lt. Frederick Downs served near Pleiku with the Fourth Division beginning in September 1967. In his memoir, *The Killing Zone*, he reports matter-of-factly:

> It was a search-and-destroy mission, which meant we searched all the hootches we found and then burned them down. Whether a single farmer's hootch or a whole village—all were burnt. . . .
>
> The first time I saw a Vietnamese family go into hysterics when their hootch was set on fire I was unsure of whether burning down their home would accomplish our mission. The mission was to deny the enemy the use of the hootches, to destroy any food we found, and to teach the people a lesson about supporting the enemy. But I quickly got used to it and accepted that this was one way to win the war.[45]

Most soldiers were not so sure that burning villages was the best way to win the war, but the logic of American military intervention proposed no alternative, except perhaps the total destruction of South Vietnam and its civilian population. The top command was not prepared to sanction such a final solution. Their attitude toward the destruction of civilian lives and property was, in fact, rife with hypocrisy. On one hand, they put soldiers under extreme pressure to pursue the enemy and bring in a big body count, and when civilians were counted among the enemy dead, most generals turned their heads or asked no questions. On the other hand, they also professed concern about minimizing civilian casualties. Accordingly, they formulated rules of engagement (ROE) to define the circumstances under which American firepower could be used and which targets might legitimately be destroyed. The ostensible goal of the ROE was to protect the lives of noncombatants, but a simple listing of the most important rules reveals that, even if they had been rigorously obeyed and enforced (and they were not), they offered slight protection to Vietnamese civilians.

According to the ROE, Vietnamese villages could be fired upon, bombed, or shelled under the following circumstances:

1. If American forces received fire from within the village. In such cases, firepower of every sort could be used without warning the inhabitants.
2. If the villages were known to give material support to the Viet Cong or the NVA. In such cases the inhabitants were supposed to receive warnings before the attack began. However, even in its language this rule was so qualified as to render it no more than a

vague guideline. Villagers were to be warned, it read, "whenever possible" and "with due regard to security and success of the mission."

3. If the civilian population was removed, the village and its environs could be declared a free-fire zone, in which case anything or anyone found there could be fired on at will.[46]

These rules rested on the flimsy assumption that the Vietnamese people had either the desire or the capacity to purge their villages of guerrillas. Any guerrilla presence in a village made it vulnerable to U.S. attack. Sometimes the villagers were warned by helicopter loudspeakers or leaflets dropped from the sky immediately in advance of air strikes and ground attacks. But the warnings often took the form of a general ultimatum that might arrive months before an attack.

Millions of warnings were printed on leaflets by the Psychological Warfare Office. Dropped from helicopters and planes, these leaflets typically contained gruesome cartoon pictures of American jets bombing Vietnamese villages, with guerrillas and civilians alike heaped on the ground in pools of blood. Under these pictures were captions (in Vietnamese) such as, "If you support the Vietcong . . . your village will look like this," or "If you let the Vietcong do this [under a picture of guerrillas shooting from village houses next to a mother and child] . . . your village will look like this [the village exploding and the woman and child dying alongside the guerrillas]." The leaflets also contained longer written ultimatums. For example:

Dear Citizens:

The U.S. Marines are fighting alongside the Government of Vietnam forces in Duc Pho in order to give the Vietnamese people a chance to live a free, happy life, without fear of hunger and suffering. But many Vietnamese have paid with their lives and their homes have been destroyed because they helped the Vietcong in an attempt to enslave the Vietnamese people. . . .

The hamlets of Hai Mon, Hai Tan, Sa Binh, Tan Binh, and many others have been destroyed because of this. We will not hesitate to destroy every hamlet that helps the Vietcong. . . .

The U.S. Marines issue this warning: THE U.S. MARINES WILL NOT HESITATE TO DESTROY IMMEDIATELY, ANY VILLAGE OR HAMLET HARBORING THE VIETCONG. . . .

The choice is yours. If you refuse to let the Vietcong use your villages . . . your homes and your lives will be saved.[47]

The threat to people was explicitly and horridly portrayed in these leaflets. However, both the leaflets and the ROE were based on the absurd claim that there were simple procedures civilians could follow to keep themselves free of danger. Would the revolutionaries leave them alone if the villagers asked them to? Not likely. If the villagers told American forces where the Viet Cong were hiding, would the Americans or South Vietnamese offer them adequate protection against retaliation? Equally unlikely. What about those civilians who politically supported the revolution but did not want to be involved militarily on either side? They would have to leave their villages or face the threat of American attack. The ROE did not so much protect noncombatants as put them in an impossible predicament that left them as vulnerable as ever. Indeed, the rules simply offered official justification for a military policy that made the killing and wounding of civilians routine. They made no commitment to separate combatants from noncombatants; they simply passed onto civilians the full responsibility for avoiding U.S. firepower.

The rules were especially evasive about the conditions under which American soldiers might fire their weapons on people. While jets and artillery could, by the ROE, fire at will on villages designated as VC strongholds, rules governing the fire of ground soldiers were either non-existent or too vague to offer clear direction. The lack of clarity is revealed in the text of a propaganda leaflet: "The Marines are here to help you. Do not run from them! If you run, they may mistake you for a Vietcong and shoot at you. Stand still and the Marines will not harm you. Tell this to your friends."[48]

What does this mean? Did soldiers have orders to shoot running villagers, or did they merely have permission to do so? Were they told not to fire but that "mistakes" do happen and would not be punished? In fact, the American military command provided no precise or consistent rules about how soldiers were to act in such situations. In practice, it was up to the field officers to control their unit's fire. Some officers issued orders to "shoot anything that moves"; some told their men that only armed villagers were legitimate targets; others offered no direction at all, leaving it entirely up to the soldiers. Even soldiers most conscientious about trying to protect civilian lives were under the weight of a profound contradiction:

the ROE offered legal justification for the complete destruction of certain villages and all their inhabitants by bombs, napalm, shells, and strafing fire. This right, however, was not (officially) offered by the high command to ground soldiers, even soldiers entering villages in the wake of such wholesale bombardments.[49]

Infantrymen felt caught in a complex web of legalistic sophistry, a nebulous and hypocritical set of rules and regulations that they believed further endangered their lives. Why, they wondered, should we be more cautious about killing civilians than the pilots who drop bombs and napalm or the artillerymen who fire thousands of rounds of "harassment and interdiction" to random coordinates within free-fire zones? After all, that fire kills civilians all the time and does so from a relatively safe distance. Why should we—the grunts, the men whose lives are most directly threatened—be held responsible for distinguishing between combatants and noncombatants? You never know when someone who looks like an ordinary civilian might pull out an AK-47 or toss a grenade or detonate a land mine. On the other hand, maybe the commanders aren't really serious about protecting civilians. Maybe it's just a public relations hoax. They may talk about respecting civilians, but in the same breath they demand higher body counts. They almost never raise an eyebrow when we call in enemy bodies without any enemy weapons to show for it. Furthermore, you can never be sure of the rules—they always change. Robert Flaherty recalls the dilemma:

> They kept changing the rules all the time. One time you could maim, pillage, do whatever the hell you wanted to do. Then they would get strict on us for a while and started making up rules and regulations about not firing on people until you got fired upon. But it got to the point where you started losing buddies by abiding by the political rules. So, after that, when you see yourself coming into a [dangerous] situation, you get on the old horn, and you call back to the rear, and you tell them that you're receiving incoming fire. You just shoot some rounds in the air and let them [the commanders in the rear] hear the "incoming" fire. Then you can call in the airstrikes and shoot up the village.[50]

In practice, the rules of engagement were largely ignored, broken, or circumvented. Many soldiers were opposed to any restrictions on their actions, believing that the rules demonstrated the government's lack of commitment to winning the war, or they saw the rules as a smokescreen to avoid public outcry against the war. Most of all, they believed any limit on their own discretion to fire put their lives in greater jeopardy. Thus, many soldiers supported the view that they would fight according to their own rules, that in the bush they would follow the unofficial rule of engagement: "If it's dead and Vietnamese, it's VC."[51]

Many soldiers, however, felt the need to have their actions justified on firmer moral ground. If they shot unarmed Vietnamese, whether intentionally or accidentally, most needed to believe they had fired upon the enemy, that their actions were legitimate, and that they had done the right thing. Sometimes the ROE provided a defense for their actions. In particular they reminded themselves of the regulations that attempted to prescribe the conduct of Vietnamese civilians. For, as we have seen, the rules of engagement placed at least as much responsibility on the Vietnamese to avoid American firepower as they did on American soldiers to avoid killing civilians. Civilians had to demonstrate their noncombatant status at every turn. They were supposed to carry identification cards certifying their loyalty to the GVN. They were subjected to curfews requiring that they be in their villages by nightfall. In many places villagers were forbidden from having lights on in their houses at night (since the Revolutionary Forces might use lights as signals). They were not to supply the enemy with food or shelter or even allow them access to the village. All enemy activities were supposed to be reported to the government. Once again, they were told to "stand still" when American forces were near.

If the villagers did not know about these regulations or did not or could not follow them, that was simply their problem. The claim that civilians broke the rules gave the American military a legal-sounding justification for both accidental and intentional slaughter. American soldiers looked to these rules to reassure themselves about the legitimacy of civilian deaths. In James Webb's novel, *Fields of Fire*, for example, a marine infantry unit received fire from a village during the night. The lieutenant immediately called in artillery strikes. The next morning, he called for more supporting fire: "Hodges listened to the rooster, wondering how it had survived the artillery of the night before. Then he smiled a bit perversely to himself. Let's see if he makes it through *this*. . . . Nam An (2) became saturated with explosions, mixes of phosphorous and high-explosive shells that rained down like a steady hailstorm, raising jets of dirt like water spurts."[52]

After this last artillery barrage, the ground troops advanced into the village. A soldier named Goodrich saw a figure moving across a porch and fired his whole magazine of bullets toward the person. It proved to be an elderly woman. Goodrich was horrified by what he had done and kneeled down beside the severely wounded woman to apologize. His squad leader said:

> "Don't be sorry. . . . She knows the rules. She shoulda been in her bunker. It's her own fault."
>
> Goodrich shook his head, his chubby face sagging in its grief. He looked down at the bleeding, decrepit creature. . . . "I should have looked more closely. I was scared. It was crazy to shoot like that."

Another man, exasperated by Goodrich's self-blame, said, "She coulda been a gook. She knew she was wrong. Look twice and you're dead."[53]

A "Kit Carson Scout" (a Vietnamese guide and interpreter who sometimes accompanied American units) called Dan asked the woman why she had left her bunker. She explained that she had been in the bunker all night but left to defecate just before the morning artillery strike. Caught amidst the shelling, she was trying to make it back to the bunker when she was shot. The marines asked Dan what he said in reply. "I say, now on, shit in bunker." The men "applauded in appreciation of Dan's wisdom."[54]

Goodrich alone expressed concern about the woman. Later in the novel Webb has Goodrich hesitate in battle for fear of shooting a child. Goodrich is wounded as a result, and a fellow marine—"Snake"—is killed rescuing Goodrich. Having Snake rescue Goodrich is crucial to the novel's politics because Snake had recently ordered the execution of an old Vietnamese couple and Goodrich (unbeknownst to Snake) had reported the atrocity. Snake's heroic death seems clearly intended to generate sympathy and forgiveness toward him and scorn for the scrupulous Goodrich. In other words, Webb is at pains to argue that Goodrich's conventional morality has no place in Vietnam, that too much concern about civilians' lives only puts you and your fellows at greater risk. Better simply to fire away and keep your mouth shut.

Nonetheless, *Fields of Fire* reveals not so much an absence of moral thought among soldiers as a desperate need to find some moral language, however strained, to justify their actions. Feeling trapped, they grasp at straws. They speak quite often of rules and right and wrong. The men attempt to persuade Goodrich that the woman he shot was at fault, that she had been wrong, that she knew the rules and had failed to obey them. The result was a twisted legalism that made an unarmed civilian responsible for the suffering inflicted by a soldier. Webb's novel is designed not to defend the ROE so much as to show that the rules made it nearly impossible to act with moral consistency (and foolhardy to try). For example, shortly after Goodrich shoots the woman, a squad leader forbids one of his men from stealing a pair of shorts from a villager. "Give'em back. . . . It's against the rules. You know that. . . . I ain't having any new Lieutenant or somebody run me in because you want a pair of shorts. Now give 'em back to the lady." Goodrich was right to shoot the woman; another soldier was wrong for stealing clothes.[55]

This contradictory morality was shaped by the ROE and by American policy in general. American leaders gave no clear or consistent guidelines to soldiers as to how they were to treat civilians. When American soldiers abused or murdered villagers, they were sometimes following direct orders. More often than not, however, they were simply operating under the vague injunction to go out and "get some Cong." Of course, not all soldiers abused civilians in face-to-face encounters. American military policy did not, in other words, make atrocities by individual soldiers inevitable, but it certainly made it inevitable that American forces as a whole would kill many civilians. More to the point, U.S. policy itself was a doctrine of atrocity. Even the constraints imposed by the oft-abused ROE sanctioned the complete destruction of villages housing unarmed civilians. Moreover, soldiers were put into situations of moral stress significantly more complex than those experienced by soldiers in wars where opposing armies fought along clear fronts. In Vietnam, soldiers were charged with killing an enemy who moved among, and was supported by, the civilian population but who was rarely seen. Americans took many of their casualties in isolation. They were ambushed, sniped at, and booby trapped, yet the enemy was either absent or in flight. Often the only Vietnamese encountered were villagers. In such circumstances it is hardly surprising that Americans and Vietnamese peasants viewed each other with hostility and suspicion. Many Americans struck out at the villagers in a desire for revenge. The range of violence was enormous and varied, from verbal abuse to destruction of property to spitting, kicking, beating, and killing. Tim O'Brien offers a commonplace example.

> When a booby-trapped artillery round blew two popular soldiers into a hedgerow, men put their fists into the faces of the nearest Vietnamese, two frightened women living in the guilty hamlet, and when

the troops were through with them, they hacked off chunks of thick black hair. The men were crying, doing this. An officer used his pistol, hammering it against a prisoner's skull.

Scraps of our friends were dropped in plastic body bags. Jet fighters were called in. The hamlet was leveled, and napalm was used. I heard screams in the burning black rubble. I heard the enemy's AK-47 rifles crack out like impotent popguns against the jets. There were Viet Cong in that hamlet. And there were babies and children and people who just didn't give a damn in there, too. But Chip and Tom were on the way to Graves Registration . . . and it was hard to be filled with pity.[56]

The soldiers wept as they beat the women. No doubt the tears reflect grief over the friends just killed, but they also symbolize the futility soldiers felt, their sense—perhaps unconscious—of the inadequacy and baseness of venting their rage on defenseless people. Whether they regretted what they had done or not, the soldiers' violence was a mere preview of the greater destruction that followed. The wholesale and impersonal annihilation caused by the air strike must have seemed to some of the men like a certificate of approval for the personal abuse of villagers by infantrymen, offering as reassurance this thought: "There's nothing we can do to them that's any worse than what that napalm is doing."[57]

The military made no body counts of civilians beaten or abused, nor did it attempt to count the number of civilians wounded or killed by gunfire and bombs. Estimates of civilian war casualties are imprecise and much disputed, but even the most conservative estimates offer some sense of the enormity of civilian losses. The most intensive effort to estimate civilian casualties in Vietnam was conducted by the Senate subcommittee on refugees in 1975. The committee estimated that 430,000 South Vietnamese civilians were killed between 1965 and 1974 and more than 1 million were wounded. Political scientist Guenter Lewy argues that American atrocities in Vietnam have been much exaggerated and claims that 300,000 South Vietnamese civilian deaths is a more accurate figure. However, there is good reason to believe that both figures are too low.[58]

Both estimates depend on differing interpretations of the numbers of wounded civilians treated in South Vietnamese hospitals. Because civilians who were killed in the war were rarely admitted to hospitals and therefore remained officially uncounted, their number was estimated by extrapolating from the ratio of killed to wounded among South Vietnamese soldiers (for every South Vietnamese soldier killed in war, there were two or three seriously wounded). Both Lewy and the Senate used this approach. However, the Senate committee also made some allowance for the probability that a sizable number of civilian wounded were not treated in hospitals. Lewy does not. More importantly, neither estimate seeks to include those civilians who were killed by American forces but who were claimed as enemy dead. This is a serious omission. Lewy acknowledges this problem without making it part of the estimate he endorses. He concedes that "in most cases villagers killed in VC-dominated or contested areas were counted as enemy dead, while others died without being counted." Lewy also points out that American forces captured only one weapon for every three people reported as enemy dead. That figure by itself does not prove that two-thirds of the dead were civilians. After all, the Revolutionary Forces tried hard to retrieve as many weapons as possible. However, the ratio of one weapon for every three enemy dead includes all the weapons found while searching arms caches throughout South Vietnam and all the weapons taken from prisoners. After firefights, U.S. units often found only one weapon for every ten people killed. Reviewing such evidence in a secret 1966 memo, Secretary of Defense Robert McNamara wrote, "The VC/NVA apparently lose only about one-sixth as many weapons as people, suggesting the possibility that many of the killed are unarmed porters or bystanders."[59]

Even Lewy, who is ideologically predisposed to downplaying civilian losses, suggests that as many as one-third of the Vietnamese claimed by the United States as enemy dead were, in fact, civilians. Using a conservative estimate of PAVN and PLAF deaths, that portion amounts to 220,000 South Vietnamese civilian deaths, thereby raising Lewy's total estimate to 522,000 and the Senate committee's estimate to 652,000. These figures do not include the 65,000 civilian deaths the U.S. government attributes to its bombing of North Vietnam.

Who caused the civilian casualties in South Vietnam? Lewy implies that the Revolutionary Forces killed as many civilians as the United States and the South Vietnamese government. His numbers, however, do not support such a conclusion. Using his estimate that at least one-third of the enemy dead claimed by the United States were civilians, even if all other civilian deaths identified by using hospital records were equally attributed to the two sides, the resulting estimate shows 437,000 killed by the United States and the GVN and 150,000 killed by the Revolutionary Forces; that is, 74 percent to 26 percent. Those figures are not so different from the percentages arrived at by Edward Herman, whom Lewy dismisses as "an antiwar publicist." Herman wrote: "A very conservative estimate would be that over 80 percent of civilian casualties were caused by U.S. and ARVN military operations."[60]

Herman and others have argued that the nature of American military policy, with its heavy reliance on firepower in and near populated areas, was far more likely to produce heavy civilian casualties than the tactics of the Revolutionary Forces. There is no doubt that the Viet Cong and North Vietnamese killed thousands of civilians. However, most of their atrocities were calculated assassinations of specific individuals. Important examples of these are described by Le Ly Hayslip in her memoir, *When Heaven and Earth Changed Places*. Hayslip herself was a teenage member of a Viet Cong self-defense force who, after returning from government imprisonment and torture, was falsely accused of leading some guerrillas into a government ambush. The Viet Cong sentenced her to death, but she was spared when her executioners decided to rape her instead. Hayslip's mother also narrowly escaped a Viet Cong execution for failing to warn Revolutionary Forces of approaching enemy troops. Four other village women were shot in the head for the same alleged offense.[61]

One enormous massacre has been attributed to Revolutionary Forces: the murder of some 2,800 South Vietnamese civilians in Hue during the Tet Offensive. While most histories of the war take it as a matter of indisputable fact that this atrocity occurred on at least this scale, the documentary evidence is still too scant to describe the event in great detail or with much authority. What evidence there is, however, does indicate that a very sizable massacre was indeed carried out by Revolutionary Forces, perhaps every bit as great as the figure of 2,800 would suggest. Without diminishing the significance of the civilian deaths in Hue, it must still be stressed that the American forces on the whole killed civilians in greater number and more indiscriminately. Of course the United States did sponsor Viet Cong-like assassinations under the Phoenix program, but the majority of civilians killed by American forces died from indiscriminate ground and air attacks in heavily populated areas. During the Tet Offensive, for example, according to the official ARVN history, more than 14,000 civilians were killed in Saigon alone, most of them by U.S. bombs and heavy weapons.[62]

American soldiers struggled to find meaning in these deaths and in the losses of their comrades. They sought to reconcile their direct experience of the war with official explanations of American intervention in Vietnam, but the battlefield realities did not match the descriptions and justifications presented by American policymakers. The contradiction between the two positions left American soldiers without a clear or compelling sense of purpose; rather, it confronted them with the wrenching prospect that they were fighting a war for nothing.

A War for Nothing

I should make it clear that while I have tried here . . . to understand the arguments of those who are called enemy, I am as deeply concerned about our own troops there as anything else. For it occurs to me that what we are submitting them to in Vietnam is not simply the brutalizing process that goes on in any war where armies face each other and seek to destroy. We are adding cynicism to the process of death, for our troops must know after a short period there that none of the things we claim to be fighting for are really involved. Before long they must know that their government has sent them into a struggle among Vietnamese, and the more sophisticated surely realize that we are on the side of the wealthy and the secure while we create a hell for the poor.
– Martin Luther King, Jr., April 1967

For soldiers, war is a directly confronted reality, not a theoretical abstraction. Their primary concern is survival, not salvation. They value quick reaction over thoughtful reflection, and with good reason: in a war zone, philosophizing can be dangerous. A soldier pondering the meaning of his experience might not see the trip wire across the trail or the sapper crawling through the weeds, and the risks are psychological as well as physical. What happens to the mind of a soldier who constantly tabulates the dangers besetting him, or who cannot stop wondering whether he is fighting for a cause that is just or worthy of the sacrifices made and the lives lost? Those who dwell on such matters risk more than increased anxiety, doubt, frustration, and guilt; they court insanity.[1]

Critical thought can also lead to various forms of dissent: desertion, rebellion, outright mutiny. Soldiers who question the meaning or purpose of the war they are ordered to fight might avoid combat, shirk their duties, or join with others to resist orders. However, dissent in the military has a high price. Even to question orders can lead to official reprimands and demotion in rank, and more serious challenges to authority risk court-martials and imprisonment. In addition to punishment, the military command attempts to stifle critical thought by saturating its soldiers with simplistic, officially prescribed explanations of the world and by branding dissenting views as traitorous, cowardly, or un-American.[2]

Thus, in war most soldiers try to focus on the demands of the moment, on the details of survival. Even during off-hours in the relative safety of rear areas, when quiet reflection is possible, they usually try to take their minds off the psychic and physical burdens of war with music, beer, letters from home, and diversions of one kind or another.

Much the same has been said about civilians in peacetime, perhaps especially about working people who spend long hours doing particularly dangerous and exhausting labor. Work so depletes their energies that they have little will or capacity for entertaining serious thoughts about the meaning or purpose of their lives. Moreover, they might not have real or attractive alternatives to ponder, so they live life a day at a time, without questioning its fundamental significance. So goes the conventional wisdom. But those, like Studs Terkel, who have really listened to working people have found an extraordinary range and depth of feelings and attitudes about work and life.[3]

So, too, with soldiers. Journalists seeking generalized statements about the justice of war from troops in a war zone often come up with empty findings, too often concluding that soldiers simply do not give the issue any thought or that they mindlessly parrot the official line of the military command. In 1966, for example, John Sack reported that American troops in Vietnam found the question of whether or not America should be fighting in Vietnam absurd and irrelevant. After all, he argued, they already were in Vietnam. Thus, to question the legitimacy of that presence was, Sack wrote, "as idly academic as the architectural pros and cons of some gingerbread mansion might be to the fire fighters in its attic trying to save it (and themselves) from annihilation."[4]

This is an important insight, as far as it goes. Soldiers in Vietnam were preoccupied with survival; but they were not blind to the reality around them, and hard as they sometimes tried to block the war from their minds, they could not help seeking as well to locate some meaning and purpose in their actions. In Vietnam, the best focus for examining American soldiers' attitudes about the war lies in the contradictory ground dividing the official justifications of the war expressed by American policymakers and the war as it was actually lived by the soldiers. Official explanations of the American mission in Vietnam failed to match the reality experienced by U.S. soldiers. Though many Americans arrived in Vietnam believing they were there to stop the spread of communism and to advance the cause of democracy, the actual nature of the war so fundamentally undermined these explanations that most American troops did not find in them a meaningful sense of purpose or legitimacy. Confusion and skepticism intensified as the war dragged on, but there was, from the beginning, significant disillusionment.

Like the rest of American society, U.S. troops were deeply divided over the question of whether or not the United States was right to go to war in Vietnam. However, whatever their views on the legitimacy of America's initial intervention, most enlisted men found the war itself to be without point or purpose. Those who generally accepted America's right to intervene in Vietnam were most disturbed by the absence of meaningful measurements of military success, a clear definition of victory. Those who questioned the legitimacy of American involvement focused more on the senselessness and futility of even trying to fight in Vietnam. They doubted that America could ever win, or they believed the only victory likely to come from American policy would require too much destruction to justify the effort.

There were complicated variations of these attitudes throughout the years of war, but a useful historical division can be made between those who fought before the Tet Offensive of 1968 and those who served in the years after Tet. In the earlier years the central thrust of disenchantment concerned the strategic aims of the war and the lack of convincing signs of progress. Among those who fought in the latter years, there was a more widespread sense that the war was not worth fighting on any terms; there was a more profound sense of the war's pointlessness. Common to soldiers throughout the war was a deep skepticism about the official justifications of the war. Many fought hard, but few found in the standard rationale a coherent or persuasive explanation for why they were fighting. Confronted by the contradictions between official explanations of the war and their own experience, most American troops concurred with the line that became the most important GI slogan about the war: "It don't mean nothin'."

OFFICIAL JUSTIFICATIONS

Vietnam is far from this quiet campus. We have no territory there, nor do we seek any. The war is dirty and brutal and difficult. And some 400 young men, born into an America bursting with opportunity and promise, have ended their lives on Vietnam's steaming soil.

Why must we take this painful road?
—President Lyndon Johnson, April 1965

American soldiers arrived in Vietnam with little idea of what they would encounter. Some could not even locate Vietnam on a world map. Only a small minority had read books about the war or the country. Their training had focused on the practicalities of their military specialties: firing weapons, fixing helicopters, dressing wounds, typing letters. As for why the war was being waged—its goals and justifications—most had heard little more than the official explanations proclaimed by Washington and echoed in the training films of basic training. Not all soldiers were familiar with even the broad outlines of those arguments. In 1967, for example, sociologist Charles Moskos found that one-quarter of the GIs he surveyed in Vietnam could not cite a single reason why America was fighting in Vietnam.[5] Those men may have been telling Moskos more about their own rejection of official justifications than about their ignorance of them. In any case, most soldiers left for Vietnam with at least a rudimentary sense of the standard arguments in defense of the American war. In fact, soldiers were more likely to have heard arguments in favor of the war rather than against it. As one veteran remarked, "To be honest, I didn't know very much about the political debates over the war but I'm sure I had a better idea of why we were supposed to fight—you know, the domino theory and to help South Vietnam—than I did with the arguments against the war."[6]

At Johns Hopkins University in April 1965, Lyndon Johnson explained his reasons for sending American soldiers to South Vietnam. This speech provides a useful catalogue of the major justifications American policymakers publicly proclaimed throughout the entire course of the war. The rationale fell into three general categories:

(1) To help South Vietnam. America, Johnson claimed, was in Vietnam to help the people of South Vietnam establish democracy in the face of communist aggression. The president described South Vietnam as an

"independent nation" that had "bravely borne . . . for so many years" the struggle to defend itself against a concerted attack from North Vietnam. But the South Vietnamese could no longer defend themselves without additional American "support." Thus, American soldiers were sent to protect "simple farmers" in "small and helpless villages" from the communist "terror" that threatened the "freedom" of this "small and brave nation." "We want nothing for ourselves, only that the people of South Vietnam be allowed to guide their own country in their own way."[7]

Throughout the war American policymakers portrayed South Vietnam as an essentially unified nation struggling to maintain independence and enhance democracy. The deep divisions within South Vietnam were not even conceded, much less explained. In Johnson's lengthy address the only hint of disunity comes in a single line: "Of course, some of the people of South Vietnam are participating in this [North Vietnamese] attack on their own government." Americans were not told the plain truth: In 1964–65 the government of South Vietnam was on the verge of collapse at the hands of *southern* revolutionaries who had a fighting force, according to U.S. estimates, of at least 200,000. At the time of Johnson's speech, the Viet Cong of the south were assisted by only a few thousand North Vietnamese troops. In March 1966, when the United States had 216,400 troops in South Vietnam, the U.S. military reported to Washington that the North Vietnamese had 13,100 PAVN soldiers south of the seventeenth parallel. These basic facts, shielded from the American public, were communicated in secret memos and meetings among U.S. policymakers in Washington and Saigon.[8]

There was no real basis for Johnson's characterization of South Vietnam as an independent nation. Its political and military leadership was, in fact, utterly dependent on American support. Equally fictitious was the portrait of the long string of American-backed regimes in Saigon as struggling democracies. They were all corruption-riddled dictatorships. For public consumption, however, these regimes were heralded as representative and reformist governments threatened not from within but from without. According to this view, the great majority of South Vietnamese looked to the United States to help them maintain an independence they never had and to improve a democracy yet to appear. American leaders promoted the illusion that American soldiers would be welcomed in Vietnam as public defenders, as saviors of freedom and self-determination. They were there to help. How a foreign power (the United States) could intervene on behalf of another people's self-determination without the taint of imperialism or hypocrisy was a question that simply did not perplex most U.S. policymakers, persuaded as they were of their own honorable intentions.[9]

(2) To contain communism. In addition to America's selfless concern for the South Vietnamese, policymakers linked the war in Vietnam to the global struggle between communism and "The Free World." Communist insurgency in Vietnam, Johnson said, reflected a "wider pattern of aggressive purpose." This was the central thrust of the domino theory, the idea that if communists succeeded in Vietnam, they would invade neighboring countries, all of them toppling, one after another, like dominoes. If the United States did not stop communism in Vietnam, communism would spread to "one country and then another . . . until all the nations of Asia are swallowed up." By extension, America itself was ultimately threatened. Failure to contain communism in Vietnam, the policymakers warned, could lead to a shift of world power so radical that the United States might eventually stand alone, surrounded by communism. At the heart of the domino theory was the idea that the fundamental source of communist insurgency was not located among South Vietnamese guerrillas, or even in Hanoi, but in Peking and Moscow. The conflicts between communist nations were either downplayed or ignored. The domino theory made all forms of left-wing insurgency a potential victory for a single power. In the early years of the Vietnam War, China was often singled out as the nation most responsible for the insurgency in South Vietnam. The centuries of conflict between China and Vietnam (a conflict that resumed in 1978 after the communist victory in Vietnam) did not figure in administration efforts to depict a uniform communist threat.[10]

(3) To preserve American credibility. The final major rationale of U.S. intervention in Vietnam was the doctrine of "credibility." If we did not prove ourselves determined to fight in small nations like Vietnam, allies throughout the world would lose faith in our commitment to freedom, and our enemies would perceive us as weak and vulnerable. Vietnam, said Johnson, was "a friend to which we are pledged." To withdraw that pledge would jeopardize our credibility throughout the world. If we failed to prevent a communist victory in Vietnam, what would other nations think of America's commitment? Who would honor our word? Who would trust our friendship? Who would respect our power?

As early as 1966 some policymakers believed the concern with credibility was the major reason for the United States to keep fighting in Vietnam. In a 1966 memorandum (published among the *Pentagon Papers* in 1971), Assistant Secretary of Defense John McNaughton wrote: "The present U.S. objective in Vietnam is to avoid humiliation. The reasons why we went into Vietnam . . . are varied; but they are now largely academic. Why we have not withdrawn from Vietnam is, by all odds, one reason: to preserve our reputation as a guarantor, and thus to preserve our effectiveness in the rest of the world. We have not hung on to save a friend, or to deny the Communists the added acres and heads."[11] As the war dragged on, concerns about honor and credibility became the central official justification of the war. By the late 1960s and 1970s it was in- creasingly obvious—even to the public—that U.S. leaders were more concerned about preserving an image of American power than they were in helping South Vietnam. Immediate withdrawal from Vietnam, Nixon argued, would prove us weak and irresolute. It would throw into doubt our will and capacity to prevail in any conflict or competition throughout the world; we would be seen as a "helpless giant."[12] Ironically, as the war continued, defended on the grounds of national honor and international prestige, America's global reputation steadily crumbled. It declined not so much because the United States was "failing" in Vietnam but because America persisted for so long in such a ruinous military intervention.

American soldiers experienced firsthand the contradictions and decep- tions of U.S. policy. Whatever leaders might say, those sent to fight the war soon realized that American intervention was not helping the people of South Vietnam, that it was not successfully containing communism, and that it was not bolstering national honor or credibility.

WHO ARE WE FIGHTING FOR?

Few Americans arrived in Vietnam with a deep-seated commitment to help the people of South Vietnam, but most were at least convinced that helping the South Vietnamese was a central purpose of their mission. While the idea of fighting for people halfway around the world did not excite great enthusiasm, American soldiers harbored quiet hopes and expectations about the way they would be received by the Vietnamese. They had, of course, grown up with romantic visions of American GIs as global liberators, riding into town on jeeps as grateful civilians pour into the streets to greet them with smiles, waves, flowers, kisses, and wine. Appealing as those images were, few soldiers sent to Vietnam, even in the first years, took them literally enough to expect similar treatment. They really did not expect to be welcomed as great American saviors. After all, they had heard enough stories about grenade-tossing children to have some doubts about how civilians regarded the Americans. Still, most took to heart official claims that the South Vietnamese needed American help. Accordingly, when soldiers arrived in Vietnam, they had the reasonable expectation that the overwhelming majority of the Vietnamese people appreciated their presence, truly wanted their support, and would at least treat them as friends and allies, if not liberators.

Such hopes were quickly dashed. Soldiers soon learned that despite U.S. boasts about helping Vietnamese friends, the Vietnamese did not seem to want the kind of help American soldiers had to offer. In *Fields of Fire*, a marine on his first patrol entered the village of Phu Phong and was shocked by the hostile attitude of the villagers, particularly the children. He said to his squad leader, "I really think these kids hate us." The squad leader offered a blunt explanation of the children's animosity: "We try to kill their papa. . . . This whole valley is VC." The new man replied, "It'll take a little getting used to. I just hadn't expected to be hated. Not by them." The squad leader put an end to the conversation by responding, "Ah, it don't mean nothing."[13] This was the standard response offered by more experienced soldiers to those who raised questions or expressed doubts about the war. It was a way of acknowledging the contradictions in American policy without directly naming or scrutinizing them. Often enough, in fact, soldiers proclaimed the war meaningless to avoid a confrontation with the war's most disturbing meanings. If everyone simply agreed that the war was crazy or insane or meaningless, there seemed less chance of going crazy oneself. The lesson of survival, passed along from the men who had survived the longest, was to take the war on its own terms, however contradictory or troubling.

Still, the widespread hostility of Vietnamese civilians toward American soldiers was not meaningless and not easy to ignore. It stood in direct contradiction to the official claim that the Vietnamese people sought U.S. military intervention. If they did, why the scorn in so many Vietnamese faces? Why were there so many incidents like this one, described by Richard Deegan? "I know one time when I was over there [1967] we was going down to get chow one morning and this little Vietnamese kid said 'Fuck you marine, goddamn Yankee go home, marine number 10.' After that I started thinking what the fuck are we doing here? We're supposed to be saving them from the Viet Cong and the Communists and all this, and they're calling us assholes, and we're no good, and all this shit."[14]

Even those who arrived in Vietnam at the beginning of the enormous American escalation of 1965 saw little evidence of Vietnamese support for their presence. A navy corpsman, recalling his 1965 tour, stated flatly, "We weren't wanted there. We knew that when we were over there."[15] An infantry captain, also in Vietnam in 1965, reported in an after-action interview: "We were moving alongside a large village complex and first the dogs started barking and then the drums started beating and Vietnamese were yelling in English: 'Marines go back! We don't want you!' or 'We don't need you.' And of course this is quite startling. The drum-beating was a signalling device to inform VC in adjacent villages or further up the line that Americans were approaching and to take warning. We found this to be true on other missions also."[16]

Many soldiers observed that the Vietnamese they encountered seemed more fearful of the Americans than hostile. A marine infantryman, Rudy Rodriquez, explained this point in an oral history conducted by the military at the end of his Vietnam tour in 1966.

> *Interviewer:* "In your observations over there did you have anything particularly noticeable about the Vietnamese people?"
>
> *Rodriquez:* "Well, the Vietnamese people were very much afraid of us. We got in a firefight. We were trapped in a village. We sent out maneuvers to get the Viet Cong out of their positions. With the rounds flying all over the place there was a lot of innocent women and kids killed, and that really brought our image in the people's eyes that we were very cruel and that we were just as bad as the communism."
>
> *Interviewer:* "Would you say, then, that a larger effort should be made toward being, well, shall we say, careful around the people?"
>
> *Rodriquez:* "This is very hard. Especially when you're in a firefight . . . because the rounds going all over the place are not particular."[17]

In a 1967 post-tour military interview, another marine, Cpl. Sherwood Freeman, echoed Rodriquez. Out in the villages, he said, the people, "didn't want to have anything to do with me. They were scared of us." But Freeman attributes the fear not merely to stray rounds killing civilians, as Rodriquez contended, but to deliberate acts of brutality by American soldiers.

> *Interviewer:* "What do you think caused the people to dislike the Marines, propaganda prior to your getting there?"

Freeman: "Nope." [At this point Freeman chuckles slightly—a haunting, complicated little laugh that seems to express incredulity that the interviewer would propose such a pat and mistaken explanation of Vietnamese hostility.] "I think what mainly made them dislike us was some of our brutality."

Interviewer: "The Marines themselves?"

Freeman: "Right."

Interviewer: "What type brutality did you see or hear of?"

Freeman: "Well, one time I saw innocent Vietnamese shot and [they] shouldn't of been shot. There was two of them. [Then the Marines] put two M-26 grenades under the [dead] bodies and just left them there so in case somebody were to come along and mess with them and roll their bodies over—BOOM, all of them would go."

Interviewer: "Were they suspected Charlie?"

Freeman: "They weren't suspected Charlie. They were just in an area where they weren't supposed to be, stealing pineapples."

Interviewer: "From whom?"

Freeman: "From nobody, because the area was emptied, you know. [The Marines] were totally clearing out [the villagers] and these two guys were going back in to steal pineapples. That's all they were going to do."[18]

The interviewer asked no more questions about the incident.

The killing, wounding, and brutalizing of Vietnamese civilians undermined any effort to believe that the war was actually helping the South Vietnamese. Frank Mathews came to Vietnam fully persuaded that he was there "to help the little guy—the South Vietnamese." His faith was sustained for some time because he served with a reconnaissance unit operating deep in the mountains. In the remote jungle and mountains there was much less contact with civilians, and when the enemy was engaged, it was usually a unit of regular, uniformed forces of North Vietnam rather than guerrilla forces of the south. Thus, Americans who fought away from population centers did not have the additional confusion of distinguishing combatants from civilians, and Frank Mathews, early in his tour, did not see the suspicion and violence characterizing the relationship between Americans and their allies. On one operation, however, he was attached to an infantry unit in a populated area and witnessed a scene that shook his faith: The U.S. troops "set up around a village and they killed everything—dogs, chickens, cats, whatever was in that village they killed. All this was done just because a few people said there were VC sympathizers in there. By killing them all like that they did the same thing as the VC did as far as I was concerned."[19] As another man put it, "We're as much a threat to the villagers as the Viet Cong are."[20]

Far from seeing themselves as liberators, many soldiers found that their search-and-destroy missions did more to promote anti-Americanism than anticommunism. Describing a unit notorious for brutalizing civilians and burning villages, a character in *Fields of Fire* comments, "I figure [they] done *made* a lot more VC than they ever end up killing."[21] However much policymakers referred to the Vietnamese as our friends and allies, the central thrust of American policy was to consider all Vietnamese potential enemies to be watched, suspected, interrogated, and if caught "where they weren't supposed to be" or among "VC sympathizers," fired upon and killed.

In his memoir, Gen. William Westmoreland describes the Vietnamese as hosts and assures the reader that every effort was made by him to instill respect for the South Vietnamese. He had cards printed and distributed to soldiers with rules of conduct admonishing the men to consider themselves guests of the Vietnamese. "I directed that every American soldier carry at all times a small card listing nine rules of conduct, such as avoiding loud and rude behavior and display of wealth and privilege, treating women with politeness and respect, giving the Vietnamese the right of way, making friends among the people, trying to learn some of the language, and in general behaving as guests in the land."[22] The soldiers could only look upon such rules as the highest form of hypocrisy. Westmoreland may have been treated as a guest in his Saigon villa, but elsewhere in the land, soldiers were deployed to root out enemies among a population far from welcoming.

Even in rear areas mutual hostility was pervasive. Rear-echelon soldiers typically encountered Vietnamese civilians in the cities, refugee camps, or makeshift shantytowns that sprang up on the outskirts of almost every American base. In these settings, most of the Vietnamese became utterly dependent on the American military presence. Many worked on large American bases as laborers or maids. Others became peddlers or hustlers, selling the GIs soft drinks, beer, trinkets, drugs, shoeshines, haircuts, and sex. As potential customers Americans were often greeted enthusiastically, but most of these relationships were strictly business. Most rear-echelon soldiers concluded that the Vietnamese looked to them not as protectors or guarantors of freedom but simply as potential customers or as marks for begging and thieving.[23]

Sociologist Charles Moskos conducted field research on army enlisted men in Vietnam, first in 1965 and again in 1967. He found the men skeptical of every justification of the war but especially unconvinced that America was fighting on behalf of South Vietnam. "They dismiss patriotic slogans or exhortations to defend democracy with 'What a crock,' 'Be serious, man,' or 'Who's kidding who?' In particular, they have little belief that they are protecting an outpost of democracy in South Vietnam. . . . The soldier definitely does not see himself fighting for South Vietnam. Quite the contrary, he thinks South Vietnam a worthless country."[24]

There was good reason for skepticism. One of the most clear-cut revelations of the *Pentagon Papers* was the fact that American policymakers had little, if any, concern about the fate of South Vietnam and its people in their own right. Rather, they regarded South Vietnam merely as the geographic focus of a global power struggle.[25]

American soldiers did not believe the Vietnamese were eager to fight communism. They were virtually unanimous in their criticisms of the capability and determination of South Vietnamese forces. While it is easy to find examples of praise for the skill and determination of the Revolutionary Forces, it is almost impossible to find American soldiers who were impressed by the ARVN or the local militias. U.S. troops typically described their military allies as untrustworthy cowards who did everything possible to avoid combat.[26]

Some soldiers began to believe the only way to survive in Vietnam was simply to treat all Vietnamese as outright enemies and make no pretense of favoring some over others. Michael Herr captures this attitude most strikingly by recounting a piece of black humor that circulated among American soldiers in Vietnam: "The joke went, 'What you do is, you load all the Friendlies [all the South Vietnamese on whose behalf America claimed to be fighting] onto ships and take them out to the South China Sea. Then you bomb the country flat. Then you sink the ships.' A lot of people knew that the country could never be won, only destroyed, and they locked into that with breathtaking concentration."[27]

American GIs fought for each other, but they surely did not feel they were fighting for the South Vietnamese. Indeed, many soldiers felt the more they worried about the welfare of civilians, the harder it was to do their job.

When Charles Moskos asked soldiers in Vietnam why they were there, most gave personal explanations. Common responses were, "My tough luck in getting drafted," "I happened to be at the wrong place at the wrong time," "I was fool enough to join this man's Army," and "My own stupidity for listening to the recruiting sergeant." Few were driven by a deep ideological commitment to the war. Nevertheless, many supported the general policy of containment and believed that stopping communism was the key objective of the American war. This view was particularly widespread in the initial years of the American buildup. In 1966 John Sack found that, at the outset of their tours, virtually every one of the approximately 170 men he studied in the First Infantry Division believed they were legitimately in Vietnam to stop the spread of communism.[28]

The justification of the war that new soldiers found most persuasive was a version of the domino theory that emphasized the threat to the United States if communism triumphed in Vietnam. The focus was not so much on the potential threat to other nations. Instead, the soldiers were most drawn to interpretations that stressed the necessity of the war to prevent a direct attack on American security. Moskos found these common responses: "The only way we'll keep them out of the States is to kill them here," "Let's get it over now, before they're too strong to stop," "They have to be stopped somewhere," and "Better to zap this country than let them do the same to us." John Sack quotes this statement as typical: "The communists win in Vietnam it'll just be Laos, Thailand, the Philippines, and then we'll have to fight in California."[29]

In 1968, Michael Herr found such views most pervasive among the top brass, who were fond of asking skeptical journalists questions like, "Would you rather fight them here or in Pasadena?" ("Maybe we could beat them in Pasadena, I'd think, but I wouldn't say it," Herr writes.) Many "lifers"— career officers and NCOs—did their best to indoctrinate their troops with this either/or proposition; either you fought in Vietnam or the entire U.S. population would be attacked. Soldiers were to believe that even though they were on the other side of the planet, they were truly fighting for the folks back home. Frank Mathews had his first experience of killing in 1966. After looking at the Viet Cong corpse, he vomited and remained sick and depressed for several days. An "old salt" sergeant tried to lift his spirits with these words: "Just figure it this way—that [man you killed] could have been the one that was in the States screwing your mama, or your wife, or your girlfriend, and that's the reason you killed him." This psychosexual version of domino theory "made a lot of sense" to the young soldier. He was a gung-ho combat volunteer and remained so through the remainder of his tour. While his motivation centered on avenging the deaths of buddies who had died—a desire to pay back the enemy—whenever he looked for a larger rationale for the war, he always returned to the sergeant's promise that the war was protecting American women.[30]

The need to perceive one's wartime service rooted in the protection or liberation of a homeland is commonplace in the history of warfare. Survey evidence amassed by Samuel A. Stouffer and his associates reveals that American GIs in World War II were more likely to view that war in terms of individual and national survival than as a moral or ideological mission on behalf of other people. In 1942, 46 percent of a sample of 6,000 enlisted men agreed with the statement, "We are not responsible for saving the world. We are in this war solely to defend the United States of America." (Thirty-eight percent disagreed and 16 percent were undecided.) In addition, 90 percent believed the war was essential to our national survival. Though Stouffer's classic study, *The American Soldier*, reveals a significant commitment to defeating fascism abroad, it concludes that the defense of the homeland was a more important motive among American servicemen.[31]

For GIs in World War II there was tangible evidence to sustain the belief that the United States was threatened. In addition to Pearl Harbor, there was the rapid conquest of Europe by Nazi Germany, and at home an entire nation was mobilized for war, a mobilization that entailed personal sacrifices and commitments throughout American society.[32]

In Vietnam, some men clung to the belief that it was necessary to fight in Indochina to prevent a war in California, and men like Frank Mathews held to the idea that his efforts were protecting American women. As men moved through their tours, however, that faith became harder to sustain. Micheal Clodfelter, who served in Vietnam from 1965 to 1966, has written, "When pressured, I upheld our presence in Vietnam by a rather feeble belief in the Domino Theory. But often I wondered how that tumbling column of dominoes . . . could possibly complete the chain reaction. . . . Try as I could, I simply could not visualize a fleet of North Vietnamese sampans and junks overcoming the U.S. Navy and landing an invasion force on the shores of California."[33]

Doubts were amplified by the recognition that millions of Americans at home felt no threat from Vietnamese communists and that, in fact, a growing number believed U.S. involvement in Vietnam was doing far more to harm the prospects of peace than to protect national security.

Most troubling to American soldiers was the awareness that the sacrifices of the war were borne disproportionately by the poor and the working class. As one veteran put it, the war demanded no "common sacrifice."

World War II was the focus of all life at home. You should see the ads in magazines like National Geographic. . . . There's a GI in every ad, or else farmers on tractors with flags or pictures of Hitler being beaten over the head with a corn cob. . . . The theme was we're all making a common sacrifice. Everyone was drafted, including lawyers, doctors—no group or stratum escaped. . . .

In Vietnam, the story was completely different. The war was unpopular at home. People were getting fat in America, but there was no common sacrifice. . . . It was a case of business as usual. Instead of everybody getting drafted, people who could go to college often did; it was those who couldn't who went into the military.[34]

In 1967, Bob Hope told American soldiers in Vietnam, "I have good news. The country is behind you—50%." The soldiers laughed, but it was a bitter laughter, founded on the knowledge that they were sent to fight a war without deep popular support. They knew as well that much of the turmoil at home was caused not by a mass mobilization for war or by a common sense of national endangerment but by the fervent debate about the legitimacy of our very involvement in Vietnam.[35]

Among American soldiers, the antiwar movement generated disturbing and contradictory responses. On one hand, the movement posed fundamental challenges to the official justifications of the war. While many soldiers were largely unaware of and misinformed about the political and intellectual substance of those challenges, simply to be aware of the existence of a growing antiwar movement made it increasingly difficult to accept uncritically the belief that the war was necessary and its goals legitimate and achievable. On the other hand, most soldiers perceived that the movement was essentially middle class. The image of the antiwar activist dominating the mass media (including the military's) was that of the college radical. For working-class soldiers, college symbolized privilege, and quite apart from the context of Vietnam, college students stirred in many a deep set of class-related emotions: resentment, anger, self-doubt, envy, and ambition. The class gulf was further exacerbated by the knowledge that college students were deferred from the draft. When college students protested the war, many soldiers took it as a personal assault, a social snubbing by those who perceived themselves intellectually and morally superior. Middle-class protest made many working-class soldiers feel angry and defensive. Even when antiwar critics were careful to distinguish their attack on government policy from any judgment of the men ordered to carry it out, soldiers often had trouble making the same separation. After all, because they were fully absorbed with prosecuting the war, soldiers had difficulty separating their identities from the war. Consequently, some soldiers felt compelled to defend a war that, by many of their own measures, was hardly defensible and to echo the justifications of policymakers that rang false in their own ears. Others sought to defend their own integrity by questioning the sincerity and courage of the antiwar activists. Micheal Clodfelter's memoir is useful in capturing the class context of these attitudes.

> To so many of us the peace phalanx parading American streets were the spoiled, gutless middle class kids who cowered in college classrooms to escape the battlefield and who, to soothe their cowards' consciences and regain their lost self-respect and their girlfriends' admiration now campaigned with ball-less envy to destroy what honor and prestige we might earn through our courage and sacrifices in battle. The peaceniks might not be attacking the integrity of American soldiers directly but they were proselytizing against the war as dishonorable and contemptible and we who were the participants in this conflict therefore felt that, by implication, we too were being made contemptible. Few of us felt any loyalty to this war, but we did possess a great loyalty and kinship to each other, to our reputations as individuals and as units. . . . We were like sons with little love left for our harsh and cruel mother, but fiercely determined to defend her name and honor against all slurs. . . . And so we often reacted bitterly to the advocates of peace who were often those more popular middle class schoolmates of ours; those who won the student body president elections, who were the valedictorians and the captains of debate teams, and who would one day pack their sportcoats and Levis . . . and leave for rooms in dorms or Greek houses while we stuffed duffel bags at an Army reception center with fatigues and khakis and were marched off to a boot camp barracks; those who would let their neatly groomed hair grow long and their narrow provincial minds expand to more liberal horizons while we had our skulls shaved to an army burr and our intellects lobotomized of all but trained responses to the military's concepts of duty, honor, tradition, and manliness.[36]

According to Clodfelter, soldiers' anger at the antiwar movement was primarily a class anger, not a reflection of their support for the war. Still, he found that most of the men in his unit in 1965–66, despite nagging doubts, generally accepted the legitimacy of American involvement. Some who did not really uphold or care about the American cause were nonetheless drawn to the emotional thrill of war. Clodfelter's memoir is a wonderful guide to that appeal. Though in a formal sense he turned against the Vietnam War, Clodfelter is unabashed about his continued enthusiasm for war. Indeed, his memoir contains some of the purplest prose of our century about the attraction of war.

Most of my compatriots mocked me for my martial desires, but a powerful infatuation for the romance and glory of war had held me spellbound from the first moment my eyes had fallen on the gunpowder smoke-shrouded lines of blue and gray charging with fixed bayonets into a blood red horizon that flamed across the illustrated pages of a Civil War history. I had remained transfixed by that haunting spell cast upon my soul by the sorcerer of death and ashes, and even now, after undergoing the true brutal reality of war, after hearing the screams of my mutilated friends and the sobs of blood-drenched women and children, after seeing the ashen stare of a man whose family had just been disintegrated by a bursting flash of napalm, still a mad love for war yet exists within me.[37]

By 1969–70 substantial numbers of soldiers opposed the war they were sent to fight. They voiced objections, avoided combat, and sometimes engaged in collective defiance of direct orders. Yet even in the latter years there remained significant animosity toward the domestic antiwar movement, to hippies and college demonstrators. In a 1970 CBS documentary, "Charlie Company," an army infantry company was filmed during an operation in which the soldiers refused to walk down a trail when ordered to do so by their captain (the men believed the trail was a likely spot for a Viet Cong ambush). The documentary also features several interviews in which enlisted men readily and openly discuss their objections to the war. They wore love beads and peace signs, and their hair and dress were far wilder than military standards prescribed. The documentary captured a small unit near the brink of mutiny. Yet one of the most remarkable moments in the film involves a group of seven or eight GIs sitting in a circle in a jungle encampment. In the midst of a discussion that includes sharp criticisms of the war, one man says, "The first thing I'm going to do when I get back to the world is beat up a hippie." The others laugh and nod. The feeling conveyed by the remark, and the men's reaction, was complex, but it seemed most of all to suggest that the antiwar protesters were enemies not because they opposed the war but because they did so (from the soldiers' perspective) at a safe and privileged distance. It was as if the grunts were saying, "Our protests against the war are the truly important ones; we are the real hippies; if anyone is going to bring the war to an end it will be grunts like us who refuse to fight and die for officers who are preoccupied with their personal advancement."[38]

Among black soldiers, the domestic antiwar movement had a somewhat different effect. Many shared with white soldiers a sense that the movement was largely elitist, lacking in compassion for the dilemma of soldiers caught in the middle of the war, and self-righteous in its moral judgments. Many also realized, however, that a number of prominent people they respected were protesting the war. When black soldiers thought about the antiwar movement, they thought not only of privileged white students; they also thought of Malcolm X, Muhammad Ali, Julian Bond, and Martin Luther King, Jr. (all of whom had taken strong positions against the war by early 1967), to name a few of the better-known figures. One of the most important civil rights organizations—the Student Nonviolent Coordinating Committee (SNCC)—publicly condemned the war in January 1966, and key members from SNCC went on to form the Black Panther party. In the late 1960s the Panthers recruited black youth from the very urban ghettos that produced so many of the men who fought in Vietnam. Only a minority of black soldiers had been active in the Panthers before going to Vietnam, but a growing number were aware of the Panthers' critique of U.S. intervention as both imperialist and racist. While white working-class soldiers like Clodfelter saw the antiwar movement as rich college kids trying to soothe their cowards' consciences and impress their girl-friends, black soldiers tended to associate domestic protest with black activists who bravely stood up against racism. Robert Sanders relates one black soldier's perspective:

Most of the people were like me; they were naive. We didn't know what the hell was really going on. We knew that Communists were supposed to be bad, and that they were trying to take the South Vietnamese's rice away from them, and that we were out there to stop them. But at the same time, the Black Panther organization, the Muslims, the Kings didn't feel that we should be out there participating in it. . . . We felt that if we were drafted we had a duty to go to war because we were Americans. But . . . we were fighting Charlie in his own backyard. We didn't really feel that we were fighting for our country; half the brothers felt it wasn't even our war and were sympathetic with Ho Chi Minh.

When I was in the Nam, Muhammad Ali was refusing to take the oath. Our reaction was that we shouldn't have taken it either. We felt that the American Dream didn't really serve us. What we experienced was the American Nightmare. . . . We felt that they put us on the front lines abroad and in the back lines at home. Most of the brothers felt the same, even though we fought right along. We wouldn't give up. We did our best to keep trucking out there in the woods, but we would always think about this. We used to sit down and have talks over it. We'd say "What the fuck are we doing in Vietnam, man? When we get back to the states, we gonna be treated shitty . . . anyway."[39]

Admired leaders at home challenged black soldiers to question the racial significance of the war. Is Vietnam a war for racial justice? Why, then, are they sending you out alongside white men to kill a yellow enemy referred to as "slopes," "zipperheads," and "gooks"? Where is the justice in that? Who are you fighting for? Will fighting in Vietnam bring you more opportunity in America? Isn't the real fight for equality back at home?

Try as they might to block critical questions from their minds and focus on survival, many soldiers were confronted by the prospect that they were fighting someone else's war, perhaps even that they were on the wrong side of a racist war. This charge came not only from critics at home, and from a growing number of GIs, but also from the Viet Cong. As Sanders recalls: "The Vietnamese constantly appealed to blacks to get out of the war. They would leave leaflets laying all over the jungle . . . [saying:] 'Blacks get out, it's not your fight,' or 'They call us gooks here and they call you niggers over there. You're the same as us. Get out, it's not your fight.' In some ways those leaflets affected morale. It made us wonder why we were there."[40]

The Viet Cong and antiwar critiques of U.S. intervention raised the level of doubt among many American troops, but especially among black soldiers. Also, blacks were more likely than whites to empathize with the Vietnamese. For example, the postwar *Legacies of Vietnam* study asked veterans to recall their wartime "feelings towards the Vietnamese in general." Among black veterans, 48 percent reported positive feelings, compared to 27 percent of white veterans. Even more strikingly, 32 percent of the white veterans admitted negative feelings toward the Vietnamese, compared to only 9 percent of blacks.[41]

However, soldiers of color were hardly immune to wartime racism toward the Vietnamese. As Dwight Williams recalls:

> Yeah, we called the Vietnamese gooks too. Almost everybody took on some racist feelings, no question. When you're in combat you don't really think about the right and wrong of it. They're just the enemy, the bad guys, the gooks. They're trying to kill you. Pretty soon, after some of your friends get killed, you can even get to hate them. It's like they ain't even human.
>
> But then, you get away from the killing and you wonder sometimes. You think, "Hey what's happening to me. I see myself changing. Maybe we ain't so different from the gooks. The white man been saying the same shit about us all these years." But mostly you don't think about it until you get back to the World. Then it really eats at you.[42]

WHAT ARE WE FIGHTING FOR?

Combat almost always has a territorial feel, the sensation of fighting for control of a specific location. Soldiers feel strong connections to the battleground, to the places where they have fought and watched friends die. Even when they do not feel strong ideological commitments to a particular cause, they can feel a sense of purpose and meaning in gaining and holding territory. In World War II, for example, even soldiers who felt little ideological commitment to the war could experience a sense of progress and purpose in the advance across Europe or the island-hopping in the Pacific that gradually moved American forces closer to Japan.[43]

American policymakers explained Vietnam as a crucial moment in a long-term effort to contain communism. Such language did not offer the promise of territorial advances, but it did draw on territorial imagery, the idea of restricting communism to a specific area. That imagery helped make the goal of containment appealing to some American soldiers. The United States would prevent the spread of communism by keeping it quarantined, by holding it behind a clear line. We will stand firm in

Vietnam, Lyndon Johnson said. The line is drawn. "To withdraw from one battlefield means only to prepare for the next. We must say in Southeast Asia . . . 'Hitherto shalt thou come, but no further.' "[44]

In Vietnam, however, despite this imagery, the mission of opposing communism offered no sense of territorial control. Revolutionary Forces had support in every province of the country, and the strategy of attrition, based not on gaining or holding territory but on killing as many of the enemy as possible, did not even attempt to preserve a recognizable line between areas that were communist and those that were not. Instead, units crisscrossed the countryside attempting to engage enemy units in battle. When combat was initiated, usually at times and places determined by the enemy, soldiers fought and moved on. Regardless of whether or not the Americans felt they had won or lost a particular firefight, the battleground was soon abandoned. Knowing that the enemy might move back into the same area was extremely demoralizing. It led many soldiers to conclude that their only function was to kill and that the war had no higher purpose.

> A current of bitterness ran through the men as they dug in for the night. . . . Many of them were beginning to experience a deep sense of futility about what they were doing. So much of the killing . . . seemed meaningless; it was take one hill, move on to the next—two days later the enemy was back again on the first. It was killing for killing's sake. . . .
>
> Above them remained two more knolls . . . each to be taken, then abandoned. And at what cost?[45]

Particularly disheartened were those who found themselves fighting on the same ground again and again. One veteran describes taking one hill— Razorback—on three different occasions: "We would go up there, spend a week and leave. Each time we lost men. There ain't nothing on that stupid-ass hill. It's out in the middle of bullshit. Walk up it getting killed and walk down the other side again. We did that three times."[46]

The Viet Cong had such widespread support throughout South Vietnam that it is doubtful any military strategy could have maintained clear territorial lines between allies and enemies. The most concerted effort made by the American military to separate "friendly" Vietnamese from the Revolutionary Forces involved uprooting hundreds of thousands of peasants from their villages and moving them into government refugee camps. The villages were then razed and the destroyed areas proclaimed free-fire zones. Vietnamese found in those zones were automatically considered Viet Cong and were subject to American fire without warning. The massive displacement of the rural population, however, utterly failed to contain or isolate the Revolutionary Forces. The refugee camps were filled with Vietnamese who supported the revolution, and many who had been politically neutral were drawn to the left by the experience of forced removal. Moreover, thousands of peasants of all political positions abandoned the camps, moving back to the countryside to rebuild their old hamlets or to the hamlets of relatives. American forces moved millions of Vietnamese, but they were never able to establish a clear military or political boundary between friends and foes.[47]

While the official goal of U.S. intervention was to prevent the spread of communism and to defend noncommunist South Vietnamese citizens, in reality American soldiers had no larger purpose than amassing high body counts. Unable to contain communism, they were sent out to kill communists. Provided with no certain way to identify communists, some soldiers came to regard all Vietnamese as legitimate targets. According to Philip Caputo, "Our mission was not to win terrain or seize positions, but simply to kill: to kill Communists and to kill as many of them as possible. Stack 'em like cordwood. Victory was a high body-count, defeat a low kill-ratio, war a matter of arithmetic. The pressure on unit commanders to produce enemy corpses was intense, and they in turn communicated it to their troops. This led to such practices as counting civilians as Viet Cong. 'If it's dead and Vietnamese, it's VC,' was a rule of thumb in the bush."[48] As Caputo indicates, even the narrowly defined goal of killing communists proved, in practice, merely an effort to produce Vietnamese corpses. The same point was made by Col. Anthony Herbert: "Regardless of what a person might have been before he was killed, afterwards he was a dink. Very damned few people ever reported killing a civilian, regardless of how unavoidable the death might have been."[49] The inability or unwillingness of the United States to distinguish between combatants and noncombatants pointed sharply to a major contradiction in American policy. On one hand, American leaders claimed there were clear and fundamental differences between North and South Vietnam and between the Viet Cong "terrorists" of South Vietnam and the South Vietnamese "friendlies." On the other hand, whenever U.S. forces killed civilians or destroyed villages, officials would bemoan the impossibility of distinguishing between combatants and civilians. Similarly, officials typically insisted that the vast majority of Vietnamese civilians opposed the Viet Cong and the leadership of Hanoi. (As late as 1974 W. W. Rostow still claimed the people of South Vietnam would not have elected Ho Chi Minh to be dog catcher.)[50] If a hamlet or a village were destroyed, however, and questions were raised about civilian casualties, a standard defense made just the opposite claim: "This ville is solid VC" or "They're all VC." This contradiction jumps to the surface in the radically different words the military used to describe the same people. Jonathan Schell found that the civilians evacuated from Ben Tre during Operation Cedar Falls were labeled "hostile civilians," a term which "hinted that all the villagers at least supported the enemy and thus all deserved to be 'relocated.'" After the village was destroyed and the civilians hauled off to camps, however, the military no longer called them hostile. They were instantly transformed into "refugees," a name "which suggested that the villagers were not themselves the enemy but were 'the people,' fleeing the enemy."[51]

Given the linguistic gymnastics required to paper over such contradictions, it is little wonder that most enlisted men made no verbal effort to distinguish among the Vietnamese. When Lt. Frederick Downs arrived in Vietnam, he was surprised to find that his men referred to the Vietnamese employees on the American base as gooks.

"I noticed you called them gooks. I thought that would be what we called the enemy. Does everybody call them gooks?"

"We do around here, sir. . . . Different units got different names for them, but it don't make no difference what you call them, you know. Friendly or not, they're all called the same. Look at them. They don't even know what good living is. They're ignorant as owl shit."[52]

Michael Herr quotes the response of one soldier when he heard a standard defense of American policy about protecting South Vietnam from communism. The soldier said, "All that's just a *load*, man. We're here to kill gooks. Period."[53]

Without doubt many soldiers, especially in the years before 1969, executed American policy with single-minded determination. According to Clodfelter, such men "did not even attempt to question the reasons for our presence, but were simply resigned to the irrevocable fact that we were there and there for one purpose only . . . to kill as many slopeheads as possible."[54] Some responded with great enthusiasm, kept careful track of their confirmed and probable kills, and fully embraced the ethic of the body count. As one veteran recalls, "There's nothing like a confirmed kill. . . . They make you crazy. You want more. You know everybody back at battalion will look at you with envy when you get back in. You scored a touchdown in front of the hometown fans. You get a lot of respect from your peers who are all doing the same thing. When somebody else got one, you'd go, 'Son of bitch, the lucky bastards. Why couldn't we have been there?' "[55]

For some, the killing became an end in itself. But more typically it was conceived as a form of payback, an effort to get back at the enemy for all the suffering the war had inflicted upon them (for the fruitless and exhausting searches, the mines and booby traps, the anxiety and confusion, and the loss of friends). Frank Mathews believes payback was the most intensely felt motivation in his marine unit (1966–67): "After about a month I had a friend—as much friendship as you can make in a month—get shot. He said, 'Pay 'em back for me.' From then on, if anybody got hurt we wanted revenge more than anything else. Every time we got psyched up for a patrol it was to pay 'em back. If another company down the road got waxed the night before, we were going out that night and pay 'em back. Payback was all we were doing."[56]

During the early years of the war there was much frustration and bitterness among U.S. troops, but soldiers expressed their feelings not so much in the determination to avoid combat as in disillusionment and confusion about what was expected of them and how their efforts would lead to victory. Out of one side of their mouths commanders screamed for high body counts. Out of the other side they periodically warned against mistreating civilians and tightened up the rules of engagement. The contradiction between the two pressures made many feel hamstrung, unable to do their jobs. Even when the rules of engagement were broken, many soldiers felt held back, and they suspected that the high command did not really intend for them to succeed. "Command gettin' in your way so you can't even do your job. Shit, last three patrols I was on we had fucking *orders* not to return fire going through the villages, that's what a fucked-up war it's gettin' to be anymore. My last tour we'd go through and that was it, we'd rip out the hedges and burn the hootches and blow all the wells and kill every chicken, pig and cow in the whole fucking ville. I mean, if we can't shoot these people, what the fuck are we doing here?"[57]

Even when soldiers felt a license to do anything, they saw no clear vision or promise of victory. To be sure, the military was always announcing great progress, but throughout the war, soldiers were wary of these official progress reports. They saw no imminent victory, no light at the end of the tunnel. They saw no decline in the opposition's will to fight, no decline in the enemy's ability to determine the time and place of battle, and no decline in their troop levels; nor did American soldiers find their own efforts rewarded by an increase in support from the Vietnamese people. Also, the American command routinely claimed as a victory any firefight in which the United States suffered fewer casualties than the enemy, but such victories often felt more like losses to the men in the field. Superiority in American firepower frequently produced high enemy body counts but only when grunts, acting as bait, managed to draw the opposition into identifiable targets. Air strikes and artillery might account for a high body count, but that itself did not necessarily translate into victorious attitudes among the soldiers.

One time we got pinned down in this dried-up riverbed. The NVA were firing at us from these bunkers in the tree line. We found out later those bunkers were reinforced with concrete. Anyway, the only place for us to hide was under these scraggly little bushes. We got our asses kicked. Any time somebody tried to move, they got hit. We lay out in that hot sun *all* day, and I mean it was baking! A few guys died from sunstroke. When we pulled one guy out later we couldn't find a single wound on him; he just died from exposure. We called in quite a few airstrikes but that didn't help much cause the NVA was just too well dug-in. We finally got out of there after dark. But we lost 12 men in that friggin' riverbed.

I don't know how many NVA we killed, but a week or so after the operation I read an article in *Stars and Stripes* all about what a great victory we had won, how we had killed something like 200 NVA and our own casualties were "light." We were out there in the open like a bunch of sitting ducks, lost twelve guys, and they said our casualties were "light." It blew my mind.[58]

By 1969 American soldiers commonly viewed the emphasis on the body count as a direct threat to their own lives, and few shared the command's desire to engage the enemy. Many officers themselves were less enthusiastic about aggressive tactics and would not take the kind of risks earlier commanders took when American lives were in jeopardy. This was particularly the case after the infamous American assault on Dong Ap Bia Mountain (Hamburger Hill) in May 1969. American units spent ten grueling days of combat in an effort to root out NVA troops fighting from well-fortified bunkers at the top of the mountain. The hill was taken, but 56 Americans were killed and 420 wounded. After all that agony to gain the objective, the command immediately decided to abandon the hilltop to search for more enemy forces.[59]

In August and November of 1969 two infantry units directly refused orders to continue their missions. In the first instance, Alpha Company, Third Battalion of the 196th Infantry, had been out on a five-day mission south of Danang in which they were repeatedly ordered to attack the same North Vietnamese bunkers. Each time they took heavy casualties. Much of the time they were under such heavy fire they could not be resupplied. They were down to forty-nine men, little more than platoon size. When the battalion commander ordered them to attack again on the fifth day, he received a radio message from his field commander, Lt. Eugene Schurtz: "I'm sorry, sir, but my men refused to go. . . . We cannot move out." The colonel responded, "Have you told them what it means to disobey orders under fire?" "I think they understand," Schurtz countered, "but some of them have simply had enough—they are broken. There are boys here who have only ninety days left in Vietnam. They want to go home in one piece. The situation is psychic here." The colonel sent some of his aides to the unit to "give them a pep talk and a kick in the ass." Eventually they convinced the men that the NVA had left the bunkers (which in fact they had) and the sixty men of Alpha Company moved out. Significantly, the battalion commander decided not to punish the men for their actions. The high command decided it was more important to downplay the incident—just "a slight ripple in the water," as the division commander put it—rather than draw attention to it with court-martial proceedings.[60]

In 1970 Capt. Brian Utermahlen of the First Cavalry Division told *Life* magazine, "Most officers frankly doubt they could get their men to fight another costly battle such as the 1969 assault on Hamburger Hill." One of his men, Pvt. Steve Wright, said, "Two of them want to kill gooks—the Captain and the Colonel—and the rest of us never want to see any again."[61]

During the years 1969–72 commanders who continued to pressure their men for high body counts were almost universally detested. In April 1969, army historians in Vietnam interviewed members of the Fourth Battalion, Forty-seventh Infantry, Ninth Infantry Division. Though interviewed by the military, the men did not refrain from voicing their criticisms. Specialist Dennis Moss was a radio operator and therefore had direct access to communications between the various levels of command. "Our Battalion Commander, in my opinion, is a very poor leader. Very poor. Every fifteen minutes he's on the horn [radio] asking me where his body count is. Every

15 minutes, he never fails. I don't even need a watch out there in the field because I know every 15 minutes the man is going to be on the horn asking where his body count is."[62] The commander was constantly hectoring Moss's company to make contact with the enemy. As another man in the unit put it, "You have to come up with some good excuses if you haven't gotten in contact! It seems he doesn't realize that you can't be in contact 24 hours a day."[63] But they were in enough contact to lose, by Moss's count, about twenty-five men each month.

> I know for a fact that the Brigade Commander, Battalion Commander and my CO are pressuring for higher rank. And I can just say if I was in their position, I wouldn't want all those men's lives on my conscience just to be a Brigadier General, a full bird colonel, and a major.
>
> They go through about 25 men a month in this company alone. . . . I can't believe this waste. I can't believe that this has actually happened to the American people. It just doesn't seem like we're accomplishing that much. They say we have, but I can't see where we have. I mean I get out there in the field and I've seen it, and I can't see where we've accomplished that much.

For Moss, American casualties were not so much the inevitable result of war but the result of ambitious officers willing to sacrifice their men for the sake of promotion. Among enlisted men (and a growing number of junior officers), however, the success of an operation was increasingly measured not by how many enemy were killed but by how few Americans, not by how much fighting occurred but by how little. Moss says at one point, for example, "It was a good night—no contact." Survival was always of paramount importance to American soldiers, but it became the overriding concern in 1969 when soldiers learned that gradual troop withdrawals might soon begin. Hopes of shortened tours arose (in most cases, for naught), and no one wanted to be among the last Americans to die in a war their country was apparently going to leave. Dennis Moss expressed the prevailing sentiment: "Maybe there's a reason, a good substantial reason, for the war, although I can say most of the men—they don't know this reason. I think most of them are fighting just to stay alive. . . . Maybe in the future this war will come to an end. I think that's mostly what's driving the men on. There's been rumors going around that the 9th Division is going to pull out. I think that's what keeps these men going, cause they darn sure don't have nothing else except for the letters back home."

Also in Moss's company was PFC William Friel:

I'd have to say that the war in Vietnam is about the biggest blunder the United States ever made. As far as I can see there's not anything over here worth 34–35,000 American lives [the number of deaths as of 1969]. . . . It just seems real senseless to me. It doesn't seem like we're fighting this war for all the people in Vietnam. The people that we come into contact with all the time—the people that live in these hootches and such—it doesn't matter to them whether or not they live under a democratic or dictatorship type government or have to live under a capitalist or communist type of economic system because, hell, alls they're gonna do is keep on living in their hootches and tending their rice paddies and water buffalo and that stuff. It seems to me alls we're fighting this war for is the people in the big cities like Saigon making a fast buck off the Americans. . . . I know if I was President for one day, I'd get all the boats and planes that we have, put every American GI on it, and get us out of here as fast as we can.

This war doesn't mean anything to us and if there's a chance that we might get killed, well then we shouldn't take the chance. If there's a couple hundred VC in the area and a chance that we might get killed then forget the couple hundred VC and keep us safe.[64]

Soldiers in Vietnam sometimes contrasted their own motivations with those of their Vietnamese opponents. Throughout the war U.S. troops expressed amazement at the dedication and discipline of the Revolutionary Forces. They wondered what explained the commitment. What made them fight on year after year? Many concluded that the enemy had a genuine sense of purpose, that he must really be fighting for a cause. It was a troubling thought because it reminded Americans of their own lack of a persuasive moral, political, or strategic purpose. "Charlie had a philosophy. . . . I would wonder what provoked a woman or a little kid to get out there and fight like this unless they honest to God felt that their beliefs were right. It was scary to me, waking me up, making me ask what I was doing there. I mean, what WERE we doing there?" As another man put it, "We're playing games and they're fighting for keeps. They've got a destination—they have to take over Saigon. We've got nothing."[65]

MORALE

In modern usage, *morale* has been trivialized. It now conveys a rather superficial meaning, not much more, really, than our daily mood, a summary of the surface emotions we display as we conduct our business. When morale is separated from stronger emotions and convictions below the surface, we treat it as a temporary condition easily responsive to minor events. We may say, for example, that a dinner out will provide a morale booster for a bad week at work. The root meaning of the word, however, suggests a more profound state of mind deeply connected to a person's moral condition. Taken seriously, morale is fundamentally shaped by the moral significance of our actions.[66]

In *A Soldier Reports*, Gen. William Westmoreland offers the following analysis of troop morale in Vietnam:

> In keeping with my belief that it was going to be a long war, the one-year tour gave a man a goal. That was good for morale. . . . I hoped it would extend the nation's staying power by forestalling public pressure to "bring the boys home."
>
> While PXs, clubs and messes, and recreational facilities primarily helped keep troops out of the cities and reduced piaster spending, they were also good for morale. So too was the R&R (rest and recuperation) program, which provided a man an interim goal to break up his one-year tour. . . . These creature comforts, plus other factors such as keeping men busy and informed, having them participate in civic action projects, and keeping the complaint channel open, helped during the period 1964–69 to generate the highest morale I have seen among U.S. soldiers in three wars. It was only after 1969 that the psychological stresses and strains of an apparently endless war began to show.[67]

Before proceeding to Westmoreland's ideas about morale, some basic falsehoods must be challenged. Most soldiers were not assigned to civic action projects, they were not well informed, and if Westmoreland did not see any morale problems before 1969, he was simply not looking. Indeed, he denies the existence of any serious problem in the military during his years as Vietnam commander (1964–68). He even implies that the My Lai massacre—the slaughter of hundreds of unarmed Vietnamese by a U.S. infantry company in early 1968—might have been avoided if he had been able to greet the unit responsible for the massacre upon its initial arrival in Vietnam: "In an effort to demonstrate that the commander cared, I tried to meet every major American unit entering the country. . . . The only major unit I was unable to meet was the 11th Infantry Brigade. . . . It is ironic that a component of that unit was destined to get into trouble at a place called My Lai."[68]

Most striking about Westmoreland's approach to morale is that it is totally removed from questions of ideology or principle. He suggests by omission that morale has nothing to do with whether or not soldiers understand and support the aims of the war or that they believe themselves engaged in an important and justifiable cause. Though he seems to believe good morale is largely contingent on having a goal, the only goal he identifies is the mere possibility of survival, the knowledge that the war will end for each man if he can survive for a one-year tour. That, along with certain creature comforts, a dose of good works (civic action), and keeping the men busy, is Westmoreland's formula for the highest morale. The purpose and meaning of the war itself is apparently irrelevant.[69]

Westmoreland is not speaking of morale in its fullest sense. Instead, he speaks the language of personnel management. He sounds like an executive of a large corporation (the largest in the United States) striving to keep his short-term employees compliant and productive. He offers a guide to some of the things that made the war merely bearable and may have served to prevent full-scale mutiny. Westmoreland concedes, in fact, that a central intention of the one-year rotation was to "forestall . . . public pressure to 'bring the boys home.'" He might well have added that the rotation policy also served to forestall GI pressure to withdraw.

While surviving a one-year tour may be, in itself, a rather unheroic goal, it very understandably became the nearly obsessive concern of most soldiers in Vietnam. At every point in their tours, most men knew precisely how much time—even to the day—they had been in Vietnam and how much remained. They drew elaborate and detailed calendars on helmet liners, flak jackets, Bibles, the sides of mechanized vehicles, and the walls of rear-area hootches.[70] With each passing day, they scratched off another square. This preoccupation was not unique to soldiers in the last years of American involvement. At every point in the war, soldiers perceived their tours in Vietnam as a kind of prison sentence, a matter of "doing time"— 365 days of it. In David Halberstam's novel, *One Very Hot Day*, set in the early 1960s, a corporal discusses the subject with two officers:

"You know what day this is? . . . Twenty-one days . . . Three weeks is all. Exactly twenty-one days to go in this country. Then home, the land of the Big PX. . . . You mind if I ask you something, Lieutenant? How many days you got left?"

Anderson smiled, almost shyly. . . . "One hundred and eighty-two."

"One hundred and eighty-two, boy, that's the best," said the Corporal, "downhill now. One hundred and eighty-three behind you, that's the important part, and nothing but downhill. . . . How many you got, Captain? You mind if I ask?"

"I don't know," Beaupre said.

"Whadya mean, you don't know," the soldier said. "Sure you know. Everybody knows. Even the Colonel knows. How many?"

"One hundred and eleven," Beaupre said.[71]

Knowing that their personal war had a finite length gave soldiers a way to structure their experience, a way to contain some of their anxiety. At least, they often reminded themselves, it will all be over in x months or days. In fact, the one-year tour was often the only concrete thing soldiers could count on in Vietnam. The rotation policy no doubt tempered GI resistance because it invited men to focus on individual survival over a specific period of time rather than collective responses to an indefinite crisis. Westmoreland's suggestion that the one-year tour increased combat motivation is not persuasive, however. In fact, virtually all the oral histories, memoirs, and novels indicate that soldiers were most willing to fight when they were least conscious of the time left in their tours. Soldiers kept track of their days left in-country throughout the course of the year, but they were most intensely aware of time at the beginning and end of their tours. In the middle of their tours, most veterans report, they were less obsessive about counting the days and most effective in carrying out their duties.

As soldiers reached the final three months of their tours, their time left in Vietnam was short enough to accord them the status of "short-timers." A wealth of lore and language describes men with "short-timers' fever." Some units called short-timers "two-digit midgets" (ninety-nine days or less), and innumerable jokes began with "I'm so short . . ." (e.g., "I'm so short I've packed my shadow so I won't lose it"). As the final weeks approached, a jolting thought absorbed the mind of the short-timer: I might actually survive this war after all! But that realization also rekindled dread. The shorter they got, the more superstitious they became.

Personal survival became an even greater preoccupation, and soldiers took as few risks as possible. In some units it became an unwritten policy to protect short-timers by finding them rear-echelon jobs. At the very least they were no longer asked to walk point or take the most dangerous assignments. Most people believed short-timers had earned the right to easy duty. They also believed short-timers could not be trusted in dangerous situations. The "fever" caused by getting short might make them overly cautious and endanger the other troops.[72]

For grunts who spent most of their time in the bush, the creature comforts cited by Westmoreland as crucial to high morale were rare indeed. To them, significant "bennies" were mail, an occasional hot meal, and the periodic "stand-downs" that returned them to rear areas for showers, rest, and beer. Other than the final day of one's tour, the most anticipated moment was the week-long R&R (usually offered to men sometime after the six-month mark). A marine grunt (marines served thirteen-month tours) writes, "These were the things that made thirteen months in the Nam bearable—a stream and a drink ahead, the objective within sight . . . a letter . . . from a girl, R and R only a month away, the bennies strung out along the way, breaking up thirteen months into chunks of weeks and days."[73]

The "Modern Living" section of *Time* magazine for 22 December 1967 features a photo-essay on the R&R trips offered to American soldiers during their Vietnam tours. The cover story is on Bob Hope—"Christmas in Vietnam"—and that, along with the R&R story, offered readers the consoling impression that America's fighting men were enjoying the holidays. They were, it seemed, either laughing at Bob Hope or basking in an exotic Asian city with bikini-clad companions. Along with photos of Asian women massaging war-weary GIs, *Time* blithely quoted the going rates for prostitutes.

No army has ever had anything quite like it—but then there has never been a war quite so frustrating as Viet Nam. It is the U.S.'s Rest and Recuperation program. . . . This month, some 30,000 will wing off from the chill monsoon rains of the DMZ or the muddy Delta for a five-day fling to a list of cities that now includes [Hong Kong, Bangkok,] Honolulu, Tokyo, Taipei, Singapore, Manila, Penang, Kuala Lumpu and, most recently, Sydney. To provide it, the Government pays Pan Am $23,500,000 a year. . . .

[In each city the soldiers are] briefed by the local R&R center (sample from Taipei: "Keep out of the buses or you may lose your wallet. Do not purchase the company of a girl for more than 24 hours at a time: they seldom look as good in the morning."). . . .

Among single men, the favorite city is Bangkok. Its Petcahburi Road offers the neon-lit Goldfinger Massage Parlor, the Whiskey A Go-Go club and some 50,000 bar girls, but also impressive temples for inspection during the recuperative hours. The companionship of a girl who also numbers English among her several skills can be secured for $11 a day or $50 for a full five days.[74]

These flings were mind-boggling experiences. Most men tried to make the week the hedonistic binge for which it was designed, but the experience often proved isolating and disappointing. Adopting the instant role of civilian-tourist-womanizer within hours of the war zone was utterly dislocating, and some men found themselves at the end of their R&R strangely eager to return to the more familiar world of war. A rare few managed to go beyond the prescribed short-term whoring and establish a rapid and intense relationship with a prostitute hired for the week or, more unusually, with a chance acquaintance. Deeply in need of affection and healing, it was not unusual for these men to fall in love and even to propose marriage. John Ketwig's memoir, *And a Hard Rain Fell*, offers an excellent account of such a relationship and its ultimate downfall. But whether R&R proved to be a great time, an alienating disappointment, or simply a drunken escape, it was, for almost everyone, an experience that simply sharpened their sense of the war's craziness. Being taken by themselves away from the war, taken just as singly and abruptly as they entered it, and deposited with a fresh set of clothes among the neon lights of a bustling, commercial city made soldiers all the more aware of how isolated their war was. Even nearby Asian capitals seemed completely removed from and oblivious to the deadly struggle in Vietnam. How, soldiers wondered, could anyone at home possibly understand what they had experienced if people in Taipei or Bangkok didn't know what was going on?

Westmoreland believed R&R gave men an interim goal. That it was. Soldiers longed for their week away, and no matter how it turned out, it was almost compulsory for men to return to their units with tall tales of blissful indulgence. But the experience underlined how the war itself had no meaningful goals.[75]

Men stationed on large bases in relatively safe areas—Long Binh, Cam Ranh Bay, Vung Tau, or Qui Nhon—had far more creature comforts than did the "boonie-rat" infantrymen. In a material sense at least, they lived in a radically different world. They could usually count on hot showers, warm meals, and electric power. They could shop at PXs stocked with everything from cigarettes and candy to cameras, radios, stereo equipment, lingerie, perfume, and jewelry. At enlisted men's clubs they could drink ten-cent beer and play slot machines. Some bases had basketball courts, nightly movies, and television. In 1966 at the enlisted men's club in Qui Nhon, soldiers could watch "The Ed Sullivan Show," "My Favorite Martian," and "Bonanza." By 1970, bases in Saigon, Tuy Hoa, Nha Trang, Qui Nhon, Pleiku, Chu Lai, Danang, and Quang Tri had a TV lineup almost as complete as that of stateside viewers, including such programs as "Star Trek," "Laugh-In," "The Mod Squad," "Get Smart," "The Beverly Hillbillies," and Red Skelton. A few bases even had swimming pools.[76]

A simple listing of amenities exaggerates the ease of life for most rear-area soldiers, even those at the best-equipped bases. For one thing, they were required to work extremely long hours at very tedious tasks. Typical working days lasted twelve hours, and most men worked six or six and a half days a week. However, there is no denying that, in contrast with grunts who lived in a state of almost constant deprivation, rear-echelon soldiers lived in relative splendor. When supply choppers occasionally took ice cream or hot meals to infantrymen in the bush, it was a rare treat, a true bennie. For grunts, a C-ration can of fruit cocktail was a highly valued possession—saved, savored, and more negotiable than cash. Some grunts only had the chance to shop at post exchanges during their week-long R&R.

These contrasts were crucial to the experience of the war and to how different soldiers perceived each other, but there is no direct or simple connection between the living conditions of various soldiers and their attitudes about the war. The creature comforts of the rear did not themselves give the war greater meaning or purpose. In fact, by some measures, rear-echelon soldiers were more demoralized than infantrymen. In the rear there were more racial conflicts, higher levels of excessive drinking and drug use, fuller exposure to black marketeering and political corruption, and deeper subjection to petty military regulations and the authority of officers.[77]

The discrepancies between official justifications of the war and its reality were no less obvious in the rear. Relationships between Americans and Vietnamese were strained and often hostile. Men were discouraged and often forbidden from leaving the base to visit nearby cities. According to Westmoreland, bases were supplied with social clubs and recreational facilities to bolster morale and "to keep troops out of the cities." The command wanted free-spending soldiers to stay out of the cities because they would exacerbate the already skyrocketing inflation of the South Vietnamese economy, but the other motive for trying to keep soldiers on base was to reduce violent conflicts between American soldiers and the local population. Told they were in Vietnam to help the South Vietnamese, rear-echelon soldiers were confined on bases, separated from the civilian allies who lived nearby.

Feeling no connection to the ostensible cause of supporting the South Vietnamese, support troops felt equally removed from the primary objective of American policy: searching for and destroying communists. Isolated on bases, subjected to a monotonous round of work, they felt simultaneously detached and vulnerable, bored and anxious. They were engulfed by the fear, suspicion, and hostility of a war zone but were not fully involved in the war itself. Many felt like witnesses or spectators to the war's destructiveness, like military voyeurs, or like actors in a mock war that might, at any moment, turn very real. The fear of a mortar and rocket attack or a ground assault through the perimeter was not always acute, but it was constant; it hung in the air as thickly and tacitly as the heat and dust.

For enlisted men, one of the most exasperating features of life on large bases was the officer corps' emphasis on "Mickey Mouse" duties and protocol—spit and polish cleaning, military etiquette, and rules and standards that seemed irrelevant and meaningless to men in a war zone. Raymond Wilson, an air force mechanic stationed in Cam Ranh Bay in 1965, recalls the disgust among enlisted men at the command's insistence on running the base as if it were in the United States rather than in a war zone. After long hours of fixing jets and helicopters, the men had to rake sand and pick up cigarette butts. "In a war zone! I mean people are getting killed and we're worrying about where you're throwing your cigarette butts! And you're supposed to rake your sand. The sand around your tent had to be raked and they would inspect twice a week. And, I swear to God, I'm not telling you a lie, it had to be raked east to west. It couldn't be raked north-south—they'd raise hell. It's crazy!"[78]

Not many rear-echelon soldiers truly envied the infantryman's ordeal of humping and the dangers of the bush, but there was almost universal envy of the relaxation of military standards common in the infantry. Everyone knew that grunts had far more leeway in how they dressed, acted, and related to officers. Indeed, when new officers joined infantry units and insisted on conventional military courtesy and tried to enforce standards of dress and protocol, they were in fast danger of losing any claim to respect or authority. Unless these officers adapted, their men would do everything possible to challenge them: carry out orders grudgingly and unenthusiastically, ignore them when possible, or even defy them outright. In combat situations, officers often loosened the reins of their authority because their very survival depended on the willingness of men to follow orders.

In the rear, where external dangers were less extreme, the gulf between officers and enlisted men was greater, and officers were less willing to forgo their prerogatives. John Ketwig describes a Fourth Division colonel who ordered rear-area soldiers to paint his jeep with a special glossy paint for use around Pleiku. When he wanted to drive to more dangerous areas, however, where a glossy jeep would be likely to draw enemy fire, he had the men sand off the gloss and repaint it olive drab. Every time the colonel returned to the rear, the glossy paint went back on, along with gold pinstripes for the fenders and seat covers made of tiger-stripe fatigue shirts. Alongside the colonel's jeep the rear-echelon mechanics spent their days fixing trucks that had been damaged by convoy ambushes or land mines. Often these trucks returned to base still dripping with the blood of the men they had carried. "It was disgusting to work on bloody trucks side by side with the colonel's 'California custom' jeep. To us, it symbolized the detachment of the officers from the suffering of the grunts." It also symbolized some of the moral dilemmas faced by rear-echelon soldiers: the guilt they felt for supporting the war without facing its greatest dangers and discomforts, and the humiliation and outrage caused by the necessity of catering to those officers who sought merely to advance their own prestige and to exercise their authority as if the bases they ran were not in a war zone but, say, built for "California custom."[79]

Westmoreland's prescription for high morale—the one-year rotation and creature comforts—did not give soldiers a goal beyond mere survival. In fact, to a large extent both factors undermined combat motivation. The inequalities between life in the bush and life in the rear infuriated combat soldiers. They had a long string of pejoratives to describe those who served in the rear ("office pogues," "Remington Raiders," "REMFs"— rear-echelon mother-fuckers). The rotation of soldiers in and out of the war created an army of individuals. No unit ever remained together for long. An individual would come to the end of his tour and leave, or he would be killed or wounded along the way. He would be replaced by a new man. When new soldiers joined their units, the other men warned them to avoid developing close friendships; friendships would be broken by the war and lead to additional grief. It was better, they said, to keep relations casual and businesslike. Most men did not know the full names of more than a few of their fellows. Nicknames helped maintain a distance.[80]

Nevertheless, in one account after another, veterans insist that, despite the obstacles to unit solidarity, they felt a profound comradeship. It was, for many, the only aspect of their Vietnam experience they could describe as valuable and meaningful. Paradoxically, the very conditions that seemed to undermine unity—the individual tours, the lack of meaningful goals or measures of success, the divisiveness at home (and in Vietnam) over the necessity of the war—might have actually provided a bond among the soldiers. One veteran put it this way: "We realized collectively we had nothing to fight for, that nobody cared about us, and we didn't give a shit about them. Our sense of motivation was a buddy system: 'we are in this and nobody cares, but at least we can care about each other.'"[81]

A soldier in Vietnam used almost the same language: "We fight for each other. We're really tight here. Nobody else cares for us."[82] Vietnam was certainly not unique in drawing men together and motivating men to fight for their buddies. The Stouffer study of GIs in World War II argues that primary group cohesion was the major motivating force among the soldiers of that war; but there is a distinct character to the unity felt by Vietnam soldiers. It was shaped not only by the common dangers of war but also by a common sense of the war's pointlessness. In World War II, by contrast, most soldiers rarely doubted the worth or significance of their sacrifices. Toward the end of World War II, the Stouffer survey asked combat soldiers, "Do you ever get the feeling that this war is not worth fighting?" Only 7 percent gave a strong affirmative, answering "very often." The rest said, "never" (40 percent), "only once in a great while" (26 percent), and "sometimes" (27 percent). When World War II soldiers did question the war's purpose, their comrades tended to reinforce the dominant view that the war was just and necessary. In Vietnam, however, soldiers drew together around the shared assumption that the war itself had no meaningful purpose, that the only meaning was located in the collective unity necessary to survive.[83]

Robert Sanders, a black infantryman who served in 1968, describes his feelings:

It takes tragedy to bring people together. . . . I felt closer to everybody in that unit at the time than I do my own blood sisters and brothers. . . . It was THE family. . . . It wasn't like a regular family that may not have enough food or jobs. In our particular family, we knew that in a few minutes everybody could be dead. . . . We was so close it was unreal. That was the first time in my life I saw that type of unity, and I haven't seen it since. And that was ten years ago. It was beautiful. It sort of chills you, brings goose bumps just to see it, just to feel it, cause the family is guys from all over the states, from New York and California, Chicago, Mississippi, 'Bama, everywhere. At first, you got all these funky types of personalities hooking up into one military unit. Everybody had their own little hatreds, their own little prejudices, biases. But after four, five, six months that disappeared. You just saw total unity and total harmony. . . . That was the only thing that really turned me on in Vietnam. That was the only thing in Vietnam that had any meaning.[84]

In the unity of the combat family there was meaning, the only meaning Sanders found in Vietnam. For many soldiers the "regular" families left behind in America faced considerable adversity and lacked food or jobs, but in Vietnam, life itself was threatened. The collective danger dissolved the little hatreds that divided them, and the unity they felt was all the more exciting for the diversity it encompassed—black and white, North and South, urban and rural. It was a precarious and temporary unity, however, deeper than anything Sanders has known before or since, but an emotion fueled by the pressures of war. For that reason we must resist romanticizing the feelings he so eloquently describes. It was, after all, a solidarity dependent on the danger and violence of a war that itself had no meaning the soldiers could embrace.

Concern about their own survival often competed with soldiers' loyalty to the group. They were torn between an intense desire to escape the exhaustion and danger of the bush and a deep commitment to the safety of their fellows. Opportunities to transfer to noncombat positions in the rear were highly sought, but not without guilt about abandoning those left behind in the bush. Still, there were some efforts to avoid combat that were widely practiced and condoned. Short-timers, for example, were expected to lay low and shirk hazardous duty. In some units almost everyone threw away the malaria pills distributed by medics. Contracting malaria meant a few weeks in the rear, and even the prospect of high fever and discomfort seemed preferable, for many, to the risks of combat. There was also nearly universal envy for those men who managed to get wounded in ways severe enough to take them out of action for the remainder of their tours yet minor enough to allow full recovery. Grunts called them "million-dollar wounds" or "tickets home." Waiting for the medevac chopper, a man wounded in this way might smile happily (and apologetically) at his comrades, who, in turn, would chide him in a friendly (but envious) way about his good luck.[85]

Some men wanted to escape the war so badly they inflicted wounds upon themselves or had a buddy do it for them. The practice was infrequent, but the temptation was almost universal. Billy Cizinski, a marine who served in 1967 recalls, "I think everybody had the thought of blowing a toe off to get out of the field. It was that much of a hell hole. But most guys couldn't do it."[86] It was generally thought of as an understandable but cowardly escape and a betrayal of the group.

Also widely condemned, at least in the early years of the war, was the practice of "ghosting," by which men feigned illnesses, invented deaths in the family, or devised other schemes that might persuade officers to grant a short return to a safe place in the rear. Another form of ghosting was to go temporarily AWOL, either during a rear-area stand-down or at the end of an R&R. These men figured that the worst punishment they might receive would be a few weeks in the stockade, a fate some considered less onerous than humping the boonies. But such practices, once again, were undercut by concerns over the well-being of the men left behind. "You never wanted to be lagging, what we called half-stepping or ghosting. Ghosting was kicking back in the rear. We didn't want to be back there ghosting and have somebody say, 'Hey man, your partner got killed.' You felt that you could have been there and helped him, you know?"[87]

In the latter years of the war, however, almost no effort to escape or avoid combat was condemned by enlisted men. By that time avoidance was, often enough, as much the collective pursuit as fighting. It was no longer so commonly perceived as an individual escape. Whole units began to half-step and ghost. The very unity that had once motivated men to fight for each other and to pay back the enemy increasingly served to enable men to avoid fighting the enemy. Even earlier in the war, when open defiance of orders was rare, some collective forms of covert combat avoidance were not uncommon. The most widespread was called sandbagging, the feigning of a mission by taking cover in a safe haven and calling in fabricated reports on field radios. Most incidents of sandbagging involved small units—squads or platoons. Squads were often sent out without an officer, and the one or two lieutenants in a platoon could sometimes be persuaded to sandbag an unpopular mission. Sandbagging usually occurred when squads were sent on nighttime patrols or ambushes. Nighttime operations tended to be more dangerous, and troops were particularly reluctant to carry them out if they came after a full day of humping. When soldiers agreed to sandbag, they simply found a concealed spot near American lines, called in periodic situation reports (using false coordinates), and slept or rested until the time they were expected to return. Tim O'Brien reports that in his company in the Americal Division, while stationed at LZ Minutemen in 1969, even the commanding officers frequently sandbagged nighttime ambushes: "If the officers decided that the men were too tired or too restless for a night's ambush, they would prepare a set of grid coordinates and call them into battalion headquarters. It would be a false report, a fake. . . . Phony ambushes were good for morale, best game we played on LZ Minutemen."[88]

By 1969 combat avoidance increasingly developed into direct "combat refusals," the military's euphemism for mutiny. The most common instances involved small units refusing to move into areas where the men believed they might get pinned down by enemy fire—a suspicious looking trail, for example, or a hill held by the enemy from well-fortified bunkers. The only official statistics so far uncovered providing any clue to the extent of such resistance were the number of soldiers convicted of "insubordination, mutiny, or other acts involving the willful refusal to perform a lawful order." The number of such cases in 1968 was 94. It rose to 128 in 1969 and 152 in 1970. Of course not all of these were combat refusals, but Senator John Stennis of the Senate Armed Forces Committee claimed that there were 35 combat refusals in the First Cavalry Division alone in 1970, suggesting that there may have been at least 245 mutinies that year among all American combat forces. In their study of "military disintegration" during the Vietnam War, *Crisis in Command*, Gabriel and Savage conclude that the extent and nature of mutiny in Vietnam was unprecedented. In Vietnam, resistance of U.S. forces was not isolated or episodic but increasingly widespread. "Unlike mutinous outbreaks of the past and in other armies, which were usually sporadic short-lived events, the *progressive* unwillingness of American soldiers to fight to the point of open disobedience took place over a four-year period between 1968 and 1971."[89]

No doubt many instances of combat avoidance and resistance were never reported or, if reported, were never adjudicated. For example, no charges were pressed against the fifty-three men of Troop B, First Squadron, First Cavalry Division, who, in 1971, refused an order to return to a combat zone from which they had just been evacuated. There were good reasons not to press charges. After all, to court-martial dissenters meant exposing a fundamental breakdown of military authority. That was not merely embarrassing to the military command; for the line officers who lost control of their men, it could be a career-ending disaster or, at the very least, a black mark on their fitness reports that would jeopardize future promotions. As soldiers became steadily less willing to carry out aggressive patrols in dangerous areas or to root out the enemy from well-entrenched positions, most officers no longer pressed their orders so hard. Some simply gave in to their men when they refused, and many officers became adept at reading the mood of their units, pushing aggressive tactics when possible and relenting to combat avoidance when necessary. Also, a growing number of junior officers shared their men's distaste for the war and joined them in placing collective survival above the priorities of the high command. Thus, many incidents that might have become mutinous were avoided through negotiation and conciliation.[90]

Finally, by 1969–70, officers were fully aware that authoritarian rule posed the ultimate risk: their own men might kill them. The "fragging" of officers increased dramatically in these years and, as with combat refusals, the threat of its occurrence shaped the relationships of officers and enlisted men far beyond its actual practice. In their most common form, fraggings were the attempted murder of officers and NCOs by their own troops. The term comes from the *frag*mentation grenades generally used to carry out the attacks (because they "don't leave fingerprints"). The army reported 126 fraggings in 1969, 271 in 1970, and 333 in 1971. These increases are particularly steep when one recalls that in the same years the total number of American troops in Vietnam dropped from over 500,000 to under 200,000. Among reported fraggings, about 80 percent of the victims were officers and NCOs.[91]

Fraggings were carried out by individuals, but few were merely personal vendettas. They often expressed the intention of other soldiers or were at least committed with the silent approval or acquiescence of a group. Soldiers commonly spoke of officers they would like to frag. Most of this talk was idle fantasy, but there were certainly collaborative attempts to murder officers. Whole units sometimes placed bounties on the heads of especially despised officers. In his novel *Going after Cacciato*,

Tim O'Brien describes a fragging ritual in which the man who volunteered to kill a second lieutenant required each of the men in his squad to touch the grenade he would use. (The lieutenant was killed because of his insistence on searching enemy tunnels, an extremely dangerous practice.)[92]

Fraggings, along with the increasing unwillingness of soldiers to fight, were indicative of such a widespread and explicit decline in morale that there were serious doubts among military experts about how long the United States could continue to field combat forces in Vietnam. In 1971 Robert Heinl, a retired officer and military analyst, toured Vietnam and wrote, "By every conceivable indicator, our army that now remains in Vietnam is in a state of approaching collapse, with individual units avoiding or having refused combat, murdering their officers and noncommissioned officers, drug-ridden and dispirited where not near-mutinous."[93] While the domestic antiwar movement is properly credited with pushing the government to withdraw U.S. forces from Vietnam, the resistance of GIs within Vietnam was an often overlooked but crucial factor in moving American leaders to the conclusion that the American ground war had to come to an end.

For soldiers still in Vietnam during the gradual American withdrawal, "peace with honor"—Nixon's rationale for the slow reduction in ground forces accompanied by bombing of unprecedented scale—was perceived as the war's crowning lie. If some soldiers continued to find some personal honor in sacrifices made on behalf of comrades, almost no one could find evidence of honor in the policy governing the final days of the American presence. It was clear that America was leaving its own sinking ship and the Vietnamese would be left to sort through the wreckage.

Perhaps nothing is more emblematic of the hollowness of official claims about fighting in Vietnam for American honor than the very "honors" awarded to U.S. soldiers. In Vietnam, American troops were presented with an unprecedented number of medals. The 3 million Americans who served in Vietnam received more bronze stars than did the 12 million men who served in World War II. The casual awarding of medals became particularly extreme in the latter years of the war, precisely when American policymakers centered their justifications of the war on the need to preserve American honor. In those final years it became commonplace for soldiers to be decorated simply for carrying out their ordinary tasks. In 1968, for example, when American deaths peaked at 14,592, there were

416,693 awards presented. In 1970, when American deaths dropped to 3,946, the number of awards rose to 523,000. During the entire Korean War only 50,258 medals were awarded.[94]

Of course, many of these awards went to men who did indeed exhibit extraordinary courage. As the narrator of Jack Fuller's *Fragments* said, "We knew they did not give the silver [star] to a grunt unless he had really done something." But even men who fully deserved their medals felt their value was cheapened by the wholesale and cynical way the military handed out more and more of them. As the war became ever more senseless, soldiers began to refer to the medals as "gongs"—meaningless and hollow.

"Bronze, silver, gold." Rumbled Jones [a character in *Fragments*]. "Some fuckin Olympics."

"Vietnam marathon," said Diaz. "You finish, you win."[95]

In 1971, more than 2,000 Vietnam veterans gathered in Washington to demand the immediate withdrawal of American forces. The most powerful expression of their rage came as the veterans gathered on the steps of the nation's capitol on the final day of their five-day demonstration. One by one they stepped forward to voice their opposition to the war. The remarks were short, pungent, and powerful, but the most searing moments were silent. After speaking, each man turned and, grasping the medals and ribbons he had won in Vietnam, hurled them at the Capitol, throwing back the honors he could no longer bear to own.[96]

To be sure, most veterans have saved their medals, and like the American population as a whole, only a minority have decisively concluded that the war in Vietnam was unjust and illegitimate. It may be especially hard for veterans to reach that conclusion. No one wants to believe they have risked their lives and lost friends in the service of a baseless cause. Many veterans strive to affirm their experience in Vietnam. In so doing, some are drawn to those, like President Reagan, who offer the comforting fiction that America's war in Vietnam was a noble cause sabotaged by liberal politicians, radical activists, and the media, and that the war might have been won if only we had allowed the soldiers to continue fighting or to fight a more total war. Such ideas pander to the war-related grief and insecurities of veterans and encourage them to agonize further over how history might have turned out differently. Yet, underlying every effort to justify, revise, or relive the past are the nagging memories of the war as it was actually experienced. With those memories return the inescapable evidence that America's policy in Vietnam blatantly contradicted the official objectives upon which it was justified. Even those soldiers who believe America was right to intervene in Vietnam and that the war should have been fought and could have been won struggle with the realization that the war they fought was not driven by a consistent or compelling moral purpose. Murray Polner interviewed more than 200 Vietnam veterans in the late 1960s and concluded, "Not one of them—hawk, dove, or haunted—was entirely free of doubt about the nature of the war and the American role in it. . . . Never before have so many questioned as much, as these veterans have, the essential rightness of what they were forced to do."[97]

What Are We Becoming?

ANOTHER WORLD

In Vietnam, American soldiers referred to the United States as The World. "When I get back to The World . . ." was a standard conversational opening. The expression signified the soldiers' feeling of radical severance from a reality of familiar meaning. The war proved so pointless, so contradictory, and so alien to any common assumption about life, they could not even locate the experience in the known world. The war seemed to belong to an unearthly place, a nether world where morality was absent or hopelessly twisted, where rational behavior felt insane and craziness merely prudent, where allies were feared and distrusted as much as enemies, where land and people were destroyed in order to save them, and where killing was the highest purpose and survival the greatest reward.

How did soldiers define and respond to this other world? They could insist that it was bizarre beyond words, beyond imagination—an unreal world. Yet it made very real demands and posed very concrete dangers. However meaningless their tasks may have felt, however removed from the pursuits and values they attributed to The World, soldiers were ordered to carry out quite specific acts. They had to hump the boonies, repair helicopters, type letters, drive convoys, and stand guard. To be sure, some men rejected these demands outright. They committed suicide, inflicted wounds on themselves, or refused orders until they were imprisoned. Several thousand deserted, abandoning their posts and hiding in the back streets of Saigon or Danang or leaving Vietnam on R&R and never returning. Most men, however, in one fashion or another, carried out the tasks assigned them, but in doing so they had to reach some accommodation with the war and make quite profound adjustments. Very simply, they had to find ways to think and act that enabled them to persist and endure. Without those adjustments soldiers might very well collapse or lose their minds.

Few men consciously decided how they would deal with the war. Most felt little control over their responses, but they could feel themselves changing as their minds moved in unclear and (so it seemed to many) uncontrollable ways to absorb the war's worst confusions and terrors. American soldiers shared a pervasive concern with survival. In moving toward that common objective, however, they developed widely differing behaviors and attitudes. Some came to accept the war entirely on its own terms and became enthralled, practically addicted, to the danger, excitement, and sense of power they found in combat. Others poured themselves into the war not out of a particular attraction to its violence but out of a strong sense of collective responsibility. They were motivated by the knowledge that other men's lives depended on their efforts and hoped to be the kind of soldier others would look to in difficult situations. This drive was often shared by men who prided themselves on the expertise they developed. They regarded themselves as skilled technicians and enjoyed the recognition their ability conferred. Others simply focused their attention as narrowly as possible on their jobs, doing only what was demanded of them but nothing more. They held back their full efforts and by so doing hoped to hold back something of their moral and emotional attachment to the war. Still others perceived the war as a kind of fantasy, a long movie in which they were merely playing a make-believe role or acting as detached spectators, witnesses to war rather than active participants. Finally, there were those who tried to reject as much of the war as possible, carving out private places, both literal and imaginative, to insulate themselves from the war's brutality. Of course, many soldiers experienced several of these responses.

Thinking of Vietnam as an antithesis to The (real) World was itself one of the most important psychological adjustments to the war. It offered men the illusion that the war existed in a physical and moral vacuum. It allowed them to interpret (and justify) their individual responses to the war as necessary and temporary reactions to an unreal environment. Soldiers made uneasy by their responses to the war tried to assure themselves that their individual transformations were not irrevocable. Perhaps they were not even real changes. After all, if the war itself seemed like an illusion, maybe one's own participation was illusory as well. In any case, wartime identities, according to this reasoning, might be quickly dropped upon return to The World, as easily shed as an astronaut's space suit. Thus, for example, soldiers faced with the troubling realization that they were beginning to enjoy killing or who began to use a great deal of heroin and wondered if they were addicted told themselves that these changes were simply short-term, reasonable responses to an insane world, not permanent alterations in their identities.

Linked to these attitudes was the idea that in a war without higher purpose or meaning than survival—a kind of Hobbesian world of brute, amoral, violence—any kind of behavior is acceptable. "The whole world gets absurd after a while. You do things that seem not right now, but which seemed right at the time. . . . You had the license to do whatever you wanted."[1] In part that sense of license grew out of soldiers' feeling used and vulnerable, little more than bait or cannon fodder. When those risks were taken without feeling a larger moral purpose, men began to believe all ethical restraints had been stripped away. Exposed to ultimate danger and indignity and unhinged from any persuasive moral imperatives, some men felt a godlike license to destroy. Fueling this impulse was the common American assumption that the Vietnam War itself was utterly lacking in moral standards. In *A Rumor of War*, Philip Caputo writes:

> As for the United States, we did not call it "the World" for nothing; it might as well have been on another planet. There was nothing familiar out where we were, no churches, no police, no newspapers, or any of the restraining influences without which the earth's population of virtuous people would be reduced by ninety-five percent. It was the dawn of creation in the Indochina bush, an ethical as well as geographical wilderness. Out there, lacking restraints, sanctioned to kill, confronted by a hostile country and a relentless enemy, we sank into a brutish state.[2]

Caputo's evocation of an ethical wilderness beyond the pale of civilization helps explain how many soldiers perceived and rationalized their own brutalization. Yet this conception also helped to loosen the sense of restraint of soldiers who sought to avoid the war. Soldiers who sandbagged operations, used drugs to relieve their anxieties, or otherwise resisted military discipline often invoked a common slogan of GIs in Vietnam: "What are they going to do about it, send me to Nam?" In comparison with the punishment of the war itself, no other threat or legal restraint seemed as fearful or onerous.

Final responsibility for the brutalization of American soldiers and their lack of moral purpose should be placed on U.S. intervention in Vietnam and the policies that shaped it. Yet because the war was fought in another, radically different world—a Third World country of peasant farmers on the other side of the planet—and because Americans were pitted against forces that dominated the terms of battle and found cover and support amidst a land and people that Americans found so utterly impenetrable and hostile, many soldiers were prompted to attribute the qualities of the war, its confusion, horror, and brutality, almost entirely to Vietnam and the Vietnamese. The men projected onto an alien world responsibility for the war's meaninglessness and savagery.

This view had wide currency in American society, and many people have used it to frame their interpretations of the whole history of the war. According to this view, American intervention in Vietnam was a well-intentioned but hopelessly naive effort to do good in a place too alien (or savage, or unpredictable, or tumultuous) to admit of American solutions. American leaders, full of optimism and high ideals, believed that each increase in American power would bring success. This faith proved misplaced as the United States slipped deeper and deeper into the "quagmire" or "bog" of Vietnam. Our failures, therefore, were not the product of twenty-five years of deliberate policy but the unfortunate combination of American innocence and Vietnamese inscrutability. Ever since the publication of the *Pentagon Papers* there has been ample evidence to contradict this interpretation. As historians like George Kahin have persuasively argued, American policymakers, far from naively optimistic, had extremely sober estimates about the odds for success in Vietnam. Their decisions were based not on the faith that victory was just around the corner but on the unquestioned belief that the United States had to do enough to avoid or forestall defeat. The United States did not inadvertently slip into the morass of war; it produced the war quite deliberately.[3]

For many supporters of the war, America's failures were attributed to tenderhearted moralism, a shameful unwillingness to use the full force of

American military might. At the heart of this view was the notion that only the most extreme brutality can triumph in a place like Vietnam—an uncivilized land whose people do not value life. General Westmoreland, for example, said in a 1974 interview, "The Oriental doesn't put the same high price on life as does the Westerner. Life is plentiful, life is cheap in the Orient. As the philosophy of the Orient expresses it, life is not important." The communists therefore commit any atrocity to advance their quest for power, and the passive civilians do not care enough about life to resist them. They live in subhuman squalor, indifferent to their own plight. Such ideas have been used not only to justify American atrocities but to argue that America was not ruthless enough. Unlike the Vietnamese, we placed too much value on life, and that was our downfall.[4]

While some soldiers embraced this view, others reached quite different conclusions. The other world of Vietnam provided soldiers a new lens through which to examine The World. They saw firsthand the extreme contrast between the wealthiest nation on earth and one of the poorest, the contrast between America's extraordinary technological power and the rudimentary material life of a peasant economy. They saw America's power unleashed, reducing much of the Vietnamese landscape to bomb-cratered wasteland. This experience raised troubling questions not only about the purpose and legitimacy of the war in Vietnam but also about the meaning of life in the United States. What values underlie American wealth and the exercise of its power? Is there any more purpose to life in the United States than there is to the war it wages in Vietnam, or is life in the United States also for nothing? Does the language of freedom and democracy used to justify the war have any more basis in the reality of American society than in the regimes it supports abroad? Are Americans, for all their wealth and technology, more civilized than the rice farmers of Vietnam, or less? And who really values life? Such questions surfaced most acutely among veterans after returning to The World, but they grew directly out of their wartime experience. David Ross, who served as a medic in the First Infantry Division (1966–67), offers these reflections:

When Americans are talking about Vietnamese or people in India or somewhere, it's not like we're looking at them like they're next-door neighbors. . . . Most of us were never able to see the Vietnamese as real people. . . .

I remember President Johnson in one of the psy-op [Psychological Operations] flicks we saw saying that the communists weren't like us—they didn't have feelings. But I always remembered . . . going into this area [after an American B-52 strike] where there was a little girl with her leg . . . traumatic amputation . . . and . . . still alive. Her mother was dead. The whole place turned upside down, a few people still wandering around with the look of the dead, a totally shocked daze.

I wondered how people would feel in Pittsburgh if the Vietnamese came over in B-52s and bombed them. . . . I'm trying to imagine a bunch of steelworkers after their wives, children, fiancees, parents, grandparents, have been blown up or are running around screaming in agony.[5]

Insights like these push some veterans to confront fully the American role in creating the other world of Vietnam and the policies that encouraged soldiers to view the Vietnamese as something other than real people. Such men are able to move beyond the narrow assumption that the war was merely a foreign affair, but they are not always better able to adjust to civilian life in America. Some have found American society as pointless and brutal as the war it waged in Southeast Asia, and they remain in a state of moral and psychological limbo, unwilling to embrace their wartime identities and unable to form new commitments in The World. Others remain wedded to the war, still wishing for another outcome and desperately clinging to the faith that if only there had been a different and better strategy or a more wholesale destruction—an invasion of North Vietnam, the use of nuclear bombs, or even more American troops—then America and its soldiers might have been victorious. Some remain bound to the war simply because nothing in postwar life has replaced the emotional extremes of Vietnam. For these men, the war, in retrospect, seems more real than life in America. At least in Vietnam, they argue, the pain and suffering were openly displayed, and life and death were on the line and directly confronted. At least in Vietnam they were among people who recognized and understood what the war exacted from them, who knew the feel of its particular horrors and absurdities, and who shared the burden of its futility.

BRUTALIZATION

In 1970, Henry Barber was stationed at Cu Chi as a casualty reporter for the Twenty-fifth Infantry Division. When American soldiers were killed or wounded, Henry wrote and typed the letters of sympathy that were sent to their families.

It was pretty much a form letter—"We regret to inform you that your son died in the Republic of South Vietnam in the service of his country . . ." but we also had to include the details of how the kid was hurt. It got pretty specific, you know—"multiple gunshot wounds in the chest and abdomen" or "severed femoral artery from a land mine." Once we received a memo asking us to tone down the letters, to just give a vague description of the wound. They told us not to write "traumatic amputation of the head" any more because it was upsetting people.[6]

If someone were so badly wounded that the soldiers at Graves Registration could not identify the body, Henry had to pull dental records and fingerprints from the files and carry them to the morgue. There he saw the young, naked bodies, ripped beyond recognition, laid out on metal tables.

Henry did this job twelve hours a day, six and a half days a week, for his entire year in Vietnam. He does not recall a day when he was not drinking or drugging, usually beginning in the morning—beer, scotch, marijuana, mescaline, speed, and all kinds of barbiturates. The drugs got him through each day, but they did not erase enough of his memory. He still has terrifying dreams about those bodies down at Graves Registration. In one nightmare, a body came alive and touched him on the shoulder. Henry woke up and his shoulder ached for a week. Most of all he dreams about the letters of sympathy. He keeps writing them over and over in his sleep: "We regret to inform you that your son has died. . . ."

As troubling as these memories are, they do not strike Henry as particularly noteworthy. He hesitates even to mention them for fear they will sound too dramatic or self-pitying, too much like exaggerated war stories. Besides, he is sure other veterans have worse experiences to relate. There was, however, something else he did want to talk about, a "small thing" that opened a new understanding of how the war had affected him. Years after the war, his younger brother asked him how to say "hello" in Vietnamese. Henry had used some Vietnamese expressions before, so it seemed like a perfectly natural question. But Henry did not know the answer. For days he searched his mind trying to recall the word and finally decided that he probably never knew it. The realization that he had not learned the most basic greeting was so disturbing because Henry measured that ignorance against the things he could say in Vietnamese. He knew how to tell someone to "get the fuck away from me," how to negotiate prices with peddlers and whores, and how to give instructions to the Vietnamese woman who shined his boots.

> I could argue with them and swear at them but I didn't know how to say hi. That may seem like a small thing but it bothers me about as much as anything else about the war.
>
> You have to understand, before I went to Vietnam I was no saint but I worked two jobs and gave all my money to my mother. I was in the CYO, captain of my high school basketball team, a pretty conscientious kid really. And I was always friendly and popular—knew everybody and was always saying hi to people. I swore a lot but I wasn't mean. It really bothers me to think how nasty I got in Vietnam.

Henry's story illustrates a crucial point about the war: the degree to which even rear-echelon soldiers could be engulfed in and traumatized by the brutality of the war. Exposed to its death, formally documenting it hour on end throughout his tour, he also found *himself* becoming increasingly hostile and angry. His postwar years have been marked by anxiety, depression, ulcers, sleeplessness, nightmares, isolation, apathy, checkered employment, uncontrollable anger, and periodic drinking binges that invariably lead to fistfights and illness. In 1983, after years of seeking psychiatric counseling at the Veterans' Administration, he was finally diagnosed as suffering from posttraumatic stress disorder. Even with that diagnosis, rendered by the chief of the psychiatric unit at a VA hospital, Henry's claim for compensation was initially rejected. After several appeals, great persistence, and the collection of a thick file of supporting testimony, Henry was granted a partial disability providing him with several hundred dollars a month in compensation. The VA rarely awards psychological disabilities to veterans who served in the rear. It generally assumes only combat soldiers are subject to psychological damage related to the war. This assumption was blatantly obvious at the final appeal hearing, when the interviewer repeatedly interrupted Henry's attempts to talk about the effect the war had on him. "Did you participate in any combat?" Henry had done some guard duty but had not been attacked. "Were you personally under fire?" There had been a few mortar and rocket attacks, but Henry had not been wounded. "Let me interrupt you again. . . ." Henry had been describing a time when he was on a work detail to collect Viet Cong bodies that had been killed on the perimeter: "There were hundreds of feet of intestine just lying there on the wire." "Would you explain to the Board, Mr. Barber, a life-threatening situation?" Henry elaborates on the rocket attacks. "Let me interrupt you for just a moment. Let's hear about how you got the Bronze Star?" "When the division invaded Cambodia in May of 1970 they asked for a casualty reporter to go along and I volunteered and they gave me the Bronze Star. But it doesn't have the V device [for valor]. It was not for bravery, just for doing a good job."[7]

Eric Stevens, a helicopter mechanic at Phu Bai in 1968, recalls the night he was on guard duty when three Viet Cong sappers tried to penetrate the perimeter. Eric and two other men on guard killed the infiltrators, leaving the bodies out in the wires until a work detail could get them in the morning. But Eric skips over this part of the story in a few words: "We were on guard duty. We had sappers in the wire. We blew them away. No big thing. It was real foggy." Because of the fog they could hardly see what they had done.

The next morning the men scheduled to take over for Eric and his friends on guard were late. It looked like they would miss breakfast. Suddenly the battalion commander made one of his rare appearances, walking around inspecting the lines. He asked Eric and the other men the questions they expected from a senior officer:

"What's your hometown son? Have you been getting your mail all right? Do you have any complaints?"

They don't really care, but it gives the troops a chance to bitch a little in a friendly kind of way. So we said, "Yeah, we missed breakfast. By the time we get in we'll be lucky to get cold oatmeal or something." Well a little later, after the colonel left, we got word over the horn that we were to go over to Headquarters to have breakfast— the best mess hall in the battalion. We're going to get eggs, real genuine eggs. So it sounded great.

Just as Eric and the other two men rounded the corner to enter the mess hall, they saw the corpses of the three sappers they had shot the night before stacked outside the mess hall.

They're all shot to shit. Like John Dillinger. Big gaping wounds, and hunks of flesh falling off, just shot to shit. The flies are beginning to come around a little. And I didn't say anything to anybody. I saw the other guys look over at the bodies and look away. So, we walked on in there and had breakfast—bacon and eggs and whole wheat toast. An excellent breakfast.

I asked myself why they would be so insensitive to just lay those people out by the mess hall. I realized later they did it for a purpose. The gooks who worked on the base were going to be coming in and filling sandbags shortly, and the bodies were put there for them to see. It was our way of saying: "This is what happens to you if you're a VC." I'm sure those bodies weren't laying out when everybody else was having breakfast. But I didn't want to dwell on it at all. I wanted to eat bacon and eggs. I chose to ignore reality for bacon and eggs. I felt bad that my price was so low—that I could see what I did and just go on in and have breakfast. It made me question what is really important to me. Is life? What do I take your life for, a dollar and a half? I tried to tell myself, ah, they're just gooks. But they weren't dead animals, they were dead people.[8]

Killing the sappers had been "no big thing." That, at least, was something Eric had expected in war. Everything he had ever heard or seen or read about war supported its necessity. Killing the enemy is what war is all about. It's kill or be killed. Such truisms helped most soldiers overcome their initial revulsion to combat death. What shocked Eric, however, was his willingness to bypass the corpses on display outside the mess hall. It was one thing to kill in self-defense and to protect others inside the perimeter. It was quite another thing to ignore the grotesque use of the dead to terrify Vietnamese civilians. Eric wondered why *he* was not terrified, why *he* was not sickened enough to skip the excellent breakfast. What has haunted Eric and so many other veterans since the war is not simply the memory of horrible sights but the knowledge that they viewed such sights without being horrified.

The brutalization of American soldiers is a central theme, perhaps the dominant one, in the war literature written by Vietnam veterans. These narratives differ in the degree and nature of the brutality they document and in their interpretations of its causes, but the common story dramatizes the process by which soldiers became (in their attitudes, if not always in their actions) increasingly callous, violent, vengeful, and sadistic. The typical movement of Vietnam literature is from initial revulsion to the war's violence to a state of psychic numbing toward it (or matter-of-fact acceptance of its necessity) to a final immersion in violence so complete that men are either destroyed by it or become addicted to it. Not all reach the end of this spectrum, but much of the Vietnam literature suggests that the war moved men inexorably in that direction. A paradigmatic example is William Huggett's novel *Body Count*. When Lt. Chris Hawkins arrives in Vietnam, he is disgusted by the slightest filth, even revolted that the men would use their dirty fingers to grab pickles from a jar. By the end he is as overcome by "kill-craze lust" as anyone: "He jammed the muzzle of the stubby shotgun into the gook's mouth as if it were a bayonet, pulling the trigger again and again."[9]

The theme of brutalization is most obvious in the novels and memoirs of combat veterans, but it also shapes accounts of life in the rear. In fact, the experience of rear-echelon soldiers often posed symbolic correlatives to the war in the bush. This relationship is illustrated, for example, in the efforts of rear-echelon soldiers to kill the rats that often infested their living quarters. In Gustav Hasford's novel, *The Short-Timers*, these killing sprees are described as gruesome metaphors for the war as a whole. One night, at Phu Bai, a group of marines set out cookies as bait to attract the rats. With the lights out, "we wait in ambush, enjoying the anticipation of violence. . . . Then the Viet Cong rats crawl out of their holes. . . . The rats skitter along the rafters, climb down the screening, then hop onto the plywood deck." Then the lights are flipped on. Most of the rats have congregated under an ammo crate where the bait was placed. One of the men pours lighter fluid into the box and throws a match.

> The rats are on fire. The rats are little flaming kamikaze animals zinging across the plywood deck, running under racks, over gear, around in circles. . . .
> "GET SOME!" Mr. Payback is screaming like a lunatic. "GET SOME! GET SOME!" He chops a rat in half with his machete. . . .
> Daytona Dave charges around and around with fixed bayonet, zeroing in on a burning rat like a fighter pilot in a dogfight. . . . He buttstrokes the rat and then bayonets him, again and again and again. "That's one confirmed!"[10]

The men who carry out this "rat race" are combat marines spending a few days in the rear before returning to the bush, but we soon learn that rat killing is a favorite pastime of rear-echelon soldiers as well. When the marine grunts take their dead rats outside for a mock funeral, they meet a group of mechanics. One of the mechanics ridicules the low body count of the grunts. "Only six? Shit. Last night my boys got seventeen. Confirmed." The grunts respond by suggesting that the mechanics were only killing "pogue" rats (rear-echelon rats), while they—the grunts—were killing "hard-core" "Viet Cong" rats.

Amidst the brutality of the war, however, most men tried to preserve some measure of humanity. Journalist Michael Herr was fascinated by American grunts and was drawn to cover them because they combined a capacity for both extreme brutality and great tenderness. For example, at Khe Sanh, "during the bad maximum incoming days of the late winter of 1968," Herr was struck by how concerned the men were with making him comfortable and safe and by "the sweetness they contained." Once at Khe Sanh some field hardened grunts sat in a circle and sang "Where Have All the Flowers Gone."[11]

They needed some outlet for their affections, some assurance that they retained the capacity to love and that they themselves were still worthy of love. The intense comradeship among soldiers, especially in combat units, is the most obvious way men resisted being overcome by the brutality of the war. A less commonly observed expression of the same yearning was the adoption of pets. "I had a dog in Vietnam. His name was Pussy. In Nam you know you have a capacity to love, but there was no one in the fucking world that loved you. The only thing I could love while I was there was a Goddamn dog. So I was very close to Pussy."[12]

Gloria Emerson went to Vietnam as a *New York Times* correspondent. Characteristically attuned to significant details overlooked by other journalists, she writes:

> The American troops loved Vietnamese dogs. It was what they loved the most in that country. They adopted dogs, none of them very big, who grew fat and playful. They were cuddled, scratched, teased, talked to, wormed, washed, and overfed. . . . There were puppies everywhere. . . .
>
> There were dogs called Dink, Gook, Slut, Pimp, Scag, Slit, Rat, Zip and Trouble. Despite the paperwork, which most soldiers loathed, in 1969 GIs took home two hundred and seventy dogs, thirty-three cats, nineteen reptiles, twenty monkeys, twenty-six birds, one fox and three lizards.[13]

Many GIs took pity on the scrawny dogs they saw in the villages or refugee camps. It made them mad when they saw the dogs neglected or mistreated. I have heard a number of veterans say that the Vietnamese, who sometimes eat dog meat, routinely kicked living dogs in the side in order to tenderize the meat; so GIs took the dogs away, believing they had rescued the animals from a life of abuse. They hoped the dogs would reward their kindness. They longed for some affection, a warm, soft body to hold amidst the fear and violence of the war. Figuratively speaking, these pets represented what many soldiers had hoped to find in their relationships with the Vietnamese people. Sent to Vietnam to save the Vietnamese from communism, soldiers hoped the Vietnamese would treat them like heroic liberators. Few Vietnamese were grateful for the American military presence, however. They regarded the Americans with fear and suspicion, when not with outright hostility. The GIs found it easier to win the trust of the dogs. They could count on the dogs, if not the people, for loyalty, affection, and gratitude.

The fact that some soldiers named the dogs "Dink" or "Gook" as well as "Pussy" suggests a kind of linguistic possession of the Vietnamese through their dogs. The GIs could own, name, and control the dogs, but the real "gooks"—the people—could not be so easily managed. Like Vietnamese civilians, there were puppies everywhere, but unlike the people, the puppies were malleable. So, too, in the rat-killing incident, the rats became surrogates of the Viet Cong, only far more easily found and killed than the real Viet Cong in the bush.

Pets aside, American soldiers slaughtered all kinds of Vietnamese animals, sometimes inadvertently in firefights but also deliberately and in situations totally removed from combat. Micheal Clodfelter's platoon of surveyors (their job was to make maps of the Vietnamese countryside) never experienced combat, but they frequently shot animals. "Some of us derived a particular bullet-cracking hedonism from riddling unfortunate animals, big and small, wild or domestic, grazing along the road as we roared by in our survey truck. . . . We rarely missed the opportunity to empty our weapons at dogs, birds, or simply the wall of a jungle canyon. It seemed unfair to us that we should have to lug our rifles around without ever getting the chance to fire them."[14]

The hedonism of destruction, though attested to by countless veterans, is commonly ignored, denied, or explained away by those who believe the natural reaction to war is (or should be) abhorrence. It is also evaded by those who believe war ennobles soldiers, that it instills courage, honor, and a greater appreciation of life. In either case, there is a tendency to portray soldiers as reluctant and regretful killers, as men who kill only on behalf of noble ideals or merely to survive or because they were ordered to do so or because they are driven to it by the most extreme physical and psychological pressures. The more troubling and complicated reality, however, is that war can engender not only the capacity to kill but the desire to kill.

> I have to admit I enjoyed killing. It gave me a great thrill while I was there. . . . There was a certain joy you had in killing, an exhilaration that is hard to explain. After a fight, guys would be really wired. "Wow, man, did you see that guy get it? Holy shit. Did you see that?"
> During ground attacks, a guy is dead and just as he is about to fall over, the volume of outgoing fire can be so intense a couple of rounds pick him up. He starts to fall over again and—whack—they pick him up. We would have contests to see how long we could keep the bodies weaving. For most people, seeing this, it's a horrible, horrible sight. We were so sadistic that we were *trying* to make it happen.[15]

In all wars, some soldiers have felt the kind of exhilaration described by this Vietnam veteran: the thrill of exercising deadly force and watching the sensational horror, the gruesome spectacle, of its results. In Vietnam, however, infantrymen used weapons with unprecedented power. *Automatic rifle* does not convey the destructiveness of the standard weapon carried by soldiers in Vietnam. Both the M14 and the M16 that replaced it (beginning in 1965) were really submachine guns. Soldiers pre-loaded their bullets into small magazines or "clips." There were twenty bullets in each clip. When fired on automatic, these weapons put out a full clip of rounds in two or three seconds. When the magazine was empty, soldiers would yank it out, jam in another, and continue firing. The M16, the standard weapon by 1967, was "fast enough," *Newsweek* reported, "to spray 700 rounds of .22 caliber bullets a minute, and powerful enough to tear off a foe's arm at 100 yards." Equally significant, the M16 was shockingly light, less than seven pounds when fully loaded (the M14 was eleven pounds). It looked and felt like a toy gun, and that was crucial to the incredible sense of power it conferred on those who used it—all those deadly rounds coming from a small, light weapon that feels like nothing more than an extension of your own arm. The lightest pressure on the trigger and, Brrrrrrrrr. So little effort for so much power; that weapon alone made some men feel invincible.[16]

Feeling invincible in the boonies was not so easy, burdened as soldiers were by their heavy packs, the impossible terrain, the unforgiving weather, the long stretches without battle, and the threat of ambush. In the villages, however, searching the hootches and interrogating the people, Americans could throw their weight around with impunity. One veteran, describing the pleasure he took in threatening villagers, recalls what he would say if a woman gave him any resistance:

> "Mama-san, you fucking shut up or I'll shoot you, too, you little VC."
> I used to love fucking with those assholes. . . . [Abusing the villagers] gave you a feeling of superiority. You're walking through the village and you got your great big old flak jacket on. You got your helmet and bandoliers all over you. You got your rifle. You tower over most of these people.
> It got to a point where you just didn't trust none of them. You don't sweet-talk them, because they ain't going to be sweet-talking *you*. . . . When you come back through here, there's going to be a booby trap to blow your fucking ass away. So we'd just try to scare the shit out of them.[17]

Though he begins by describing how superior he felt abusing the villagers, how much fun it was to have such power over them, he quickly shifts to his feeling of distrust and vulnerability. For all those bandoliers of ammo, the little villagers might set out deadly weapons of their own. Suddenly, the big old flak jacket does not seem so protective.

In fact, the exhilaration some found in violence cannot be understood apart from other emotions fueled by the war—anxiety, frustration, helplessness. They were like two responses to the same drug—a temporary high followed by a terrible low. Billy Cizinski recalls: "Your emotions were up and down, up and down, up and down. After a firefight you'd walk around three feet off the ground. Sometimes you got incredibly high, almost like a sexual release. But then there were times when you were mortared or when you were paranoid that something terrible was going to happen. Then you felt like a little rat in the corner of a hole."[18]

Since the war thousands of veterans have sought to understand how the war affected their emotions and why they thought and acted as they did. Yet even during their tours in Vietnam, soldiers needed explanations for the changes they felt themselves undergoing. They wanted to know why they were no longer so repulsed by the death they witnessed, why they were becoming so brutal to civilians, why they were becoming increasingly suspicious and distrustful, or why they came to take sadistic delight in the violence they committed. They needed answers because they needed to believe that these transformations were attributable to forces beyond their control, that the changes were not permanent, and that they retained some claim to personal morality.

These issues are highlighted in the way combat veterans explain the practice of mutilating Vietnamese corpses. Mutilation was not universally practiced by American infantrymen; but in some units it was common-place, and most combat veterans at least witnessed it. There is a common pattern to the accounts of mutilation. Often veterans begin by describing an operation on which they encountered bodies of American soldiers that had been mutilated by the Viet Cong or the NVA. This event becomes the impetus for mutilating the enemy as a form of revenge. The continuation of mutilation is then justified as a form of psychological warfare. Next, mutilation is viewed as a way of marking the number of kills one has made, a kind of personal body count. Collecting enemy ears is a way of proving how many people one has killed. Finally, mutilation becomes mere sadism. One veteran suggests something of this process in a brief description: "At first—this was 1966—they nailed ears, almost always right ears, to a tree. This was supposed to scare the Cong. Then they started wearing them in strings or hanging them up in hootches on strings. Then they started saving them in jars, with alcohol to preserve them."[19]

Another veteran, whose story was the subject of "Frank," a PBS documentary, relates his experience:

> I guess the point of insanity for me came . . . on a sweep. . . . We were working our way up this hill . . . and we came to this clear little ridge like, and there were four stakes in the ground. . . . There were four American [heads] on these stakes. . . . I remember looking at it and just saying, "My God. No." . . . The guys had been decapitated and they had their gonads in their mouths.
>
> [A few days later on another patrol] we set up an ambush and we got two people . . . and now I had a buck knife. I remember running up to the body and . . . looking at their teeth—seeing if they had any gold. And, while I was doing this, out came the knife, and I started mutilating. It was . . . this overwhelming sense of, "I've got to. You're gonna pay." And I remember stabbing over and over, just stabbing, and ripping at the body.
>
> I guess my justification is revenge. I mean I saw it done to us first. So I guess that made it OK.[20]

The justification was revenge, but Frank's feelings at the time were not really so calculated: "I was hyper, I was like somebody on speed. . . . I was not Frank. Y'know? I was John Wayne, I was Steve McQueen. I was Clint Eastwood. . . . I was living a fantasy."

Robert Flaherty was in Vietnam in 1965 with the Third Battalion, Third Marines:

> After you come across some eighteen year old [American] kid who's been beheaded, with his head stuck on a stake and his testicles stuffed in his mouth, it starts to play with your mind, and you want to do something to stop that shit.
>
> And you've been watching these people [the Vietnamese]. They come out in the morning and they defecate in the rice paddies, and that defecation fertilizes the rice, which they eat again, the old recycle trip. Some of these people are ninety years old and they haven't been outside a grid square—about two or three city blocks, in their whole life. They're human beings, but you start saying to yourself: Is that human being's life worth my friend Tommy Ionello who is over here doing whatever he can do for these people and their country?
>
> Then you say to yourself, these people just exist. They're Buddhists and they believe if they die an honorable death they'll come back as a nightingale or mayor of the town or some bullshit—they won't be a peasant anymore. So they're only too eager to rush up and die.
>
> So we started to do anything to make those people afraid of us—cutting ears, taking gold teeth. In my unit cutting off trigger-fingers was the big deal.[21]

According to the conventional wisdom of American grunts, the Vietnamese dreaded nothing more than having their bodies mutilated because they believed it would prevent reincarnation. This defense of mutilation was not unique to the Vietnam War. A version of it was expressed by a John Wayne character in the 1956 film *The Searchers*, set in the late 1860s. The Texas Rangers ride into the western plains in pursuit of a Comanche war party. The Rangers seek to avenge an Indian attack on an Anglo farmstead. They come across an Indian who has died from his wounds. One of the Rangers, Ethan Edwards (John Wayne), takes out his pistol and shoots out the eyes of the dead man. The captain of the Rangers, who is also a preacher, is aghast.

"What good did that do you?" he asks Edwards.

"By what you preach, none," Edwards replies. "But what that Comanche believes . . . ain't got no eyes, he can't enter the spirit land. Has to wander forever between the winds."

Kevin Leblanc, a medic in the First Cavalry Division, says his unit justified mutilation as a form of psychological warfare, but some came to enjoy it:

> Now with them [the Vietnamese], if you lose a part of your body and you're buried without it, there's no reincarnation. They would just be floating, walking the earth in a state of limbo, like the Catholic's Purgatory. So it was a psychological thing. In the beginning, this was the justification for doing it, that it was just psychological warfare. But it got to the point where we were just doing it for the hell of it, like getting a gook ear was some kind of a trophy, a prized possession. We even cut off testicles and stuck them in the gook's mouth. That was the bottom line.[22]

What gives these testimonies such sadness is not just the horror of the events described but the desperate struggle of veterans to account for their participation. Each of them is faced with the most difficult moral legacy of the war: coming to terms with their individual responsibility. No matter how persuasively they explain the various pressures, emotions, or motivations that caused certain kinds of behavior, they are left to reflect upon their own particular behavior and the nature and meaning of their accountability. Whether others view their actions as insane or normal, criminal or honorable, tragic or heroic, the shocking memory of the brutalization they experienced can never be fully or finally evaded. One might argue, as I have, that atrocity was intrinsic to the very nature of American intervention in Vietnam, that given the policy of fighting a counterrevolutionary war on behalf of a client state incapable of winning widespread support among its people, American atrocities were inevitable. It was not inevitable, however, that everyone would participate in the atrocity of the war to the same degree or in the same manner. This variability is a key reason why the issues of complicity and culpability are so complex. In truth, American soldiers were not responsible for the war. Most were not even old enough to vote. (The voting age was not lowered from twenty-one to eighteen until 1971.) Had they voted for the victorious presidents of 1964 and 1968, however, they would have voted for one man who promised not to send American boys to Vietnam (Johnson) and another who claimed to have a secret plan to bring the war to a rapid end (Nixon). In each case, of course, the promises were not fulfilled. But American soldiers, like everyone, do bear a measure of responsibility for their own actions, however inhuman the circumstances. In that sense, many were no more responsible for the war's atrocities than were those Americans who watched the war at home on television and who, like Eric Stevens, turned away from the carnage before their eyes in order to eat their bacon and eggs. Others, however, carry heavier portions of guilt.

Jerry Samuels was in Vietnam in 1969 with the Sixty-fifth Engineers battalion:

> One time we went into this village that was south of Tay Ninh, not far from the Cambodian border, in the parrot's beak. . . . Man, we went into that village and we were dragging the people kicking and scream-ing into this one corner of the village [for interrogation]. All of a sudden it was mayhem; there was no order at all; it was just a sudden thing of, wow! man, these people are resisting. Bursts went off; people hit the ground; GIs were firing into the crowd of people now and then, and there was yelling and screaming and biting and kicking. Yes, there were pregnant women, kids. I was having trouble with these two boys about fourteen or fifteen, trying to get them into the crowd, and finally I shouldered them into the crowd and kind of lost sight of them. I was so pissed off at them as they'd been kicking me in the stomach and biting me that I unslung my weapon and fired a burst into the crowd. About four people dropped. I let off about eight rounds, a two or three second burst. Instantly, I felt shitty. But I was still pissed off at these people, they were almost fighting us and I heard the sergeants yelling, "Vietcong bastards! You little mother-fucking commie gooks!"—I pictured them as the enemy. Finally, things started calming down after about two hours of this bullshit, laying people on the ground, standing on their backs, slapping them around.[23]

After things calmed down, Jerry and three other men took four Viet-namese girls outside the village and raped them ("they were forcibly willing—they'd rather do that than get shot"). When one of the girls "yelled some derogatory thing at the guy who'd balled her . . . he just reached down for his weapon and blew her away." This prompted the other three men, including Jerry, to kill the other girls. "It was just a spontaneous, instantaneous type thing. . . . We just picked up our weapons without giving it a second thought and fired up the rest."

In the village, as the Americans herded the villagers together, some of the Vietnamese began to scream and kick. The soldiers began to fire. It was, Jerry says, a "sudden type thing," prompted by the feeling that the villagers were "almost fighting us." Yet the account does not fully support the claims of spontaneity. The brutality, if not the killing, continued for about two hours. The rapes took place only after things had calmed down. Once again, though, Jerry describes the killing of the women as spontaneous. But as he talks through the event, it is clear that he cannot account for his actions as a mere result of blind, sudden, emotion. His mind moved in more complicated ways. He recalls that firing his weapon brought an "instantaneous feeling of satisfaction." But that was quickly followed by a "feeling of doubt about yourself"—"Instantly I felt shitty." "And in order to justify what you've done you've got to do it again. You've got to keep doing it."

Even as the killings were taking place, the actions of the soldiers were defined by justificatory language, the need to believe the villagers were resisting and that they were, as the sergeants yelled, "commie gooks"— the enemy. Officers, Jerry points out, were instrumental in promoting this view: "There was a second louie there and he had this thing about treating everyone as if they were VC." High-ranking officers had frequently demanded higher body counts with speeches such as, "I want kills, I want them gooks to be wiped out. I want to see you guys come back with kills." Moreover, American commanders had declared the village a free-fire zone. To Jerry this meant, "You can assume, especially in a free-fire zone, that you can fire on anything that moves." But the orders were vague. Jerry felt that many of the officers encouraged the shooting of villagers, or at least invited it, but refrained from offering clear and unambiguous orders to do so. The message seemed to be, Go ahead and shoot—we need kills—but you're on your own if there is an investigation. Some officers presented an opposing view: "Believe it or not, there're a lot of young officers, especially a lot out of ROTC, who really preach against the genocidal thing."

Yet, for most of his tour in Vietnam, Jerry fully accepted the view that every Vietnamese was a legitimate target of American violence. In fact, the villagers were even more infuriating to many American soldiers than were the main-force guerrilla units. The guerrillas were hidden away, but their loyalties were open. They were clear-cut enemies, armed and obviously dangerous. The villagers posed a more troubling presence. They lived in the open, but their loyalties were hidden. American troops came and went, the bombs fell, and the guerrillas waited in ambush. Amidst it all, the villagers had the audacity to carry on with their lives—working their fields, tending their animals, and raising their children. All the fear, frustration, and pressure generated by the American effort to make contact with the NVA and the Viet Cong was heightened by the mysterious role of the Vietnamese people. It was clear that few supported the Americans, but it was not clear what role they actually did play, when or how and to what extent they might be supporting the revolution. Interrogations, for all the brutality with which they were commonly conducted, rarely provided useful information. Added to this was the cynicism created among soldiers by the knowledge that the official justification of the war was to protect these very people from communism. Thus, for many, the villagers were viewed both as cause and embodiment of all the war's contradictions and confusions. As Jerry Samuels put it: "In Vietnam you identify every gook with the enemy. . . . You feel it's their fault we're there. If it weren't for the Vietnamese, we wouldn't be there."

After about six months in Vietnam, Jerry had deep reservations about his participation in atrocities. He could no longer justify his actions. He could offer many explanations of the conditions that "allowed [atrocities] to happen," but he could not deny that his participation was willful. Most troubling was the sense of power and pleasure he derived from killing. "Whether it's a basic human trait, I don't know. Whether it's the result of a violent society, I don't know, all I can tell you is how I felt. There is a certain satisfaction in killing somebody. . . . All I can remember is the temporary satisfaction of defeating something, of making a conquest type thing. . . . It's not an enormous fantastic, majestic thing at all; it's just . . . the satisfaction of holding the power of life and death over somebody." Significantly, Jerry's own sense of guilt came to the surface largely because of his experience as a witness to the atrocities committed not by ground troops but by American air strikes. Frequently his unit was sent out to conduct Personnel Damage Assessments (PDAs) in the wake of U.S. bombing. Their job was to search for bodies. One time in particular, his unit counted eighty-eight bodies. Though the dead included women and children, all of the deaths were counted as confirmed Viet Cong kills.

Another time Jerry's unit was sent across the Vietnamese border to do a PDA in a Cambodian village. They found a school destroyed by fire. The children had been incinerated, many of them still sitting at their desks. "Now this came out in the *Stars and Stripes*. . . . It said the NVA had completely massacred a village which was 'common procedure for the

NVA.' [But] I never heard of the NVA or VC having napalm. *It was a napalm strike by U.S. jets, man.* It's the simplest thing in the world to tell the difference between flame-throwers, which the paper said the NVA had used on the village, and napalm. Because when napalm is through burning it is still hanging around; it looks like snot hanging from the trees."

Jerry went to see a psychiatrist at the mental hygiene clinic at Cu Chi to talk about the growing uneasiness he felt about his involvement in atrocities, both as witness and participant. "I wanted them to either justify it and show me it was the right thing to do . . . or take me under their wing and tell me, yes, you are messed up and we'll see to it that it doesn't happen again." But the psychiatrist "just gave me some pills to take to relax me and slapped me on the back and said not to worry about it." After that, Jerry went to a chaplain. "The whole time I was talking to him, tears streaming down my face, he just had this grin on his face and reassured me that I was doing what was right for the country."

Finally, following the advice of a young officer, Jerry reenlisted. By reenlisting, the officer pointed out, he would be granted a thirty-day leave to the United States before returning to Vietnam. He could desert while on leave. The leave was not granted for two more months, but when Jerry got back to the United States, he went to Canada to live in exile.

Though many soldiers did not directly participate in atrocities, few made the effort to protest against those they witnessed. After all, who would listen? Who would take the charges seriously enough to do something about them? And if they did, what actions would they take? Who would be held responsible? What were the risks of protest? These issues were explored by reporter Daniel Lang in his study of an American infantryman who witnessed the rape and murder of a Vietnamese girl. In his 1967 report, *Casualties of War,* Lang gave his subject the pseudonym Sven Erikkson to protect him from possible reprisals or harassment. (A 1987 film with the same name was based on this book.) In 1966, Sven was sent on a five-man reconnaissance patrol. Prior to the mission the sergeant in command announced to the other men that they would leave early in order to kidnap a Vietnamese girl. The girl would be taken, reported one of the men, "for the purpose of boom-boom, or sexual intercourse, and at the end of five days we would kill her." Sven was shocked by the plan and considered reporting it to an officer, but he was persuaded by a friend that the sergeant could not have been serious. However, the plan was serious. A young woman named Mao was kidnapped, raped, and murdered. Sven went along with the patrol but refused to participate in the crimes. His passive resistance proved to be a great risk. When he declined to take his turn at raping the girl, the sergeant and another man threatened to kill him and report his death as a combat casualty.[24]

Sven was not killed, perhaps because the mission was ended prematurely by a firefight in which additional American troops were called in for support. After returning to the base, he brought charges against the other four men, an action that brought him into further jeopardy of retribution. Yet, "I knew I wouldn't rest until something was done about Mao's murder. It was the least I could do—I had failed her in so many ways." Sven was tormented by the fact that he had not taken some action to save Mao's life, however futile any such action might have been. He had pledged to himself that, if he survived, he would at least seek to have the crimes punished. The captain who heard Sven's charges promised to handle the investigation but delayed reporting it to higher authorities. Finally, Sven found a chaplain who called the Criminal Investigation Division, and a court-martial was initiated.[25]

At the military trial, the defense counsel for the accused said, "There's one thing that stands out about this particular offense. . . . It did not occur in the United States. Indeed, there are some that would say it did not even occur in civilization." All four were convicted; but one man was eventually acquitted, and the others received significantly reduced sentences.[26]

Erikkson attributed his actions to theological convictions which, though sown in a rural Minnesota Lutheran upbringing, grew stronger in Vietnam:

> We all figured we might be dead in the next minute, so what difference did it make what we did? But the longer I was over there, the more I became convinced that it was the other way around that counted—that *because* we might not be around much longer, we had to take extra care how we behaved. Anyway, that's what made me believe I was interested in religion. Another man might have called it something else, but the idea was simply that we had to answer for what we did. We had to answer to something, to someone—maybe just to ourselves.[27]

Not all who committed atrocities like the ones Sven observed have had to answer to criminal tribunals, but they have had to answer to themselves. So too have the far greater number of veterans who, like Sven, were witnesses to atrocity rather than participants. That answering is central to the postwar psychological traumas suffered by, according to the Veterans' Administration, at least 500,000 Vietnam veterans.[28]

It is also important to note, however, that the events reported by Sven were typical of the cases adjudicated by the American military: that is, incidents in which individual soldiers could be isolated for punishment without challenging the larger context of American military policy in Vietnam. At no time, for example, did American courts try the legality of air strikes on populated areas, the legality of rules of engagement that called for the shooting of Vietnamese who fled American forces (whether armed or not), or the legality of counting dead civilians as part of enemy body counts.

These reflections do not justify the individual crimes reported by Sven Erikkson, but they do point to the discrepancy in moral accountability in the war. While enlisted men and low-ranking officers were sometimes brought to trial, the high command remained virtually exempt from legal scrutiny. This point is best illustrated by the military's response to the most notorious and (so far as we know) largest single instance of American atrocity, the My Lai massacre of hundreds of unarmed villagers.

On 16 March 1968, Charlie Company, First Battalion, Twentieth Infantry, Americal Division, made a combat assault on Xom Lang, a subhamlet of Tu Cung in Song My village, Quang Ngai province. The U.S. military typically put numbers after hamlet names to reduce complexity, but sometimes, as in this case, even the hamlet name was wrong. The United States called Xom Lang My Lai-4. For several weeks prior to the massacre, the company had patrolled the region in fruitless efforts to make contact with the enemy. They had, however, suffered a number of casualties from booby traps and sniper fire. In preparation for the My Lai assault, Capt. Ernest Medina gave an emotional pep talk to the men of Charlie Company. Sound intelligence, he told them, indicated a large enemy presence in the hamlet, 250 to 280 members of the "hard-core" Forty-eighth Viet Cong Battalion. This mission, he promised, would be different from the frustrating humps without contact. Finally they would meet the enemy face-to-face. Charlie Company had "a score to even up," and the attack on My Lai would be "your chance to get revenge on these people" for the buddies killed in the previous weeks.

According to most accounts, Medina did not specifically order the killing of all villagers, whether armed or unarmed, men or women, old or young. But many recalled lines from his briefing which implied precisely that:

"When we go into My Lai, it's open season. When we leave, nothing will be living. Everything's going to go." "Nothing [will] be walking, growing, or crawling." "They're all VCs, now go in and get them. We owe them something."[29]

Dropped outside the village by helicopter, the company received no fire. The LZ was cold. The Americans entered the village completely unopposed, and they remained unopposed throughout the day. They did not see a single Vietnamese even carrying a weapon. According to the military investigation conducted by Gen. W. R. Peers a year and a half after the massacre, "At no time was enemy fire received by Charlie Company after it landed at My Lai-4."[30]

There were about 700 people in My Lai-4 that day, almost all of them women, children, and old men. As the Americans advanced toward the village, they opened fire on several people working the rice fields or walking along the roads. Once inside the hamlet, the killing became wholesale and systematic. Soldiers stormed into the Vietnamese homes and killed the families inside, or they set fire to the thatch roofs and killed the people as they ran out the doorways. Some men rounded up groups of people and executed them en masse. Grenades were tossed into family bomb shelters crammed with people. One group of at least 75 women, children, and old men were thrown into a large ditch and sprayed with automatic fire. As the killing spread throughout the hamlet, villagers were running in all directions, and some GIs focused on these people, picking them off one at a time as they tried to escape. The killing was more methodical than spontaneous. It took place over a period of at least two hours. Between killings many men raped women and girls. Some took time out from the carnage to smoke cigarettes or eat C-rations. Others decided to kill the animals as well as the people. A military correspondent saw a group of ten to fifteen GIs pouring bullets into one cow. Then they spotted a woman nearby and turned their fire on her. One soldier was seen running after a duck with a knife. Another man borrowed an M79 grenade launcher to kill a water buffalo. "I hit that sucker right in the head; went down like a shot. You don't get to shoot water buffalo with an M79 every day."[31]

No one knows precisely how many people were killed. The Peers investigation, describing its estimate as conservative, places the figure at 175 to 200 women, children, and old men in My Lai-4. Another military study, conducted by the Criminal Investigation Division, estimated 347 civilian deaths. Seymour Hersh, the journalist who first brought the story to national attention, believes 450 to 500 were killed, as does Richard Falk, an expert in international law who investigated the massacre.[32]

The massacre was not revealed to the American public until November 1969, a full twenty months after the fact. The military report of the My Lai assault described the operation as a great American victory in which U.S. troops engaged the enemy and killed 128 Viet Cong. It also reported 2 Americans killed in action and 11 wounded. (In fact, the only American casualty was a GI named Herb Carter who shot himself in the foot, intentionally according to some sources, accidentally according to others.) On 17 March 1968 the *New York Times* and other American newspapers dutifully reported the military version of the My Lai operation. The *Times* did change one thing, however, describing the enemy dead as members of an NVA unit rather than Viet Cong guerrillas, as reported by the military. The key military version of My Lai was the after-action report filed by Lt. Col. Frank Barker, Jr., commander of the three-company unit specially formed to conduct operations in the My Lai area (Task Force Barker). The "operation," he wrote, "was well planned, well executed and successful. . . . The enemy suffered heavily." Barker confirmed the fabricated body count of 128 VC dead and upheld the lie that American soldiers were fired upon by Viet Cong forces: "During the operation . . . two local [Viet Cong] force companies supported by two to three local guerrilla platoons opposed the friendly forces. . . . The many hedge rows offered the enemy considerable cover and concealment. . . . However the clear weather permitted maximum utilization of reconnaissance aircraft and helicopter gunships to seek out and destroy enemy defensive positions. . . . [Charlie Company] attacked to the east receiving small arms fire as they pressed forward."[33]

Barker viewed the assault from his command helicopter at an altitude of about 1,000 feet. It is not certain that the clear weather allowed him to see the massacre below from that height, but at one point his chopper touched down to evacuate Herb Carter. According to the crew members, a stack of at least twenty Vietnamese corpses was plainly in view a few feet away. Barker's report made no specific mention of civilian deaths, but it did include the following: "On this operation the civilian population supporting the VC in the area numbered approximately 200. This created a problem in population control and medical care of those civilians caught in fires of the opposing forces. However, the infantry unit on the ground and helicopters were able to assist civilians in leaving the area and in caring for and/or evacuating the wounded."

Barker's report was filed almost two weeks after the massacre. By that time Hugh Thompson, the pilot of an American helicopter gunship, had filed a complaint about the killing of civilians at My Lai. He had landed his helicopter several times in the midst of the carnage and had made several attempts to stop it. Details of his complaint were heard by officers at every level of command, including Colonel Barker. Also, within a few days of the massacre, the Viet Cong circulated leaflets throughout the area claiming 500 Vietnamese villagers had been killed and providing detailed charges:

> At Xom Lang Sub-Hamlet . . . they routed all the civilians out of their bunkers and herded them, at bayonet point, into a group near a ditch in front of Mr. Nhieu's gate. . . . About 100 civilians who squatted in a single line were killed instantly by bursts of automatic rifle fire and M79 rounds. Bodies were sprawled about, blood was all over. . . .
>
> Some entire families were massacred. . . . Mr. Huong Tho, 72 years old, was beaten, his beard was cut, and he was pushed into a well and shot with automatic rifle fire until his body submerged. Nguyet, 12 years old, after being raped, was bayoneted in the vagina and rest of her body.[34]

These claims, along with Hugh Thompson's complaint, prompted Col. Oran Henderson, commander of the Eleventh Infantry Brigade, to begin an informal investigation. His report, however, upheld almost every detail of Barker's original after-action report. Henderson did make one modification. While Barker had claimed no civilian deaths, Henderson wrote that twenty civilians had been "inadvertently killed" in "the cross fires of the US and VC forces." But he explicitly denied that Americans deliberately killed hundreds of civilians without receiving any hostile fire: "The allegation that US Forces shot and killed 450–500 civilians is obviously a Viet Cong propaganda move to discredit the United States in the eyes of the Vietnamese people."[35]

Two years after My Lai, General Peers's inquiry revealed that the initial reports and investigations were nothing less than a massive and deliberate coverup extending all the way up to the divisional command of Gen. Samuel Koster. Koster, along with at least fifty commanding officers, had significant knowledge of the massacre, either through firsthand observation or eyewitness reports. Yet all supported the coverup, either by actively suppressing the truth or by refusing to act upon the information they received.[36]

Criminal charges were brought against eighteen officers, including two generals, three colonels, five majors, three captains, and five lieutenants. All but Lt. William Calley had their charges dismissed without a trial or were acquitted. Calley was convicted of killing twenty-two civilians and was sentenced to life imprisonment. However, with President Nixon's de facto pardon, Calley was paroled after three and a half years under house arrest.[37]

Though exceptional in its scale, the My Lai massacre reflected the patterns and psychology of brutalization that were at the heart of American military operations in South Vietnam. Since the war, however, it has virtually disappeared from public debate or memory. Throughout the 1980s very few students even recognized the name.[38]

GETTING A DISTANCE ON THE WAR

Many soldiers tried to transmute the war into another kind of experience, or they found ways to deflect reality, to avoid a direct confrontation with the danger they faced and the damage that might already have been inflicted on their minds and bodies. They sought to gain some mental distance from the brutality that engulfed them. Some found a measure of pride and self-worth in their alternative perceptions of the war. Others found excitement and exhilaration. Most escapes from the real war, however, were either temporary, illusory, or dangerous.

One way of gaining a distance on the war was to concentrate on the skills of soldiering. By focusing attention on the particular techniques and challenges of their duties, some men avoided reflecting on the implications of their work. They were like dedicated technicians concerned with the problems at hand. These were men who thought of themselves not as killers, pawns, counterrevolutionaries, anticommunists, or even as soldiers. They were skilled laborers or technicians who tried to master a particular job. They were machine gunners who learned to put out thousands of rounds of suppressing fire without interruption and without melting the barrels of their guns, point men who developed a keen ability to spot trip wires and to sniff out enemy ambushes, grenadiers who could tilt their M79 "blokers" at just the right angle to pop a grenade into a sniper's hideout at a distance of 150 meters, and medics who moved from man to man amidst the cross fire, making instant triage decisions as they applied pressure bandages and injected morphine, blocking from their minds both the dangers they faced and the gaping wounds before their eyes.

In Vietnam ordinary soldiers not only had access to a wide variety of sophisticated weapons, they were often called upon to make important tactical decisions. The most common deployments of combat soldiers in Vietnam were platoon- and company-sized patrols. Very often the only officers in the field were one or two lieutenants. If they were killed or wounded, command decisions fell to NCOs, to specialist-4s (corporals who did not share all the privileges of full NCOs), or to whoever happened to be in a position to see what was going on. Even on larger operations, squads of eight men led by lance corporals or corporals often got detached from their commanding officer. Patrolling in thick jungle terrain required that units move single file in columns. The men were continually reminded not to bunch up. By staying spread out, at intervals of about five meters, fewer men were endangered by an ambush or booby trap. Thus a company-sized column of 100 men could stretch out over one-third of a mile. The nearest officer might be on the other side of a ridge or halfway down a treacherous slope.

When firefights began, officers were expected to coordinate movements, notify base commanders, and call in supporting fire. In practice, these roles were often filled by enlisted men. To call in air strikes and artillery required a series of rapid and crucial calculations. Getting the coordinates wrong endangered everyone. A former marine infantry captain, asked to talk about the men in his company, was most impressed by their ability to learn these kinds of skills despite their young age and lack of formal education:

> It was very complicated. You go out there with a radio and you get hit and you start calling in artillery and air and naval gunfire and you're nineteen years old and you don't have a helluva lot of education. There are a whole lot of things you have to wrestle with—three-dimensional conceptions of where you are and what the relationship is between the artillery and the various types of rounds. . . . You know, the conception is that an infantryman has to be dumb. But there are no dumb infantrymen as far as I'm concerned—they're all dead.[39]

GIs in Vietnam believed that men were most likely to die during their first months in Vietnam and that experience improved their chances for survival. Along with the skills they developed, soldiers began to find some calm and confidence amid the chaos and uncertainty of battle. Central to this process was a reconciliation toward the possibility of death. Paradoxically, chances for survival seemed greatest when survival itself was less a preoccupation. Gene Holiday describes this transition as a growing "acceptance of death." He felt it happen around the fourth or fifth month of his tour. In the first months he had thought constantly about the possibility of dying. "But I never *accepted* it." Instead he kept worrying about what he could do to survive, how he could assert some control over his fate. Gradually he stopped associating death with personal control and responsibility; rather, he came to view it as a matter of fate. "Once you accept that you're never going to see your 20th birthday and once you accept that you're going to die at nineteen, your job becomes a lot easier and you see a lot straighter and you're a lot clearer."[40]

However, Gene insists, "accepting death" was not the same as believing it absolutely inevitable. "If you're sure it's going to happen, then you're still a little frightened about it I think. But when you accept it, it frees you a lot." That freedom allowed Gene to do his job with greater skill and clarity.

You start to get real good at it. And you can see it happening to the other guys in your unit. After you've been together for awhile, it's amazing how well people do their jobs. You walk into an ambush and everybody knows just what to do. When you first get to Vietnam you fall down, shit your pants, and freeze up. Some guys are so scared they can't even return fire. But after awhile you'll be out in the bush and a firefight starts and right away people are getting into good positions, putting out rounds, covering for their buddies, tossing extra ammo to the machine-gunners; nobody's screaming or crying, its just working together, doing what has to be done.

Gene took pride in the teamwork of battle, the coordinated and often unspoken, intuitive effort of collective survival. For him, there was nothing particularly alluring or seductive about killing. The real thrill of combat was found in the deep sense of interdependence, the pride he felt not so much in fighting for his own survival but in the knowledge that each man's life depended on everyone doing what had to be done. As another veteran put it: "The biggest turn-on in Nam was having other men depend on me. In my whole life, no one had ever depended on me for nothing. In 'Nam they depended on me for their lives."[41]

Combat medics (called corpsmen by the navy and marines) were among those soldiers most likely to draw motivation and pride from performing a skill crucial to their fellows. Many medics entered the service with high school educations. In Vietnam they were invariably called "Doc," and with good reason.

When I was training back in the states the officers and doctors were always lording it over us. They ran the show and we were only corpsmen. It had nothing to do with how much medicine you knew, it was your rank that mattered. In Vietnam it was a completely different ballgame. No one asked you if you had a medical license, they just wanted to know if you could save lives. I performed operations in the field that only a surgeon would be allowed to do in the states, or at least a resident. It gave me a real feeling of comeuppance.[42]

In Vietnam, soldiers used skills that meant the difference between life and death. Their talents were accorded respect proportionate to their ability to support the survival of the whole. Often this brought an inversion of social orientation. Men who, in the United States, had been treated as ephemeral subordinates were, in Vietnam, vital and important. Men who had never been entrusted with responsibility suddenly found people trusting them with their lives. Men who had never felt a sense of individual power found themselves carrying a whole arsenal of powerful weapons.

Sometimes pride in wartime skills seemed to have a narrower focus: the sheer thrill of doing dangerous things coolly and masterfully. This quality was especially appealing to Michael Herr, whose brilliant war correspondence itself was a venture in developing cool under fire.

The crew chief was a young Marine who moved around the chopper without a safety line hooked to his flight suit, so comfortable with the rolling and shaking of the ship that you couldn't even pause to admire his daredevil nerve; you cut straight through to his easy grace and control, marveling as he hunkered down by the open door to rig the broken seat up again with pliers and a length of wire. At 1,500 feet he stood there in the gale-sucking door . . . his hands resting naturally on his hips, as though he were just standing around on a street corner somewhere, waiting. He knew he was good, an artist, he knew we were digging it, but it wasn't for us at all; it was his, private; he was the man who was never going to fall out of any damn helicopter.[43]

Like aesthetes who pursue art for its own sake, savoring its pleasures without regard to the moral or political significance of the artistic endeavor, some soldiers became aesthetes of war, connoisseurs of its skills, sensations, and spectacles. Some, like this helicopter crew chief, were themselves artists. Others were spectators. Often the roles of actor and viewer were intertwined. In any case, these soldiers felt an aesthetic detachment from the war. Perhaps the most common example of this phenomenon was the sensation of participating in the making and watching of a movie. In *A Rumor of War*, for example, Philip Caputo repeatedly links his experience of combat to the world of film. "Strangest of all had been that sensation of watching myself in a movie. One part of me was doing something while the other part watched from a distance, shocked by the things it saw, yet powerless to stop them from happening."[44] For Caputo, the metaphor of motion pictures helps explain a two-sided emotion: the feeling of participating in events far beyond ordinary experience (blown up on a huge screen) yet being powerless to control the outcome of the story. He feels at once the heady self-importance of the movie star and the helplessness of the moviegoer, impotent to affect the actions unfolding on the screen.

Frank Mathews, a marine in the Third Reconnaissance Battalion, learned that thinking of the war as a movie could be dangerous:

> We had gone on so many patrols it got to where it wasn't that big a thing worrying about getting shot anymore. We'd take chances. Once in the middle of a firefight I decided to pull a John Wayne stunt. I saw a VC wide open, but it was just too easy [to kill him immediately]. So I hollared at him first so he'd see me. Then I took off toward this log, jumped over, wanting to pop up shooting on the other side. But I broke my arm trying to pull that stunt. I wrote a letter to John Wayne telling him there was no damn way that stunt could work cause I broke my wrist trying it. I never did get an answer, but I sure wrote him.[45]

During the war some journalists were struck by the detail and precision with which American soldiers discussed the arsenal of war—the range and power of all manner of rifles, machine guns, artillery, and explosives. "See, ma'am," a soldier told one reporter, "that canister round has something like seven thousand oblong bearings in it, with a range of four hundred meters, and it just rips everything to pieces out there, even trees." After a few months in-country, their ears learned subtle distinctions. They could tell not only whether a shell was incoming or outgoing but what exactly was fired, where it came from, and how much it could destroy. Even years later, in the rap groups formed by veterans to grapple with the emotional and psychological traumas of the war, men frequently discuss the intricacies of various weapons. Such talk is often initiated as a way of avoiding discussion of more complicated and painful memories. The hardware of war offers solid footing. Voices become animated. Men who remained silent during talk about loss, or guilt, or powerlessness might jump eagerly into a conversation about weaponry. Long debates ensue about the relative merit of a particular rifle, helicopter, or armored personnel carrier.[46]

Infantrymen were not alone in their appreciation of America's enormous firepower. On bases throughout Vietnam, American soldiers sat outside in the evening to watch distant firefights flashing through the dark. Passing around joints of marijuana, the men could view the war as a spectacular light show. The best light shows were provided by an American gunship known as "Spooky" or "Puff the Magic Dragon." On the outside these planes were military relics—old C-47 transports and DC-3s powered by propeller engines and looking like something out of World War II. But their insides had been gutted and outfitted with a whole warehouse of powerful guns and ammunition. Mounted in the windows and cargo doors of these old planes were at least three multibarrel 7.62 mm miniguns. By flying the plane in slow, banking turns, pilots could train the guns on a specific target area. Each gun spewed forth 6,000 rounds a minute, enough firepower to put a bullet in every square yard of an area the size of a football field in sixty seconds.[47]

Puff the Magic Dragon was a name taken from the Peter, Paul, and Mary song about a peaceful, playful dragon. The gunship was hardly peaceful, but to stoned-out soldiers who watched Puff work out in the surrounding jungle, the name seemed wonderfully ironic and appropriate. For one thing, the military was always using peaceful-sounding euphemisms to describe the devastation of Vietnam. For example, operations in which villages were destroyed and the peasants hauled off to refugee camps were a key element of the "pacification" program designed to "win the hearts and minds" of the Vietnamese people. Also, the song "Puff, the Magic Dragon," was widely thought to be about the pleasures of pot smoking. Puffing on marijuana, soldiers watched a magic dragon that quite literally breathed fire. The spectacle was extraordinary. Every fifth round from the miniguns was a tracer, a bullet that flashes bright red to help mark the target. Because the rounds were expelled so rapidly, the tracers made a connecting line of red that streaked across the sky. As the gunship slowly circled above, long red ropes of fire linked it to the ground, dancing and whipping across the sky and visible for miles. Illumination flares were periodically dropped over the target, adding additional color to the fireworks.

Drugs were central to the response of American soldiers to the war in Vietnam. Marijuana was the drug of choice. Grown throughout Indochina, it was widely available to GIs at prices the Americans found absurdly and joyously low. Making a connection did not require much stealth or savvy. Drugs were openly hawked outside every American base, and as convoys moved along Vietnamese roads, dealers of all ages approached the trucks. To the amazement of GIs, you could buy cartons of marijuana that were, apart from their contents, indistinguishable from cartons of American cigarettes. The Vietnamese emptied the tobacco from the cigarettes, refilled them with grass, and put them back in packs of Kools or Salems. They even resealed the plastic wrappers. A whole carton of filter-tipped marijuana cigarettes could be purchased for under $5 or in exchange for a carton of American cigarettes.[48]

In the first years of full-scale escalation, 1965–67, most American soldiers probably did not use drugs other than alcohol. Granting that surveys may seriously underestimate usage, a 1967 study found that 29 percent of returning soldiers admitted to smoking marijuana in Vietnam, and 7 percent said they did it more than twenty times. By 1969, studies placed total users at 50 percent, with 30 percent in the "heavy use" category. By 1971, the total figure approached 60 percent.[49]

In part, of course, these figures reflect a growing incidence of marijuana use in the United States. Yet among men who were heavy users in Vietnam, only about one-half had been heavy users before the war. Moreover, the marijuana commonly available in the United States was not nearly as strong as the drug found in Vietnam. Before 1975, most grass available in the United States had a THC content (the active drug in marijuana) of around 1 percent. In Indochina, marijuana had THC levels of at least 5 percent, and one researcher found readings as high as 20 percent. Also, much of the grass available in Vietnam was treated with opium, usually by rubbing a liquid opiate on the paper of the cigarette.[50]

Drugs are too commonly equated in a simplistic way with the rise of dissent among American troops, however. Drug use parallels but does not explain the increase in combat refusals, fraggings, and other acts of insubordination or dissent. In a general way, of course, higher drug use reflected the growing alienation of U.S. forces, but drug use did not necessarily make soldiers less willing to fight. It might be, in fact, that drugs actually helped soldiers endure the doubt, fatigue, and confusion of the war. For many it was a form of self-medication that made the war more endurable. Nor was all drug use unofficial. Amphetamines were commonly available from medics to help grunts get through long patrols. Some soldiers think this speed made them more edgy, aggressive, and brutal. Nick D'Allesandro was a Green Beret squad leader who reported to sociologist Murray Polner that he had participated in killing at least 100 civilians in the Iadrang Valley in 1964. "I'm not copping out [but] I was usually under the influence of dextrine diamphetamine sulphate, fifteen-milligram pills. . . . You just can't believe the incredible aggravation you feel when you come down from amphetamines. That time at Plei Me I was so pissed off at the world that I would've shot children in the streets and not even flinched. I know, because when I wasn't on them, I once asked to be removed from an operation in which an unusually large number of civilians had been killed."[51]

The effect of marijuana on soldiers was varied, but it was most valued for its ability to provide euphoric escape from the anxiety of the war. Most combat soldiers did not smoke out in the field on operations, but when the men returned to base camps, the drug was often at the center of small group parties. It was a social drug, a form of collective release.

We'd get together in a hootch or sometimes we'd sneak out to this Buddhist temple near the base. It was very powerful stuff and everybody got real happy. At first we'd laugh and joke and talk about silly shit. But after awhile it got real mellow and we might even talk about things that bothered us. Or we'd just lay back and get off on the designs in the temple. Most of the time I hated everything about Vietnam. But when I was stoned I could really appreciate the beauty of the country. You'd look out over the valley and everything seemed really peaceful. And even if there was a firefight going on out in the jungle we wouldn't think "Hey, there are people getting blown away out there." It was more like, "Wow, man, take a look at those colors!"[52]

Heroin was not widely available in Vietnam before 1969, but in 1970 it appeared throughout the country. It was 95 percent pure, and small vials could be had for $2 (the same quantity in the United States had a street value of $100 to $200). Usually it came in powder form and was snorted or mixed with tobacco and smoked. Many soldiers mistakenly believed that because they did not inject the heroin, they would not become addicted. By 1971, however, some studies indicate that at least 10 percent of American soldiers were hooked and more than 20 percent were occasional users. Several factors help explain the use of heroin. It was even more powerful than marijuana in suppressing anxiety, and unlike marijuana, which had the effect of slowing down time, heroin gave users the feeling that time was flying by. "It makes time go away. The days go bip, bip, bip." For some men, heroin seemed to offer the perfect psychological solution to their preoccupation with getting through their 365-day tour as rapidly as possible. Also, in 1969 the military began a crackdown on marijuana. The crackdown did not make a significant dent in the supply and use of marijuana (indeed usage continued to rise), but enough soldiers were busted to make others more nervous and cautious about smoking it openly. While grass is very pungent and relatively bulky, heroin is odorless and comes in small doses, easily hidden. Thus, some men switched from grass to heroin simply because it seemed safer. There was a common expression among those who smoked heroin: "I can salute an officer with one hand, and take a drag of heroin with the other."[53]

In the latter years of the war many soldiers gleaned some personal satisfaction in their noncompliance with military regulations. They prided themselves less on what they did than on what they refused to do, on how little of themselves they could give to the war. Outwardly they went through the motions of compliance (saluting officers), but inwardly they sought to preserve an identity apart from the war (taking drugs). It became increasingly uncommon for soldiers to draw self-respect from the jobs they performed. This was especially true in rear areas, where individual assignments were less directly linked to the safety of others. While combat soldiers might still have to fight hard for their individual and collective survival, in the rear there was little motivation to work hard. Some men withheld their best efforts as a way of preserving a sense of integrity, not wanting to capitulate to a meaningless cause. Others simply put all their thoughts and energies into their free time. In *The Other War*, Charles Anderson writes about the elaborate efforts rear-echelon soldiers gave to improving their living quarters. They used blowtorches to burnish their plywood walls ("paneling"), hung brightly colored parachute silk from their ceilings, and installed elaborate shelves, tables, and partitions. Whenever possible, men would bunk with people of common interests. When this happened, the men would outfit their "hootches" accordingly. There were hootches for "juicers" (sometimes called "boozers' heaven"), with elaborate bars, and hootches for "heads," with stereos, candles, incense, and fancy bongs for smoking dope. Anderson also describes a "jockhouse," where the men turned their quarters into a weight-lifting gym, and a "library," "whose occupants used the Book-of-the-Month Club to further their insulation from the war."

> Victory to the rear-echelon-unit member was not measured in terms of dead bodies or captured weapons. . . . Victory was measured in terms of completeness of isolation from the war. To push away as far as possible a frustrating no-progress war . . . was to secure the objective.
> Complete victory was defined as the perfect reproduction in Vietnam of all conditions and luxuries of life in the States, the real world.[54]

These efforts to withdraw from the war helped many cope with the drudgery and anxiety of their year in Vietnam. Yet, some veterans have felt a loss of self-esteem in their postwar lives for not having given more of themselves to the war or, more accurately, for not having had a war to which they were moved to extend themselves. As Eric Stevens expresses it:

> One of the things that bothers me most about Vietnam was that I didn't give it my best effort. I only did what I had to do. There was just no motivation to do a good job, the whole thing seemed pointless. I really didn't give a fuck. Having that attitude helped me survive. It was like I was saying to myself, "I'm not really here because I'm not giving everything I've got." But it also made me feel bad. In my heart I think I wanted to be in a war that would inspire me to do something great, you know, "above and beyond the call of duty."[55]

"THAT'S HOW POOR THOSE PEOPLE ARE"

When Bob Foley arrived in Vietnam, the American ground war was—gradually—winding down. It was 1971, and traveling by bus to Cha Rang, where he would be a clerk for the 160th Heavy Equipment Maintenance Company, Bob noticed an abandoned American compound. The unit once housed there had been withdrawn from Vietnam. Left behind were rows of empty barracks, sandbagged bunkers, perimeter wire, and a 5,000-gallon water tank. It looked like a dusted-over ghost town. Passing the same spot a few weeks later, however, Bob did a double take. The base had disappeared. The entire place had been stripped clean; all that remained was the huge water tank. He asked his first sergeant for an explanation and was told that the local Vietnamese had dismantled the compound piece by piece, salvaging every scrap. "Well, at least they didn't get the tanker!" said Bob, laughing nervously. The sergeant casually responded, "Oh, they just haven't figured out a way to get it down yet. Give 'em a couple of weeks and it'll be gone." And it was.[56]

Telling that story reminds Bob of an afternoon when the commanding officer called everyone out in front of the company area to test-fire their weapons. The men enjoyed these "mad minutes": they provided a release from their normal rear-area duties and helped to ease the tension that had been building over the possibility of a Viet Cong attack. The men fired thousands of rounds of ammunition into a nearby hillside until they stood ankle-deep in brass shell casings. Within minutes after the firing stopped, local people arrived by the score. "They came out of the woodwork—two or three hundred Vietnamese. They were all over the place." They raced around picking up the brass, "just grabbing it up like it was money." For the Vietnamese, it was money, and they had many uses for the shells, among which Bob recalls one in particular: they made brass ashtrays and sold them to American GIs.[57]

Another veteran remembers an American dump where dozens of Vietnamese, many of them children, sorted through the garbage, dividing it, cleaning it, and putting it in special piles: "That dump was the neatest, cleanest place I've ever been to in my life. I mean, *nothing* was wasted." Vietnam veterans tell many versions of these salvaging stories. Each conveys a vivid sense of the fact that many Vietnamese people quite literally survived on what the Americans threw away or left behind.[58]

Veterans use such stories to make a variety of conflicting points. Some portray the Vietnamese as greedy parasites and try to evade the most shocking implications of the scavenging by casting it as a kind of war profiteering. Others focus on the material wastefulness of the American military, often using it as a metaphor for the greater waste of the war as a whole. Others want to dramatize the extraordinary economic dependence the United States imposed on Vietnam. But most veterans share a need to describe, in some form, the profound and pervasive poverty they witnessed in Vietnam. Even veterans still hostile toward the Vietnamese commonly echo the words of Bob Foley: "I never in my life saw anything like the poverty I saw in Vietnam." Not all sympathize with the Vietnamese who scooped up American refuse "like it was money," but each, in his own way, wrestles with the painful memories of having waged a war amidst and against a people far poorer than most Americans can begin to imagine.

Growing up in Birmingham, Alabama, Bob lived "on the poor side of town." His father sold shoes and his mother was a bookkeeper for a small business. Though there was always food on the table and a roof overhead, the family enjoyed few luxuries. Bob's experience in Vietnam confirmed his identity as a working-class American. In fact, it made him more acutely aware of his subordinate status in the United States. Why, he wondered, were there so few men in his unit from privileged families? The awareness that the war was fought mostly by working-class Americans like himself, however, did not finally lead Bob to a firmer grasp of his social identity or a clearer understanding of how to live, for in Vietnam his identity was linked to international inequality. The outcome produced deep confusion and a contradictory guilt. "In Vietnam I was a rich Yankee, dropping shell casings all over the ground. But back home I was just a poor southern kid. It made me real confused. I still feel bad that I'm not a very successful American. I'd *like* to have a lot of money and a house. But I also think about those people in Vietnam and I feel guilty for living in a country that has more money than it knows what to do with." In Vietnam, American soldiers saw their social condition through a new and perplexing lens. Though most were poor and working-class Americans, they carried out the foreign policy of the richest nation on earth, and they did so in a country where the people were poorer than they.

Even without the many additional dangers and hardships brought by the war, living conditions in Vietnam were meager. Most people lived in thatched houses with dirt floors. Toilets, running water, refrigeration, electricity—these were luxuries only the urban elite could afford. In the countryside, three-fourths of the people were tenant farmers working small plots or rice paddies. These Vietnamese peasants defined their class positions in categories roughly translated as "middle farmers," "poor farmers," and "very poor farmers." The distinctions were important, but they were essentially differences within a hard-pressed subsistence.[59]

One of the most wrenching impacts of American military policy was the forced displacement of millions of rural Vietnamese. Some had their land destroyed and fled to the cities or to the outskirts of American bases in search of work. Many more were systematically removed from areas governed by the NLF and placed in refugee camps. All told, the American war was responsible for the displacement of at least 5 million South Vietnamese (of a population of 17 million). These refugees were the Vietnamese most frequently encountered by American GIs. While combat soldiers had direct contact with rural peasants, most Americans—support troops housed in large, rear-area bases—were more likely to have interactions with the displaced people living in makeshift shantytowns and refugee camps.

Living conditions in the refugee camps and base-area slums were often more appalling than in the countryside. While the best rural hamlets were neat and orderly with carefully built houses and well-kept hedgerows, most of the camps and slums were filthy and chaotic, patched together from whatever was at hand. American veterans have vivid memories of Vietnamese dwellings made entirely from American garbage—whole walls constructed of flattened tin cans, looking like surreal and grotesque advertisements for Coca-Cola, Pepsi, Schlitz, Budweiser, and other American products.[60]

Most of the refugees and urban Vietnamese became in some way dependent on the American military, which officially employed about 100,000 Vietnamese civilians. Countless others survived on what they could sell to the Americans (or scavenge or steal). In the early 1960s, South Vietnam was a major exporter of rice. By 1966, because of the destroyed farmland and the displacement of peasants, it had to begin importing rice to feed the swelling urban population. As the war continued, the South Vietnamese economy became increasingly based on servicing the American military. When Vietnamese students at a Saigon teachers college were asked, on an English exam, to list fifteen occupations, "almost every student included launderer, car-washer, bar-girl, shoe-shine boy, soldier, interpreter, and journalist. Almost none of the students thought to write down doctor, engineer, . . . or even their own chosen profession, teacher."[61]

This economic dependence is crucial to an understanding of relationships between U.S. soldiers and Vietnamese civilians. To the Vietnamese, American soldiers were rarely considered allies. At best, they were most commonly perceived as potential employers or customers. This was a strange role for many American troops, men who by no means considered themselves wealthy. In America it would have seemed unimaginable to hire others to clean and cook. The parents of many U.S. soldiers were themselves service workers of one kind or another. Nor did their military pay provide soldiers much reason to consider themselves advantaged, at least not by American standards. During the height of the war the lowest-ranking American soldiers were paid between $150 and $200 a month for serving in Vietnam. This included a bonus of $50 to $65 a month for hazardous duty.[62]

By Vietnamese standards, however, American soldiers were wealthy indeed. American soldiers found that their money could command a wide variety of goods and services. On many American bases, privates and corporals could hire Vietnamese women to make their beds, clean their boots, sweep their floors, and wash and iron their clothes. The soldiers called them "hootch girls." In 1970, at Tay Ninh, base camp for the First Brigade of the Twenty-fifth Infantry Division, 800 Vietnamese girls and women were employed by American servicemen. A staff sergeant told Gloria Emerson that only men of his rank and above had official permission to hire hootch maids. "But," he said, "what the hell, everyone seems to have them." One of the hootch girls at Tay Ninh was a forty-one-year-old woman named Nguyen Thi Khao. She worked for seven soldiers and earned $33 a month. Five dollars a month per man was the standard rate. Hootch girls that were also prostitutes could earn more, and Nguyen Thi Khao was particularly upset by the prostitution. She told Emerson, "American soldiers have much money and it seems that they are all sexually hungry all the time. Our poor girls. With money and a little patience, the Americans can get them very easily."[63]

A soldier who was in Vietnam much earlier, in 1963, gives this account: "All of us felt we were entitled to our servants. Twenty guys in a hootch would chip in and pay twenty dollars for a woman to come and do all the cleaning, make all the beds and shine all the boots. And for that woman, twenty dollars a month was a lot of money. We didn't make much in the Army—fifty or sixty dollars a month, that's what it was when I started. For us to be able to afford a servant just had mind-expanding or -exploding consequences."[64]

Americans responded to their relative prosperity in various ways ranging from compassion to violence (and complicated combinations of the two). Some were deeply moved by the poverty they encountered and wanted to help. This impulse led some to support a favored servant, giving her (or him) special attention, gifts, and extra money. Others went further, volunteering their service to orphanages, schools, or hospitals. Not all such relationships were so clearly marked by the conventions of charity, however. Some men reached out toward the Vietnamese on a more equal footing.

Richard Marlotas served in Vietnam as a dockworker in the 116th

Transportation Company at Cam Ranh Bay. He was among the poorest Americans to go to Vietnam. He was raised in Pawtucket, Rhode Island, by his mother, a cleaning woman for a local factory. For Richard, even basic necessities were frequently absent or inadequate. He commonly went to bed hungry, and during the days, at school, the other children "used to pick on me cause they had more than we did. I had nothing. I used to wear the same clothes. We had no money to buy stuff—food or anything."[65]

Life got worse for Richard after he returned from Vietnam. For almost thirteen years he was homeless, living on the streets of Boston and sleeping under a bridge near Kenmore Square. Given all that he has endured—extreme poverty, harsh winters, years of heavy drinking and drug taking, loneliness and depression, what he has called "all this confusion and mayhem"—it sometimes amazes him that he has survived until age forty-four.

One day, while thinking back on his year in Vietnam and his memories of the Vietnamese and about their poverty in relation to his own, Richard said, "You know, those people don't have anything either." He has an especially vivid memory of Vietnamese children walking around naked: "Naked, for christsakes, *naked*!" And the dwellings: "They lived in little cardboard houses—whatever they could make."

The Vietnamese Richard saw lived in a village near the American base at Cam Ranh Bay. The village was off-limits to the American soldiers, but like many others, Richard occasionally slipped off base and went to the Vietnamese community. He visited prostitutes, but he also developed a relationship with a "regular" girl. Sometimes he brought her small gifts— a bar of soap, for example. He remembers how happy Vietnamese girls were to receive such gifts. "They *loved* them! In that country they don't have things like that. Small things like that they look at as great—a bar of soap! That's how poor those people are! Then I came home and found out I couldn't afford a bar of soap either."

Richard measures his own condition—his years of homelessness and poverty—not only in relation to other Americans, most of whom are far better off than he, but also by comparison with the hardship he witnessed among the people of Vietnam. Yet it is no relief to him that others elsewhere are at least as poor. There is little compensation in the knowledge that the Vietnamese "don't have anything either." Rather, it reminds him all the more powerfully of how nearly impossible it is for the very poor to maintain a sense of dignity in a country as generally wealthy as the United States. He keeps thinking of those "small" gifts he was able to buy for women in Vietnam, and this leads him to a painful realization: he cannot afford the gifts that might be appreciated by most Americans. Just imagine, he said, offering a plain little bar of soap as a present to an American woman. "She'd think you were nuts!"

At one point during his tour, Richard had hopes of marrying the Vietnamese woman he befriended. He gave up, though, when people told him it would require all kinds of paperwork, that there would be lots of red tape. American officials discouraged such marriages. Nevertheless, in 1969, despite the obstacles, 455 Americans received permission to marry Vietnamese women and take them to the United States.[66]

Richard found some satisfaction in his relationship to the Vietnamese. For one of the few times in his life, he felt a sense of individual strength and realized his own capacity for generosity. Other Americans, however, responded to the Vietnamese quite differently, for even many well-intentioned Americans found their empathy eroded by the nature of the war and the U.S. role in Vietnam.

American soldiers were told they were in Vietnam to help the people, and some brought to the war a vision of themselves modeled on the GIs of World War II lore, handing out candy to children and waving at pretty girls along the road. They were invariably disappointed. The children, it turned out, did not respond as the Americans wanted. If some were shy, docile, and grateful (the sort of responses most endearing to would-be benefactors), many soon became persistently and aggressively demanding.

Some saw the relationship as an evolving antagonism. Jonathan Schell, a journalist reporting on the war in 1967, wrote:

At first, the G.I.s, charmed by the shyness and reserve of the Vietnamese children and wanting to be friendly, offer pieces of candy or gum. Perhaps the children accept and politely offer thanks, but the next time there is less hesitation, and after several times the children far from hesitating, demand the handouts. Walking along the road [an American] soldier would often be virtually attacked by groups of children. . . . They ran at him screaming, "O.K.! O.K.! O.K.! O.K.!" and turn[ed] smiles full of excitement and anticipation up to him as they grabbed both his hands and rifled his pockets.

When Americans refused such demands, they were frequently met with shouted insults: "Cheap Charlie!" the children yelled, or "You Number Ten!" Some Vietnamese used the nastier taunts they had learned from Americans. They might flip the bird and scream, "Fuck you, G.I.!"[67]

Some Americans came to despise the Vietnamese after the briefest, most superficial contact. Mike Dowling, from a midwestern, middle-class family, was drafted out of graduate school in 1970. (He is now a history professor.) As a student Mike had opposed the war. He agreed to serve in an army intelligence unit (the Army Security Agency), having been told that such service would probably keep him out of Vietnam. He was, in fact, sent to Saigon. His round of work and leisure did not require much contact with the Vietnamese, nor did he seek any. He had a Vietnamese hootch maid and other casual associations, but when I asked him if he had ever established a relationship with a Vietnamese, he responded:

> One, and it was a totally unsatisfactory thing. During our lunch hour we would often go outside of the building and sit in the sun, or exercise, or whatever. The guy came up to me one day and he started a conversation in rather halting English. So I chatted with him. Next day he came up and we chatted very briefly. The third day he came up to me and asked if I could buy him cigarettes at the PX, which, when I told him no, ended our relationship. I have to be really honest, and I don't want this to sound racist. But maybe it is. I didn't particularly care for the Vietnamese people I associated with. I had a very good friend who got out in the countryside and he said that Saigon gave a very misleading impression of what the Vietnamese were like. But the ones I saw were grasping, dishonest, and greedy.[68]

Mike's response to the Vietnamese is similar to another veteran's: "Hey, we're over here fighting *their* lousy war, risking *our* lives, and these people expect us to be Santa Claus. And when you aren't they feel cheated."[69] The anger and resentment of fighting on behalf of people who did not view the American war as their own prevented most soldiers from seeking a truer understanding of the Vietnamese. Many did not look beyond examples of "greed" to the poverty exacerbated by economic dependence on the United States or to the aggression American military policy visited on Vietnamese civilians.

Having once determined that the Vietnamese were "grasping" and "dishonest," it was not a long step to attribute such qualities to race. Thus, "gooks" were, by their very nature, beggars and thieves. Faced with Vietnamese civilian participation in the anti-American revolution, American soldiers began to interpret Vietnamese poverty not as a factor in their willingness to risk revolution but as proof of willful animalism. Sven Erikkson explains:

From one day to the next, you could see for yourself changes coming over guys on our side—decent fellows, who wouldn't dream of calling an Oriental a "gook" or a "slopehead" back home. But they were halfway around the world now, in a strange country, where they couldn't tell who was their friend and who wasn't. Day after day, out on patrol, we'd come to a narrow dirt path leading through some shabby village, and the elders would welcome us and the children come running with smiles on their faces, waiting for the candy we'd give them. But at the other end of the path, just as we were leaving the village behind, the enemy would open up on us, and there was bitterness among us that the villagers hadn't given us warning. All that many of us could think at such times was that we were fools to be ready to die for people who defecated in public, whose food was dirtier than anything in our garbage cans back home. Thinking like that— well, as I say, it could change some fellows. It could keep them from believing that life was so valuable—anyone's life, I mean, even their own.[70]

Some soldiers expressed their rage in brutal attacks on Vietnamese civilians. The range of such attacks covered a huge spectrum, from taunts and insults to kicks and shoves to murder. One commonly reported form of brutality is particularly relevant in this context. As American troops traveled by truck, they often passed groups of Vietnamese children calling for food or cigarettes. Some soldiers made a game of throwing cans of C-rations at the children—not tossing the cans as charity but throwing them, as hard as possible, as weapons. An army combat engineer gives this account: "We threw full C-ration cans at kids on the side of the road. Kids would be lined up on the side of the road. They'd be yelling out, 'Chop, chop; chop, chop,' and they wanted food. They knew we carried C-rations. Well, just for a joke, these guys would take a full can . . . and throw it as hard as they could at a kid's head. I saw several kids' heads split wide open, knocked off the road, knocked into tires of vehicles behind."[71]

A marine who served at the opposite end of South Vietnam offers a similar testimony:

When they originally get in country [Americans] feel very friendly toward the Vietnamese and they like to toss candy at the kids. But as they become hardened to it and kind of embittered against the war, as you drive through the ville you take the cans of C-rats and the cases and you peg 'em at the kids; you try to belt them over the head. And one of the fun games that always went was you dropped the C-rats cans or the candy off the back of your truck just so that the kid will have time to dash out, grab the candy, and get run over by the next truck. One of the other fun games was, you take the candy and you toss it out on a concertina wire. The kids are so much dying for the candy that they'll tear their flesh and their clothing trying to get at this candy which you've thrown inside the barbed wire.[72]

In Gustav Hasford's *Short-Timers*, a soldier tells a new man, "You'll know you're salty when you stop throwing C-ration cans *to* the kids and start throwing the cans *at* them."[73]

This is not easy to understand, and veterans who are plagued with guilt for incidents like this do not themselves fully understand what led them to behave so cruelly or how they might have found in it a "joke" or a "fun game." Somehow those roadside children became the emblems and the targets of the war's contradictions. They cried out of a need the Americans could not satisfy, in tones that stripped the official American claims of their legitimacy: they said, in effect, "You soldiers cannot help us and we do not want you in our country, but now we depend on you, and we'll take what we can get." The soldiers responded, "You ungrateful, double-crossing bastards, you want some food? *Here's* some food!" Some men found amusement and a temporary sense of power in lashing out at the children, but the awful "joke" of using C-rations as weapons was rooted as much in a sense of tormented impotence as in feelings of superiority. The soldiers had the advantage of size, and they carried the weight of American wealth and power; but often enough they felt as dependent and helpless as the Vietnamese children. Mark Sampson recalls:

God forbid you should do something good for them, cause then they're on you like flies on shit. And if you don't do anything good for them they're on you anyway. But once you do something good for them it's like you're the brave white God. You can't do too much good and you can't do wrong. It's just, I don't know. You give C-rations to kids—you see that they're really hungry, I mean swollen stomachs and stuff—but sometimes you'd just want to, you know [he points an imaginary rifle], go "Hut" and drop one of them and just say: "Fuck you."[74]

Many American soldiers felt more empathy with the Viet Cong and the North Vietnamese Army than with Vietnamese civilians. They developed deep respect for the determination of opposing forces to fight on year after year, surviving in the jungles and mountains on little else but cold balls of rice and walking hundreds of miles in thin, rubber slippers. Their efforts testified to an extraordinary commitment, and American soldiers, lacking a clear sense of purpose, came to envy the Revolutionary Forces for having a cause that inspired such devotion. The poverty of civilians, however, posed another set of troubling challenges. It stood as a constant reminder of the futility of the American war effort, of what little common purpose was shared between the allies, and of America's role in exacerbating the suffering of the Vietnamese and furthering the antagonism between the two peoples.[75]

Much of the anguish described in this chapter had its most wrenching impact on the minds of American soldiers after their return to the United States. Away from the war, veterans found it difficult to numb themselves to the suffering they endured, witnessed, and inflicted. The radical contrast between the misery left in Vietnam and the comfortable abundance of most Americans often triggered such anguish. In "Coming to Terms with Vietnam," Peter Marin describes a Vietnam veteran's initial moments back in the United States. The soldier, just a long plane flight away from the war, was met by his parents at the airport:

> They drove home in silence and then sat together in the kitchen, and his mother, in passing, apologized for there being "nothing in the house to eat." That did it; he broke. Raging, he went from cupboard to cupboard, shelf to shelf, flinging doors open, pulling down cans and boxes and bags, piling them higher and higher on the table until they spilled over onto the floor and everything edible in the house was spread out in front of them.
>
> "I couldn't believe it," he said, shaking his head as he told me. "I'd been over there . . . killing those poor bastards who were living in their tunnels like rats and had nothing to eat but mud and a few goddamn moldy grains of rice, and who watched their kids starve to death or go up in smoke, and she said *nothing to eat*, and I ended up in the kitchen crying and shouting: *Nothing to eat, nothing to eat!*"[76]

Beyond this veteran's rage one can imagine the hurt and confusion of his parents. If they were like most families of Vietnam veterans, they might rightly point out that, by American standards, they lived quite plainly. Yet the experience of Vietnam had made poor and working-class soldiers the representatives of American national wealth and power. The fact that they themselves were not wealthy only made their identity more troubling and precarious. American soldiers found in Vietnam a painful and confusing mirror in which to reflect upon their place in American society. "Poor" in one society, they were "rich" (but "cheap") in another. They were caught in the middle of a struggle between the First World and the Third, a struggle that left thousands of veterans feeling utterly adrift, like homeless and abandoned executors of American power.

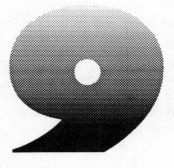

Am I Right or Wrong?

In 1969, a Vietnam veteran "wearing paint-spattered overalls . . . with a pair of work gloves hanging from his back pocket" stood on the sidewalk of a midwestern city. He watched a parade of several thousand antiwar demonstrators, most of them students, march along a downtown street. Soon, his face "livid with rage," the veteran began screaming at the protesters. Among the peace marchers was a contingent of Vietnam Veterans Against the War. One of them, a blue-collar vet from Milwaukee, approached the angry counterdemonstrator and managed to strike up a conversation. It turned out both had served in the First Cavalry Division. Soon the antiwar veteran said, "Look, we were over there—we know what was going on."

"Damn right," the other replied.
"Well, hell, you know we should have never gotten in there in the first place—you know we didn't belong there."
"Yeah," the other guy said dubiously.
"Well, that's all we're saying. . . ."
"Yeah, but I just can't take them damn kids who don't know what we went through, saying we're all a bunch of killers, and that the Viet Cong are all saints."

"I got six ounces of lead in my ass that shows that's not true. But I just don't want anyone else killed in that mess."

"I agree with you on that, but I just can't stand these hippies."

The counterdemonstrator was angry at the students, not so much because they opposed the war, but because he believed they opposed him, that they were attacking his morality without sharing his sacrifices or understanding his experience. He felt the students were labeling him a killer while romanticizing the Viet Cong, but his dislike of the hippies did not constitute support for the war. Andrew Levison, the writer who witnessed this episode, offers the insightful suggestion that the real issue at work in the veteran's response to the antiwar demonstration was "class and class distinction." "Looking at the rows of students passing by, that counterdemonstrator was furiously hostile. With a guy whom he recognized as a peer, both as veteran and worker, what appeared like inflexible reaction was converted into a viewpoint not so very different from that of the people marching by."[1]

To many veterans, the protests of college students felt like moral and social putdowns, expressions not of principle and commitment but simply of class privilege and arrogance. These feelings often come out most explicitly in long interviews. Steve Harper, a veteran from Akron, Ohio, was one of the nine subjects of Murray Polner's valuable book *No Victory Parades* (1971). Harper told Polner: "The critics are picking on us, just 'cause we had to fight this war. Where were their sons? In fancy colleges? Where were the sons of all the big shots who supported the war? Not in my platoon. Our guys' people were workers and things like that. . . . Still, we did things that made me sore. Like stopping the bombing—and maybe even putting us in Vietnam in the first place. If the war was so important, why didn't our leaders put everyone's son in there, why only us?"[2] For Harper, debate about the war often seemed like a personal attack because so much of it was carried on by "big shots" who did not have to fight the war. The critics and architects of the war did the talking, while the sons of workers did the fighting. Surely, he concluded, whatever the privileged might say about the war, they must be against grunts like him.

Harper's own views about the war, as he readily conceded, were confused. In the same breath he could denounce limitations on American bombing and the initial U.S. intervention in Vietnam. That is not necessarily a contradictory position. In effect he said, we should have won the war or stayed out. A simple enough argument to state, but one that evades the questions of whether the war could have been won or whether it was worth winning (that is, a just cause) and the further question of why it would be right to continue trying to win a war in which the original intervention was wrong or misguided. When those questions are broached, Harper's conflicted feelings and those of many veterans are drawn to the surface. A 1979 Harris survey found that a vast majority of veterans (89 percent) agreed with the statement, "The trouble in Vietnam was that our troops were asked to fight in a war which our political leaders in Washington would not let them win." Yet a clear majority of veterans (59 percent) also agreed with a completely contrary viewpoint: "The trouble in Vietnam was that our troops were asked to fight in a war we could never win."[3] The general public shared this contradictory view (73 and 65 percent agreeing with each statement, respectively). Of course, both formulations have a common appeal: they put the onus of responsibility for the war and its outcome on American leaders, not on ordinary soldiers and civilians. They also pose the same attractive alternatives suggested by Harper: win or stay out.

As for the moral legitimacy of the war, Steve Harper struggled to defend U.S. intervention. The United States, he said, was helping the people of Vietnam, people who "wanted us there" and who "wanted their freedom." Hard as he tried to sustain that view, however, his memories of the war kept contradicting it. He could not forget how the Vietnamese almost always seemed to be helping the Viet Cong ("they take all the Americans have to offer and give us nothin' and give the VC all they have"). Nor did he try to disguise his disdain for the Vietnamese military and government, which he saw as riddled with corruption and unable and unwilling to fight successfully against the Viet Cong ("they'd turn and run, from their officers on down"). Finally, Harper could only resolve the contradictions between his faith in the American mission and the realities he experienced by arguing, "We were there to help but Vietnamese are so stupid they can't understand that a great people want to help a weak people."[4]

In the end, Harper's defense of the war came down to a simple affirmation that American soldiers were right to go to Vietnam, that they were doing their duty. Perhaps because his own testimony about the war punched gaping holes in official justifications of American intervention, Harper returned repeatedly to a defense, not of U.S. policy, but of soldiers like himself. "We were soldiers, doing our jobs. We didn't want to bring disgrace on ourselves and our folks. We were right in being there." So much self-worth and dignity depended on his belief that his own actions were right. That is the crucial point. Harper's defense of American intervention was not insincere, but in defending the war, he expressed his stronger need to defend himself. At times he entertained the possibility that the United States was wrong to involve itself in Vietnam. Yet, he could not fully embrace that position because it suggested to him that simply doing his duty might also have been wrong. Clinging to the idea that he was right in being there, he felt he must also conclude that the nation was right to send him.

Harper's effort to link the moral integrity of individual soldiers and the justice of the war was shaken by his knowledge of the class inequalities of military service. If the war were really so important, truly a just war, he was sure the leaders would ask everyone to fight. While he insisted that he had done the right thing by going to Vietnam, he could not ignore the obvious presence of millions of young Americans who thought it was their duty, not to fight in the war, but actively to resist it.

> Last week, I had to be in Chicago; I ran into a "Resist the Draft" rally on the street. At first I smile: kids at it again, just a fad. Then I started getting sore. About how I had to go and they could stay out. Cosco went in and he was the straightest guy I ever knew. My Negro buddy didn't like the war, but he went in too. I just stood there and got sore at those rich kids telling people to "resist the draft." What about us poor people? For every guy who resists the draft one of us gotta go and he gets sent out into the boonies to get his backside shot at. One of their signs read "We've Already Given Enough." And I thought, "What *have* they given?"[5]

Because of the class gulf between most protesters and veterans, the specific political message of the antiwar demonstrators was mostly inconsequential to veterans like Harper. "We've Already Given Enough" or "Bring the Boys Home" were slogans intended to support the lives of soldiers and surely offended him less than the waving of Viet Cong flags or the chant "Ho Ho Ho Chi Minh, the NLF is going to win." To many veterans, however, all protest seemed like yet another class privilege enjoyed by wealthier peers, and even moderate objections to the war, if made by draft-immune college students, were often read as personal attacks. Student protests put into bold relief the contrast between the experiences of the two groups. Watching protest marches reminded some veterans of their own marches in Vietnam—those endless, exhausting, and dangerous humps. While they were enduring the hardship and danger of war, college students were—in the eyes of many soldiers—frolicking on campus in a blissful round of sex, drugs, and rock 'n roll *and* getting the credentials necessary to gain high-paying jobs. Then, too, simply the physical appearance of protesters, their long hair and shaggy dress, could anger veterans. Of course, soldiers in Vietnam also stretched conventional military rules related to dress and hair, so much so that by 1968 it was not uncommon to find men in the boonies wearing unofficial medallions, beads, and headgear and displaying wild graffiti ("eat the apple, fuck the Corps") on their flak jackets and helmet liners. Vets, however, had the perception that their own assertions had been harder won, that the kids on campus seemed to get away with everything. Then, too, they were especially irritated by nonveterans who dressed up in military uniforms, a popular fashion of the time. It was not so much that the old uniforms mocked the military; few people were as scornful of the military as most vets, but they felt you had to earn the right to wear the uniform in a casual way and that nonvets who did it were insulting those who had worn them in combat.

The resentment and jealousy vets felt toward protesters were based on more than anger that those at home seemed to have such a wonderful, safe time while those in Vietnam faced such danger. They also resented and envied the pride and conviction protesters took in their activism. For veterans torn by confusion about the war they had fought, and struggling to feel some pride in what they had done, the protesters' passion, self-assurance, and sense of purpose could generate a nagging—if unspoken—envy. Faced with people so sure the war was wrong, vets were convinced their own morality was under siege.

Victor Belloti, a captain in the Boston Fire Department, went to Vietnam in 1965 as a combat medic. He was the first of three generations to graduate from high school, and after the war he earned a college degree at the University of Massachusetts in Boston. He was reminded of his strong feelings about college students while talking about the attitude of combat soldiers toward men who served in rear areas. He laughed about all the ribbing the grunts used to give men in the rear, how they called them office pogies and "Remington Raiders," and how he would say things to them like, "You ought to come out in the field with us sometime and see the *real* war." When asked how deep the antagonism was between the two groups of soldiers, Belloti said that while there was some tension, most of his complaints were made in fun. By way of comparison he thought of his feelings for college students who demonstrated against the war.

I didn't have anywhere near the contempt or resentment for people in the rear that I had for the university students I met after the war. To me most of them were the arch-liberals from suburban communities, having never really worked in their lives. They were kids who had never had anything go wrong with them and they went on "marches" and they protested the Vietnam War. They didn't have the slightest idea what was going on over there. Politically they were right, I'm not saying they weren't. But this shit about baby-killers. I know guys who sacrificed a lot for women and children in ambush situations and going through villages. The political rightness or wrongness of the situation? We weren't wanted there. We knew that when we were over there.[6]

Belloti's contempt for campus protesters clearly draws on a keenly felt sense of class inequality, but what was "this shit about baby-killers"? The line, so crucial to his claim that protesters did not understand the reality of Vietnam (however right they might be about the "politics") is tossed into the account with an offhandedness that assumes we know precisely what he means, that the point is beyond dispute, and that no further explanation is necessary. In fact, understanding its significance is a complicated but essential way of getting at one of the central moral legacies of military service in Vietnam.

Among most veterans, Belloti's reference to "baby-killers" would be accepted with a knowing nod of recognition. Many take it as axiomatic that the antiwar movement regarded them as immoral killers. Stories certifying that commonplace were passed around among veterans with a frequency and resonance that imbued them with a mythic quality. David Chambers, interviewed in the late 1960s, reported: "At Travis Air Force Base an incident occurred which—true or not—spread like wildfire in Nam, and I think was believed by the guys. It seemed very possible to me, too. A vet, just back, was in the men's room when a hippie came up to him. He asked the vet if he had just returned from Nam and when he said yes, he had, the guy shot him in the arm."[7] Chambers makes a key point. Though the story is dubious (how, for one thing, would a hippie even make it onto the base?), it seemed plausible to many veterans. Even before returning home, these men anticipated rejection. Stories like this gained such currency that they were quickly generalized beyond individual anecdotes to statements such as "The protesters are calling us baby-killers" or "Hippies are spitting at veterans." By the 1980s, these images became widely accepted throughout American culture as literal representations of the homecoming received by most veterans. The archetypal story featured a returning veteran arriving at an airport (usually in California). He is wearing his dress uniform with campaign ribbons. As the vet walks through the terminal, a hippie, often a girl, approaches, calls him a baby-killer, and spits at him.

Were veterans really spit upon by hippies or protesters? In the late 1980s journalist Bob Greene posed this question in his syndicated column and received more than a thousand letters, some of which he collected in a book (*Homecoming*). Greene was persuaded that spittings had indeed occurred and devoted the first third of his collection to letters from men claiming it had happened to them. However, Greene concedes that there is an "apparent sameness" to these letters, a sameness that should, I think, make one wary of their literal truthfulness. Here is a typical sample: "I arrived at Los Angeles International Airport. . . . On my way to the taxis, I passed two young women in the waiting area. One of these young women approached me and, in a low voice, called me a 'baby killer' and spat on my ribbons. I was in uniform and wearing the Vietnamese Service Medal, the Vietnamese Campaign Medal, an Air Force Commendation Medal, and the Purple Heart."[8] The remainder of the letters in Greene's book are from veterans who either express deep skepticism about the spitting allegations or who believe being spit at was an uncommon experience. Many even testify to acts of great kindness from strangers upon returning home. The most commonplace letters were in many respects the most poignant. They came from men simply struggling to express the pain, confusion, and isolation they felt upon returning to the United States, how uncomfortable people seemed to be around them, or how little people seemed to want to know about their experience.

Alongside the stories of war protesters standing guard at airports to taunt returning veterans should be placed a surprising survey. In 1979 Harris pollsters used a "feeling thermometer" to measure public attitudes toward Vietnam veterans. On a scale of 1 to 10, with 10 being the warmest possible feeling and 1 the coolest, a sample of 237 "antiwar activists" rated Vietnam veterans 8.9, far above their rating of military leaders (4.7) and congressional representatives (5.0), and even higher than their ranking of "people who demonstrated against the war in Vietnam" (7.7—not all antiwar activists endorsed public demonstrations as a useful tactic to end the war). Though the attitudes of antiwar activists may have been cooler toward veterans during the war years (the poll came several years later), a total reversal in feeling seems unlikely.

While antiwar activists claimed warmer feelings toward Vietnam vets than the "baby-killer" stories suggest, the Harris survey found that veterans had a very low opinion of protesters. The sample of 1,179 Vietnam veterans ranked protesters at 3.3, a response pollsters consider "very cool." Veterans gave an even lower score (1.9) to people who left the country to avoid the draft. Antiwar activists had much more respect for draft evaders, ranking them at 7.1.[9]

Granting that most people in the peace movement did not hate veterans and did not abuse them, many veterans certainly perceived the antiwar movement as a personal rejection. A key reason, as discussed, was that Vietnam was a working-class war wealthier students had the best chance of avoiding. Moreover, protesters were not always careful to distinguish between the managers of the war and the workers who did the fighting. The antiwar movement openly and fervently attacked not only the political decision to intervene in Vietnam but the conduct of the war as well. How else, activists might argue, could they make Americans aware of the discrepancy between official justifications of the war and its reality? The war's injustice could not be fully demonstrated unless it was shown that the military was burning down Vietnamese villages, killing civilians, and supporting corrupt, dictatorial regimes. How could those realities be exposed without making soldiers feel morally suspect? Furthermore, some protesters simply did not make a clear distinction between the war and those who fought it, and they regarded American soldiers as ready and willing killers or ignorant dupes.

When Gene Holiday returned from Vietnam, he was curious to meet some people on "the hippie side." "They never really called me a baby-killer, but they said I was a marine and I was one of those kind of people." He got especially upset the day he saw an antiwar demonstration in 1971. "I got real angry at a couple people for carrying the North Vietnamese flag. [I told them]: 'You're 18, you don't even know what the hell went on. What are you carrying that thing for?' I took the flag and started ripping it up." The argument quickly escalated into a brutal fight between Gene and three demonstrators. It ended when all four were arrested.[10]

By the late 1960s, moreover, a minority within the antiwar movement wanted not simply an end to American intervention but a victory for Vietnamese left-wing revolutionary nationalism. As Todd Gitlin has pointed out, among the New Left wing of the peace movement, at least among its late 1960s leadership, there was a strong tendency to romanticize Third World revolutionaries: "With the United States pulverizing and bullying small countries, it seemed the most natural thing in the world to go prospecting among them for heroes. Their resistance was so brave, their enemies so implacable, their nationalism so noble, we could take their passions, even their slogans and styles of speech . . . for our own. . . . It no longer felt sufficient . . . to say no to aggressive war; we felt driven to say yes to revolt."

Gitlin, an important New Left figure, recalls that American flags almost always outnumbered NLF flags at antiwar demonstrations. However, the NLF flags received "a disproportionate share of the media spotlight." Student activists who championed the NLF comprised a rather small portion of American college students. In the late 1960s about 7 to 10 percent of college students described themselves as radicals, and of these, probably only a fraction sided with the Vietnamese Revolutionary Forces. However, those who did embrace America's official enemy contributed to the isolation of the antiwar movement. As Gitlin writes, "Surely those NLF flags were part of the explanation for one of the stunning political facts of the decade: that as the war steadily lost popularity in the late Sixties, *so did the antiwar movement*."[11] Of course the movement's loss of support was largely fueled by the attacks of government officials like President Nixon and Vice-President Agnew who tried to persuade the public that the entire movement sided with the enemy. While many veterans were receptive to this wildly distorted claim, they were by no means alone.

While the antiwar movement has been branded with far too much blame for the mistreatment of Vietnam veterans, society as a whole was certainly unable and unwilling to receive these men with the support and understanding they needed. The most common experiences of rejection were not explicit acts of hostility but quieter, sometimes more devastating forms of withdrawal, suspicion, and indifference. When veterans told new acquaintances that they had served in Vietnam, it was not uncommon for people to treat them warily. Veterans could feel themselves making other people nervous and uneasy. They often wondered if they were just being paranoid or if others were in fact being remote and detached, keeping them at arm's length. Some veterans began to expect such behavior, and their expectation of tension helped to create it. For some, all contact with nonveterans became uncomfortable, even intolerable.

Tony Almeida, son of a firefighter, returned from Vietnam in 1969. At an outdoor rock concert he struck up a conversation with a young woman and some of her friends:

They were my own age but they were college kids—definitely not from the type of upbringing I'd come from, for sure. One thing led to another and to get to the point I ended up in bed with this girl. We were about to make love and some question she asked me—I don't remember the question but I remember responding, "Yeah, I was in the marines."

She looked at me and she said, "Then you were in Vietnam?"

I said, "Yeah, I just came back from Vietnam, in fact, not too long ago."

She just completely withdrew and sat up on one elbow and said, "Sorry." No, wait, she didn't say she was sorry, she just said, "You have to leave now."

I could have punched her right in the face at that point. That's when I started to feel guilty, I guess, about participating in the war. That's when I started to realize that there was this whole *other* set of experiences that had happened with other people and there must have been some reason why they were making those connections. I don't know what stopped me from saying "Who the fuck are you?" But I just took it, got up and got dressed and left. I didn't talk about Vietnam again with anybody except other vets until 1978.[12]

Faced with society's indifference, uneasiness, and outright rejection and gripped by their own troubled memories of the war, thousands of veterans lapsed into the sort of silence reported by Tony Almeida. For years—a full decade, sometimes longer—a startling number of men who fought in Vietnam—who knows how many—would not talk about their experience with nonveterans, would not even volunteer that they had been in a war. If asked directly, they might reveal a piece of their experience, some stock anecdote they had practiced enough to feel comfortable telling: an amusing story about some crazy GI who booby trapped the shitter; the time on guard duty when they were attacked by rock apes (gorillas—guerrillas, get it?); or how there were these bizarre lizards that made this spooky cry in the night that sounded exactly like "fuck you" ("they were called geckos, but most of us just called them 'fuck-you lizards'"). Some veterans could go on at such length and with such enthusiasm telling these stories that even good friends might fail to realize that they were only hearing about a sliver of experience, that underneath the easy stories was a profound silence, and that anything approaching the real pain and confusion of the war was packed away. Of course, there were some veterans for whom no war story was easy, men who simply would not talk.

In part, the silence reflected the conviction that others simply did not care about the war, wanted to forget it, could not possibly understand what it was like, or would be so appalled by what they heard they would condemn the storyteller. It is also true that many veterans did not want to risk the pain of talking about the war, even with sympathetic listeners. Veterans, too, wanted to bury the war, to put it behind them. After all, to discuss it seriously and honestly was to court emotional turmoil. In other words, the silence of veterans had as much to do with the nature of the war as it did with the lack of support for returning soldiers. For many, Vietnam was so meaningless, so frustrating and confusing, and so morally wrenching, they almost surely would have had postwar problems regardless of the homecoming they received (though more support, especially better benefits and psychological services, would have made things much better for many). While most Americans were all too able to forget the war, many veterans could not. Try as they might to bury the war, its unresolved emotions and memories festered below the surface, sometimes coming out in indirect, unpredictable, dangerous, and self-destructive ways: sudden flashes of anger, hard drinking or drug use, panic attacks, extreme distrust, inability to care about anything or anybody. Meanwhile, the sources of so much of this pain were largely unknown or unexpressed. The silence of so many veterans, so profound during the 1960s and 1970s but, for some, lasting much longer, is one of the most significant and psychologically destructive examples of group self-censorship in American social history.

Many veterans had trouble even establishing contact with other veterans. After World War II, such connections were virtually ready-made. Most men returned within a two-year period, and virtually the whole generation had served. The men who returned from Vietnam drifted home in isolation, one at a time. Even meeting new friends who had served in Vietnam could be tough since the entire group represented only 10 percent of the generation. Old friends from the neighborhood who had gone to Vietnam might well have moved or never returned. Nor did many veterans try hard to contact those they served with in Vietnam. Like most Americans they, too, were trying to forget the war. As a result, most veterans had no idea what had happened to the men they left behind in Vietnam. Veterans often find the first visit to the Vietnam Memorial emotionally wrenching in large part because it is, in many cases, the first time they learn the fate of wartime buddies.

Perhaps the veterans best able to find a voice during the latter years of the war and through much of the 1970s were those who actively opposed the war. Founded in 1967, Vietnam Veterans Against the War (VVAW) gradually grew by 1971 into the most significant antiwar veterans' movement spawned by any American war. In 1970, feeling the need to talk about the war collectively, VVAW began organizing informal rap groups. Though the veterans sometimes asked psychiatrists, such as Robert Jay Lifton, to attend their meetings, they insisted on retaining primary control over the structure of the meetings and the issues addressed, a radical departure from conventional models of group therapy. Drawing on his work with veterans, Lifton wrote *Home from the War* (1973), in which he makes the case that political activism helped antiwar veterans recover from much of the emotional and psychological trauma of their wartime experience. These men, he argues, by developing a critique of the war and speaking out against it, found a renewed faith in their own moral integrity.[13]

For antiwar veterans a crucial element of their political development was their speaking about their own experience of the war's immorality. To do so meant accepting some personal complicity for what they viewed as wrong. Yet it also allowed them to place their own actions in a larger context of national policy and decision making that located primary responsibility at the highest level of political and military power. Their acts of confession and witness were not merely psychologically cathartic. By talking through the worst of their experience and attaching those experiences to a political condemnation of the war, antiwar veterans grew more hopeful about the prospects for shaping a new and positive postwar identity. There were two key public moments when this process was engaged collectively. In January 1971, 150 antiwar veterans gathered in Detroit for the Winter Soldier Investigation, where they testified to American atrocities they had either committed or witnessed in Vietnam. A few months later, a much larger group—more than a thousand—rallied in Washington to lobby congressional representatives, testify before the Senate Foreign Relations Committee, and stage antiwar demonstrations.[14]

It may be, however, that Lifton was too sanguine about the postwar recovery of antiwar veterans. He wrote in the early 1970s, and many of the more than 500,000 Vietnam veterans who suffered some form of post-traumatic stress syndrome did not experience the worst symptoms until five or even ten years after their tours. Moreover, in the 1970s antiwar veterans had a level of support within the larger culture that was much reduced in the Reagan era. While antiwar veterans, like everyone in the peace movement, always had their motives and patriotism challenged by the right wing, they were looked upon as political mavericks, even heroes, by significant numbers of people who had turned against the war. When veterans themselves spoke out against the war, their testimony was prized as firsthand confirmation of what the movement had been arguing all along. Of course, Vietnam veterans had a healthy suspicion of their reception by the civilian antiwar movement; they were alert to the possibility that the warmth of their welcome was commensurate with their ideological purity and might evaporate with any sign of political backsliding. Many antiwar vets, therefore, preferred to maintain a certain distance from other peace groups. Nonetheless, surely they found in the larger peace movement a measure of social respect and political legitimation.

Still, throughout the 1960s and much of the 1970s, Vietnam veterans rarely received respectful attention in mainstream culture. On the rare occasions when Vietnam vets were portrayed in film and television, they were typically represented as psycopathic misfits. With some notable exceptions, such as Gloria Emerson's superb book *Winners and Losers* (1976) and works written by veterans themselves, there was little wider cultural effort to investigate the experiences of Vietnam veterans. When veterans gained brief moments in the national spotlight, their appearances were political gestures more symbolic than substantive, as when American POWs were wined and dined at the Nixon White House in 1973 or when antiwar veteran Ron Kovic was invited to speak at the 1976 Democratic convention.

A more serious moment in popular culture's treatment of Vietnam veterans came in 1978 with the appearance of the film *Coming Home*. Despite some fine moments, the film finally reduced the complexity of veterans' experiences to a sanctimonious political parable, evading such crucial issues as the working-class status of most vets, the particular nature of the war experiences that caused so much trauma, and the reasons why most veterans did not come to share the unconflicted antiwar convictions of the film's hero.

The film opens promisingly with a group of wounded veterans playing pool in a VA hospital and discussing the war. The scene has an extraordinary documentary texture, establishing an instant sense that one is witnessing real veterans in a moment of honest confrontation with the meaning of their experience. Their talk focuses on one man's claim that, if asked, he would fight again in Vietnam. His halting but dignified effort to defend his position and the debate it stimulates pose some of the most important questions veterans have faced in coming to terms with the war: Was the war worth fighting? Were the sacrifices necessary? Was going to Vietnam personally right or wrong? Was there any real choice?

In fact, it is not uncommon to hear veterans express a willingness, even a desire, to fight again. Some simply hold to the conviction that they did their duty by fighting in Vietnam and would do it again, not because they are hooked on war or because the cause was clear or convincing, but because they believe when their nation goes to war, citizens should serve. Others entertain the idea of going to war again as a way of reimagining their first experience, this time projecting a positive outcome. Others simply became addicted to the thrill of combat and have found nothing in civilian life to match the existential high of risking death and causing it. Some of these men, a small but significant number impossible to count, have acted on that impulse by joining mercenary armies to fight in remote corners of Africa and Latin America. Others who miss the exhilaration of war have taken more moderate steps, such as playing survival war games in the woods with guns that fire paint pellets or immersing themselves in the fantasies of *Soldier of Fortune* magazine. Others who would "do it again" are driven by more obscure impulses, desires to avenge particular buddies, to purge themselves of survivor guilt, or to court death.

Though *Coming Home* begins with the promise of exploring such responses, along with those of antiwar veterans, the first scene ends tellingly by giving the final and decisive word to a veteran who argues that vets who still support the war are simply "lying to themselves," that they have to "justify being paralyzed" (or in some other way wounded by the war) so they "justify killing people." "But how many guys you know can make the reality and say, 'What I did was wrong and all this other shit was wrong, man' and still be able to live with themselves?" How, that is, can someone permanently damaged by the war have the courage to argue that the damage was done in pursuit of an unjust cause? It is a good and tough question, but the remainder of the film is devoted not to the complex implications of the question but simply to embracing the unexplained radicalization of a veteran, Luke Martin (Jon Voight), who comes to just that position.

Luke, an enlisted man paralyzed from the waist down, moves from anguished and bitter casualty of the war to compassionate and committed antiwar activist. While recovering he meets Sally Hyde (Jane Fonda), a conservative officer's wife who is transformed by her experience as a volunteer at the VA hospital where she meets Luke and other wounded veterans. Suddenly she begins wearing hip clothes, buys a sports car, lets her hair go natural, and berates other officers' wives for ignoring the plight of wounded GIs. She and Luke fall in love while her husband, Capt. Robert Hyde (Bruce Dern), is away in Vietnam. Though Sally's own views on the war are never articulated, it is clear that she comes to embrace Luke's emerging radicalism. Indeed, she asks to sleep with Luke for the first time on the night he is arrested for chaining shut the gates of the Marine Corps Training Depot. Her political and sexual liberation are ratified that night when she experiences her first orgasm.

When Sally's husband returns from Vietnam, he is troubled, hard-drinking, explosive, and ultimately suicidal. He learns of his wife's infidelity from FBI agents who have been trailing Luke since his act of civil disobedience. Robert confronts Sally with a loaded rifle, telling her he knows about the affair with Luke. She says, "I wanted to talk to you. You seemed so far away from me since you came back. I've been scared. I love you. I do. I'm not going to make excuses for what happened. It happened. I needed somebody. I was lonely."

At this point, Luke, sensing trouble, arrives at the house, further igniting Robert's rage. Looking pious and mournful, Luke tries to calm Robert by saying that he understands. Even more enraged, Robert yells, "Bullshit, you Jody motherfucker." Undaunted, Luke continues his effort to pacify Robert: "I can understand because I'm a brother and I've been in the same place you're at right now. . . . But she's here because she loves you and there was never any question of that. . . . You give her a chance, she can help you." Robert now seems on the verge of shooting Luke and issues an ominous threat: "Say something else Fuck." Unruffled, Luke does say more: "I'm not the enemy. Maybe the enemy is the fucking war. But you don't want to kill anyone here. You have enough ghosts to carry around." Given the fact that Luke has slept with Robert's wife, one might imagine that Robert does indeed have reason to regard Luke as an enemy. When one recalls that the part of Sally is played by Jane Fonda, loathed by many veterans for her trip to Hanoi in 1972, where she was photographed smiling among North Vietnamese antiaircraft guns, veterans sympathetic to Robert may read the affair between Luke and Sally as a sexual *and* political betrayal. But Luke's sanctimonious speech works, and Robert backs down. He apologizes, puts down his rifle, and mutters, "I'm fucked." He has been successfully disarmed by the two lovers, and as if we hadn't gotten the point fully, Luke grabs the rifle out of Robert's hand, drops the bayonet, and takes the rounds out of the chamber. Meanwhile, Robert breaks down in front of Sally, saying, "I just want to be a hero, that's all. I just want to be a fucking hero. One day in my life. One moment."

What follows is a series of crosscuts. We see Robert decorated with a bronze star (a baseless honor since we know it was given for an accidental, self-inflicted wound). Then we see Luke giving a moving speech to high school boys: "I *wanted* to be a war hero. I *wanted* to go out and kill for my country. Now I'm here to tell you that I have killed for my country, or whatever, and I don't feel good about it. Because there's just not enough reason, man, to feel a person die in your hands or to see your best buddy blown away. . . . And there's a lot of shit I did over there that I find fucking hard to live with. . . . I'm just telling you, there's a choice to be made here." As he speaks, we cut back and forth between Luke and Robert, who goes to the beach, strips off his dress uniform, and swims out to sea in an apparent suicide. The choice that Luke encourages appears to the film audience as a choice between a veteran like Luke, who has turned against the war, and Robert, who still clings to a military identity that has been so ravaged he is led to suicide.

The final scene shows Sally Hyde and a friend entering a grocery store, and in the final frame we see an exit sign that reads "Lucky Out." In terms of the film's pious antiwar politics, Robert's suicide is indeed a lucky out. His departure spares us from confronting fully the real sadness and complexity represented by the thousands of suicidal Vietnam veterans. Because our knowledge of Robert is so sketchy and his character is presented so unsympathetically, we are not encouraged to grieve at his death. (However, Bruce Dern's performance is so strong that many viewers might be able to imagine beyond the limitations of the screenplay to reach a fuller empathy with Robert's sense of estrangement and betrayal.) In addition to reducing political and psychological complexity, Robert's suicide relieves us of the threat of violence his character represents. Luke poses no such threat. In addition to his nonviolent politics, he is confined to a wheelchair. Finally, the film resolves the romantic conflict of the movie, suggesting that Luke and Sally's affair can continue without the inconvenience of a disturbed spouse.

Even the soundtrack seems to assure us that Robert was beyond hope, that he was simply too out of touch to be saved. The song that covers his suicide (and also accompanies Robert's first appearance in the film) is "Out of Time" by the Rolling Stones. The song becomes Robert's epitaph and, at least by implication, the theme song intended for all veterans who fail to break with their military identity and have been away too long and are too "out of touch" to "know what's goin' on."

Coming Home makes an attractive hero of a wounded veteran who witnesses against the war, but it gives little voice to the majority of veterans who remained ambivalent about or supportive of the war. It even oversimplifies the political development of antiwar veterans, most of whom testify about how hard it was to establish an identity in opposition to the war and to reject the official versions of reality they had grown up with. As one man put it, "I grew up with all the patriotism, the VFW crap, and it hurt to change. I went through hell."[15] In *Coming Home* we learn something of Luke's agonizing recovery from his wound, but we are left essentially clueless as to how and why he turned against the war. (The same criticism applies to the more recent film about a paralyzed Vietnam veteran, *Born on the Fourth of July* [1989].)

Unlike Robert Hyde, most veterans did not return from Vietnam still hoping to be a war hero, but many did expect a measure of respect for having fought a tough war. Convinced, as many were, that antiwar people would be against them, veterans often looked to supporters of the war for sympathetic and welcoming company. Surely, they thought, veterans of earlier wars, members of the American Legion or the VFW, would understand what they had gone through and accept them as comrades. But most Vietnam veterans were as disillusioned by the right as they were by the left. Their stories about the rejection they felt among older veterans are as commonplace as the ones about antagonistic peaceniks. Just as many vets believed the antiwar movement looked at them as immoral, lower-class baby-killers, they were equally convinced that older vets and prowar hawks regarded them as pitiful losers.

When Todd Dasher returned from Vietnam, he recalls his father saying, "You guys ain't really veterans, you didn't win the war. You didn't win your war."[16] The father would not even acknowledge his son's status as a veteran. Worse, he made Tom feel personally responsible for the war's outcome, as if it had been his war to win or lose. The younger veterans believed the older men who fought in Korea and World War II looked upon them as losers, crybabies, dopers, and deadbeats who had not even fought in a real war but had only fought in a little skirmish, a "conflict." In part, the generational friction between veterans was inevitable. Many conservative older veterans took great stock in America's military record, and the Vietnam War was, to them, a great blot. Vietnam veterans could not help but feel that the older men who railed at the government, the media, and the antiwar movement for undermining the American war effort were also casting aspersions on the competence of American troops. It is certainly true that the traditional service organizations—the VFW and American Legion—were dominated in the 1960s and 1970s by World War II veterans and gave scant attention to the needs of returning Vietnam veterans. Moreover, Vietnam veterans themselves were not especially eager to conform to the traditional ways of the conservative organizations. While the older men were often content to sit around the bar drinking beer and reminiscing, the younger men might want to smoke grass and listen to rock music or plan a community project. Nor were they always so red, white, and blue, so convinced that the war in Vietnam was worth winning and a simple matter of pouring on more firepower, as the older men often argued.

Even David Chambers, who returned from Vietnam to Fair Lawn, New Jersey, still very committed to the American cause, found it difficult to abide the patly hawkish views of the men down at the American Legion hall:

In the [American Legion] Hall I found myself listening to middle-aged men telling me how it was in a "real war." They didn't know or care about what we went through.

Then one night a fat guy, an accountant from Passaic, who said he had been with Patton in Germany, came in with a letter from his nephew in Vietnam. The nephew had come on some GIs who had been cut up badly. So his outfit went into a neighboring village and searched for the VC. They also asked the people. Nobody would admit seeing them. Everybody knew they were lying so they ordered the M-48 tanks to destroy every hooch in the village. The nephew had written: "If you don't think an M-48 doesn't scare somebody, it does!"

"That's the only way!" the accountant said. . . . And then another guy chipped in, angry: "We should use the H-bomb if necessary to get it over with." Everybody agreed, and he went on about communism and freedom . . . and again everyone seemed to approve. At that point I got up to leave. He was right, in some ways; I'd do it again if my country asked me to, but it wasn't quite the same as me or my buddies saying it; and this guy, maybe forty-five or fifty, was parading around like a hotshot while his own kid was probably deferred. . . . [In a slightly different context he added,] Their arguments were so pat; they all seemed so damn sure. But I was *there*.[17]

Because he was there, he knew the war was not so easy to win. He remembered that he and his fellow marines were still being shelled at Con Thien long after a magazine article claimed the shelling had stopped. He also knew that South Vietnam was a society torn up by internal conflict and corruption. So, convinced as he was that America was right in fighting the war, he could not be so sure as the older vets. Indeed, he concedes, "I might one day conclude it was all for nothing. Who knows?"

When David enrolled at a state teachers college, he hung around with other Vietnam vets. "It was easy to talk with them and we all felt different from the civilians and the old vets. One of the vets was an out-and-out 'dove,' but I could take that very easily from him because he had been there, too, and drew an honest conclusion. The only test we had was: were you there?" During a class debate a member of Young Americans for Freedom made a hawkish speech in support of David's position, and David chimed in to ask why, if he "felt so strongly about it," he "still hung onto his 2-S [student deferment] card?" "I still think we could win over there. . . . But nobody who hasn't been there can tell it to me that way. In his mouth the words sounded dirty."[18]

David continually drew a line between Vietnam veterans and everyone else. For him, you were either an insider or an outsider. If you had not been there, you could not really know what went on, and your views were inherently suspect. Many Vietnam veterans have drawn that kind of boundary. Indeed, veterans of all wars have had a tendency to think of their experiences as beyond the comprehension of civilians, but with Vietnam veterans, this attitude has often had an additional, more divisive, component. Most veterans of previous wars believed that while civilians might not understand what soldiers did in war, at least very few were opposed to what they did. However, many Vietnam veterans have had the extra anxiety that outsiders not only fail to understand them but disrespect them as well.

This anxiety is one important element in explaining a high level of distrust among Vietnam veterans. For those with the most acute suspicion of nonvets, a common characteristic among men suffering from posttraumatic stress disorder, outsiders could be viewed as potentially hostile in every realm of life. Such veterans have varying levels of what can loosely be understood as paranoia. The term is used here in the nontechnical, everyday sense to refer to a condition of extreme and disproportionate anxiety and suspicion about other people's intentions and behavior—the assumption that "everyone's out to get you." Some psychiatrists, wanting to distinguish between veterans who suffer from clinical paranoia (a full-fledged psychosis) and the far greater number who have extreme nervous anxiety and suspicion around other people, have preferred such terms as *hypervigilance* or *pansuspiciousness*.[19] In any case, specialists tend to find common ground in their descriptions of the symptoms. According to Herbert Hendin and Ann Haas, "This ['paranoid' adaptation] to combat trauma involves eternal vigilance in dealings with others, an expectation that any argument is a prelude to a violent fight. . . . Under such emotional pressure, the veteran perceives civilian life as an extension of the war and almost everyone . . . is seen as a potential enemy. . . . [They have] a perpetual readiness for attack, even when no danger exists."[20]

Vietnam was, for American soldiers, the perfect training ground for paranoia. To assume that everyone was a potential enemy was, in fact, a reasonable psychological response to the realities of counterguerrilla warfare. As the sergeant told Larry Hughes when he arrived in Vietnam, "Be alert from this moment and don't trust nobody with slanted eyes!" Paranoia thrived in a war zone where Americans could never be sure of Vietnamese loyalties. Is the barber a Viet Cong informant? Is the hootch maid counting steps when she walks across the compound to help the Viet Cong fix their targets for a rocket attack? Have the villagers booby trapped the trail? Does this child have a satchel charge taped to his stomach? Such suspicions might prove to be groundless, but they were not unreasonable. Hypervigilant soldiers might make mistakes, be too hasty to lash out, or assume wrongly that a civilian posed a threat; but they were determined to survive, and a strong dose of paranoia could be as necessary to survival as a clean rifle.[21]

GI distrust was not limited to the Vietnamese. In many ways the nature of the war encouraged soldiers to suspect everyone, even other Americans. Experience taught men to watch out for the new guys who were thrust into combat units only a few days after leaving the States. So green and scared, these guys could panic and get everybody killed. Equally suspect were officers bucking for promotion and all too eager to put their units in jeopardy to build up a good body count. Then there was supporting fire to worry about—an artillery unit, for example, with a reputation for screwing up coordinates and putting its rounds on top of American grunts. Better to suspect everyone. Trust that extended beyond the squad level was a combat equivalent of blind faith.

Suspicion ran so deep that Americans sometimes questioned not only the competence but the loyalty of their own troops. At a more complex psychological level, I would further suggest that many soldiers were concerned about their own political loyalty to the American cause and sometimes projected that concern outward onto others—fellow soldiers, Vietnamese civilians, Americans at home. Some GI folklore gives expression to anxiety about the tenuous bonds holding individuals together as "one side." One legend features an American grunt who defects to the other side and fights alongside the Viet Cong against his countrymen. He is typically described as a blond, ghostlike figure, responsible for a great many American deaths, who is impossible to track down and kill. This legendary defector figures in Robert Roth's novel, *Sand in the Wind*, where he is described by marine grunts as the Phantom Bloker because of his alleged skill at firing a grenade launcher (a "bloker") on U.S. positions. In *No Bugles, No Drums*, Charles Durden goes beyond the legend to have one of his main characters, a black GI named Jinx, defect and fight for the Viet Cong. Tim O'Brien's novel, *Going after Cacciato*, centers on a squad of American grunts on a fantastic mission to capture Cacciato, a member of their unit who deserted. Among his many guises, Cacciato sometimes appears as a Viet Cong guerrilla, thus becoming, at times, a metaphorical defector. The idea of defection was scary because it confronted men with the possibility of disloyalty within their own units and because it raised the troubling proposition that the American cause offered too little sense of purpose to hold everyone's conviction, that, in fact, the other side might have a more devout sense of mission.[22]

In *The Great War and Modern Memory*, Paul Fussell makes the intriguing suggestion that the structure of combat during World War I—the trench warfare—promoted a way of thinking about the world that persistently divided things into two. That is, the war so locked its participants into an "us versus them" mentality that it nourished a tendency to see all experience as binary, polarized, and adversarial. "Prolonged trench warfare, with its collective isolation, its 'defensiveness,' and its nervous obsession with what 'the other side' is up to, establishes a model of modern political, social, artistic, and psychological polarization."[23]

It may be too much to argue that wartime experience has quite the causal weight Fussell sometimes implies. After all, dualistic, binary thinking can be linked to other major historical transformations such as the scientific revolution, the Protestant Reformation, or the rise of industrial capitalism. But the psychological responses to warfare surely have an impact on civilian life, especially among the people most profoundly affected by the war. If trench warfare was a model of polarization, the American military experience in Vietnam was more nearly a model of paranoia. In Vietnam, there were rarely the clear sides of trench warfare. The sense of isolation was often as individual as it was collective. Soldiers experienced the deepest uncertainty about whom to trust; about who represented the other side; about where, if anyplace, they could be safe; and even about where, in literal terms, they were.

The distrust fostered by Vietnam went deeper than a sense of vulnerability to external threats. Often it has been accompanied by a deep-seated internal suspicion, a distrust of oneself. At the heart of this distrust is moral self-doubt and pain. The war's most serious psychological traumas lie in the moral distress many veterans have carried from the war itself: the hurt and guilt that come with confronting the prospect that one risked, witnessed, and inflicted violence on behalf of an unjustifiable cause, that one participated in forms of brutality that were not only often excessive and arbitrary but were unconnected to a persuasive or consistent political mission.

Of course, significant numbers of veterans insist the war has not left them with doubt or regret or guilt, and we should not facilely assume that these men are simply repressing or denying their true feelings. Many soldiers, especially among the large contingent of rear-echelon soldiers, were able to find ways to insulate themselves from the worst of the war. Psychiatrists Hendin and Haas have found that the veterans they studied who suffered the least guilt (or the need to deny guilt) were those who were not involved in acts of unnecessary, gratuitous, or excessive violence. Studies of veterans also suggest that men from stable, middle-class backgrounds were considerably less likely to have serious postwar problems than the majority from working-class families. In part this may reflect the fact that middle-class men were far more likely to receive rear-area assignments, thereby avoiding the heavy combat that is closely linked to most severe cases of posttraumatic stress. There is not yet conclusive evidence that middle-class men who experienced heavy combat were less likely than other combat veterans to have postwar psychological problems.[24]

One can hardly ignore the documentation of unprecedented levels of psychological turmoil experienced by Vietnam veterans. Even the Veterans' Administration, an agency that for ten years refused even to acknowledge the existence of psychological problems specifically related to service in Vietnam, eventually conceded that at least 500,000 veterans suffered from Vietnam Delayed Stress Syndrome or, as it is now most commonly known, posttraumatic stress disorder. Specialists who treat this disorder usually place the figure a good deal higher, at about 800,000, and extensive interviews with veterans suggest that for every man who might be clinically diagnosed with the syndrome, there are just as many who share a number of its symptoms or suffer a milder form. Furthermore, among the many veterans who have lived stable and productive civilian lives, a considerable number have indeed denied or repressed their war-related pain or attributed it to some other, more manageable source.[25]

As Peter Marin has persuasively argued, however, the moral distress of Vietnam has been denied less by veterans than by American culture as a whole. After a decade of virtual silence about Vietnam veterans, the media in the 1980s gradually "discovered" this forgotten, working-class segment of the baby boom generation; but for the most part, the attention was superficial. The focus was on a new, long-belated effort to recognize and honor the sacrifices of Vietnam veterans. Suddenly images of veterans began to appear in movies, commercials, television shows, and popular music. Contingents of veterans began marching in Memorial Day parades and receiving warm, emotional applause. Some magazine articles began describing Vietnam veterans as new cultural heroes. There was widespread feeling that these men had been unfairly treated and neglected. At best, the attention brought some scrutiny to such crucial issues as the massive use by U.S. forces of Agent Orange, a dioxin with extraordinary levels of toxicity that poisoned thousands of American veterans along with the land and people of Vietnam. There was also some recognition of the inadequacy of medical, psychological, and educational benefits for veterans. Then, too, as *posttraumatic stress disorder* entered the nation's vocabulary, people began to associate it with a list of very real and disturbing symptoms—depression, flashbacks, nightmares, anxiety, extreme mood swings, anger, paranoia, emotional numbing, and so on. But the sources of that psychic turmoil, and its social, political, and moral significance, were little examined. To do so would mean a serious reexamination of the war itself. Instead, most public discourse about veterans suggested that their problems were primarily ones of readjustment, that veterans returning individually from war lacked collective reentry rituals, that they reentered civilian society so rapidly they did not have enough time to "decompress," and that society failed to offer veterans the gratitude and welcome so necessary to the reestablishment of a positive civilian identity. While those matters are not unimportant, the simplistic implication of much commentary about veterans was that everything would have been fine had these men simply been given a parade, a pat on the back, and a few more benefits. However, to follow Peter Marin's argument once again, society has not yet adequately addressed "the unacknowledged source of much of the vets' pain and anger: profound moral distress, arising from the realization that one has committed acts with real and terrible consequences."[26]

Eating at the souls of many veterans is the knowledge that in Vietnam they committed acts and took risks they never imagined themselves capable of—from the most heroic to the most savage—in pursuit of a cause they could neither win nor identify nor embrace. Soldiers in all wars fight for survival, but they do not find meaning in their action unless they can attach it to a just and positive purpose. In Vietnam, Americans had only the negative goals of destruction and survival. Their postwar efforts to find positive goals in civilian life have often hinged on their ability to free themselves from an inflated sense of personal responsibility for the war's conduct and outcome. As William Mahedy and others have argued, veterans come to terms with the war most successfully not by denying the worst of the war and their participation in it but by identifying all that was wrong about the war and sharing responsibility for it with the larger society.[27] Only then can they fully locate what is still right and whole in themselves. This complex business has been made harder because the larger culture has yet to acknowledge the war's grave injustices or its complicity in making or allowing them to occur. Thus the veterans have had to confront the war in social and moral isolation, an isolation exacerbated by the class inequalities of the war. The working class not only shouldered a disproportionate share of the war's fighting but a disproportionate share of its moral turmoil. The recent acceptance of veterans will do nothing to help this struggle if it simply covers their experience in the warm glow of tributes and parades. It will be helpful only if America as a whole confronts the social and moral cruelty of the Vietnam War and accepts the collective responsibility to become accountable for that history and the future it continues to shape.

Notes

INTRODUCTION

1. Hemingway, *Farewell to Arms*, pp. 177–78.
2. Emerson, *Winners and Losers*, p. 4.
3. Brende and Parson, *Vietnam Veterans*, pp. 203–40.
4. In a newly opened vet center, I began one of my first interviews for this project as a nearby television showed pictures of former hostages being cheered as they paraded through the streets of Washington, D.C. Many Vietnam veterans found these homecoming ceremonies deeply upsetting. Billy Cizinski interview, 27 Jan. 1981. Unless indicated otherwise, all interviews are from my personal files.
5. While I argue that survivor-heroes were primarily a 1980s phenomenon, H. Bruce Franklin provides persuasive evidence that the political effort to make American POWs dominant symbols of the Vietnam War began as early as the first Nixon administration. See "The POW/MIA Myth," *Atlantic*, Dec. 1991.
6. The Reagan quotations are from Gibson, *The Perfect War*, p. 5, and Capps, *The Unfinished War*, p. 147. Capps describes a White House ceremony of February 1981 during which Reagan awarded the Medal of Honor to a Vietnam veteran and lamented the fact that the veterans had not received the sort of homecoming bestowed on the recently returned hostages. Bush's words are from Sifry and Cerf, *The Gulf War Reader*, p. 313. For a brilliant early analysis of this right-wing interpretation of the war within the military see Burdick, "Vietnam Revisioned."
7. *Newsweek*, 14 Dec. 1981. Goldman and Fuller's *Charlie Company* is more penetrating than the magazine story out of which it grew. It too, however, presents the war almost exclusively through the memories of veterans. The authors adopt the voices of the veterans, largely avoiding the effort to assess or interpret their memories against other sources. Similarly, MacPherson offers "cascades" of "subjective remembrances and opinions" from Vietnam veterans without placing their views in a sufficient historical context to explore fully the meaning of their experiences. See *Long Time Passing*, p. 7. Authorial reticence also characterizes the four major oral histories of Vietnam veterans. In each case the author collects and edits, presenting the material with little context or comment. See Baker, *Nam*; Goff and Sanders, *Brothers*; Santoli, *Everything We Had*; and Terry, *Bloods*.
8. "Remembering Vietnam," *Atlantic*, May 1985, p. 9.
9. Contrast the Vietnam movies with three of the most famous photographic images of the war: (1) a Buddhist monk burning to death, having immolated himself to protest the repressive government of Ngo Dinh Diem, the American-backed ruler of South Vietnam, (2) a young South Vietnamese girl running naked toward the camera, her skin burning with napalm dropped by American jets, and (3) a South Vietnamese officer firing a pistol at the temple of a Viet Cong prisoner. Single photographs do not have as much potential as film to provide political or historical context, yet each of these images raises more fundamental questions about the Vietnam War than most scenes in Hollywood movies about Vietnam.
10. The figures on work-related deaths come from Levison, *Working-Class*

Majority, p. 77. Data on the class backgrounds of American soldiers is presented in chapter 1, below. I use *enlisted men* to refer to all members of the American military who were not commissioned officers. The term includes both draftees and volunteers as well as noncommissioned officers. However, the major focus here is on the young, low-ranking, noncareer soldiers who comprised the great bulk of the American military in Vietnam. Also, while marines are not, properly speaking, *soldiers*, their mission in Vietnam was certainly that of soldiers, and I use that term to refer to all American ground troops in Vietnam. This is essentially a study of the men who served on the ground in the army and the marines. The air war was crucial to the experience of ground soldiers and is addressed in that context, but the experiences of pilots and crewmen are not examined. A further clarification is necessary: in chapters 5–7 the major focus is on combat soldiers—the grunts. Yet I have tried in a general way in those chapters, and more extensively elsewhere, to address the experiences of rear-echelon support troops as well. Still, frontline troops receive the closest scrutiny.

11. Hersh, *My Lai 4*, pp. 46–47.

12. Brende and Parson, *Vietnam Veterans*, p. 75; Hendin and Haas, *Wounds of War*, pp. 160–82. As early as 1971 the National Council of Churches estimated that 49,000 veterans had died from various causes after returning home.

13. Rap Group Notes, 17 Aug. 1984. From November 1981 until April 1988 I attended weekly rap groups for Vietnam veterans at the Dorchester Multi-Service Center in Boston.

14. *Inaugural Addresses*, pp. 336, 348. Though Vietnam was not named until 1981, it should be noted that Eisenhower, in his 1953 inaugural, saluted "the French soldier who dies in Indo-China" (p. 296).

15. Foucault, *Power/Knowledge*, pp. 78–92.

CHAPTER ONE

1. Dan Shaw interview, 21 July 1982.

2. Casualties by town were provided by Friends of the Vietnam Memorial (Washington, D.C.) from software derived from the *Vietnam Veterans Memorial: Directory of Names*; the Illinois study is Willis, "Who Died in Vietnam."

3. On Levittown, N.Y., see Dobriner, *Class in Suburbia*; also useful is Berger's *Working-Class Suburb*.

4. Kovic, *Born on the Fourth of July*, pp. 99–100.

5. The *Newsday* quotation is found in Useem, *Conscription, Protest, and Social Conflict*, p. 83.

6. These towns are taken from random pages of the *Vietnam Veterans Memorial: Directory of Names*, pp. 18, 77, 163, 754. Populations are taken from the 1970 census. The 8 percent figure is based on a random sample of 1,200 men listed in the directory.

7. Information about Talladega and Mountain Brook is from the 1970 federal census.

8. Clodfelter, *Pawns of Dishonor*, p. 109.

9. *U.S. Casualties in Southeast Asia*, p. 4.

10. The discussion of "third country forces" is drawn primarily from Kahin, *Intervention*, pp. 332–36.

11. This view is expressed in works as diverse as Kahin, *Intervention*; Herring, *America's Longest War*; Sheehan, *A Bright Shining Lie*; Lewy, *America in Vietnam*; and Karnow, *Vietnam*.

12. John Hendricks interview, 3 Sept. 1985.

13. As early as 1961, Secretary of Defense Robert McNamara and the Joint Chiefs of Staff drafted memos for Kennedy arguing that some 200,000 American troops might be needed in Vietnam. See Gravel, *Pentagon Papers*, 2:78–79, 108.

14. Baskir and Strauss, *Chance and Circumstance*, p. 5.

15. Helmer, *Bringing the War Home*, pp. 4–5.

16. Glick, *Soldiers, Scholars, and Society*, pp. 18–20; Moskos, *American Enlisted Man*, pp. 113–16; Binkin and Eitelberg, *Blacks and the Military*, pp. 75–78.

17. A full transcript of King's Riverside Church address can be found in Reese Williams's *Unwinding the War*, pp. 427–40.

18. Ibid.; *New York Times*, 26 Feb. 1967, p. 10.

19. Lewy, *America in Vietnam*, pp. 154–55; Gettleman et al., *Vietnam and America*, p. 320; *New York Times*, 29 Apr. 1968, p. 16. The conscious effort to reduce black casualties may have been unique to the army. In the marines, black combat deaths were about 13 percent throughout the war.

20. Young, "When the Negroes in Vietnam Come Home," p. 63; Thomas A. Johnson, "Negroes in 'the Nam,'" p. 38.

21. Young, "When the Negroes in Vietnam Come Home," p. 63. Reenlistment rates are in Moskos, "The American Dilemma in Uniform," p. 103.

22. Figures on black officers can be found in Glick, *Soldiers, Scholars, and Society*, pp. 18–20; test scores for blacks are in Moskos, *American Enlisted Man*, pp. 116, 216.

23. The study that found 90 percent of black Vietnam veterans working-class or poor is Egendorf et al., *Legacies of Vietnam*, pp. 106–9; bonuses are in Glick, *Soldiers, Scholars, and Society*; disproportionate combat assignments for blacks who scored in the highest category can be found in Moskos, *American Enlisted Man*.

24. For how working-class jobs are often ill-defined as white collar see Braverman, *Labor and Monopoly Capital*, pp. 283–411; also see Levison, *Working-Class Majority*, pp. 21–29.

25. Kolko, *Wealth and Power in America*, pp. 72, 76.

26. Bane, *Here to Stay*, p. 119.

27. Atkinson, *The Long Gray Line*, p. 29.

28. Gabriel and Savage, *Crisis in Command*, pp. 51–96.

29. Egendorf et al., *Legacies of Vietnam*, p. 142.

30. Ibid., pp. 105–9.

31. Bell, *The Coming of the Post-Industrial Society*, pp. 216–17; Egendorf et al., *Legacies of Vietnam*, p. 13.

32. On two-year college enrollments see Bowles and Gintis, *Schooling in Capitalist America*, p. 209, and Levison, *Working-Class Majority*, p. 119. For Harvard survey see Fallows, "What Did You Do in the Class War, Daddy." For combat rate of high school dropouts compared to college graduates see Veterans' Administration, *Myths and Realities*, p. 10.

33. Brende and Parson, *Vietnam Veterans*, pp. 19–20; *New York Times*, 10 Nov. 1965, p. 5.

34. On the West Point class of 1966 see Atkinson, *The Long Gray Line*; Glass, "Draftees Shoulder Burden," pp. 1747–55.

35. Flynn, *Lewis B. Hershey*, pp. 195–96; Baskir and Strauss, *Chance and Circumstance*, pp. 14–17.

36. Baskir and Strauss, *Chance and Circumstance*, pp. 20–21.

37. Moynihan's views are from *The New Republic*, 5 Nov. 1966, p. 20; Davis and Dolbeare, *Little Groups of Neighbors*, p. 134.

38. Baskir and Strauss, *Chance and Circumstance*, pp. 125–26.

39. Ibid., pp. 124, 129; Davis and Dolbeare, *Little Groups of Neighbors*, p. 136.

40. Helmer, *Bringing the War Home*, p. 9.

41. Graham Greene, *The Quiet American*, p. 60.

42. Barnes, *Pawns*, p. 68; Baskir and Strauss, *Chance and Circumstance*, pp. 126–30.

43. Baskir and Strauss, *Chance and Circumstance*, p. 47.

44. Ibid., pp. 36–48.

45. Ibid.

46. Davis and Dolbeare, *Little Groups of Neighbors*, pp. 78–83; Baskir and Strauss, *Chance and Circumstance*, pp. 24–25.

47. In some rural counties of Wisconsin, for example, the local boards gave occupational deferments to milk tank truck drivers and cheesemakers even though these jobs were not on the critical skills list distributed by the national headquarters.

48. Davis and Dolbeare, *Little Groups of Neighbors*, pp. 57–59, 82.

49. Flynn, *Lewis B. Hershey*, p. 254.

50. Davis and Dolbeare, *Little Groups of Neighbors*, p. 137.

51. Baskir and Strauss, *Chance and Circumstance*, p. 23.

52. Helmer, *Bringing the War Home*, p. 6.

53. Teodori, *The New Left*, p. 297.

54. Halberstam, *The Best and the Brightest*, p. 593.

55. Baskir and Strauss, *Chance and Circumstance*, pp. 48–52.

56. Glick, *Soldiers, Scholars, and Society*, pp. 27–28.

57. Wallace quotation found in Levison, *Working-Class Majority*, p. 164.

58. Cook, "Hard-Hats," pp. 712–19; see also Andy Logan, *The New Yorker*, 6 June 1970, pp. 104–8.

59. *Time*, 1 June 1970, p. 12.

60. Cited in Levison, *Working-Class Majority*, p. 136.

61. Ehrenreich, *Fear of Falling*, pp. 107, 124. Though I had virtually finished this section before reading Ehrenreich's book, I am grateful for her fine analysis of the "discovery of the working-class" in the late 1960s.

62. Coles, *The Middle Americans*, pp. 131–34.

63. Cincinnatus, *Self-Destruction*, p. 27.

CHAPTER TWO

1. Rap Group Notes, 30 Mar. 1982.

2. Hodgson, *America in Our Time*, pp. 466, 482; Binkin and Eitelberg, *Blacks and the Military*, p. 68; Helmer, *Bringing the War Home*, p. 108.

3. Ralph Blumenthal, "Glens Falls and the War," *New York Times*, 12 July 1967, p. 4.

4. Franks, *Waiting out a War*, pp. 42–43.

5. MacPherson, *Long Time Passing*, p. 76.

6. Chris Debeau interview, 12 May 1982.

7. Baskir and Strauss, *Chance and Circumstance*, p. 55.

8. Raymond Wilson interview, 13 Sept. 1981.

9. Ken Lombardi interview, 12 May 1981.

10. Helmer, *Bringing the War Home*, p. 110.

11. See the discussion in Moskos, *American Enlisted Man*, p. 117. The 1968 Defense Department survey of enlistment motivations does not include racial breakdowns.

12. On minimum enlistment requirements see ibid., p. 48; Mike Dowling interview, 8 Apr. 1982.

13. Mark Sampson interview, 14 Mar. 1982.

14. John Stevens interview, 29 Jan. 1984.

15. Mike Dowling interview, 8 Apr. 1982.

16. Mark Jennings interview, 15 Oct. 1984.

17. Baker, *Nam*, p. 33.

18. O'Brien, *If I Die*, p. 29.

19. Ibid., pp. 32–33.

20. Ibid., p. 29.

21. Ibid., p. 34.

22. Stewart Bushnell interview, 4 Sept. 1981.

23. Baker, *Nam*, pp. 27–28.

24. Nick Green interview, 6 July 1982.

25. Egendorf et al., *Legacies of Vietnam*, pp. 383–85.

26. This yearbook can be found in the Dorchester High School library.

27. Cited in Helmer, *Bringing the War Home*, pp. 106–7.

28. Ed Johnson interview, 15 Oct. 1982.

29. Sennett and Cobb, *Hidden Injuries*, p. 121.

30. Todd Dasher interview, 12 Jan. 1981.

31. Dan Shaw interview, 21 July 1982.

32. Joseph, *Good Times*, pp. 451–52.

33. Billy Cizinski interview, 10 July 1981.

34. Baker, *Nam*, pp. 33–34.

35. O'Brien, *If I Die*, p. 22.

36. Kovic, *Born on the Fourth of July*, pp. 54–56.

37. Ibid., p. 73.

38. Terry, *Bloods*, pp. 6–7.

39. Roger Neville Williams, *The New Exiles*, p. 133.

40. Billy Cizinski interviews, 27 Jan., 10 July 1981.

41. Kennedy's inaugural address can be found in many places, including Cohen's *Vietnam*, pp. 74–76.

42. Lloyd B. Lewis, *The Tainted War*, pp. 37–41; Duncan, *The New Legions*, pp. 146–55.

43. Bob Foley interviews, 9 and 15 Sept. 1981.

44. Rap Group Notes, 3 Dec. 1983.

45. Frank Mathews interviews, 3 and 14 Sept. 1981.

46. Richard Deegan interview, 21 June 1982.

47. Dwight Williams interview, 14 May 1982.

48. Carlos Martinez interview, 9 May 1983.

49. Davis and Dolbeare, *Little Groups of Neighbors*, p. 134.

50. Fussell, *The Great War and Modern Memory*, p. 335.

51. Appy, "Vietnam According to Oliver Stone," pp. 187–89; Leed, *No Man's Land*, p. 19.

52. Eric Stevens interview, 13 May 1982.

53. O'Brien, *Going after Cacciato*, pp. 218–19.

54. See, for example, Baker, *Nam*, p. 28.

55. Raymond Wilson interview, 13 Sept. 1981.

56. Ken Lombardi interview, 12 May 1981.

57. Frank Mathews interviews, 3 and 14 Sept. 1981.

58. O'Brien, *Going after Cacciato*, p. 313.

CHAPTER THREE

1. Roth, *Sand in the Wind*, p. 95.

2. Kovic, *Born on the Fourth of July*, p. 77.

3. Hasford, *The Short-Timers*, p. 4.

4. Kovic, *Born on the Fourth of July*, pp. 78–79.

5. Ibid., p. 81.

6. Ibid., p. 84.

7. On "toilet training" see Roth, *Sand in the Wind*, p. 119. While there were, of course, major differences between basic training and Nazi concentration camps, the "welcoming ceremonies" of each might usefully be compared. Barrington Moore offers the following description of the Nazi camps: "Upon entering the camps the prisoners faced 'welcoming ceremonies' of a thoroughly brutalizing nature. . . . These traumatic rites of passage had two closely related effects. The first was straightforward degradation, the destruction of the prisoner's self-respect, the obliteration of whatever individuality and status he or she may have enjoyed in the outside world. Second, the camp officials 'processed' the prisoners to make them as much alike as possible by issuing them uniforms and numbers after confiscating all personal possessions.

"These actions were the beginning of a regime that deprived the prisoners of all but a minimum of food and minimum of sleep. As soon as possible, camp officials controlled nearly every moment of the prisoners' waking life, even to the point of giving them only limited and selected periods of time for urination and defecation" (*Injustice*, p. 65).

8. Robert Flaherty interview, 7 July 1982.

9. Rap Group Notes, 21 Feb. 1985.

10. Barnes, *Pawns*, pp. 93–98.

11. Gene Holiday interview, 8 May 1984.

12. Barnes, *Pawns*, pp. 86 and 101; *Time*, 10 Dec. 1965, p. 31.

13. Hathaway, *A World of Hurt*, pp. 19–20.

14. Ibid., p. 8.

15. Barnes, *Pawns*, p. 131.

16. Roth, *Sand in the Wind*, p. 115.

17. Barnes, *Pawns*, pp. 101–2.

18. Ibid., pp. 103–4.

19. Tauber, *Sunshine Soldiers*.

20. Ibid., p. 24.

21. Roger Neville Williams, *The New Exiles*, pp. 103–14; Cortright, *Soldiers in Revolt*, pp. 10–15; Helmer, *Bringing the War Home*, pp. 36–39; Baskir and Strauss, *Chance and Circumstance*, pp. 109–66.

22. Roger Neville Williams, *The New Exiles*, p. 140.

23. Emerick, *War Resisters Canada*, pp. 83–84.

24. Stan Bodner interview, 17 Mar. 1981.

25. Barnes, *Pawns*, p. 111.

26. Robert Flaherty interview, 7 July 1982.

27. Hathaway, *A World of Hurt*, p. 14.

28. Robert Flaherty interview, 7 July 1982. For another account of a "blanket party" see Hasford, *The Short-Timers*, pp. 16–17.

29. Franks, *Waiting out a War*, p. 56.

30. Ibid., p. 57.

31. Roth, *Sand in the Wind*, pp. 99–100.

32. Ibid., p. 113.

33. Ibid., p. 99.

34. Ibid., pp. 102–3.

35. Short and Seidenberg, "A Matter of Conscience," p. 83.

36. Roth, *Sand in the Wind*, pp. 142–43.

37. O'Brien, *If I Die*, p. 59.

38. Bob Foley interview, 15 Sept. 1981.

39. Hasford, *The Short-Timers*, pp. 12–13.

40. Sandee Shaffer Johnson, *Cadences*, p. 139; Tauber, *Sunshine Soldiers*, pp. 129–30.

41. Barnes, *Pawns*, p. 99.

42. Goff and Sanders, *Brothers*, p. 6; Roth, *Sand in the Wind*, p. 138.

43. Emerick, *War Resisters Canada*, p. 84.

44. Gene Holiday interview, 8 May 1984.

45. Rap Group Notes, 10 Jan. 1983.

46. Photographs of the first two billboards appear in Maitland and McInerney, *Contagion*, p. 30. The Fort Dix sign is described in Citizens Commission of Inquiry, *Dellums Committee Hearings*, p. 161.

47. Terry, *Bloods*, p. 8.

48. Luke Jensen interview, 24 Apr. 1983.

49. Baker, *Nam*, pp. 37–38.

50. O'Brien, *If I Die*, p. 45.

51. Tauber, *Sunshine Soldiers*, pp. 141, 204.

52. Barnes, *Pawns*, p. 136; Baskir and Strauss, *Chance and Circumstance*, p. 120.

53. Mark Sampson interview, 14 Mar. 1982.

54. Todd Dasher interview, 12 Jan. 1981.

55. Frank Mathews interview, 3 Sept. 1981.

56. For a description of a drill instructor's Vietnam-related threats see Roger Neville Williams, *The New Exiles*, p. 137. On the use of computers for tour assignments see Baskir and Strauss, *Chance and Circumstance*, pp. 55–56.

57. O'Brien, *If I Die*, p. 67.

58. Baker, *Nam*, pp. 40–41.

59. Baskir and Strauss, *Chance and Circumstance*, p. 122.

60. Tauber, *Sunshine Soldiers*, p. 250.

61. Sack, *M*, pp. 79–81.

62. This memorandum, dated 11 August 1966, was provided to the author through the courtesy of Gen. Edwin Simmons, author of the memo and longtime director of the Marine Corps History and Museums Division. A copy is on file in the archives of the Marine Corps Historical Center (hereafter MHC) in the Washington, D.C., Navy Yard.

CHAPTER FOUR

1. Maitland and McInerney, *Contagion*, p. 12.

2. Caputo, *A Rumor of War*, p. 50; for a similar example see Santoli, *Everything We Had*, p. 35.

3. Ogden, *Green Knight, Red Mourning*, pp. 22–26; also described in Maitland and McInerney, *Contagion*, p. 8.

4. Brennan, *Brennan's War*, p. 4.

5. Robert Flaherty interview, 7 July 1982. Flaherty arrived in Okinawa with the Second Battalion, Fifth Marines. This unit became the Third Battalion, Ninth Marines, upon arrival in Vietnam. He later transferred to 3/3. For corroboration of these unit transfers see Shulimson and Johnson, *U.S. Marines in Vietnam*, p. 55n.

6. Martin, *The GI War*, pp. 273–78.

7. Raymond Wilson interview, 13 Sept. 1981.

8. Sheehan et al., *Pentagon Papers*, pp. 477–78.

9. Col. James B. Soper, "A View from FMF Pac," pp. 202–17.

10. Baker, *Nam*, p. 61; Riggan, *Free Fire Zone*, p. 4.

11. Charles R. Anderson, *Grunts*, pp. 22–23.

12. Westmoreland, *A Soldier Reports*, p. 49.

13. Jim Barrett interview, 12 Sept. 1981.

14. Richard Deegan interview, 21 June 1982.

15. Downs, *The Killing Zone*, p. 4.

16. Jim Barrett interview, 12 Sept. 1981.

17. Corder, *The Deerhunter*, p. 54. This novel is based on the screenplay written by Deric Washburn. The lines quoted are the same in the film version; Stone and Boyle, *Platoon and Salvador*, p. 20.

18. Eric Stevens interview, 12 May 1982.

19. Fuller, *Fragments*, p. 45.

20. Richard Deegan interview, 21 June 1982; Dan Simpson interview, 21 July 1982; Baker, *Nam*, p. 71.

21. Jim Barrett interview, 12 Sept. 1981.

22. Ehrhart, *Vietnam-Perkasie*, p. 20.

23. See the description of a nuoc mam factory in Hasselblad's *Lucky-Lucky*, pp. 135–36.

24. Mark Sampson interview, 14 Mar. 1982.

25. Baker, *Nam*, p. 54.

26. Gettleman et al., *Vietnam and America*, pp. 461–69; Riggan, *Free Fire Zone*, p. 8.

27. Stewart Bushnell interview, 4 Sept. 1981.

28. Ketwig, *And a Hard Rain Fell*, p. 33.

29. Baker, *Nam*, pp. 51–52.

30. Riggan, *Free Fire Zone*, p. 5.
31. Ketwig, *And a Hard Rain Fell*, p. 33.
32. Parks, *GI Diary*, p. 49.
33. Ketwig, *And a Hard Rain Fell*, p. 32.
34. Hughes, *You Can See a Lot*, p. 24.
35. Dick Boyer interview, 25 July 1984.
36. Groom, *Better Times*, p. 114.
37. Ibid., pp. 115–16.
38. Ibid., p. 117.
39. Clodfelter, *Pawns of Dishonor*, p. 40; for similar examples see Ketwig, *And a Hard Rain Fell*, pp. 44, 70–73, 195.
40. Fuller, *Fragments*, pp. 50–51.
41. Citizens Commission of Inquiry, *Dellums Committee Hearings*, p. 161.
42. Groom, *Better Times*, p. 133.
43. Webb, *Fields of Fire*, pp. 49–50.
44. Sam Warren interview, 29 Apr. 1982.
45. Baker, *Nam*, p. 54.
46. Frank Mathews interview, 3 Sept. 1981.
47. O'Brien, *If I Die*, p. 97.
48. Vietnam Oral History Collection, MHC. During the war both the army and the Marine Corps conducted field interviews with American troops in Vietnam. The Marine Corps archive is quite extensive, with approximately 5,000 taped interviews with men of all ranks. The army collected far fewer oral histories from Vietnam (several hundred), and most are with high-ranking officers. These archives are largely unknown to Vietnam War scholars but can be of use. The major deficiency in the interviews with enlisted men is their almost exclusive focus on detailed narratives of tactics, terrain, weaponry, and so on; interviewers made little effort to elicit critical or attitudinal responses. Thus, these tapes offer a quite narrow view of GI thought and experience. The few slightly open-ended questions focused on practical military or tactical matters rather than wide-ranging critical perspectives: for example, "What lessons did you learn on this operation?" or "What advice would you give to other Marines coming over to Vietnam?" In response to the latter question the most common responses were "Don't try to be John Wayne," "Keep your head down, and listen to your squad leader," or "Don't try to be gung-ho. Just do your job." See, for examples, Vietnam Oral History Tape #3671, MHC.
49. Suddick, *A Few Good Men*, p. 60.
50. Cincinnatus, *Self-Destruction*, pp. 157–60.
51. Helmer, *Bringing the War Home*, p. 76.
52. Sam Warren interview, 29 Apr. 1982.
53. John Lafite interview, 1 Apr. 1982.
54. Baker, *Nam*, pp. 70–79. For convenience, I have provided the pseudonym Carl Shepard. Baker uses no names in his excellent oral history.
55. Ibid., p. 74.

CHAPTER FIVE

1. Fall, *Two Viet-Nams*, p. 3.
2. For brief accounts of the development of Vietnamese nationalism see Karnow,

Vietnam, pp. 89–127, and Gettleman et al., *Vietnam and America*, pp. 5–17. A fuller treatment can be found in the works of Marr: *Vietnamese Anticolonialism* and *Vietnamese Tradition on Trial*.

3. Patti, *Why Viet Nam?*, pp. 220–80.

4. Kahin, *Intervention*, chaps. 1–2.

5. Ibid., pp. 52–65; Kolko, *Anatomy of a War*, pp. 62–65; Karnow, *Vietnam*, pp. 198–205; Gettleman et al., *Vietnam and America*, pp. 70–80.

6. Fitzgerald, *Fire in the Lake*, p. 69; Kahin, *Intervention*, chap. 3.

7. Fitzgerald, *Fire in the Lake*, pp. 72–137; Gettleman et al., *Vietnam and America*, pp. 109–61.

8. Kahin, *Intervention*, p. 98.

9. Ibid., chap. 4.

10. Gettleman et al., *Vietnam and America*, p. 250; Karnow, *Vietnam*, pp. 357–76; for a striking firsthand account of the Gulf of Tonkin incident see Willenson, *The Bad War*, pp. 28–35.

11. Turley, *The Second Indochina War*, p. 89; Gibson, *The Perfect War*, chaps. 9–12.

12. Cohen, *Vietnam*, pp. 115–21; Fall, *Two Viet-Nams*, p. 4.

13. Caputo, *A Rumor of War*, p. 57; Herr, *Dispatches*, p. 156.

14. Cohen, *Vietnam*, p. 117; *Medallion World Atlas* (Maplewood, N.J.: Hammond, 1974), p. 190; Westmoreland, *A Soldier Reports*, p. 62.

15. Wright, *Meditations in Green*, pp. 7–8.

16. Whitlow, *U.S. Marines in Vietnam*, pp. 23–24; Spector, *Advice and Support*; Weigley, *The American Way of War*; for examples of search-and-destroy tactics in the period 1959–64 see Fall, *Two Viet-Nams*, pp. 379–84.

17. Westmoreland, *A Soldier Reports*, pp. 174–96; Cincinnatus, *Self-Destruction*, pp. 59–72.

18. Westmoreland, *A Soldier Reports*; Gallucci, *Neither Peace nor Honor*, pp. 68–129; Sheehan et al., *Pentagon Papers*, pp. 578–79.

19. Lewy, *America in Vietnam*, pp. 50–63.

20. Westmoreland, *A Soldier Reports*, pp. 99–100.

21. Ibid.

22. Hersh, *My Lai 4*, p. 9; Lewy, *America in Vietnam*, pp. 79–80; Cincinnatus, *Self-Destruction*, pp. 75–91.

23. Halberstam, *The Best and the Brightest*, p. 249.

24. The tent pin example comes from Command Chronology, 3d Battalion, 27th Marines, Combat After Action Report, Operation Allen Brook, 4 Aug. 1968, tab B, p. 10, MHC.

25. Gibson, *The Perfect War*, p. 275.

26. Lewy, *America in Vietnam*, p. 63; Gibson, *The Perfect War*, pp. 270–315.

27. Lewy, *America in Vietnam*, pp. 125, 191–95; Fitzgerald, *Fire in the Lake*, pp. 339–45.

28. For a chronology of major U.S. operations in Vietnam see Stanton, *Vietnam*.

29. Hayslip, *When Heaven and Earth Changed Places*; Webb, *Fields of Fire*.

30. Command Chronology, 1st Marine Division, Combat Operations After Action Report, Operation Pipestone Canyon, Nov. 1969, p. 52, MHC.

31. Shulimson, *U.S. Marines in Vietnam*, p. 204, my emphasis. For example of command emphasis on "maintaining contact" see Vietnam Interview Tape #331, tape 1/6, U.S. Army Center for Military History (hereafter CMH).

32. Marshall, *Vietnam*, p. 2.

33. Ibid., p. 6.

34. Ibid., p. 7.

35. Ibid., p. 9.

36. Lewy, *America in Vietnam*, pp. 451–53.

37. Doyle and Lipsman, *America Takes Over*, p. 72; Gravel, *Pentagon Papers*, 4:462.

38. Lewy, *America in Vietnam*, pp. 82–83; *Time*, 24 Sept. 1965, p. 34.

39. Baritz, *Backfire*, pp. 252–64; Brewin and Shaw, *Vietnam on Trial*.

40. Westmoreland quotation from Karnow, *Vietnam*, p. 514; Adams, "Vietnam Cover-Up."

41. Brewin and Shaw, *Vietnam on Trial*, pp. 312–43; *Nation*, 5, 12 July 1986, p. 6.

42. Baritz, *Backfire*, p. 257.

43. Ibid., p. 260.

44. Ibid., p. 254; Lewy, *America in Vietnam*, p. 455.

45. Duiker, *Communist Road to Power*, p. 236; Charles R. Anderson, *Grunts*, p. xi; Cincinnatus, *Self-Destruction*, p. 147.

46. Fall, *Two Viet-Nams*, pp. 396–97.

47. Corson, *The Betrayal*, pp. 161–62.

48. West, *Small Unit Action*, p. 1.

49. Lewy, *America in Vietnam*, p. 309. Lewy cites a Defense Department study of American casualties between January 1967 and September 1968 which found that 23.7 percent of U.S. combat deaths were caused by mines and booby traps.

50. Ibid., p. 101.

51. West, *Small Unit Action*, pp. 1–14.

52. Lewy, *America in Vietnam*, p. 309.

53. Participation of G Company, 2d Battalion, 27th Marines, in Operation Allen Brook, Vietnam Oral History Tape #3045, MHC; for other examples of booby trap markings noticed by American infantrymen see Goff and Sanders, *Brothers*, p. 57.

54. O'Brien, *If I Die*, pp. 152–53. The following is a list of the most commonly encountered mines and booby traps:

1. Booby trapped grenade: "This device is probably the most common of all booby-traps. It consists of a trip wire attached to a small bush or tree, stretched across a footpath, and connected to a grenade with a friction type fuse. When the wire is tripped, the grenade is detonated." (From an information sheet produced by the Ninth Marine Regiment in 1966 and provided to me by Gen. Edwin Simmons. It is also in the archives of the MHC.)
2. "Bouncing Betty": A very common pressure-release land mine. It is buried underground, and when the release mechanism is stepped on, the mine "bounces" into the air and explodes at about waist level.
3. Bombs, mortars, and artillery rounds: These high-explosive rounds were the most destructive of all. They were placed in trees, shrubs, gates, or underground and could be triggered by trip wire, pressure release, or command detonation.

55. Fitzgerald, *Fire in the Lake*, p. 142; Mangold and Penycate, *Tunnels of Cu Chi*.

56. Del Vecchio, *The 13th Valley*, pp. 245–46.

57. Goldman and Fuller, *Charlie Company*, pp. 123–24.

58. Kolko, *Anatomy of a War*, pp. 148, 185.

59. Gen. O. M. Barsanti, "Fighting on the Coastal Plains," in *A Distant Challenge*, ed. Infantry Magazine, pp. 106–7.

60. Documentation of the command emphasis on firepower and mobility is abundant. See, for example, the Vietnam reportage of Schell, now conveniently collected under the title *The Real War*, and Cincinnatus, *Self-Destruction*, pp. 60–75.

CHAPTER SIX

1. *Time*, 24 Sept. 1965, p. 34.

2. There are pictures and descriptions of American helicopters throughout the fourteen-volume series *The Vietnam Experience*, published by Boston Pub. Co., Boston, Mass. A useful collection of photographs with technical information can be found in Stanton, *Vietnam*, pp. 279–80, 286–93. The 1967 figure is from Westmoreland, *A Soldier Reports*, p. 248.

3. For such an image one might study the remarkable photograph taken by Larry Burrows of a marine unit on patrol in Operation Prairie. This picture has been widely reproduced but first appeared in *Life*, 28 Oct. 1966, p. 30.

4. Del Vecchio, *The 13th Valley*, pp. 149–54.

5. Caputo, *A Rumor of War*, p. 79.

6. Roth, *Sand in the Wind*, p. 168.

7. Fuller, *Fragments*, p. 68; Charles R. Anderson, *Grunts*, pp. 69–83.

8. Mayer, *The Weary Falcon*, pp. 12–13.

9. Roth, *Sand in the Wind*, p. 176.

10. Caputo, *A Rumor of War*, p. 222.

11. Charles R. Anderson, *Grunts*, p. 49.

12. Huggett, *Body Count*, p. 39.

13. Goldman and Fuller, *Charlie Company*, p. 126.

14. A copy of this essay was given to me by the author in May 1983.

15. Charles R. Anderson, *Grunts*, pp. 35–97.

16. Participation of E Company, 2d Battalion, 7th Marines, in Operation Allen Brook, Vietnam Oral History Tape #2806, MHC.

17. Participation of G Company, 2d Battalion, 27th Marines, in Operation Allen Brook, Vietnam Oral History Tape #3045, MHC.

18. Westmoreland, *A Soldier Reports*, p. 175.

19. Webb, *Fields of Fire*, p. 155.

20. Groom, *Better Times*, p. 200.

21. Garland, *Infantry in Vietnam*, pp. 97–103.

22. Gibson, *The Perfect War*, pp. 93–154, esp. p. 103.

23. George Burch interview, 29 Sept. 1981.

24. Goff and Sanders, *Brothers*, pp. 32–33.

25. Hackworth, *About Face*, pp. 594–95; Wilson, *The LBJ Brigade*; Thomas Taylor, *A Piece of This Country*.

26. Del Vecchio, *The 13th Valley*, p. 250.

27. Charles R. Anderson, *Grunts*, p. 101.

28. Groom, *Better Times*, p. 175.

29. Participation of B Company, 1st Battalion, 27th Marines, in Operation Allen Brook, PFC David A. Harmon, Vietnam Oral History Tape #3055, MHC.

30. Frank Mathews interview, 9 Sept. 1981.

31. *Time*, 6 Oct. 1967.

32. Herr, *Dispatches*, p. 149.

33. See Westmoreland's preface to Shore, *Battle for Khe Sanh*, p. vii.

34. Karnow, *Vietnam*, p. 542.

35. Goldman and Fuller, *Charlie Company*, p. 46.

36. Ibid., p. 55.

37. Ibid., p. 58.

38. Participation of M Company, 3d Battalion, 27th Marines, in Operation Allen Brook, Vietnam Oral History Tape #2873, MHC.

39. Frank Mathews interview, 9 Sept. 1981.

40. Hersh, *My Lai 4*, pp. 3–43; Schell, *Village of Ben Suc*, pp. 35–37.

41. Schell, *Village of Ben Suc*, pp. 33–34.

42. Ellsberg, *Papers on the War*, p. 250.

43. Ibid., p. 251.

44. Brennan, *Brennan's War*, pp. 32–34.

45. Downs, *The Killing Zone*, p. 22.

46. Walzer, *Just and Unjust Wars*, pp. 188–96; Schell, *The Military Half*, pp. 14–15; Lewy, *America in Vietnam*, pp. 102–3.

47. Schell, *The Military Half*, pp. 17–18.

48. Ibid., pp. 20–21.

49. Lewy, *America in Vietnam*, pp. 234–37.

50. Robert Flaherty interview, 7 July 1982.

51. Caputo, *A Rumor of War*, p. xix.

52. Webb, *Fields of Fire*, pp. 96–97.

53. Ibid., p. 99.

54. Ibid., p. 103.

55. Ibid., pp. 100–101.

56. O'Brien, *If I Die*, pp. 147–48.

57. Mark Sampson interview, 14 Mar. 1982.

58. Lewy, *America in Vietnam*, pp. 442–46.

59. Ibid., pp. 443, 451–53; the McNamara memo is in Sheehan et al., *Pentagon Papers*, p. 534.

60. Lewy, *America in Vietnam*, pp. 442–53; Herman, *Atrocities in Vietnam*, p. 43.

61. Hayslip, *When Heaven and Earth Changed Places*, pp. 85–97, 109–11.

62. Chomsky and Herman, *The Washington Connection*, pp. 345–54; Karnow, *Vietnam*, pp. 529–31; Sheehan, *Bright Shining Lie*, pp. 719–20.

CHAPTER SEVEN

1. Gray, *The Warriors*, pp. 12–28; Herr, *Dispatches*, pp. 20–21.

2. Barnes, *Pawns*, pp. 181–239; Sherrill, *Military Justice*, pp. 62–97, 158–90.

3. Rubin, *Worlds of Pain*, pp. 155–84, 232; Terkel, *Working*.

4. Sack, *M*, p. 132.

5. Moskos, *American Enlisted Man*, pp. 149–50.

6. Luke Jensen interview, 24 Apr. 1983.

7. Gettleman, *Vietnam*, pp. 323–30. An excellent single-volume introduction to competing interpretations of American intervention is Kimball's *To Reason Why*.

8. Gettleman, *Vietnam*, p. 324; Gravel, *Pentagon Papers*, 3:392, 438–40, 4:295; Kahin, *Intervention*, pp. 290–91, 306–8.

9. Early in his first term, President Nixon also gave considerable public emphasis to the goal of helping South Vietnam achieve self-determination. In 1969, for example, he said, "We have to understand our essential objective: we seek the opportunity for the South Vietnamese to determine their own political future without outside interference" (in Wills, *Nixon Agonistes*, p. 429). Wills offers a brilliant analysis of the contradictions of "self-determination" as a guiding principle of American foreign policy; see pp. 419–33.

10. Gettleman, *Vietnam*, p. 325; Kimball, *To Reason Why*, pp. 27–70.

11. Sheehan et al., *Pentagon Papers*, pp. 502–3; Schell, *Time of Illusion*, p. 10.

12. Gettleman et al., *Vietnam and America*, pp. 428–39; for a superb critique of the doctrine of credibility see Zinn, *Logic of Withdrawal*.

13. Webb, *Fields of Fire*, p. 90.

14. Richard Deegan interview, 21 June 1982.

15. Victor Belloti interview, 8 Aug. 1981.

16. Vietnam Oral History Tape #150, MHC.

17. Vietnam Oral History Tape #150, MHC.

18. Vietnam Oral History Tape #5024, MHC.

19. Frank Mathews interview, 3 Sept. 1981.

20. Goldman and Fuller, *Charlie Company*, p. 126.

21. Webb, *Fields of Fire*, p. 171.

22. Westmoreland, *A Soldier Reports*, p. 299.

23. Fitzgerald, *Fire in the Lake*, pp. 349–53; Schell, *Village of Ben Suc*, pp. 117–18; Pelfrey, *The Big V*, pp. 16–21.

24. Moskos, *American Enlisted Man*, pp. 148–49. Moskos conducted in-depth interviews with thirty-four men and believes his findings were confirmed in shorter discussions with hundreds of American soldiers in Vietnam.

25. See Kahin's *Intervention* for a thorough survey of decision making from 1945 to 1965. "Credibility," in Schell's *Time of Illusion*, is perhaps the best concise source for policymakers' lack of concern about South Vietnam. See also Kimball, *To Reason Why*, pp. 255–99.

26. Moskos found this attitude "endemic" among American soldiers; see *American Enlisted Man*, p. 151. For testimonies of how South Vietnamese forces fled from battle during a VC attack on Cam Lo see Vietnam Tape #2587–2589, MHC. For an example of GI criticism of ARVN forces see Goff and Sanders, *Brothers*, p. 133.

27. Herr, *Dispatches*, p. 59.

28. Moskos, *American Enlisted Man*, pp. 149–50; Sack, *M*, p. 131.

29. See note 28 above.

30. Herr, *Dispatches*, p. 63; Frank Mathews interview, 3 Sept. 1981.

31. Stouffer et al., *The American Soldier*, 1:432.

32. In August 1945, 71 percent of American servicemen believed "most" or "almost all" of "the people back home are doing all they should to help win the war" (Stouffer et al., *The American Soldier*, 2:583).

33. Clodfelter, *Pawns of Dishonor*, p. 112.

34. Brecher and Costello, *Common Sense*, pp. 196–97.

35. *Time*, 22 Dec. 1967, p. 59.

36. Clodfelter, *Pawns of Dishonor*, pp. 110–11.

37. Ibid., p. 97.

38. The quotation from "Charlie Company" should be considered a close para-phrase based on notes taken after viewing the film.

39. Goff and Sanders, *Brothers*, pp. 132–33.

40. Ibid., pp. 131–32.

41. Brende and Parson, *Vietnam Veterans*, pp. 138–65; Egendorf et al., *Legacies of Vietnam*, p. 392.

42. Dwight Williams interview, 14 May 1982.

43. Stouffer et al., *The American Soldier*, 2:170–71.

44. Gettleman, *Vietnam*, p. 325.

45. Groom, *Better Times*, pp. 220–21. For another example see Goldman and Fuller, *Charlie Company*, p. 254.

46. Baker, *Nam*, p. 233.

47. The best case study of the massive forced relocation of Vietnamese civilians remains Jonathan Schell's *Village of Ben Suc*.

48. Caputo, *A Rumor of War*, p. xix.

49. Herbert, *Soldier*, p. 238.

50. Rostow makes this statement in Peter Davis's documentary "Hearts and Minds" (1975).

51. Schell, *The Real War*, p. 127.

52. Downs, *The Killing Zone*, pp. 6–7.

53. Herr, *Dispatches*, p. 20.

54. Clodfelter, *Pawns of Dishonor*, p. 113.

55. Baker, *Nam*, p. 101.

56. Frank Mathews interview, 3 Sept. 1981.

57. Herr, *Dispatches*, p. 29.

58. Luke Jensen interview, 24 Apr. 1983. For similar examples see Halstead, *GIs Speak Out*, pp. 62–63, and Terry, *Bloods*, p. 23.

59. Lewy, *America in Vietnam*, pp. 144–46.

60. Boyle, *Flower of the Dragon*, pp. 85–104.

61. *Life*, 23 Oct. 1970, pp. 31–32.

62. Vietnam Oral History Tape #379, CMH. Moss's description of the pressure for body counts is fully corroborated by the other men interviewed from his unit. Another radio man, Sgt. Stephen Kraycar, said, "The battalion commander is stressing his VC kills very much lately. I don't know if he's being pressured from brigade or not, but I know every five minutes on the radio he comes down and asks how many Victor Charlie have we killed recently." Also see Goldman and Fuller, *Charlie Company*, pp. 94–104.

63. Vietnam Oral History Tape #379, CMH.

64. Vietnam Oral History Tape #379, CMH.

65. Goff and Sanders, *Brothers*, p. 148; Goldman and Fuller, *Charlie Company*, p. 127.

66. See the entry for *morale* in the *Oxford English Dictionary*.

67. Westmoreland, *A Soldier Reports*, pp. 358–59.

68. Ibid.

69. Westmoreland's view of morale is also documented in a CBS news documen-

tary, "Morley Safer's Vietnam." See Arlen's review of the documentary in *Living-Room War*, pp. 61–65.

70. Herr, *Dispatches*, p. 118.
71. Halberstam, *One Very Hot Day*, p. 20.
72. Pelfrey, *The Big V*, p. 19; Ketwig, *And a Hard Rain Fell*, p. 178.
73. Charles R. Anderson, *Grunts*, p. 47.
74. *Time*, 22 Dec. 1967, pp. 52–57.
75. Ketwig, *And a Hard Rain Fell*.
76. Herbert, *Soldier*, pp. 124–31; Hughes, *You Can See a Lot*, pp. 158–59; for the television offerings see *Stars and Stripes*, 4 May 1970.
77. Linden, "Demoralization."
78. Raymond Wilson interview, 13 Sept. 1981.
79. Ketwig, *And a Hard Rain Fell*, pp. 107–8.
80. O'Brien, *If I Die*, p. 101.
81. MacPherson, *Long Time Passing*, p. 570.
82. Emerson, *Winners and Losers*, p. 67.
83. Stouffer et al., *The American Soldier*, 1:440. The affirmative responses were considerably higher earlier in the war and dropped somewhat after VJ day; see 2:588.
84. Goff and Sanders, *Brothers*, p. 60.
85. Charles R. Anderson, *Grunts*, pp. 85–124.
86. Billy Cizinski interview, 27 Jan. 1981; for an example of a soldier getting a buddy to injure him to get out of combat see Roth, *Sand in the Wind*, p. 340.
87. Goff and Sanders, *Brothers*, p. 87.
88. O'Brien, *If I Die*, pp. 107, 131–32. For another example see Roth, *Sand in the Wind*, pp. 460–61.
89. Gabriel and Savage, *Crisis in Command*, pp. 45–46, emphasis in original; Lewy, *America in Vietnam*, p. 157; Lipsman and Doyle, *Fighting for Time*, pp. 99–100.
90. Hauser, *America's Army in Crisis*, p. 99.
91. Lewy, *America in Vietnam*, p. 156; Johnson and Wilson, *Army in Anguish*.
92. O'Brien, *Going after Cacciato*, p. 281.
93. Heinl, "Collapse of the Armed Forces," p. 30.
94. *New York Times*, 29 Nov. 1971; Cincinnatus, *Self-Destruction*, p. 161.
95. Fuller, *Fragments*, p. 80. The *Random House Dictionary* offers this definition of *gong*: "a large bronze disk of Oriental origin that produces a vibrant, hollow tone when struck."
96. Emerson, *Winners and Losers*, pp. 329–32. Photographs of Vietnam veterans throwing away their medals at this demonstration can be found in Kerry et al., *The New Soldier*, pp. 132–45.
97. Polner, *No Victory Parades*, p. 165.

CHAPTER EIGHT

1. Ed Johnson interview, 15 Oct. 1982.
2. Caputo, *A Rumor of War*, p. xx.
3. The view that America inadvertently slipped into the quagmire of Vietnam can be found in Schlesinger's *The Bitter Heritage*. Daniel Ellsberg's superb cri-

tique of this interpretation, "The Quagmire Myth and the Stalemate Machine," can be found in his *Papers on the War*, pp. 47–131.

4. The Westmoreland quotation is from the Peter Davis documentary "Hearts and Minds" (1975).

5. Capps, *The Unfinished War*, p. 90.

6. Henry Barber interview, 25 May 1983.

7. Transcript of hearing before the Veterans' Administration, Boston, Mass., 12 Oct. 1983. Provided to the author by Henry Barber.

8. Eric Stevens interview, 13 May 1982.

9. Huggett, *Body Count*, pp. 33, 430.

10. Hasford, *The Short-Timers*, pp. 67–70.

11. Herr, *Dispatches*, p. 158.

12. Baker, *Nam*, p. 242.

13. Emerson, *Winners and Losers*, p. 239.

14. Clodfelter, *Pawns of Dishonor*, p. 178.

15. Baker, *Nam*, p. 204.

16. Doyle and Lipsman, *America Takes Over*, pp. 116–17.

17. Baker, *Nam*, p. 194.

18. Billy Cizinski interview, 27 Jan. 1981.

19. Lane, *Conversations with Americans*, p. 123.

20. "Frank: A Vietnam Veteran" was produced by WGBH and Canzoneri/Simon Productions. It was originally broadcast on WGBH-TV, Boston, on 25 May 1981. Transcripts available from WGBH Transcripts, 125 Western Ave., Boston, MA 02134.

21. Robert Flaherty interview, 7 July 1982.

22. Kevin Leblanc interview, 1 Apr. 1982.

23. Roger Neville Williams, *The New Exiles*, pp. 271–87.

24. Lang, *Casualties of War*, pp. 26, 35.

25. Ibid., pp. 54, 75–77.

26. Ibid., p. 102.

27. Ibid., p. 110.

28. MacPherson, *Long Time Passing*, pp. 177–96, 247–58.

29. Hersh, *My Lai 4*, pp. 39–41.

30. Peers, *My Lai*, p. 202.

31. Hersh, *My Lai 4*, p. 56.

32. Peers, *My Lai*, p. 180; Hersh, *My Lai 4*, p. 75.

33. Hersh, *My Lai 4*, pp. 69, 79; Peers, *My Lai*, pp. 268–71.

34. Peers, *My Lai*, pp. 66–76, 284.

35. Ibid., pp. 272–73.

36. Ibid., pp. 199–209.

37. Ibid., pp. 221–28.

38. Most of the books published about the war in the 1980s either omit My Lai entirely or make only passing, and often careless, reference to it. For example, Stanley Karnow's long and useful history, *Vietnam* (the companion book to the thirteen-part PBS documentary, "Vietnam: A Television History"), makes several one-line references to My Lai. In one passage he puts the death toll at "more than three hundred"; in another, "a hundred" (see pp. 24, 530). My teaching experience throughout the decade leads to my conclusion that most students had not heard of My Lai.

39. John Worthington interview, 21 June 1982.

40. Gene Holiday interview, 8 May 1984.

41. Ralph Brown interview, 9 Oct. 1983.

42. Victor Belloti interview, 8 Aug. 1981.

43. Herr, *Dispatches*, pp. 146–47.

44. Caputo, *A Rumor of War*, p. 289.

45. Frank Mathews interview, 3 Sept. 1981.

46. Emerson, *Winners and Losers*, p. 194; Schell, *Village of Ben Suc*, p. 45; Rap Group Notes, 1981–86.

47. Morrocco, *Thunder from Above*, p. 80.

48. U.S. Congress, Committee on the Judiciary, *Hearings*, pp. 6263–6759; numerous personal interviews, e.g., Jackson Baylor interview, 10 Sept. 1981.

49. Helmer, *Bringing the War Home*, p. 75.

50. Novak, *High Culture*, pp. 174–97.

51. Polner, *No Victory Parades*, p. 116.

52. Peter Wright interview, 16 Nov. 1984.

53. Helmer, *Bringing the War Home*, p. 79; Ed Johnson interview, 15 Oct. 1982.

54. Charles R. Anderson, *Vietnam*, pp. 32–33.

55. Eric Stevens interview, 13 May 1982.

56. Bob Foley interviews, 9 and 15 Sept. 1981.

57. Foley is describing a version of what American soldiers called a mad minute, a time (usually short but sometimes much longer than a minute) when weapons were fired, often at maximum rates of output, with no enemy in sight. Targets varied or were nonexistent. Usually the soldiers simply gathered along the perimeter and fired at random into a nearby hillside or wood line. The purpose and meaning of the mad minute varied. For the enlisted men it was usually perceived as a kind of recreation, a release from boredom and tension, and it was sometimes initiated by them without orders. Some commanders called for mad minutes knowing that they were good for morale. Mad minutes were also thought, by some commanders, to serve a tactical purpose. They might be ordered in the middle of the night when an enemy attack or "probe" was expected, in hopes that the mad minute might trigger a firefight before the attackers were fully prepared. This was sometimes called recon-by-fire (reconnaissance by fire).

58. Dennis Johnson interview, 8 Feb. 1982.

59. For Vietnamese descriptions of class see Hunt, "Organizing for Revolution," esp. pp. 107–31. This useful essay is based on 285 interviews with Vietnamese peasants conducted by the RAND Corporation. For the figure on tenant farming see Corson, *The Betrayal*, p. 129.

60. Fitzgerald, *Fire in the Lake*, pp. 349–53.

61. For the figure on military employees and the teachers college quotation see Luce and Sommer, *Viet Nam*, p. 286. In 1963 South Vietnam exported 800,000 tons of rice. By 1967 it had to import over a million tons. See Corson, *The Betrayal*, p. 222.

62. For a brief discussion of the wage scale of American servicemen during the war see Baskir and Strauss, *Chance and Circumstance*, p. 116. For more detailed information see House Committee on Armed Services, "Pay and Allowances of the Uniformed Services," 91st Cong., 1969–70, 1 (no. 3): 30–53, and *Congressional Quarterly*, 3 Apr. 1970, p. 931.

63. *New York Times*, 5 July 1970, p. 4. Some American units, such as the First

Infantry Division at Lai Khe and the Fourth Infantry Division at Pleiku, established official military brothels. See Brownmiller, *Against Our Will*, pp. 95–97.

64. Santoli, *Everything We Had*, pp. 7–8.

65. Richard Marlotas interview, 26 July 1982. Though the quotations are drawn from this interview, the general analysis is based on frequent meetings over a seven-year period.

66. Emerson, *Winners and Losers*, p. 239.

67. Schell, *Village of Ben Suc*, pp. 117–18; MacPherson, *Long Time Passing*, p. 228.

68. Mike Dowling interview, 8 Apr. 1982.

69. Todd Dasher interview, 12 Jan. 1981.

70. Lang, *Casualties of War*, pp. 19–20.

71. Vietnam Veterans Against the War, *Winter Soldier Investigation*, p. 22.

72. Ibid., p. 36; for another example see p. 80. Also see Trullinger, *Village at War*, p. 117.

73. Hasford, *The Short-Timers*, p. 66.

74. Mark Sampson interview, 14 Mar. 1982.

75. Levy, "ARVN as Faggots," pp. 18–27. Both the Viet Cong and the NVA wore rubber slippers comparable to American shower slippers, or flip-flops. Many were made from tire scraps. American soldiers called them Ho Chi Minh sandals.

76. Marin, "Coming to Terms," pp. 49–50.

CHAPTER NINE

1. Levison, *Working-Class Majority*, pp. 157–58.

2. Polner, *No Victory Parades*, p. 27.

3. Veterans' Administration, *Myths and Realities*, p. 60.

4. Polner, *No Victory Parades*, pp. 28, 24, 26.

5. Ibid., p. 29.

6. Victor Belloti interview, 8 Aug. 1981.

7. Polner, *No Victory Parades*, p. 10.

8. Bob Greene, *Homecoming*, p. 62.

9. Veterans' Administration, *Myths and Realities*, pp. 89–90.

10. Gene Holiday interview, 8 May 1984.

11. Gitlin, *The Sixties*, pp. 261–63, emphasis in original.

12. Tony Almeida interview, 29 June 1982. A similar experience is described in Baker, *Nam*, p. 279.

13. Lifton, *Home from the War*.

14. Kerry et al., *The New Soldier*; Vietnam Veterans Against the War, *Winter Soldier Investigation*.

15. Sennett and Cobb, *Hidden Injuries*, p. 147.

16. Todd Dasher interview, 12 Jan. 1981.

17. Polner, *No Victory Parades*, pp. 9–10, 7.

18. Ibid., p. 15.

19. Brende and Parson, *Vietnam Veterans*, pp. 104–5.

20. Hendin and Haas, *Wounds of War*, pp. 88–89.

21. Hughes, *You Can See a Lot*, p. 24.

22. Roth, *Sand in the Wind*; Durden, *No Bugles, No Drums*; O'Brien, *Going after Cacciato*.

23. Fussell, *The Great War and Modern Memory*, p. 76.

24. Egendorf et al., *Legacies of Vietnam*, pp. 539–74; Hendin and Haas, *Wounds of War*, pp. 203–31.

25. Brende and Parson, *Vietnam Veterans*, pp. 1, 65–83.

26. Marin, "Living in Moral Pain," p. 72.

27. Mahedy, *Out of the Night*; Figley and Leventman, *Strangers at Home*.

Bibliography

ARCHIVAL SOURCES

Marine Corps Historical Center (MHC). Located in Washington, D.C., the MHC is the headquarters of the Marine Corps History and Museums Division. It holds an enormous archive of Vietnam-related materials, including command chronologies, after-action reports, and operational journal files. Most useful to this study was its massive collection of oral histories. Marine Corps historians conducted approximately 5,000 taped interviews with marines of all ranks who served in Vietnam.

U.S. Army Center for Military History (CMH). The CMH, in Washington, D.C., contains an extensive Vietnam archive, but my research there was brief and primarily confined to the taped interviews. The army's Vietnam oral history collection includes several hundred interviews, mostly with officers.

Personal Files. These include tapes and transcripts of interviews I conducted between 1981 and 1987 with approximately 100 Vietnam veterans.

ORAL HISTORIES, MEMOIRS, DIARIES, AND LETTERS

Adler, Bill. *Letters from Vietnam*. New York: Dutton, 1967.
Anderson, Charles R. *The Grunts*. Novato, Calif.: Presidio Press, 1976.
————. *Vietnam: The Other War*. Novato, Calif.: Presidio Press, 1982.
Baker, Mark. *Nam: The Vietnam War in the Words of the Men and Women Who Fought There*. New York: William Morrow, 1981.
Brandon, Heather. *Casualties*. New York: St. Martin's Press, 1984.
Brennan, Matthew. *Brennan's War*. New York: Pocket Books, 1986.
Brown, Fred Leo. *Call Me No Name*. New York: Vantage Press, 1973.
Broyles, William, Jr. *Brothers in Arms*. New York: Knopf, 1986.
Caputo, Philip. *A Rumor of War*. New York: Holt, Rinehart and Winston, 1977.
Chanoff, David, and Doan Van Toai. *Portrait of the Enemy*. New York: Random House, 1986.
Clark, Johnnie M. *Guns Up!* New York: Ballantine Books, 1984.
Clodfelter, Micheal. *The Pawns of Dishonor*. Boston: Branden Press, 1976.
Corson, Lt. Col. William R. *The Betrayal*. New York: W. W. Norton, 1968.
Downs, Frederick. *The Killing Zone*. New York: W. W. Norton, 1978.
Duncan, Donald. *The New Legions*. New York: Pocket Books, 1967.
Edelman, Bernard, ed. *Dear America: Letters Home from Vietnam*. New York: W. W. Norton, 1985.
Ehrhart, W. D. *Vietnam-Perkasie: A Combat Marine Memoir*. London: McFarland, 1983.
Elkins, Frank Callihan. *The Heart of Man*. New York: W. W. Norton, 1973.
Goff, Stanley, and Robert Sanders. *Brothers: Black Soldiers in the Nam*. Novato, Calif.: Presidio Press, 1982.

Greene, Bob. *Homecoming: When the Soldiers Returned from Vietnam*. New York: G. P. Putnam's Sons, 1989.

Hackworth, Col. David H. *About Face: The Odyssey of an American Warrior*. New York: Simon and Schuster, 1989.

Halstead, Fred. *GIs Speak Out against the War: The Case of the Ft. Jackson 8*. New York: Pathfinder Press, 1970.

Herbert, Lt. Col. Anthony B. *Soldier*. New York: Dell Pub. Co., 1973.

Hughes, Larry. *You Can See a Lot Standing under a Flare in the Republic of Vietnam*. New York: William Morrow, 1969.

Joseph, Peter. *Good Times: An Oral History of America in the Nineteen Sixties*. New York: William Morrow, 1974.

Kerry, John, and Vietnam Veterans against the War. *The New Soldier*. New York: Collier Books, 1971.

Kovic, Ron. *Born on the Fourth of July*. New York: McGraw-Hill, 1976.

Lane, Mark. *Conversations with Americans*. New York: Simon and Schuster, 1970.

Luce, Don, and John Sommer. *Viet Nam: The Unheard Voices*. Ithaca, N.Y.: Cornell University Press, 1969.

Martin, Ralph G. *The GI War*. Boston: Little, Brown and Co., 1967.

Mason, Robert. *Chickenhawk*. New York: Penguin Books, 1984.

Norman, Michael. *These Good Men*. New York: Pocket Books, 1991.

O'Brien, Tim. *If I Die in a Combat Zone*. New York: Delacorte Press, 1973.

Ogden, Richard E. *Green Knight, Red Mourning*. New York: Zebra Books, 1985.

Parks, David. *GI Diary*. New York: Harper and Row, 1968.

Polner, Murray. *No Victory Parades*. New York: Harcourt, Brace and World, 1971.

Santoli, Al. *Everything We Had: An Oral History of the Vietnam War by Thirty-Three American Soldiers Who Fought There*. New York: Random House, 1981.

Tauber, Peter. *The Sunshine Soldiers*. New York: Simon and Schuster, 1971.

Terry, Wallace. *Bloods: An Oral History of the Vietnam War*. New York: Random House, 1984.

Truong Nhu Tang, with David Chanoff and Doan Van Toai. *A Vietcong Memoir*. New York: Vintage Books, 1986.

Vance, Samuel. *The Courageous and the Proud*. New York: W. W. Norton, 1970.

Westmoreland, Gen. William C. *A Soldier Reports*. Garden City, N.Y.: Doubleday, 1976.

Wheeler, John. *Touched with Fire*. New York: Franklin Watts, 1984.

Willenson, Kim. *The Bad War: An Oral History of the Vietnam War*. New York: New American Library, 1987.

NOVELS AND SHORT STORIES

Anderson, Robert A. *Cooks and Bakers*. New York: Avon Books, 1982.

Corder, E. M. *The Deerhunter*. New York: Jove Publications, 1978.

Del Vecchio, John M. *The 13th Valley*. New York: Bantam Books, 1982.

Dodge, Ed. *Dau*. New York: Berkley Books, 1984.

Durden, Charles. *No Bugles, No Drums*. New York: Viking Press, 1976.

Fuller, Jack. *Fragments*. New York: William Morrow, 1981.

Greene, Graham. *The Quiet American*. London: Penguin Books, 1955.
Groom, Winston. *Better Times Than These*. New York: Summit Books, 1978.
Halberstam, David. *One Very Hot Day*. Boston: Houghton Mifflin, 1967.
Hasford, Gustav. *The Short-Timers*. New York: Harper and Row, 1979.
Hathaway, Bo. *A World of Hurt*. New York: Taplinger Pub. Co., 1981.
Heinemann, Larry. *Close Quarters*. New York: Farrar, Straus and Giroux, 1977.
———. *Paco's Story*. New York: Farrar, Straus and Giroux, 1986.
Hemingway, Ernest. *A Farewell to Arms*. New York: Charles Scribner's Sons, 1957.
Huggett, William Turner. *Body Count*. New York: Dell Pub. Co., 1973.
Ketwig, John. *And a Hard Rain Fell*. New York: Pocket Books, 1986.
Klinkowitz, Jerome, and John Somer, eds. *Writing under Fire: Stories of the Vietnam War*. New York: Dell Pub. Co., 1978.
Kolpacoff, Victor. *The Prisoners of Quai Dong*. London: Secker and Warburg, 1967.
Mason, Bobbie Ann. *In Country*. New York: Harper and Row, 1985.
Mayer, Tom. *The Weary Falcon*. Boston: Houghton Mifflin, 1971.
Moore, Robin. *Search and Destroy*. New York: Popham Press, 1978.
O'Brien, Tim. *Going after Cacciato*. New York: Delacorte Press, 1978.
———. *The Things They Carried*. New York: Penguin, 1991.
Pelfrey, William. *The Big V*. New York: Avon Books, 1972.
Riggan, Rob. *Free Fire Zone*. New York: Ballantine Books, 1984.
Roth, Robert. *Sand in the Wind*. Los Angeles: Pinnacle Books, 1973.
Stone, Robert. *Dog Soldiers*. Boston: Houghton Mifflin, 1974.
Suddick, Tom. *A Few Good Men*. New York: Avon Books, 1978.
Taylor, Thomas. *A Piece of This Country*. New York: W. W. Norton, 1970.
Webb, James. *Fields of Fire*. New York: Bantam Books, 1978.
Werder, Albert D. *A Spartan Education*. Brooklyn Heights: Beekman Publishers, 1978.
Wilson, William. *The LBJ Brigade*. Los Angeles: Apocalypse Corp., 1966.
Wright, Stephen. *Meditations in Green*. New York: Bantam Books, 1984.

OTHER SOURCES

Adams, Sam. "Vietnam Cover-Up." *Harper's*, May 1975.
Appy, Christian G. "Vietnam According to Oliver Stone." *Commonweal*, 23 Mar. 1990.
Arlen, Michael J. *Living-Room War*. New York: Viking Press, 1966.
———. *The View from Highway 1*. New York: Farrar, Straus and Giroux, 1976.
Atkinson, Rick. *The Long Gray Line*. Boston: Houghton Mifflin, 1989.
Badillo, Gilbert, and David G. Curry. "The Social Incidence of Vietnam Casualties: Social Class or Race?" *Armed Forces and Society* 2 (1976).
Bain, David Haward. *After-Shocks*. New York: Penguin Books, 1986.
Bane, Mary Jo. *Here to Stay: American Families in the Twentieth Century*. New York: Basic Books, 1976.
Baritz, Loren. *Backfire*. New York: William Morrow, 1985.
Barnes, Peter. *Pawns: The Plight of the Citizen-Soldiers*. New York: Knopf, 1972.

Baskir, Lawrence M., and William A. Strauss. *Chance and Circumstance: The Draft, the War, and the Vietnam Generation.* New York: Knopf, 1978.

Baxter, Gordon. *Vietnam: Search and Destroy.* New York: World Pub. Co., 1967.

Bell, Daniel. *The Coming of the Post-Industrial Society.* New York: Basic Books, 1973.

Berger, Bennett M. *Working-Class Suburb: A Study of Auto Workers in Suburbia.* Berkeley: University of California Press, 1960.

Berman, Larry. *Planning a Tragedy: The Americanization of the War in Vietnam.* New York: W. W. Norton, 1982.

Binkin, Martin, and Mark J. Eitelberg. *Blacks and the Military.* Washington, D.C.: Brookings Institute, 1982.

Bourne, Peter G. *Men, Stress, and Vietnam.* Boston: Little, Brown and Co., 1970.

Bowles, Samuel, and Herbert Gintis. *Schooling in Capitalist America.* New York: Basic Books, 1976.

Boyle, Richard. *The Flower of the Dragon.* San Francisco: Ramparts Press, 1972.

Braverman, Harry. *Labor and Monopoly Capital.* New York: Monthly Review Press, 1974.

Brecher, Jeremy, and Tim Costello. *Common Sense for Hard Times.* Boston: South End Press, 1976.

Brende, Joel Osler, and Erwin Randolph Parson. *Vietnam Veterans: The Road to Recovery.* New York: Plenum Press, 1985.

Brewin, Bob, and Sydney Shaw. *Vietnam on Trial: Westmoreland vs. CBS.* New York: Atheneum, 1987.

Brooks, John. *The Great Leap.* New York: Harper Colophon Books, 1968.

Brownmiller, Susan. *Against Our Will: Men, Women and Rape.* New York: Bantam Books, 1976.

Bryan, C. D. B. *Friendly Fire.* New York: G. P. Putnam's Sons, 1976.

Burchett, Wilfred G. *Vietnam: Inside Story of the Guerilla War.* New York: International Publishers, 1965.

Burdick, Frank A. "Vietnam Revisioned: The Military Campaign against Civilian Control." *democracy,* Jan. 1981.

Buttinger, Joseph. *Vietnam: The Unforgettable Tragedy.* New York: Horizon Press, 1977.

Capps, Walter H. *The Unfinished War: Vietnam and the American Conscience.* Boston: Beacon Press, 1982.

Chomsky, Noam. *American Power and the New Mandarins.* New York: Vintage Books, 1969.

———. *At War with Asia.* New York: Vintage Books, 1970.

Chomsky, Noam, and Edward S. Herman. *The Washington Connection and Third World Fascism.* Boston: South End Press, 1979.

Cincinnatus. *Self-Destruction: The Disintegration and Decay of the United States Army during the Vietnam War.* New York: W. W. Norton, 1981.

Citizens Commission of Inquiry, ed. *The Dellums Committee Hearings on War Crimes in Vietnam.* New York: Vintage Books, 1972.

Coffey, Raymond R. "When the Blacks Come Home." *The Progressive,* Nov. 1968.

Cohen, Steven, ed. *Vietnam: Anthology and Guide to a Television History.* New York: Knopf, 1983.

Coles, Robert. *The Middle Americans.* Boston: Little, Brown and Co., 1971.

Cook, Fred J. "Hard-Hats: The Rampaging Patriots." *Nation,* 15 June 1970.

Cortright, David. *Soldiers in Revolt: The American Military Today*. Garden City, N.Y.: Doubleday, 1975.

Davis, James W., and Kenneth M. Dolbeare. *Little Groups of Neighbors: The Selective Service System*. Chicago: Markham Publishing, 1968.

Dellinger, David. *Vietnam Revisited*. Boston: South End Press, 1986.

Dobriner, William M. *Class in Suburbia*. Englewood Cliffs, N.J.: Prentice-Hall, 1961.

Donovan, Col. James A. *Militarism, U.S.A.* New York: Charles Scribner's Sons, 1970.

Doyle, Edward, and Samuel Lipsman. *America Takes Over*. Boston: Boston Pub. Co., 1983.

Duiker, William J. *The Communist Road to Power in Vietnam*. Boulder, Colo.: Westview Press, 1981.

Egendorf, Arthur, et al. *Legacies of Vietnam: Comparative Adjustments of Veterans and Their Peers*. Washington, D.C.: Government Printing Office, 1981.

Ehrenreich, Barbara. *Fear of Falling*. New York: Pantheon Books, 1989.

Ellsberg, Daniel. *Papers on the War*. New York: Simon and Schuster, 1972.

Emerick, Kenneth Fred. *War Resisters Canada*. Knox: Knox, Pennsylvania, Free Press, 1972.

Emerson, Gloria. *Winners and Losers: Battles, Retreats, Gains, Losses, and Ruins from a Long War*. New York: Random House, 1976.

Falk, Richard A., ed. *The Vietnam War and International Law*. 4 vols. Princeton, N.J.: Princeton University Press, 1969.

Fall, Bernard. *Last Reflections on a War*. Garden City, N.Y.: Doubleday, 1967.

———. *The Two Viet-Nams*. New York: Praeger, 1967.

Fallows, James. *National Defense*. New York: Random House, 1981.

———. "What Did You Do in the Class War, Daddy?" *Washington Monthly*, Oct. 1975.

Figley, Charles R., and Seymour Leventman, eds. *Strangers at Home: Vietnam Veterans since the War*. New York: Praeger, 1980.

Fitzgerald, Frances. *Fire in the Lake: The Vietnamese and the Americans in Vietnam*. Boston: Atlantic/Little, Brown Books, 1972.

Flynn, George Q. *Lewis B. Hershey, Mr. Selective Service*. Chapel Hill: University of North Carolina Press, 1985.

Foucault, Michel. *Power/Knowledge: Selected Interviews and Other Writings*. New York: Pantheon Books, 1980.

Franks, Lucinda. *Waiting out a War*. New York: Coward, McCann, and Geoghegan, 1974.

Fulbright, J. William. *The Vietnam Hearings*. New York: Vintage Books, 1966.

Furlong, William Barry. "Training for the Front-All-Around-You War." *New York Times Magazine*, 24 Oct. 1965.

Fussell, Paul. *The Great War and Modern Memory*. New York: Oxford University Press, 1975.

Gabriel, Richard A., and Paul L. Savage. *Crisis in Command*. New York: Hill and Wang, 1978.

Gallucci, Robert L. *Neither Peace nor Honor: The Politics of American Military Policy in Vietnam*. Baltimore: Johns Hopkins University Press, 1975.

Garland, Albert N., ed. *Infantry in Vietnam*. Nashville: Battery Press, 1967.

Gaylin, Willard. *In the Service of Their Country: War Resisters in Prison*. New York: Viking Press, 1970.

Gelb, Leslie H., and Richard Betts. *The Irony of Vietnam: The System Worked*. Washington, D.C.: Brookings Institution, 1979.

Gershen, Martin. *Destroy or Die: The True Story of Mylai*. New Rochelle, N.Y.: Arlington House, 1971.

Gettleman, Marvin E., ed. *Vietnam: History, Documents, and Opinions*. New York: New American Library Mentor, 1970.

———— et al. *Vietnam and America: A Documented History*. New York: Grove Press, 1985.

Gibson, James William. *The Perfect War: Technowar in Vietnam*. Boston: Atlantic Monthly Press, 1986.

Gitlin, Todd. *The Sixties*. New York: Bantam Books, 1987.

————. *The Whole World Is Watching*. Berkeley: University of California Press, 1980.

Glass, Andrew. "Defense Report: Draftees Shoulder Burden of Fighting and Dying in Vietnam." *National Journal*, 15 Aug. 1970.

Glasser, Ronald J. *365 Days*. New York: Bantam Books, 1971.

Glick, Edward B. *Soldiers, Scholars and Society: The Social Impact of the American Military*. Palisades, Calif.: Goodyear Publishing, 1971.

Goldman, Peter, and Tony Fuller. *Charlie Company: What Vietnam Did to Us*. New York: William Morrow, 1983.

Grant, Zalin. "Vietnam as Fable." *New Republic*, 25 Mar. 1978.

————. "Whites against Blacks in Vietnam." *New Republic*, 18 Jan. 1969.

Gravel, Senator Mike, ed. *The Pentagon Papers*. 5 vols. Boston: Beacon Press, 1971.

Gray, J. Glenn. *The Warriors: Reflections on Men in Battle*. New York: Harcourt Brace, 1958.

Griffen, William L., and John Marciano. *Lessons of the Vietnam War*. Totowa, N.J.: Rowman and Allanheld, 1979.

Halberstam, David. *The Best and the Brightest*. New York: Random House, 1972.

Hallin, Daniel. *The "Uncensored War."* Berkeley: University of California Press, 1989.

Harrington, Michael. *The Other America*. Baltimore: Penguin Books, 1963.

Harvey, Frank. *Air War—Vietnam*. New York: Bantam Books, 1967.

Hasselblad, Marva. *Lucky-Lucky*. Greenwich, Conn.: Fawcett Publications, 1967.

Hauser, William L. *America's Army in Crisis*. Baltimore: Johns Hopkins University Press, 1973.

Hayslip, Le Ly, with Jay Wurts. *When Heaven and Earth Changed Places*. New York: Plume, 1989.

Heinl, Robert. "The Collapse of the Armed Forces." *Armed Forces Journal*, 7 June 1971.

Hellmann, John. *American Myth and the Legacy of Vietnam*. New York: Columbia University Press, 1986.

Helmer, John. *Bringing the War Home: The American Soldier in Vietnam and After*. New York: Free Press, 1974.

Hendin, Herbert, and Ann Pollinger Haas. *Wounds of War*. New York: Basic Books, 1984.

Herman, Edward S. *Atrocities in Vietnam: Myths and Realities*. Philadelphia: Pilgrim Press, 1970.

Herr, Michael. *Dispatches*. New York: Knopf, 1977.

Herring, George C. *America's Longest War*. New York: Wiley, 1979.

Hersh, Seymour M. *Cover-Up*. New York: Random House, 1972.

———. "The Decline and Near Fall of the U.S. Army." *Saturday Review*, 18 Nov. 1972.

———. *My Lai 4*. New York: Vintage Books, 1970.

———. *The Price of Power: Kissinger in the Nixon White House*. New York: Summit Books, 1983.

Hickey, Gerald. *Village in Vietnam*. New Haven: Yale University Press, 1964.

Hochschild, Adam. "Reserve and Guard: A More Selective Service." *Washington Monthly*, Jan. 1971.

Hodgson, Godfrey. *America in Our Time*. New York: Vintage Books, 1976.

Horne, A. D., ed. *The Wounded Generation: America after Vietnam*. Englewood Cliffs, N.J.: Prentice-Hall, 1981.

Howell, Joseph T. *Hard Living on Clay Street: Portraits of Blue Collar Families*. Garden City, N.Y.: Doubleday, 1973.

Hunt, David. "Organizing for Revolution in Vietnam: Study of a Mekong Delta Province." *Radical America*, Jan.–Apr. 1974.

Inaugural Addresses of the Presidents of the United States. Washington, D.C.: Government Printing Office, 1989.

Infantry Magazine, ed. *A Distant Challenge: The U.S. Infantryman in Vietnam, 1967–1972*. Nashville: Battery Press, 1983.

Janowitz, Morris. *The Professional Soldier*. New York: Free Press, 1960.

Johnson, Haynes, and George C. Wilson. *Army in Anguish: A Washington Post National Report*. New York: Simon and Schuster, 1971.

Johnson, Sandee Shaffer. *Cadences: The Jody Call Book, No. 1*. Canton, Ohio: Daring Books, 1983.

Johnson, Thomas A. "Negroes in 'the Nam.'" *Ebony*, Aug. 1968.

Just, Ward. *Military Men*. New York: Knopf, 1970.

Kahin, George McT. *Intervention*. New York: Knopf, 1986.

Kahin, George McT., and John W. Lewis. *The United States in Vietnam*. New York: Delta Press, 1967.

Karnow, Stanley. *Vietnam: A History*. New York: Viking Press, 1983.

Keegan, John. *The Face of Battle*. New York: Penguin Books, 1978.

Kimball, Jeffrey P. *To Reason Why*. Philadelphia: Temple University Press, 1990.

Knightley, Phillip. *The First Casualty*. New York: Harcourt Brace Jovanovich, 1975.

Knoll, Erwin, and Judith Nies McFadden. *War Crimes and the American Conscience*. New York: Holt, Rinehart and Winston, 1970.

Kolko, Gabriel. *Anatomy of a War*. New York: Pantheon Books, 1985.

———. *Wealth and Power in America*. New York: Praeger, 1962.

Ladinsky, J. "Vietnam, the Veterans, and the Veterans Administration." *Armed Forces and Society* 2 (1976).

Lang, Daniel. *Casualties of War*. New York: McGraw-Hill, 1969.

Leed, Eric. *No Man's Land: Combat and Identity in World War I*. Cambridge: Cambridge University Press, 1979.

Levison, Andrew. *The Working-Class Majority*. New York: Penguin Books, 1975.

Levy, Charles J. "ARVN as Faggots: Inverted Warfare in Vietnam." *Transaction*, Oct. 1971.

Lewis, David L. *King*. Chicago: University of Illinois Press, 1978.

Lewis, Lloyd B. *The Tainted War: Culture and Identity in Vietnam War Narratives*. Westport, Conn.: Greenwood Press, 1985.

Lewy, Guenter. *America in Vietnam*. New York: Oxford University Press, 1978.

Lifton, Robert Jay. *Home from the War*. New York: Simon and Schuster, 1973.

Linden, Eugene. "Demoralization." *Saturday Review*, 8 Jan. 1972.

Lipsman, Samuel, and Edward Doyle. *Fighting for Time*. Boston: Boston Pub. Co., 1983.

McAlister, John T. *Vietnam: The Origins of Revolution*. Garden City, N.Y.: Anchor Books, 1971.

McCarthy, Mary. *The Seventeenth Degree*. New York: Harcourt Brace Jovanovich, 1974.

MacPherson, Myra. *Long Time Passing: Vietnam and the Haunted Generation*. Garden City, N.Y.: Doubleday, 1984.

Mahedy, William P. *Out of the Night: The Spiritual Journey of Vietnam Veterans*. New York: Ballantine Books, 1986.

Maitland, Terrence, and Peter McInerney. *A Contagion of War*. Boston: Boston Pub. Co., 1983.

Manchester, William. *The Glory and the Dream*. New York: Bantam Books, 1975.

Mangold, Tom, and John Penycate. *The Tunnels of Cu Chi*. New York: Berkley Books, 1986.

Marin, Peter. "Coming to Terms with Vietnam." *Harper's*, Dec. 1980.

———. "Living in Moral Pain." *Psychology Today*, Nov. 1981.

Marr, David G. *Vietnamese Anticolonialism 1895–1925*. Berkeley: University of California Press, 1971.

———. *Vietnamese Tradition on Trial 1920–1945*. Berkeley: University of California Press, 1981.

Marshall, S. L. A. *Vietnam: Three Battles*. New York: Da Capo Press, 1971.

Melman, Seymour. *In the Name of America*. Annandale, Va.: Turnpike Press, 1968.

Moore, Barrington, Jr. *Injustice*. White Plains, N.Y.: M. E. Sharpe, 1978.

Morrocco, John. *Thunder from Above*. Boston: Boston Pub. Co., 1984.

Moskos, Charles C. "The American Dilemma in Uniform: Race in the Armed Forces." *The Annals of the American Academy of Political and Social Science*, ed. Adam Yarmolinsky. Philadelphia, Mar. 1973.

———. *The American Enlisted Man: The Rank and File in Today's Military*. New York: Russell Sage Foundation, 1970.

———. "Why Men Fight." *Trans-Action*, Nov. 1969.

Novak, William. *High Culture: Marijuana in the Lives of Americans*. New York: Knopf, 1980.

Oberdorfer, Don. *Tet!* New York: Doubleday, 1971.

Palmer, Gen. Bruce, Jr. *The 25-Year War: America's Military Role in Vietnam*. New York: Touchstone, 1985.

Palmer, Laura. *Shrapnel in the Heart*. New York: Vintage Books, 1988.

Patti, Archimedes L. A. *Why Viet Nam? Prelude to America's Albatross*. Berkeley: University of California Press, 1980.

Peers, Lt. Gen. W. R. *The My Lai Inquiry*. New York: W. W. Norton, 1979.

Podhoretz, Norman. *Why We Were in Vietnam*. New York: Simon and Schuster, 1982.

Polenberg, Richard. *One Nation Divisible*. New York: Viking Press, 1980.

Popkin, Samuel L. *The Rational Peasant*. Berkeley: University of California Press, 1979.

Pratt, John Clark. *Vietnam Voices*. New York: Penguin Books, 1984.

President's Task Force on Manpower Conservation. *One Third of a Nation*. Washington, D.C.: Government Printing Office, 1964.

Race, Jeffrey. *War Comes to Long An*. Berkeley: University of California Press, 1972.

Record, Jeffrey. "Maximizing COBRA Utilization." *Washington Monthly*, Apr. 1971.

Report of the National Advisory Commission on Civil Disorders. New York: Bantam Books, 1968.

Rosenberger, John W. "How the Soldiers View Vietnam." *The Progressive*, Mar. 1968.

Rubin, Lillian Breslow. *Worlds of Pain: Life in the Working-Class Family*. New York: Basic Books, 1976.

Sack, John. *Lieutenant Calley: His Own Story*. New York: Viking Press, 1971.

———. *M*. New York: New American Library, 1967.

Salisbury, Harrison E., ed. *Vietnam Reconsidered*. New York: Harper Torchbooks, 1984.

Schandler, Herbert Y. *Lyndon Johnson and Vietnam: The Unmaking of a President*. Princeton, N.J.: Princeton University Press, 1977.

Schell, Jonathan. *The Military Half*. New York: Knopf, 1968.

———. *The Real War*. New York: Knopf, 1987.

———. *The Time of Illusion*. New York: Knopf, 1976.

———. *The Village of Ben Suc*. New York: Knopf, 1967.

Scheurer, Timothy E. "Myth to Madness: American, Vietnam and Popular Culture." *Journal of American Culture*, Summer 1981.

Schlesinger, Arthur M., Jr. *The Bitter Heritage: Vietnam and American Democracy, 1941–1966*. New York: Houghton Mifflin, 1967.

Sennett, Richard. *Authority*. New York: Vintage Books, 1981.

Sennett, Richard, and Jonathan Cobb. *The Hidden Injuries of Class*. New York: Vintage Books, 1973.

Sexton, Patricia Cayo, and Brendan Sexton. *Blue Collars and Hard Hats*. New York: Vintage Books, 1971.

Shawcross, William. *Sideshow*. New York: Simon and Schuster, 1979.

Sheehan, Neil. *A Bright Shining Lie*. New York: Random House, 1988.

———, ed. "Letters from Hamburger Hill." *Harper's*, Nov. 1969.

——— et al. *The Pentagon Papers: As Published by the New York Times*. New York: Quadrangle Books, 1971.

Sherrill, Robert. *Military Justice Is to Justice as Military Music Is to Music*. New York: Harper and Row, 1970.

Shore, Capt. Moyers S., II. *The Battle for Khe Sanh*. Washington, D.C.: Government Printing Office, 1969.

Short, William, and Willa Seidenberg. "A Matter of Conscience: Resistance within the U.S. Military during the Vietnam War." *Vietnam Generation*, Winter 1989.

Shulimson, Jack. *U.S. Marines in Vietnam: An Expanding War, 1966*. Washington, D.C.: Government Printing Office, 1982.

Shulimson, Jack, and Maj. Charles M. Johnson. *The U.S. Marines in Vietnam: The Landing and the Buildup, 1965*. Washington, D.C.: Government Printing Office, 1978.

Sifry, Micah L., and Christopher Cerf. *The Gulf War Reader*. New York: Random House, 1991.

Soper, Col. James B. "A View from FMF Pac of Logistics in the Western Pacific, 1965–1971." In *The Marines in Vietnam, 1954–1973: An Anthology and Annotated Bibliography*. Washington, D.C.: Government Printing Office, 1974.

Spector, Ronald H. *Advice and Support: The Early Years*. New York: Free Press, 1985.

Stack, Carol. *All Our Kin: Strategies for Survival in a Black Community*. New York: Harper Colophon Books, 1974.

Stanton, Shelby L. *Vietnam: Order of Battle*. Washington, D.C.: U.S. News Books, 1981.

Starr, Paul. *The Discarded Army: Veterans after Vietnam*. New York: Charterhouse, 1973.

Stone, Oliver, and Richard Boyle. *Platoon and Salvador: The Original Screenplays*. New York: Vintage Books, 1987.

Stouffer, Samuel A., et al. *The American Soldier*. 2 vols. Princeton, N.J.: Princeton University Press, 1949.

Suid, H. Lawrence. *Guts and Glory: Great American War Movies*. Reading, Mass.: Addison-Wesley, 1978.

Summers, Harry G. *On Strategy*. Novato, Calif.: Presidio Press, 1982.

Taylor, Clyde, ed. *Vietnam and Black America: An Anthology of Protest and Resistance*. Garden City, N.Y.: Doubleday, 1973.

Teodori, Massimo, ed. *The New Left: A Documentary History*. New York: Bobbs-Merrill, 1969.

Terkel, Studs. *American Dreams: Lost and Found*. New York: Pantheon Books, 1980.

———. *Division Street: America*. New York: Avon Books, 1967.

———. *The Good War: An Oral History of World War Two*. New York: Pantheon Books, 1984.

———. *Working*. New York: Pantheon Books, 1974.

Thompson, E. P. *The Making of the English Working Class*. New York: Vintage Books, 1966.

Trillin, Calvin. "The War in Kansas." *New Yorker*, 22 Apr. 1967.

Trullinger, James Walker, Jr. *Village at War: An Account of Revolution in Vietnam*. New York: Longman, 1980.

Turley, William S. *The Second Indochina War*. New York: Mentor, 1987.

U.S. Congress. Committee on the Judiciary. *Hearings before the Subcommittee to Investigate Juvenile Delinquency: Drug Abuse in the Armed Forces*. 91st Cong., 1969–70. Vol. 34.

U.S. Casualties in Southeast Asia. Washington, D.C.: Government Printing Office, 1985.

Useem, Michael. *Conscription, Protest, and Social Conflict: The Life and Death of a Draft Resistance Movement*. New York: Wiley, 1973.

Veterans' Administration. *Data on Vietnam Era Veterans*. Washington, D.C.: Veterans' Administration, 1977.

———. *Myths and Realities: A Study of Attitudes Toward Vietnam Era Veterans*. Washington, D.C.: Government Printing Office, 1980.

Vietnam Veterans Against the War. *The Winter Soldier Investigation: An Inquiry into American War Crimes*. Boston: Beacon Press, 1972.

Vo Nguyen Giap. *The Military Art of People's War*. New York: Monthly Review Press, 1970.

Walzer, Michael. *Just and Unjust Wars*. New York: Basic Books, 1977.

Weigley, Russell F. *The American Way of War*. New York: Macmillan, 1973.

West, Capt. Francis J., Jr. *Small Unit Action in Vietnam*. New York: Arno Press, 1967.

Whitlow, Capt. Robert H. *U.S. Marines in Vietnam: The Advisory and Combat Assistance Era, 1954–1964*. Washington, D.C.: Government Printing Office, 1977.

Williams, Reese, ed. *Unwinding the War*. Seattle: Real Comet Press, 1987.

Williams, Roger Neville. *The New Exiles: American War Resisters in Canada*. New York: Liveright, 1971.

Willis, John Martin. "Who Died in Vietnam: An Analysis of the Social Background of Vietnam War Casualties." Ph.D. diss., Purdue University, 1975.

Wills, Garry. *The Kennedy Imprisonment*. Boston: Atlantic/Little, Brown, 1982.

———. *Nixon Agonistes*. Boston: Houghton Mifflin, 1970.

Young, Whitney. "When the Negroes in Vietnam Come Home." *Harper's*, June 1967.

Zaroulis, Nancy, and Gerald Sullivan. *Who Spoke Up?* New York: Holt, Rinehart and Winston, 1984.

Zinberg, Norman. "GIs and OJs in Vietnam." *New York Times Magazine*, 5 Dec. 1971.

Zinn, Howard. *The Logic of Withdrawal*. Boston: Beacon Press, 1967.

———. *The Politics of History*. Boston: Beacon Press, 1970.

Index

Debeau, Chris, 45–46
Deegan, Richard, 74–76, 110, 124, 213
Deer Hunter, The, 81–82, 125
Del Vecchio, John M., 171; *The 13th Valley*, 171–72, 185
Democracy: and U.S. military effectiveness, 5; as official justification for war, 7, 132, 152, 207–8, 209, 210, 217
Dern, Bruce, 312, 313
Desertion, 95, 109, 112, 251, 271
Diem, Ngo Dinh. *See* Ngo Dinh Diem
Dienbienphu, battle of (1954), 149
Dishonorable discharge, 90, 91, 92
Dong Ap Bia Mountain (Hamburger Hill), 230–31
Dorchester, Mass., 11, 12, 15, 55
Douglas, William O., 149
Dowling, Mike, 50–51, 293
Downs, Frederick, 124, 194–95, 228; *The Killing Zone*, 124, 195
Draft: escalation of inductions, 18, 26, 31; avoidance, 18, 34, 36–37, 50–52, 63, 305; graduate school deferments, 26, 35, 36; age of eligibility, 27; proportion of soldiers from, 28; enlistment motivated by, 28, 29, 36, 46–47; working-class vulnerability to, 28–30, 33, 34, 35, 37, 45–46; college-student deferments, 29, 30, 35, 45–46, 69, 220, 301; lottery, 29, 36; occupational deferments, 29–30, 35–36, 326 (n. 47); admission standards, 30–32; classification categories, 31, 80; medical exemptions, 33–34, 36; local boards, 34–35, 326 (n. 47); resistance, 36, 51, 301; tour commitment, 49–50; middle class and, 50–52, 53
Drug use, 93–94, 140–41, 190, 253, 283–85
Durden, Charles: *No Bugles, No Drums*, 318

Edwards, Reginald, 62
Ehrhart, W. D.: *Vietnam-Perkasie*, 128
Ellsberg, Daniel, 193–94
Emerson, Gloria, 2, 261, 290, 310; *Winners and Losers*, 310

Empire, Ala., 14, 15
Enlistment, 44, 46–49, 54–78 passim, 96; draft-motivated, 28, 29, 36, 46–47
Enthoven, Alain, 163
Erikkson, Sven, 271–72, 273, 293–94

Falk, Richard, 274–75
Firebase Julie, 188–89
Fitzgerald, Frances, 149, 171
Flaherty, Robert, 88–89, 97, 119–20, 198, 266
Flynn, George, 30
FNGs (fuckin' new guys), 138–41
Foley, Bob, 69–72, 82–83, 101, 286–88, 340 (n. 57)
Fonda, Jane, 312–13
Foucault, Michel, 10
"Fragging," 185, 246–47, 283
France, 113, 145, 147–49, 154
"Frank: A Vietnam Veteran" (PBS), 265–66
"Freedom Birds," 123
Free-fire zones, 194, 196, 226–27, 269
Freeman, Sherwood, 214–15
"Free World forces," 16
Friel, William, 233
Friendly fire, 8, 185
Fuller, Jack: *Fragments*, 136, 248
Fuller, Tony, and Peter Goldman, 189; *Charlie Company*, 323 (n. 7)
Full Metal Jacket, 6, 87
Fussell, Paul: *The Great War and Modern Memory*, 81, 318

Gabriel, Richard A., and Paul L. Savage: *Crisis in Command*, 245
Geneva Accords (1954), 149
"Ghosting," 244
Gibson, James William, 158, 183
Gitlin, Todd, 305–6
Glens Falls, N.Y., 45
Goff, Stanley, 184
Goldman, Peter. *See* Fuller, Tony, and Peter Goldman
Go Noi island, 160
Great Depression, 58–59
Great Society, 19, 32, 33, 39
Green, Nick, 54–55

Green Berets (Special Forces), 66
Green Berets, The, 66
Greene, Bob: *Homecoming*, 304
Greene, Graham: *The Quiet American*, 32, 83
Gregory, Dick, 20
Groom, Winston, 133, 135; *Better Times Than These*, 133–36, 182, 186
Guam: casualties from, 15–16
Gulf of Tonkin Resolution (1964), 18, 151
Guthrie, Arlo, 34

Haas, Ann, 317, 319
Hackworth, David, 185
Halberstam, David, 37, 156, 235–36; *One Very Hot Day*, 235–36
Hamburger Hill, 230–31
Hamlet Evaluation System (HES), 158–59
Harmon, David, 186
Harper, Steve, 11, 299–301
Harris poll, 300, 304, 305
Harvard University, 26
Hasford, Gustav, 87, 260, 295; *The Short-Timers*, 87, 102, 260, 295
Hathaway, Bo: *A World of Hurt*, 91–92
Hawkins, Gains, 165
Hayslip, Le Ly: *When Heaven and Earth Changed Places*, 160, 204
Heinl, Robert, 247
Helicopter warfare, 174–75, 176
Helmer, John, 48, 49
Hemingway, Ernest: *A Farewell to Arms*, 2
Henderson, Oran, 276
Hendin, Herbert, 317, 319
Herbert, Anthony, 227
Herman, Edward, 203–4
Herr, Michael, 44, 152, 217, 218, 228, 261, 280
Hersh, Seymour, 274–75
Hershey, Lewis B., 30, 35, 36
Hispanic Americans, 15, 19
Ho Chi Minh, 16, 148, 149, 150, 224, 228
Ho Chi Minh Trail, 146
Holiday, Gene, 86, 90, 105, 110, 279, 305
Homosexuality, 101–2

Hope, Bob, 220, 237
Hue: civilian massacre at, 204
Huggett, William: *Body Count*, 260
Hughes, Larry, 132–33, 317

Illinois: casualties from, 12
Infantry, 112, 176, 179, 240–41; First Division, 1, 117, 179, 188, 218; Fourth Division, 117; Twenty-fifth Division, 117, 171, 290; Ninth Division, 117, 179, 231; Third Battalion, 196th Brigade, 231; Eleventh Brigade, 235

Jackson, George L., 20–21
Japan: occupation of Vietnam by, 145, 148
Jensen, Luke, 117
"Jody," 106, 312
Johnson, Ed, 56, 57
Johnson, Lyndon B.: Guam conference, 15–16; U.S. troop escalation, 17, 121; efforts to contain antiwar sentiment, 19, 36–37, 121, 122; and communism, 67, 211, 225–26, 254–55; on Vietnam, 146, 209–10; official justifications for war, 209–12; campaign promises, 267
Johnson, Thomas, 21

Kahin, George McT., 148, 253
Karnow, Stanley: *Vietnam*, 339 (n. 38)
Kennedy, John F., 17, 63, 64–66, 67, 149
Kent State University: killings at, 39, 40
Ketwig, John, 129, 131, 132, 238, 241; *And a Hard Rain Fell*, 238
Khe Sanh base, 187–88, 261; siege of, 141–42, 188
KIA (killed in action), 17, 156, 170, 189. *See also* Casualties
King, Rev. Martin Luther, Jr., 19–20, 77, 206, 223
Korean War: U.S. troop composition, 18, 30; blacks in, 21; ambiguous conclusion of, 61, 145; and Vietnam policy, 148; medals awarded in, 248; veterans of, 314

National Opinion Research Center (NORC), 23–24, 49
Native Americans, 19, 61
New York City: antiwar riot in, 39–40, 41
New Zealand: combat forces from, 16
Ngo Dinh Diem, 149–50, 323 (n. 9)
Nguyen Thi Khao, 290
Nixon, Richard M., 17, 145–46, 310; and "silent majority," 39; and antiwar movement, 39, 306; and U.S. credibility, 212; and "peace with honor," 247; campaign promises, 267; pardon of Calley, 277; and South Vietnamese "self-determination," 336 (n. 9)
Noncommissioned officers (NCOs), 135, 140, 218, 246, 278
North Vietnam: creation of, 149, 150; U.S. raids into, 150–51; U.S. bombing of, 151, 203; in official U.S. policy, 153, 209–10
North Vietnamese Army (NVA; People's Army of Vietnam, PAVN), 106n, 146n; siege of Khe Sanh, 141, 187–88; attack on Firebase Julie, 188–89; supposed Cambodian massacre, 270–71. *See also* Revolutionary Forces

O'Brien, Tim: *If I Die in a Combat Zone*, 52; and the draft, 52–53, 60; *Going after Cacciato*, 83–84, 85, 246–47, 318; and basic training, 101, 108; as new guy, 139–40; and land mines, 170–71; on brutality toward civilians, 201–2; on sandbagging, 245; on fragging, 246–47
Officer Basic School, 113–14
Officer candidate school, 21–22, 24
Officers: and My Lai massacre, 8–9, 276–77; blacks, 22; social class, 24; and treatment of civilians, 135, 197, 269; combat tours, 140; in combat areas, 142, 278; pressure for body counts, 156, 184, 229, 231–32, 269, 317, 337 (n. 62); use of soldiers as bait, 188–89; and official justification for war, 218; soldiers' defiance of, 223, 231, 241, 245, 246; relaxation of aggressive tactics, 230, 231, 245, 246; insistence on protocol and discipline, 240–41; fragging of, 246–47
Ogen, Richard: *Green Knight, Red Mourning*, 118–19
One Third of a Nation (President's Task Force on Manpower Conservation), 31

Pace College, 40
"Pacification" program, 157–58, 159–60, 282
Paranoia, 316–17, 319
Paratroopers, 96, 119, 175
Parks, David, 131–32
Patriotism, 47, 48, 61, 64, 67, 83, 310
Patton, 145–46
Peace Corps, 66
Peers, W. R., 274, 276
Pentagon Papers, 211–12, 217, 253
People's Army of Vietnam (PAVN). *See* North Vietnamese Army
People's Liberation Armed Forces (PLAF). *See* Viet Cong
Persian Gulf War, 4–5
Personnel Damage Assessments (PDA), 270
Philippines: combat forces from, 16
Phoenix program, 158, 204
Picciano, John, 45, 98–99
Platoon, 6, 82, 125–26, 187
Polner, Murray, 249, 284, 299; *No Victory Parades*, 299
Posttraumatic stress disorder, 128, 257, 272–73, 309–10, 316–17, 319–20
Poverty: American, 31, 32, 288; Vietnamese, 131, 132, 287–88, 290, 291, 293
Powell, Adam Clayton, 20
Project 100,000, 32–33, 37, 80
Prostitution, 132, 179, 237, 238, 290, 291
Psychological Operations, 254–55
Psychological warfare, 265, 267
Psychological Warfare Office, 196
Puerto Rico: casualties from, 15
"Puff the Magic Dragon," 282–83

Quayle, Dan, 51

Racial discrimination, 21–22, 31
Racism, 38, 101, 223, 224–25, 293
Rape, 268, 271–72
Reagan, Ronald, 4, 5, 9, 48, 248, 323
  (n. 6)
Rear-echelon soldiers: combat-support
  ratios, 167; and Vietnamese civilians, 216–17, 239–40, 289, 290;
  short-timers, 237; living conditions,
  238–39, 285–86; demoralization, 239,
  240, 241; and military protocol and
  discipline, 240–41, 285; combat soldiers' hostility toward, 241, 302; brutalization of, 257, 260; insulation
  from war, 286, 319
Reenlistment, 21, 22, 271
Refugee camps, 159, 194, 226, 227, 282,
  288–89
Reserve Officer Training Corps
  (ROTC), 24, 269
Reserves, 30, 36–37, 94
Rest and recuperation (R&R) program, 156, 234, 237–38, 244, 251
Revolutionary Forces, 150; civilian
  support for, 106, 136, 146, 158, 163,
  165–66, 167–68, 191, 192, 195, 197,
  214, 216, 226, 300; attacks on U.S.
  forces, 139, 141, 161, 163–64, 171–72,
  182–83, 187, 189–90; Tet Offensive,
  141, 188, 204; casualties, 143, 162–
  63, 172–73, 189, 190, 203, 218, 230;
  advantages over U.S. forces, 145,
  146–47, 151, 166, 171, 173; defined,
  146n; search-and-destroy missions
  and, 154, 155, 163, 166, 182, 193, 216;
  attrition strategy against, 155–56,
  163, 226; control of hamlets, 158, 159,
  160, 226; troop strength, 164–65,
  166, 167, 210; "irregular" guerrillas,
  165–66; difficulty of locating, 171–
  72, 175, 182, 193, 194, 270; U.S. soldiers as bait for, 182, 184, 187–89; air
  strikes on, 184–86; killing of civilians, 204; Americans' respect for,
  217, 233, 295–96; refugee resettlement program and, 226–27; mutilation of corpses, 265; U.S. antiwar

movement and, 298, 299, 306. *See
also* North Vietnamese Army; Viet
Cong
Reynolds, Jerry, 45
Riggan, Rob, 122, 129, 131; *Free Fire
Zone*, 122, 129
Rodriquez, Rudy, 214
Rogers, Richard, 188–89
Ross, David, 254
Rostow, W. W., 228
Roth, Robert: *Sand in the Wind*, 92,
  99, 100, 318
Rules of engagement (ROE), 195–96,
  197–99, 200–201, 229, 273

Sack, John, 113, 207, 218
Sadler, Barry: "The Ballad of the
  Green Berets," 66
Saigon, Vietnam, 204, 233
Sampson, Mark, 110, 295
Samuels, Jerry, 268–69, 270–71
Sandbagging, 244–45, 253
Sanders, Robert, 223–24, 242–43
Sapper attacks, 190
Savage, Paul L. *See* Gabriel, Rich-
  ard A., and Paul L. Savage
Schell, Jonathan, 191, 228, 292
Schurtz, Eugene, 231
Search-and-destroy operations, 153,
  155; as bait for enemy attacks, 8,
  182; Westmoreland and "distortion"
  of, 156; combat battalions devoted
  to, 158; futility of, 163; and Viet-
  namese villages, 166, 193, 195, 216
Selective Service Qualifying Test, 35
Selective Service System, 28, 29–30,
  34, 37. *See also* Draft
Sennett, Richard, 56
Shaw, Dan, 11–12, 53, 58
Shepard, Carl, 141–44, 331 (n. 54)
"Short-timers," 236–37, 243
Shulimson, Jack, 161
Simmons, Edwin H., 113–15
Snipers, 142, 171, 172, 181, 193
Soldiers, 323–24 (n. 10); killed in Viet-
  nam, 1, 7, 8, 14–15, 16, 19, 29, 163,
  233, 247–48; number of in Vietnam,
  6, 17–18, 121, 163, 168; movie por-
  trayals of, 6, 81–82, 125–26; work-

ing-class, 6–7, 12, 14–15, 22–25, 27–28, 221, 288, 319; Vietnamese hostility toward, 7, 132, 168–69, 213–15, 230, 292; demoralization, 7, 163, 239, 247; and official justifications for war, 7, 204–5, 207–8, 209, 212, 217–18, 225, 228, 248–49, 300–301; enemy attacks on, 7–8, 163–64, 171–72, 181, 189–90; and body counts, 8, 156, 183, 227, 228–29, 230, 231–32, 265, 317; as bait for enemy attacks, 8, 182–83, 184, 187–89; and meaninglessness of war, 8, 208, 213, 226, 233, 250–53, 321; blacks, 19, 20–22, 25, 223–25; reenlistment, 21, 22, 271; middle-class, 23, 27, 319; educational attainment, 25–26; ages of, 27; draft/volunteer ratio, 28; antiwar protests by, 43, 94, 222, 248, 302; and war movies, 60, 124–25; brutalization of, 82, 252–53, 255–72, 277; lack of understanding about the war, 85, 119, 201, 209, 232–33; conscientious objector applications, 94–95; desertion, 95, 112, 251; advanced training, 96, 111–12; imperative to kill Vietnamese, 107, 137, 156, 227, 228–29, 269, 273; assignment to Vietnam, 111–12, 113; training for Vietnam, 113–16; arrival in Vietnam, 117–24, 125–26, 127–28, 130; departure from Vietnam, 123–24, 296; "new guys," 126–27, 137–44, 317; contempt for Vietnam and Vietnamese, 128–29, 217, 228, 255; ambivalence toward Vietnamese, 130–36, 212–13, 216–17, 224–25, 292–94, 296; brutality and atrocities against Vietnamese, 133, 136, 201–2, 214–16, 255, 259, 264–66, 267–75, 294–95; combat tour duration, 140, 235–36; drug use, 140–41, 143, 282, 283–85; inurement to death and killing, 143–44, 259, 278–79; enemy advantages over, 145, 146–47, 166, 171, 173; search-and-destroy missions, 153, 155, 163, 182, 191–95, 216; rear-echelon, 167, 238–41, 257, 260, 285–86,

302, 319; land mines and, 169, 170–71; and air-support strikes, 172, 183, 184–87, 278, 317–18; "humping the boonies," 175–82, 183–84; deprived of basic information, 178–79, 188–89, 201; friendly fire casualties, 185; fragging of officers, 185, 246–47; laying waste to villages, 193–95, 196, 215–16; and rules of engagement, 195–96, 197–201, 229; survival imperative, 206, 207, 232, 235, 236, 241–42, 251, 321; and critical thought about the war, 206–8, 218–20, 224, 254–55; and antiwar protesters, 220–24, 305; enthusiasm for war and killing, 222, 228–29, 251, 260, 262–63, 270; mutiny ("combat refusal"), 222, 231, 245–46, 247; respect for enemy, 233, 295–96; morale, 234–35, 237, 240, 241, 247; short-timers, 236–37, 243; rest and recuperation (R&R), 237–38; group solidarity, 242–43; combat avoidance, 243–45, 247; medals awarded to, 247–48; psychological traumas, 257–58, 272–73, 317–18, 319; concentration on skills of soldiering, 277–82; and Vietnamese poverty, 286–89, 290–92, 293, 296–97; salaries, 289–90; marriage to Vietnamese women, 292; field interviews with, 331 (n. 48). *See also* Veterans

South Korea: combat forces from, 16

South Vietnam, 316; official justifications for war in, 7, 132, 152–53, 209–13, 217, 227–28; government dictatorship, 8, 149–50, 210; U.S. support for, 16, 17, 32, 149, 155, 156, 209–11; U.S. troop withdrawal and, 39, 155; revolutionaries of, 106n, 114, 146, 150, 163, 166, 167, 210, 211; chemical defoliation of, 129; regional history, 147–48; creation of, 149, 150; ground combat in, 150, 151, 171; U.S. bombing of, 151; geography and climate of, 151–52; government political control in, 156, 158–59, 199; casualties, 202–3, 204; "self-determination," 210–11, 336 (n. 9); refugee resettlement, 226–27; inflation in, 240; economic dependency, 289, 340 (n. 61). *See also* Army of the Republic of Vietnam

Soviet Union, 66–67, 149, 211

Spector, Ronald, 154

Spellman, Francis, Cardinal, 149

Springsteen, Bruce: "Born in the U.S.A.," 48

Squad leaders, 140

Stars and Stripes, 230, 270–71

Stennis, John, 245

Stevens, Eric, 126–27, 258–59, 268, 286

Stone, Oliver, 125–26

Stouffer, Samuel A., 219, 242; *The American Soldier*, 219

Strauss, William A. *See* Baskir, Lawrence M., and William A. Strauss

Student Nonviolent Coordinating Committee (SNCC), 223

Suddick, Tom: *A Few Good Men*, 140

Suicide, 9, 92, 251, 313

Supporting fire. *See* Air strikes

Talladega, Ala., 14–15

Tauber, Peter, 93, 94, 108–9, 112; *The Sunshine Soldiers*, 93

Taylor, Thomas: *A Piece of This Country*, 185

Terkel, Studs, 207

Tet Offensive, 141, 188, 204, 208

Thailand: combat forces from, 16

Thompson, Hugh, 276

Tompkins, Rathvon, 188

Tonkin Gulf incidents, 8, 150–51

Travis Air Force Base, 303

"Uncounted Enemy" (CBS), 164

Unemployment, 45, 58–59

United States: Vietnam casualties, 1, 7, 163, 169, 170, 233, 247–48; bombing of Vietnam, 5, 151; official justifications for war, 7, 132, 152–53, 209–12; responsibility for Indochinese casualties, 8, 16–17, 19, 203–4; military strategy, 8, 144, 153–54, 155–56, 182, 204; aid to allied governments, 16; support of South Vietnamese government, 16, 17, 32, 149–50, 155, 156, 209–11; troop levels in Vietnam, 16, 17–18, 111, 121, 163, 166–67, 168, 210; intervention in Vietnam, 16, 148, 253–54, 299–300; escalation of the war, 17–18, 111, 121, 151, 163, 214; troop withdrawals, 18, 39, 112, 247; invasions and bombing of Cambodia and Laos, 39, 151, 270–71; invincibility myth, 145–46; containment doctrine, 148, 149, 211, 218, 225–26; raids on North Vietnam, 150–51; attempt to win over Vietnamese people, 157–59; assassinations, 158, 204; "credibility" doctrine, 211–12; as "The World," 250, 252, 255; marijuana in, 283; economic dependence of Vietnam on, 287, 293

U.S. Air Force, 49, 120

U.S. Army, 70; enlistment age, 27; draftee/volunteer ratio, 28; Army National Guard, 37; draft-motivated enlistment, 46, 49; tour commitment, 49; basic training, 90–91, 92–94, 96, 99, 112; advanced training, 96, 111; class composition, 108; human-waste burning, 129; I Corps, 170; fraggings, 246; troop salaries, 289–90; black casualties, 325 (n. 19); field interviews, 331 (n. 48)

U.S. Congress, 35, 151; Senate subcommittee on refugees, 202–3; Senate Foreign Relations Committee, 309

U.S. Department of Defense, 20–21, 33

U.S. Joint Chiefs of Staff, 163, 325 (n. 13)

U.S. Marine Corps, 323–24 (n. 10); enlistment age, 27; draftee/volunteer ratio, 28; tour commitment, 49, 237; volunteers, 62, 77; basic training, 86–87, 89, 90–92, 94, 96, 97–98, 110, 111, 114–15; arrivals in Vietnam, 118–19; in World War II, 119; Vietnam bases, 141, 144, 187–88; Vietnam strategy, 154; military operations, 160; helicopters, 174; civilian warnings, 196, 197; civilian hostility toward, 214–15; black casualties, 325 (n. 19); field interviews, 331 (n. 48)

—units: First Division, 117; Third Division, 117, 161; Second Battalion, Third Regiment, 118; First Battalion, Third Regiment, 180–81; Third Battalion, Ninth Regiment, 119; Ninth Regiment, 170

U.S. Military Academy (West Point), 24, 28

U.S. Navy, 49

U.S. Supreme Court, 94–95

United Technologies Corporation, 5–6, 10

Utermahlen, Brian, 231

"Vertical envelopment," 175

Veterans: symbolic political gestures toward, 3–4, 5–6, 310, 320; hostile U.S. reception of, 5, 7, 303–5, 306–7, 310, 314–16; difficulties in returning to civilian life, 5, 307–9, 311, 316–17, 320–21; perceptions of war experiences, 8, 9, 248, 249, 296, 297, 300, 309, 316, 319; suicides, 9, 313; World War II and Korea, 13, 314–15; social class backgrounds, 24, 301, 305, 319; education, 25–26; prewar innocence, 81, 82, 83; oral histories, 82, 323 (n. 7); and new arrivals, 123–24, 125; movie portrayals of, 125–26, 310–14; psychological traumas, 128, 272–73, 309–10, 316, 319–21; antiwar protests by, 248, 298, 302, 309, 310, 314; and brutalization, 259, 260, 272–73; and antiwar protesters, 298–99, 301–2, 305, 306; postwar deaths, 324 (n. 12). See also Soldiers

Veterans' Administration, 24, 257, 272–73, 319–20

Veterans of Foreign Wars (VFW), 314, 315

Viet Cong (People's Liberation Armed Forces, PLAF), 146n, 318; basic training and, 105, 106–7, 114–15; defined, 106n, 114, 150; civilian dead counted as, 199, 227–28, 270, 275, 276; killing of civilians, 204; and black American soldiers, 224; Forty-eighth Battalion, 273. See also Revolutionary Forces

Viet Cong infrastructure (VCI), 158, 166

Viet Minh, 148–49

Vietnam: independence, 19, 148; nationalism, 32, 147, 150, 305–6; soldiers' assignment to, 111–12, 113; French in, 113, 147–49, 154; soldier training for, 113–16, 132, 209; soldiers' arrival in, 117–24, 125–26, 132; heat and smell, 127–28, 129–30, 152, 177–78; chemical defoliation, 128, 129; Chinese rule of, 145, 147, 211; U.S. intervention in, 148, 149, 150, 152–53, 207–8, 211, 253; popularity of Ho in, 149; partition of, 149, 150; climate and rainfall, 152; and brutalization of soldiers, 251, 253, 254; economic dependence of, 287, 288. See also North Vietnam; South Vietnam

Vietnam Delayed Stress Syndrome, 320

Vietnamese civilians: hostility toward Americans, 7, 132, 168–69, 213–15, 230, 292; casualties, 8, 16, 17, 202–4, 274–75, 276; racism toward, 101, 224–25, 293; soldiers' suspicion of, 106, 132, 135, 136–37, 317; U.S. mission to protect, 106, 132, 212–13, 227, 240, 270; support for Viet Cong, 106, 158, 163, 165, 167–69, 192, 196–97, 226–28, 300; soldiers' contempt for, 128–29, 217, 228, 254–55; soldiers' ambivalence toward, 130–36, 212–13, 216–17, 224–25, 292–94, 296; poverty of, 132, 286–88, 289, 290–92, 293, 296–97; soldiers' brutality and atrocities against, 133, 136, 201–2, 214–16, 255, 259, 264–66, 267–75, 294–95; ambiguity of soldiers' instructions on, 135–36, 192–93, 197–98, 201, 229, 269, 273–74; killed by South Vietnamese government, 150; U.S. "pacification" of, 157–58, 159–60, 282; refugee resettlement, 159, 194, 226–27, 228, 288–89; knowledge of American movements, 179; uncooperativeness of, 191–92, 193, 270; counted as enemy dead, 195, 199, 227–28, 270, 273, 275, 276; rules of engagement and, 195–98, 199–201, 229, 273; Viet Cong killings of, 204; rear-echelon soldiers and, 216–17, 239–40, 289, 290; empathy of soldiers for, 255, 290, 291–92; My Lai massacre, 273–76; marriage to Americans, 292

Vietnamese Communist Party, 146n, 150

Vietnam Memorial, 1–3, 9, 14, 17, 309

Vietnam Veterans Against the War (VVAW), 298, 309

Vietnam War, 3; political conservatives and, 4–5, 9–10, 248; official justifications for, 7, 106, 209–12, 248–49; U.S. responsibility for, 8, 16, 253–54; U.S. escalation, 17–18, 39, 151, 163; criticisms of, 19–20, 223–24; media images of, 38, 323 (n. 9); public support for, 40–41, 220; U.S. strategy, 153–56; soldiers and justness of, 204–5, 207–8, 209, 212, 218–19, 222, 233, 249, 254, 299–301, 319; and containment of communism, 211, 218, 225–26; U.S. withdrawal from, 247

Voight, Jon, 311

Wallace, George, 38–39

War on poverty, 19–20, 32

Warren, Sam, 138, 141

Wave assaults, 164, 189–90

Wayne, John, 60, 61, 62, 66, 75, 125, 266, 281

Weapons: rifles, 102, 263; training, 104; captured, 203; soldiers' expertise on, 281–82; "mad minutes," 287, 340 (n. 57); C-rations used as, 294–95

Webb, James, 137, 160, 182, 199–201; *Fields of Fire*, 137, 160, 182, 199–201, 213, 216

Westmoreland, William C.: troop requests, 121; attrition strategy, 155–56; and search-and-destroy tactic, 156, 182; enemy troop level estimates, 164, 165–66; and soldiers' conduct, 216; *A Soldier Reports*, 234; on troop morale, 234–35, 236, 237, 238, 240, 241; on "Orientals," 254

Williams, Dwight, 76–78, 225

Wilson, Raymond, 46, 84, 120–21, 240

Wilson, William: *The LBJ Brigade*, 185

Winter Soldier Investigation, 309

Women: prohibited from draft boards, 35; antiwar sentiment, 41; in basic-training symbolism, 101, 102; domino theory and, 218–19; Vietnamese, 290, 291–92

Working class: proportion of soldiers from, 6, 22, 23, 24–25, 27; Vietnam service, 6–7, 11–13, 15, 28, 220, 288, 305; attitudes toward military service, 7, 48, 49, 53, 55–56, 58–59, 61; war deaths, 12, 14–15; black soldiers, 22, 24; education levels, 25, 26; draft vulnerability, 28, 33, 34, 35, 37, 50, 51; hawkish stereotype of, 38–39, 40–41; and antiwar movement, 39–40, 41–42, 45, 66, 220–21, 305; and war experience, 81, 82, 84, 319, 321; and basic training, 100, 107, 108, 109–11

World War I, 81, 318

World War II, 5; veterans, 13, 58, 308, 314, 315; universality of service in, 18, 59, 220; black soldiers, 21; age of soldiers, 27; and draft system, 30; and working class, 58–59; in movies, 60–61, 75, 124–25, 281; influence on Vietnam recruits, 60–61, 118, 119, 124–25, 292; Vietnam in, 148; soldiers' attitudes in, 219, 225, 242; medals awarded in, 247

Wright, Stephen, 153, 231; *Meditations in Green*, 153

Young, Whitney, 21